READINGS IN THE PHILOSOPHY OF EDUCATION

Second Edition

edited by
JOHN MARTIN RICH
UNIVERSITY OF TEXAS AT AUSTIN

WADSWORTH PUBLISHING COMPANY, INC.
BELMONT, CALIFORNIA

Cover Designer: Steve Renick
Production Editor: Sandra Mangurian
Copy Editor: Sandra Craig

ISBN: 0-534-00204-8

L. C. Cat. Card No.: 72-85028

Printed in the United States of America

1 2 3 4 5 6 7 8 9 10—76 75 74 73 72

PREFACE TO THE FIRST EDITION

This book differs from previous anthologies devoted to philosophy of education in a number of significant ways. First of all, its organization is based on the conviction that philosophy of education is a branch of social philosophy. As a social philosophy, it examines educational aims, develops theories of human nature and their meaning for education and social life, philosophically formulates the place and function of education within the social order, and interprets educational values and their role in shaping the development of youth. With these tasks in mind, the book is arranged in three major parts. The first part deals with the major areas surrounding the conception of philosophy of education as a social philosophy. The second part focuses on the problems of knowledge and philosophical analysis. The third part presents the nature and function of philosophy of education.

Particular care has been taken to choose readings appropriate—as well as comprehensible—for those studying philosophy of education for the first time. The readings are quoted in their entirety, or at considerable length, in order that each position will be as understandable as possible. Selections are not limited to contemporary writers, but also draw on a number of great works of the past which are relevant to present educational concerns. The selections are taken from social and political thought as well as education and philosophy.

Whenever feasible, an attempt has been made to choose selections that represent the ideas of a leading figure on each of the major positions on each topic, so that students can confront the major positions and their leading proponents. The task of understanding and contrasting each position stimulates the student to think philosophically, to sustain and reorganize his thought, and develop and defend a philosophical position of his own.

Introductions are provided for each of the seven sections to assist the reader in gaining an overview and perspective on the readings; questions for discussion, designed to stimulate further thought and analysis, follow each section.

PREFACE TO THE SECOND EDITION

Several important assumptions underlie the organization of this second edition. Certain persistent educational concerns and problems which raise important philosophical questions are used as a basis for the organizational structure of the book. Inquiry is more likely to be generated by problem situations than by a study of philosophical systems. Thus, students are encouraged to engage in philosophical thinking about education. Moreover, they immediately begin working with educational problems with which they are concerned, thereby overcoming the remoteness and lack of "relevance" which they frequently find in other approaches.

Another feature of this revised edition is that major positions by leading philosophers of education are presented in such a manner that they contrast sufficiently with one another to promote philosophical thinking. Learning is better facilitated when the individual is faced with conflicting positions and problematic situations rather than authoritative answers.

A revision reflects the latest developments in philosophy of education since the first edition. Noteworthy of these developments is the philosophical interest displayed in education as a discipline or field of study. A full chapter is devoted to these concerns and placed, along with the chapter on the nature and function of philosophy of education, in a new section dealing with the study of education.

Other recent developments are reflected in new essays in the areas of educational aims, knowledge and education, the conceptual structure of education, the question of man, and education and the social order. Nearly two-thirds of the selections are new, representing the latest developments and concerns in philosophy of education. Besides new introductions to each chapter and new discussion questions following the chapters, the reader will also find in this edition suggested readings, biographical sketches, and an index.

CONTENTS

PART ONE /

SOCIETY, VALUES, AND EDUCATION

CHAPTER ONE /

AIMS OF EDUCATION

THERE have been countless expressions of aims throughout the history of education, and educators from Plato to Dewey have been concerned with their formulation. Aims give direction and purpose to the learner and offer benchmarks for evaluating educational programs.

Today there is greater concern with technology—the hardware and software of education—than with aims. Educators have concentrated on the improvement of techniques and have given less attention to aims. However, it would be erroneous to conclude that this lack of attention is due to widespread public agreement on aims. Nothing could be further from the truth. We are not altogether clear whether our primary aim is liberal education or vocational preparation, whether we wish to create the capacities for appreciating humane culture or to prepare students for citizenship responsibilities. There still is no agreement on whether schools should serve strictly to develop intellectual abilities or whether they should assume responsibility for the total development of students. Resources cannot be allocated for educating the gifted or culturally different learners without a clear sense of aims. It is commonly asserted that schools should provide a liberal education or should produce educated persons, but we cannot advocate these aims with the confidence and certainty of educators of the past.

One way in which this state of affairs may be ameliorated would be to devote greater attention to the formulation of aims. There is no shortage of aims; rather, the problem in a number of cases is the way they are formulated. Aims are usually stated in terms of supernaturalistic results—such as perfecting oneself in the image of divinity or learning to know and abide by God's will—or naturalistic outcomes—such as encouraging a commitment to liberty and equality or fostering a willingness to promote the cause of human betterment. The problem with such aims is the difficulty of determining what actions by students can be counted as evidence of having fulfilled the aims. The use of abstractions, metaphors, and ambiguous terms is inappropriate for formulating aims. When aims are stated in such a manner that no empirical procedures can falsify or confirm them, it is likely that they serve the function of slogans; they persuade, entice, or propel people to act on the basis of high-sounding phrases that strike a responsive emotional chord. If aims are to promote clarity and precision of purpose, they must be formulated in such manner that evidence can show when they are attained or to what extent students fail to fulfill them.

It is commonly held that education is extrinsically valuable—that is, that education is desirable for what it will do for the individual (for example, a better job, a larger income, higher status) or for society (meet manpower needs, develop good citizens, teach students to respect authority, for example). Persons of this persuasion usually consider education exclusively in extrinsic rather than intrinsic terms.

Both John Dewey and Richard S. Peters have conceived education in an intrinsic sense. For Dewey, life is development and development is growth. Because the characteristic of life is growth, education is one with growing. Additionally, since growth is relative to nothing but further growth, education is not subordinate to anything except more education. Education, Dewey says, is a continuous reorganization, reconstruction, and transformation of experience that adds to the meaning of experience and improves the ability to deal with subsequent experience.

Peters takes a somewhat different approach. He holds that education is the initiation of the young into worthwhile activities. It would be contradictory to say that someone had been educated but that he had not improved. Such an interpretation of education does not tell us what should be the content of education; rather, its purpose is limited to the clarification of the term *education.* When we ask questions about aims, we are attempting to clarify and to focus attention on what is worth achieving. We are not asking for a statement of ends extrinsic to education. Also, to speak of someone as educated is to imply that the person has understanding, can give reasons for things, and has developed standards for appraisal. For Peters, education is concerned with the development of desirable states of knowledge and understanding. Simply stated, Peters' conception of education is similar to some interpretations of "liberal education"—namely, that such education is worthwhile and desirable, needs no justification beyond itself, and leads to both depth and breadth of knowledge and understanding.

There is disagreement about whether universal aims can be established. Some educators believe that the purpose of education is to develop the mind and that this purpose is the same for all societies at all times. Others argue that aims cannot be universal, that they must be formulated in terms of the situation and the characteristics of the school population; moreover, the available resources and the abilities of the educators involved must be considered if aims are to be stated realistically. Still other educators believe that both positions are inadequate. Instead, they insist that the perilous conditions that face civilization in the immediate future make it imperative that the world's leaders cooperate in establishing international priorities, including educational aims that best help to meet these priorities.

Aims are expressions of values—what is considered worthwhile and desirable. Before we can formulate aims, we must understand our value system; and to understand values we must not only know what they are but have defensible reasons for holding them. Aims may be studied historically by the factors that led to their adoption and support. Sociological studies conducted by surveys and questionnaires are another approach to the study of aims. However, aims are basically philosophic in character. The philosopher of education needs to be aware of public views, but he may also consider whether public preferences and desires are actually desirable. For instance, in rural school systems local citizens commonly expected the schools to prepare youth for rural life and farming, even though farming was rapidly declining as a source of employment. It is also possible to survey occupational skills of workers in the community, thereby providing a job analysis that can be used as a basis of the school's program. The difficulty with this approach is the assumption that the way occupations are conducted is the way they ought to be conducted.

In some cases aims issue from a philosophy of education. Aims in this instance would be an integral part of the philosophical system, mutually consistent with the other aspects of the system. An idealist, for example, might hold certain basic convictions about mind, spirit, or ideas. The aim that might follow from these assumptions is that man (finite mind) should strive to perfect himself in the image of a Universal and Infinite Mind. When aims are connected this closely to a philosophical system, effective criticism of the aims must also be a criticism of the tenets of the system.

The following selections are concerned with problems of educational aims. Note that Herbert Spencer distinguishes between ornamental and useful knowledge. Try to determine the basis on which he makes the distinction and whether he offers adequate grounds for doing so. Then see why Spencer elects to establish priorities and look for the connection between priorities and his previous distinction.

Robert Hutchins takes a different approach. Look closely at Hutchins' attempt to delineate man's nature and the way he relates his findings to educational aims. Does Hutchins believe that aims are universal or relative to the situation?

The essay by Edward Thorndike and Arthur Gates first establishes what is valuable as a basis for determining aims, beginning on the level of the individual and moving to the level of the society. Look for the reasons for this shift in context. Later in the essay the authors offer criticisms that could be applied to some educators in this chapter.

John Dewey's conception of the purpose of education is based on concepts of experience and growth. He uses two criteria to explain the basis of his definition. He also distinguishes education from routine and capricious activities and attempts to show a connection between ends and processes.

Richard S. Peters objects to the ways in which educators have customarily thought about aims. A key factor in his essay is the role of procedural principles in the educational process.

1 / HERBERT SPENCER

What Knowledge Is of Most Worth?

It has been truly remarked that, in order of time, decoration precedes dress. Among people who submit to great physical suffering that they may have themselves handsomely tattooed, extremes of temperature are borne with but little attempt at mitigation. Humboldt tells us that an Orinoco Indian, though quite regardless of bodily comfort, will yet labor for a fortnight to purchase pigment wherewith to make himself admired; and that the same woman who would not hesitate to leave her hut without a fragment of clothing on, would not dare to commit such a breach of decorum as to go out unpainted. Voyagers uniformly find that colored beads and trinkets are much more prized by wild tribes than are calicoes or broadcloths. And the anecdotes we have of the ways in which, when shirts and coats are given, they turn them to some ludi-

Herbert Spencer, "What Knowledge Is of Most Worth?" from *Education: Intellectual, Moral and Physical* (New York: James B. Millar and Co., 1884), Chap. I.

Herbert Spencer (1820–1903) has been referred to as "the second founding father of sociology" (Auguste Comte was the first). After a brief tenure as editor of the *Economist,* he supported himself by maintaining a list of subscribers to his major treatises, which were published in installments. The doctrine of laissez faire remained a dominant motif in his sociological and political writings, and the thesis that the organism develops from homogeneity of structure to heterogeneity or multiformity was an essential feature of his biological theory. In 1860 he undertook a prodigious writing project to unify all the theoretical sciences of his day, a series of works that included physics, biology, psychology, sociology, and ethics. Spencer is best known in education for the influence his educational ideas exerted on the formulation of the Cardinal Principles of Education (1918).

crous display, show how completely the idea of ornament predominates over that of use. Nay, there are still more extreme illustrations: witness the fact narrated by Captain Speke of his African attendants, who strutted about in their goat skin mantles when the weather was fine, but when it was wet, took them off, folded them up, and went about naked, shivering in the rain! Indeed, the facts of aboriginal life seem to indicate that dress is developed out of decorations. And when we remember that even among ourselves most think more about the fineness of the fabric than its warmth, and more about the cut than the convenience—when we see that the function is still in great measure subordinated to the appearance—we have further reason for inferring such an origin.

It is not a little curious that the like relations hold with the mind. Among mental as among bodily acquisitions, the ornamental comes before the useful. Not only in times past, but almost as much in our own era, that knowledge which conduces to personal well-being has been postponed to that which brings applause. In the Greek schools, music, poetry, rhetoric, and a philosophy which, until Socrates taught, had but little bearing upon action, were the dominant subjects; while knowledge aiding the arts of life had a very subordinate place. And in our own universities and schools at the present moment the like antithesis holds. We are guilty of something like a platitude when we say that throughout his after-career a boy, in nine cases out of ten, applies his Latin and Greek to no practical purposes. The remark is trite that in his shop, or his office, in managing his estate or his family, in playing his part as director of a bank or a railway, he is very little aided by this knowledge he took so many years to acquire—so little, that generally the greater part of it drops out of his memory; and if he occasionally vents a Latin quotation or alludes to some Greek myth, it is less to throw light on the topic in hand than for the sake of effect. If we inquire what is the real motive for giving boys a classical education, we find it to be simply conformity to public opinion. Men dress their children's minds as they do their bodies, in the prevailing fashion. As the Orinoco Indian puts on his paint before leaving his hut, not with a view to any direct benefit, but because he would be ashamed to be seen without it; so a boy's drilling in Latin and Greek is insisted on, not because of their intrinsic value, but that he may not be disgraced by being found ignorant of them—that he may have "the education of a gentleman"—the badge marking a certain social position, and bringing a consequent respect.

This parallel is still more clearly displayed in the case of the other sex. In the treatment of both mind and body, the decorative element has continued to predominate in a greater degree among women than among men. Originally personal adornment occupied the attention of both sexes equally. In these latter days of civilization, however, we see that in the dress of men the regard for appearance has, in a considerable degree, yielded to the regard for comfort; while in their education the useful has of late been trenching on the ornamental. In neither direction has this change gone so far with women. The wearing of ear-rings, finger-rings, bracelets; the elaborate dressings of the hair; the still occasional use of paint; the immense labor bestowed in making habiliments sufficiently attractive; and the great discomfort that will be submitted to for the sake of conformity, show how greatly, in the attiring of women, the desire of approbation overrides the desire for warmth and convenience. And similarly in their education, the immense preponderance of "accomplishments" proves how here, too, use is subordinated to display. Dancing, deportment, the piano, singing, drawing—what a large space do these occupy! If you ask why Italian and German are learned, you will find that, under all the sham reasons given, the real reason is, that a knowledge of those tongues is thought ladylike. It is not that the books written in them may be utilized, which they scarcely ever are; but that Italian and German songs may be sung, and that the extent of attainment may bring whispered admiration. The births, deaths, and marriages of kings, and other like historic trivialities, are committed to memory, not because of any direct benefits that can possibly result from knowing them, but because society considers them parts of a good education—because the absence of such knowledge may bring the contempt of others. When we have named reading, writing, spelling, grammar, arithmetic, and sewing, we have named about all the things a girl is taught with a view to their direct uses in life; and even some of these have more reference to the good opinion of others than to immediate personal welfare.

Thoroughly to realize the truth that with the mind as with the body the ornamental precedes the useful, it is needful to glance at its rationale. This lies in the fact that, from the far past down even to the present, social needs have subordinated individual needs, and that the chief social need has been the control of individuals. It is not, as we commonly suppose, that there are no governments but those of monarchs, and parliaments, and constituted authorities. These acknowledged governments are supplemented by other unacknowledged ones, that grow up in all circles, in which every man or woman strives to be king or queen or lesser dignitary. To get above some and be reverenced by them, and to propitiate those who are above us, is the universal struggle in which the chief energies of life are expended. By the accumulation of wealth, by style of living, by beauty of dress, by display of knowledge or intellect, each tries to subjugate others, and so aids in weaving that ramified network of restraints by which society is kept in order. It is not the savage chief only who, in formidable warpaint, with scalps at his belt, aims to strike awe into his inferiors; it is not only the belle who, by elaborate toilet, polished manners, and numerous accomplishments, strives to "make conquests," but the scholar, the historian, the philosopher, use their acquirements to the same end. We are none of us content with quietly unfolding our own individualities to the full in all directions, but have a restless craving to impress our individualities upon others, and in some way subordinate them.

And this it is which determines the character of our education. Not what knowledge is of most real worth is the consideration, but what will bring most applause, honor, respect—what will most conduce to social position and influence—what will be most imposing. As throughout life not what we are, but what we shall be thought, is the question; so in education, the question is, not the intrinsic value of knowledge, so much as its extrinsic effects on others. And this being one dominant idea, direct utility is scarcely more regarded than by the barbarian when filing his teeth and staining his nails.

If there needs any further evidence of the rude, undeveloped character of our education, we have it in the fact that the comparative worths of different kinds of knowledge have been as yet scarcely even discussed—much less discussed in a methodic way with definite results. Not only is it that no standard or relative values has yet been agreed upon, but the existence of any such standard has not been conceived in any clear manner. And not only is it that the existence of any such standard has not been clearly conceived, but the need for it seems to have been scarcely even felt. Men read books on this topic, and attend lectures on that; decide that their children shall be instructed in these branches of knowledge, and shall not be instructed in those; and all under the guidance of mere custom, or liking, or prejudice, without ever considering the enormous importance of determining in some rational way what things are really most worth learning. It is true that in all circles we have occasional remarks on the importance of this or the other order of information. But whether the degree of its importance justifies the expenditure of the time needed to acquire it, and whether there are not things of more importance to which the time might be better devoted, are queries which, if raised at all, are disposed of quite summarily, according to personal predilections. It is true, also, that from time to time we hear revived the standing controversy respecting the comparative merits of classics and mathematics. Not only, however, is this controversy carried on in an empirical manner, with no reference to an ascertained criterion, but the question at issue is totally insignificant when compared with the general question of which it is part. To suppose that deciding whether a mathematical or a classical education is the best, is deciding what is the proper *curriculum*, is much the same thing as to suppose that the whole of dietetics lies in determining whether or not bread is more nutritive than potatoes.

The question which we contend is of such transcendent moment, is, not whether such or such knowledge is of worth, but what is its *relative* worth? When they have named certain advantages which a given course of study has secured them, persons are apt to assume that they have justified themselves; quite forgetting that the adequateness of the advantages is the point to be judged. There is, perhaps, not a subject to which men devote attention that has not *some* value. A year diligently spent in getting up heraldry would very possibly give a little further insight into ancient manners and morals, and into the origin of names. Any one who should learn the distances between all the towns in England might, in the course of his life, find one or two of the thousand facts he had acquired of some slight service when arranging a journey. Gathering together all the small gossip of a county, profitless occupation as it would be, might yet occasionally help to establish some useful fact —say, a good example of hereditary transmission. But in these cases every one would admit that there was no proportion between the required labor and the probable benefits. No one would tolerate the proposal to devote some years of a boy's time to getting such information, at the cost of much more valuable information which he might else have got.

And if here the test of relative value is appealed to and held conclusive, then should it be appealed to and held conclusive throughout. Had we time to master all subjects we need not be particular. To quote the old song:

Could a man be secure
That his days would endure
As of old, for a thousand long years,
What things might he know!
What deeds might he do!
And all without hurry or care.

"But we that have but span-long lives" must ever bear in mind our limited time for acquisition. And remembering how narrowly this time is limited, not only by the shortness of life but also still more by the business of life, we ought to be especially solicitous to employ what time we have to the greatest advantage. Before devoting years to some subject which fashion or fancy suggests, it is surely wise to weigh with great care the worth of various alternative results which the same years might bring if otherwise applied.

In education, then, this is the question of questions, which it is high time we discussed in some methodic way. The first in importance, though the last to be considered, is the problem how to decide among the conflicting claims of various subjects on our attention. Before there can be a rational *curriculum*, we must settle which things it most concerns us to know; or, to use a word of Bacon's, now unfortunately obsolete, we must determine the relative values of knowledges.

To this end a measure of value is the first requisite. And happily, respecting the true measure of value, as expressed in general terms, there can be no dispute. Every one in contending for the worth of any particular order of information, does so by showing its bearing upon some part of life. In reply to the question, "Of what use is it?" the mathematician, linguist, naturalist, or philosopher explains the way in which his learning beneficially influences action—saves from evil or secures good—conduces to happiness. When the teacher of writing has pointed out how great an aid writing is to success in business—that is, to the obtaining of sustenance—that is, to satisfactory living—he is held to have proved his case. And when the collector of dead facts (say a numismatist) fails to make clear any appreciable effects which these facts can produce on human welfare, he is obliged to admit that they are comparatively valueless. All then, either directly or by implication, appeal to this as the ultimate test.

How to live?—that is the essential question for us. Not how to live in the mere material sense only, but in the widest sense. The general problem which comprehends every special problem is the right ruling of conduct in all directions under all circumstances. In what way to treat the body; in what way to treat the mind; in what way to manage our affairs; in what way to bring up a family; in what way to behave as a citizen; in what way to utilize all those sources of happiness which nature supplies—how to use our faculties to the greatest advantage of ourselves and others—how to live completely? And this being the great thing needful for us to learn, is, by consequence, the great thing which education has to teach. To prepare us for complete living is the function which education has to discharge; and the only rational mode of judging of any educational course is to judge in what degree it discharges such function.

This test, never used in its entirety, but rarely even partially used, and used then in a vague, half-conscious way, has to be applied consciously, methodically, and throughout all cases. It behooves us to set before ourselves, and ever to keep clearly in view, complete living as the end to be achieved; so that in bringing up our children we may choose subjects and methods of instruction with deliberate reference to this end. Not only ought we to cease from the mere unthinking adoption of the current fashion in education, which has no better warrant than any other fashion, but we must also rise above that rude, empirical style of judging displayed by those more intelligent people who do bestow some care in overseeing the cultivation of their children's minds. It must not suffice simply to *think* that such or such information will be useful in after life, or that this kind of knowledge is of more practical value than that; but we must seek out some process of estimating their respective values, so that as far as possible we may positively *know* which are most deserving of attention.

Doubtless the task is difficult—perhaps never to be more than approximately achieved. But considering the vastness of the interests at stake, its difficulty is no reason for pusillanimously passing it by, but rather for devoting every energy to its mastery. And if we only proceed systematically, we may very soon get at results of no small moment.

Our first step must obviously be to classify, in the order of their importance, the leading kinds of activity which constitute human life. They may naturally be arranged into, 1. Those activities which directly minister to self-preservation; 2. Those activities which, by securing the necessaries of life, indirectly minister to self-preservation; 3. Those activities which have for their end the rearing and discipline of offspring; 4. Those activities which are involved in the maintenance of proper social and political relations; 5. Those miscellaneous activities which make up the leisure part of life, devoted to the gratification of the tastes and feelings.

That these stand in something like their true order of subordination, it needs no long consideration to show. The actions and precautions by which, from moment to moment, we secure personal safety must clearly take precedence of all others. Could there be a man, ignorant as an infant of all surrounding objects and movements, or how to guide himself among them, he would pretty certainly lose his life the first time he went into the street, notwithstanding any amount of learning he might have on other matters. And as entire ignorance in all other directions would be less promptly fatal than entire ignorance in this direction, it must be admitted that knowledge immediately conductive to self-preservation is of primary importance.

That next after direct self-preservation comes the indirect self-preservation, which consists in acquiring the means of living, none will question. That a man's industrial functions must be considered before his parental ones is manifest from the fact that, speaking generally, the discharge of the parental functions is made possible only by the previous discharge of the industrial ones. The power of self-maintenance necessarily preceding the power of maintaining offspring, it follows that knowledge needful for self-maintenance has stronger claims than knowledge for family welfare—is second in value to none save knowledge needful for immediate self-preservation.

As the family comes before the state in order of time—as the bringing up of children is possible before the state exists, or when it has ceased to be, whereas the state is rendered possible only by the bringing up of children—it follows that the duties of the parent demand closer attention than those of the citizen. Or, to use a further argument, since the goodness of a society ultimately depends on the nature of its citizens, and since the nature of its citizens is more modifiable by early training than by anything else, we must conclude that the welfare of the family underlies the welfare of society. And hence knowledge directly conducing to the first must take precedence of knowledge directly conducing to the last.

Those various forms of pleasurable occupation which fill up the leisure left by graver occupations—the enjoyments of music, poetry, painting, etc.—manifestly imply a pre-existing society. Not only is a considerable development of them impossible without a long-established social union, but their very subject matter consists in great part of social sentiments and sympathies. Not only does society supply the conditions to their growth, but also the ideas and sentiments they express. And consequently that part of human conduct which constitutes good citizenship is of more moment than that which goes out in accomplishments or exercise of the tastes; and, in education, preparation for the one rank before preparation for the other.

Such then, we repeat, is something like the rational order of subordination: that education which prepares for direct self-preservation; that which prepares for indirect self-preservation; that which prepares for parenthood; that which prepares for citizenship; that which prepares for the miscellaneous refinements of life. We do not mean to say that these divisions are definitely separable. We do not deny that they are intricately entangled with each other in such way that there can be no training for any that is not in some measure a training for all. Nor do we question that of each division there are portions more important than certain portions of the preceding divisions: that, for instance, a man of much skill in business, but little other faculty, may fall farther below the standard of complete living than one of but moderate power of acquiring money but great judgment as a parent; or that exhaustive information bearing on right social action, joined with entire want of general culture in literature and the fine arts, is less desirable than a more moderate share of the one joined with some of the other. But after making all qualifications, there still remain these broadly-marked divisions; and it still continues substantially true that these divisions subordinate one another in the foregoing order, because the corresponding divisions of life make one another *possible* in that order.

Of course the ideal of education is complete preparation in all these divisions. But failing this ideal, as in our phase of civilization every one must do more or less, the aim should be to maintain *a due proportion* between the degrees of preparation in each. Not exhaustive cultivation in any one, supremely important though it may be—not even an exclusive attention to the two, three, or four divisions of greatest importance; but an attention to all—greatest where the value is greatest, less where the value is less, least where the value is least. For the average man (not to forget the cases in which peculiar aptitude for some one department of knowledge rightly makes that one the bread-winning occupation)—for the average man, we say, the desideratum is a training that approaches nearest to perfection in the things which most subserve complete living, and falls more and more below perfection in the things that have more and more remote bearings on complete living.

In regulating education by this standard there are some general considerations that should be ever present to us. The worth of any kind of culture, as aiding complete living, may be either necessary or more or less contingent. There is knowledge of intrinsic value, knowledge of quasi-intrinsic value, and knowledge of conventional value. Such facts as that sensations of numbness and tingling commonly precede paralysis, that the resistance of water to a body moving through it varies as the square of the velocity, that chlorine is a disinfectant—these, and the truths of science in general, are of intrinsic value: they will bear on human conduct ten thousand years hence as they do now. The extra knowledge of our own language, which is given by an acquaintance with Latin and Greek, may be considered to have a value that is quasi-intrinsic;

it must exist for us and for other races whose languages owe much to these sources, but will last only as long as our languages last. While that kind of information which, in our schools, usurps the name History—the mere tissue of names and dates and dead unmeaning events—has a conventional value only, it has not the remotest bearing upon any of our actions, and it is of use only for the avoidance of those unpleasant criticisms which current opinion passes upon its absence. Of course, as those facts which concern all mankind throughout all time must be held of greater moment than those which concern only a portion of them during a limited era, and of far greater moment than those which concern only a portion of them during the continuance of a fashion, it follows that in a rational estimate, knowledge of intrinsic worth must, other things equal, take precedence of knowledge that is of quasi-intrinsic or conventional worth.

One further preliminary. Acquirement of every kind has two values—value as *knowledge* and value as *discipline*. Besides its use for guidance in conduct, the acquisition of each order of facts has also its use as mental exercise; and its effects as a preparative for complete living have to be considered under both these heads.

These, then, are the general ideas with which we must set out in discussing a *curriculum*: life as divided into several kinds of activity of successively decreasing importance; the worth of each order of facts as regulating these several kinds of activity, intrinsically, quasi-intrinsically, and conventionally; and their regulative influences estimated both as knowledge and discipline.

And now we come to that remaining division of human life which includes the relaxations, pleasures, and amusements filling leisure hours. After considering what training best fits for self-preservation, for the obtaining of sustenance, for the discharge of parental duties, and for the regulation of social and political conduct, we have now to consider what training best fits for the miscellaneous ends not included in these—for the enjoyments of nature, of literature, and of the fine arts, in all their forms. Postponing them as we do to things that bear more vitally upon human welfare, and bringing everything, as we have, to the list of actual value, it will perhaps be inferred that we are inclined to slight these less essential things. No greater mistake could be made, however. We yield to none in the value we attach to aesthetic culture and its pleasures. Without painting, sculpture, music, poetry, and the emotions produced by natural beauty of every kind, life would lose half its charm. So far from thinking that the training and gratification of the tastes are unimportant, we believe that the time will come when they will occupy a much larger share of human life than now. When the forces of nature have been fully conquered to man's use—when the means of production have been brought to perfection—when labor has been economized to the highest degree—when education has been so systematized that a preparation for the more essential activities may be made with comparative rapidity—and when, consequently, there is a great increase of spare time, then will the poetry, both of art and nature, rightly fill a large space in the minds of all.

But it is one thing to admit that aesthetic culture is in a high degree conducive to human happiness, and another thing to admit that it is a fundamental requisite to human happiness. However important it may be, it must yield precedence to those kinds of culture which bear more directly upon the duties of life. As before hinted, literature and the fine arts are made possible by those activities which make individual and social life possible; and manifestly, that which is made possible must be postponed to that which makes it possible. A florist cultivates a plant for the sake of its flower, and regards the roots and leaves as of value chiefly because they are instrumental in producing the flower. But while, as an ultimate product, the flower is the thing to which everything else is subordinate, the florist very well knows that the root and leaves are intrinsically of greater importance, because on them the evolution of the flower depends. He bestows every care in rearing a healthy plant, and knows it would be folly if, in his anxiety to obtain the flower, he were to neglect the plant. Similarly in the case before us. Architecture, sculpture, painting, music, poetry, etc., may be truly called the efflorescence of civilized life. But even supposing them to be of such transcendent worth as to subordinate the civilized life out of which they grow (which can hardly be asserted), it will still be admitted that the production of a healthy civilized life must be the first consideration, and that the knowledge conducing to this must occupy the highest place.

And here we see most distinctly the vice of our educational system. It neglects the plant for the sake of the flower. In anxiety for elegance it forgets substance. While it gives no knowledge conducive to self-preservation—while of knowledge that facilitates gaining a livelihood it gives but the rudiments, and leaves the greater part to be picked up anyhow in after life—while for the discharge of parental functions it makes not the slightest provision—and while for the duties of citizenship it prepares by imparting a mass of facts, most of which are irrelevant, and the rest without a key, it is diligent in teaching everything that adds to refinement, polish, eclat. However fully we may admit that extensive acquaintance with modern languages is a valuable accomplishment, which, through reading, conversation, and travel, aids in giving a certain finish, it by no means follows that this result is rightly purchased at the cost of that vitally important knowledge sacrificed to it. Supposing it true that classical education conduces to elegance and correctness of style, it can not be said that elegance and correctness of style are comparable in importance to a familiarity with the principles that should guide the rearing of children. Grant that the taste may be greatly improved by reading all the poetry written in extinct languages, yet it is not to be inferred that such improvement of taste is equivalent in value to an acquaintance with the laws of health. Accomplishments, the fine arts, *belles-lettres*, and all those things which, as we say, constitute the efflorescence of civilization, should be wholly subordinate to that knowledge and discipline in which civilization rests. *As they occupy the leisure part of life, so should they occupy the leisure part of education.*

Thus far our question has been the worth of knowledge of this or that kind for purposes of guidance. We have now to judge the relative values of different kinds of knowledge for purposes of discipline. This division of our subject we are obliged to treat with comparative brevity; and happily no very lengthened treatment of it is needed. Having found what is best for the one end, we have by implication found what is best for the other. We may be quite sure that the acquirement of those classes of facts which are most useful for regulating conduct involves a mental exercise best fitted for strengthening the faculties. It would be utterly contrary to the beautiful economy of nature if one kind of culture were needed for the gaining of information and another kind were needed as a mental gymnastic. Everywhere throughout creation we find faculties developed through the performance of those functions which it is their office to perform, not through the performance of artificial exercises devised to fit them for these functions. The red Indian acquires the swiftness and agility which make him a successful hunter by the actual pursuit of animals; and by the miscellaneous activities of his life he gains a better balance of physical powers than gymnastics ever give. That skill in tracking enemies and prey which he has reached by long practice implies a subtlety of perception far exceeding anything produced by artificial training. And similarly throughout. From the Bushman, whose eye, which being habitually employed in identifying distant objects that are to be pursued or fled from, has acquired a quite telescopic range, to the accountant whose daily practice enables him to add up several columns of figures simultaneously, we find that the highest power of a faculty results from the discharge of those duties which the conditions of life require it to discharge. And we may be certain, *a priori*, that the same law holds throughout education. The education of most value for guidance must at the same time be the education of most value for discipline.

We conclude, then, that for discipline as well as for guidance, science is of chiefest value. In all its effects, learning the meaning of things is better than learning the meaning of words. Whether for intellectual, moral, or religious training, the study of surrounding phenomena is immensely superior to the study of grammars and lexicons.

Thus to the question with which we set out, What knowledge is of most worth? the uniform reply is—science. This is the verdict on all the counts. For direct self-preservation, or the maintenance of life and health, the all-important knowledge is—science. For that indirect self-preservation which we call gaining a livelihood, the knowledge of greatest value is—science. For the due discharge of parental functions, the proper guidance is to be found only in—science. For that interpretation of national life, past and present, without which the citizen can not rightly regulate his conduct, the indispensable key is—science. Alike for the most perfect production and highest enjoyment of art in all its forms, the needful preparation is still—science. And for the purposes of discipline—intellectual, moral, religious—the most efficient study is, once more—science. The question which at first seemed so perplexed has become, in the course of our inquiry, comparatively simple. We have not to estimate the degrees of importance of different orders of human activity, and different studies as severally fitting us for them, since we find that the study of science, in its most comprehensive meaning, is the best preparation for all these orders of activity. We have not to decide between the claims of knowledge of great though conventional value, and knowledge of less though intrinsic value, seeing that the knowledge which we find to be of most value in all other respects is intrinsically most valuable: its worth is not dependent upon opinion, but is as fixed as is the relation of man to the surrounding world. Necessary and eternal as are its truths, all science concerns all mankind for all time. Equally at present and in the remotest future must it be of incalculable importance for the regulation of their conduct that men should understand the science of life, physical, mental, and social, and that they should understand all other science as a key to the science of life.

And yet the knowledge which is of such transcendent value is that which, in our age of boasted education, receives the least attention. While this which we call civilization could never have arisen had it not been for science, science forms scarcely an appreciable element in what men consider civilized training. Though to the progress of science we owe it that millions find support where once there was food only for thousands, yet of these millions but a few thousand pay any respect to that which has made their existence possible. Though this increasing knowledge of the properties and relations of things has not only enabled wandering tribes to grow into populous nations, but has given to the countless members of those populous nations comforts and pleasures which their few naked ancestors never even conceived, or could have believed, yet is this kind of knowledge only now receiving a grudging recognition in our highest educational institutions. To the slowly growing acquaintance with the uniform coexistences and sequences of phenomena—to the establishment of invariable laws—we owe our emancipation from the grossest superstitions. But for science we should be still worshipping fetishes, or, with hecatombs of victims, propitiating diabolical deities.

Paraphrasing an Eastern fable, we may say that in the family of knowledges, science is the household drudge, who, in obscurity, hides unrecognized perfections. To her has been committed all the work; by her skill, intelligence, and devotion have all the conveniences and gratifications been obtained; and while ceaselessly occupied ministering to the rest, she has been kept in the background, that her haughty sisters might flaunt their fripperies in the eyes of the world. This parallel holds yet further. For we are fast coming to the *dénouement*, when the positions will be changed; and while these haughty sisters sink into merited neglect, science, proclaimed as highest alike in worth and beauty, will reign supreme.

2 / ROBERT M. HUTCHINS

The Basis of Education

The obvious failures of the doctrines of adaptation, immediate needs, social reform, and of the doctrine that we need no doctrine at all may suggest to us that we require a better definition of education. Let us concede that every society must have some system that attempts to adapt the young to their social and political environment. If the society is bad, in the sense, for example, in which the Nazi state was bad, the system will aim at the same bad ends. To the extent that it makes men bad in order that they may be tractable subjects of a bad state, the system may help to achieve the social ideals of the society. It may be what the society wants; it may even be what the society needs, if it is to perpetuate its form and accomplish its aims. In pragmatic terms, in terms of success in the society, it may be a "good" system.

But it seems to me clearer to say that, though it may be a system of training, or instruction, or adaptation, or meeting immediate needs, it is not a system of education. It seems clearer to say that the purpose of education is to improve men. Any system that tries to make them bad is not education, but something else. If, for example, democracy is the best form of society, a system that adapts the young to it will be an educational system. If despotism is a bad form of society, a system that adapts the young to it will not be an educational system, and the better it succeeds in adapting them the less educational it will be.

Every man has a function as a man. The function of a citizen or a subject

Robert M. Hutchins, "The Basis of Education," from *The Conflict in Education*, pp. 67–76. Copyright 1953 by Harper & Row, Publishers, Inc. Reprinted by permission of the publisher.

Robert M. Hutchins (1899–) has served as dean of the Yale School of Law, president and later chancellor of the University of Chicago, associate director of the Ford Foundation, and since 1954, president of the Fund for the Republic. He is known as an advocate of the great books programs and for his ideas on liberal education, which are contained in such works as *The Higher Learning in America, Education for Freedom, The Conflict in Education,* and *The Learning Society*.

may vary from society to society, and the system of training, or adaptation, or instruction, or meeting immediate needs may vary with it. But the function of a man as man is the same in every age and in every society, since it results from his nature as a man. The aim of an educational system is the same in every age and in every society where such a system can exist: it is to improve man as man.

If we are going to talk about improving men and societies, we have to believe that there is some difference between good and bad. This difference must not be, as the positivists think it is, merely conventional. We cannot tell this difference by any examination of the effectiveness of a given program as the pragmatists propose; the time required to estimate these effects is usually too long and the complexity of society is always too great for us to say that the consequences of a given program are altogether clear. We cannot discover the difference between good and bad by going to the laboratory, for men and societies are not laboratory animals. If we believe that there is no truth, there is no knowledge, and there are no values except those which are validated by laboratory experiment, we cannot talk about the improvement of men and societies, for we can have no standard of judging anything that takes place among men or in societies.

Society is to be improved, not by forcing a program of social reform down its throat, through the schools or otherwise, but by the improvement of the individuals who compose it. As Plato said, "Governments reflect human nature. States are not made out of stone or wood, but out of the characters of their citizens: these turn the scale and draw everything after them." The individual is the heart of society.

To talk about making men better we must have some idea of what men are, because if we have none, we can have no idea of what is good or bad for them. If men are brutes like other animals, then there is no reason why they should not be treated like brutes by anybody who can gain power over them. And there is no reason why they should not be trained as brutes are trained. A sound philosophy in general suggests that men are rational, moral, and spiritual beings and that the improvement of men means the fullest development of their rational, moral, and spiritual powers. All men have these powers, and all men should develop them to the fullest extent.

Man is by nature free, and he is by nature social. To use his freedom rightly he needs discipline. To live in society he needs the moral virtues. Good moral and intellectual habits are required for the fullest development of the nature of man.

To develop fully as a social, political animal man needs participation in his own government. A benevolent despotism will not do. You cannot expect the slave to show the virtues of the free man unless you first set him free. Only democracy, in which all men rule and are ruled in turn for the good life of the whole community, can be an absolutely good form of government.

The community rests on the social nature of men. It requires communication among its members. They do not have to agree with one another; but they must be able to understand one another. And their philosophy in general must supply them with a common purpose and a common concept of man and society adequate to hold the community together. Civilization is the deliberate pursuit of a common ideal. The good society is not just a society we happen to like or to be used to. It is a community of good men.

Education deals with the development of the intellectual powers of men. Their moral and spiritual powers are the sphere of the family and the church. All three agencies must work in harmony; for, though a man has three aspects he is still one man. But the schools cannot take over the role of the family and the church without promoting the atrophy of those institutions and failing in the task that is proper to the schools.

We cannot talk about the intellectual powers of men, though we can talk about training them, or amusing them, or adapting them, and meeting their immediate needs, unless our philosophy in general tells us that there is knowledge and that there is a difference between true and false. We must believe, too, that there are other means of obtaining knowledge than scientific experimentation. If knowledge can be sought only in the laboratory, many fields in which we thought we had knowledge will offer us nothing but opinion or superstition, and we shall be forced to conclude that we cannot know anything about the most important aspects of man and society. If we are to set about developing the intellectual powers of men through having them acquire knowledge of the most important subjects, we have to begin with the proposition that experimentation and empirical data will be of only limited use to us, contrary to the convictions of many American social scientists, and that philosophy, history, literature, and art give us knowledge, and significant knowledge, on the most significant issues.

If the object of education is the improvement of men, then any system of education that is without values is a contradiction in terms. A system that seeks bad values is bad. A system that denies the existence of values denies the possibility of education. Relativism, scientism, skepticism, and anti-intellectualism, the four horsemen of the philosophical apocalypse, have produced that chaos in education which will end in the disintegration of the West.

The prime object of education is to know what is good for man. It is to know the goods in their order. There is a hierarchy of values. The task of education is to help us understand it, establish it, and live by it. This Aristotle had in mind when he said: "It is not the possessions but the desires of men that must be equalized, and this is impossible unless they have a sufficient education according to the nature of things."

Such an education is far removed from the triviality of that produced by the doctrines of adaptation, of immediate needs, of social reform, or of the doctrine of no doctrine at all. Such an education will not adapt the young to a bad environment, but it will encourage them to make it good. It will not overlook immediate needs, but it will place these needs in their proper relationship to more distant, less tangible, and more important goods. It will be the only effective means of reforming society.

This is the education appropriate to free men. It is liberal education. If all men are to be free, all men must have this education. It makes no difference how they are to earn their living or what their special interests or aptitudes may be. They can learn to make a living, and they can develop their special interests and aptitudes, after they have laid the foundation of free and responsible manhood through liberal education. It will not do to say that they are incapable of such education. This claim is made by those who are too indolent or unconvinced to make the effort to give such education to the masses.

Nor will it do to say that there is not enough time to give everybody a liberal education before he becomes a specialist. In America, at least, the waste and frivolity of the educational system are so great that it would be possible through getting rid of them to give every citizen a liberal education and make him a qualified specialist, too, in less time than is now consumed in turning out uneducated specialists.

A liberal education aims to develop the powers of understanding and judgment. It is impossible that too many people can be educated in this sense, because there cannot be too many people with understanding and judgment. We hear a great deal today about the dangers that will come upon us through the frustration of educated people who have got educated in the expectation that education will get them a better job, and who then fail to get it. But surely this depends on the representations that are made to the young about what education is. If we allow them to believe that education will get them better jobs and encourage them to get educated with this end in view, they are entitled to a sense of frustration if, when they have got the education, they do not get the jobs. But, if we say that they should be educated in order to be men, and that everybody, whether he is a ditch-digger or a bank president, should have this education because he is a man, then the ditch-digger may still feel frustrated, but not because of his education.

Nor is it possible for a person to have too much liberal education, because it is impossible to have too much understanding and judgment. But it is possible to undertake too much in the name of liberal education in youth. The object of liberal education in youth is not to teach the young all they will ever need to know. It is to give them the habits, ideas, and techniques that they need to continue to educate themselves. Thus the object of formal institutional liberal education in youth is to prepare the young to educate themselves throughout their lives.

I would remind you of the impossibility of learning to understand and judge many of the most important things in youth. The judgment and understanding of practical affairs can amount to little in the absence of experience with practical affairs. Subjects that cannot be understood without experience should not be taught to those who are without experience. Or, if these subjects are taught to those who are without experience, it should be clear that these subjects can be taught only by way of introduction and that their value to the student depends on his continuing to study them as he acquires experience. The tragedy in America is that economics, ethics, politics, history, and literature are studied in youth, and seldom studied again. Therefore the graduates of American universities seldom understand them.

This pedagogical principle, that subjects requiring experience can be learned only by the experienced, leads to the conclusion that the most important branch of education is the education of adults. We sometimes seem to think of education as something like the mumps, measles, whooping-cough, or chicken-pox. If a person has had education in childhood, he need not, in fact he cannot, have it again. But the pedagogical principle that the most important things can be learned only in mature life is supported by a sound philosophy in general. Men are rational animals. They achieve their terrestrial felicity by the use of reason. And this means that they have to use it for their entire lives. To say that they should learn only in childhood would mean that they were human only in childhood.

And it would mean that they were unfit to be citizens of a republic.[1] A republic, a true *res publica*, can maintain justice, peace, freedom, and order only by the exercise of intelligence. When we speak of the consent of the governed, we mean, since men are not angels who seek the truth intuitively and do not have to learn it, that every act of assent on the part of the governed is a product of learning. A republic is really a common educational life in process. So Montesquieu said that, whereas the principle of a monarchy was honor, and the principle of a tyranny was fear, the principle of a republic was education.

Hence the ideal republic is the republic of learning. It is the utopia by which all actual political republics are measured. The goal toward which we started with the Athenians twenty-five centuries ago is an unlimited republic of learning and a world-wide political republic mutually supporting each other.

All men are capable of learning. Learning does not stop as long as a man lives, unless his learning power atrophies because he does not use it. Political freedom cannot endure unless it is accompanied by provision for the unlimited acquisition of knowledge. Truth is not long retained in human affairs without continual learning and relearning. Peace is unlikely unless there are continuous, unlimited opportunities for learning and unless men continuously avail themselves of them. The world of law and justice for which we yearn, the world-

[1] I owe this discussion to the suggestions of Scott Buchanan.

wide political republic, cannot be realized without the world-wide republic of learning. The civilization we seek will be achieved when all men are citizens of the world republic of law and justice and of the republic of learning all their lives long.

3 / EDWARD L. THORNDIKE and ARTHUR I. GATES

The Ultimate Aims of Education

Aims of Education in Terms of Human Wants

Need of Definite Formulation of Aims. In the preceding chapter it was said that the effect of education is to produce changes in human nature and in other things in the world. It was said furthermore that by educating himself and others, man aims to produce those changes which result in improving his condition, in achieving a better relation between himself and the rest of the world, in increasing his welfare, or in making his life better and richer. Such statements obviously leave the purpose of education rather vague. The acute reader will at once inquire: "What do you mean by an improved condition, a better relation, an increase in welfare, or a richer life?" "On what basis are we to decide what is a bad, indifferent, or good condition of life?" These are very pertinent questions, which have long engaged the attention of thoughtful

Edward L. Thorndike and Arthur I. Gates; "The Ultimate Aims of Education," from *Elementary Principles of Education* (New York: The Macmillan Company, 1929), pp. 15–30. Reprinted by permission of the authors.

Edward L. Thorndike (1874–1949) was an early behaviorist and educational psychologist at Teachers College, Columbia University (1899–1940). He conducted important studies of animal behavior which led to the formulation of his famous "laws" of learning. In Thorndike's early work his psychology was based on a mentalistic pleasure principle and a molecular physiological reductionism; later his approach became more molar and functionalistic. He rejected Binet's intelligence tests because they were based on the assumption of a general mental ability; the rationale of relatively independent abilities was used as a basis for Thorndike's tests.

Arthur I. Gates (1890–) was a full-time member of the faculty at Teachers College, Columbia University, from 1917 to 1965 and is now professor emeritus. During different periods he served as head of the Department of Educational Psychology and director of the Division of Foundations of Education. He has written extensively in the areas of educational research, educational psychology, reading, and educational measurement.

men. They are pertinent because every person interested or active in education should have some idea of its aims or objectives. Statements of these aims or objectives should express the ultimate purposes of education in such a way that they may be used as definite, intelligible principles of guidance by those who seek to educate effectively. They should be so stated as to be helpful in deciding on particular steps in education such as the desirability of teaching this fact, establishing that habit, encouraging the other skill, inculcating another ideal.

What Determines Values. Education seeks to secure for men things that are good instead of bad, conditions that satisfy instead of annoy, activities that are right and beneficial instead of wrong and harmful. Things are not good or bad in and of themselves; a man's acts are neither right nor wrong apart from their effects; no condition is either satisfying or annoying in isolation. Things, conditions, and acts can be classified as good or bad, beneficial or harmful, satisfying or annoying, or as otherwise possessing value and significance only when viewed from some point of view. In the last analysis, decisions as to the value and significance of things with which education is concerned are based on desires, wants, cravings, or urges. To justify and explain this statement, we must take a short excursion into the field of psychology, the science which undertakes to explain human conduct as it is.

The Rôle of Human Wants. According to modern psychology, all human activity is initiated and sustained by some urge, craving, desire, or want. The young infant is largely immobile until it experiences the craving for food, or the urge of thirst, or the desire for physical activity, or some other want. It then becomes active and the activity continues until the infant's craving is satisfied, until it secures what it wants, unless the desire subsides or is overcome by some other urge such as the craving to rest from the effects of its own exertions. Unless the infant wants something, there is no occasion for striving. When it is actively seeking to satisfy one urge, such as hunger, the object of that urge, food, is supremely important, valuable, good, whereas other things such as noises, movements, toys are at the time relatively unimportant and undesired. To the infant, then, things take on value and importance as they serve to satisfy some childish want.

What is true of infancy is fundamentally true of all ages. Human cravings, in the last analysis, initiate and sustain action. Without them, "the human organism would become inert like a wonderful clockwork whose springs had been removed or an engine whose fires had been drawn." Wants, furthermore, are the final determinants of good and bad, useful and useless, right and wrong, beautiful and ugly. Things have value and importance only as they serve to satisfy the urges which lie back of somebody's strivings;

they are called useless, bad, wrong, and the like only as they fail to contribute to, or positively thwart, some conscious being's efforts to satisfy his cravings.

A thing or event or act or condition is not then, in the last analysis, desirable because it is valuable. It is valuable because it is desirable—because it satisfies a want or craving or impulse of some man or other conscious being. Suppose, for instance, that all creatures had been, and now and in the future were to be, blind. The most beautiful painting would be no better than the ugliest; for it could make no difference to anybody. Suppose that all beings, past, present, and future, existed equally well and equally happily without, as with, food—that no one wanted food or drink. Temperance would be no longer a virtue, and gluttony no longer a sin. They would simply be accidental qualities like the color of one's eyes. For the temperate man would satisfy no want of his own or anyone else's, nor would the glutton's acts imply deprivation for anybody else. Value or worth or goodness means power to satisfy wants. One thing or condition or act is more valuable or more worthy or better than another because it satisfies wants more fully, or satisfies more wants, or causes less deprivation of wants.

Aim of Education Stated in Terms of Human Wants. Life is activity initiated and sustained to satisfy wants. Since this is the case, we may say provisionally that the ultimate aim of education for man[1] is to secure the fullest satisfaction of human wants. Observe that this statement contains the word *fullest*; this implication of this word we should emphasize and explain.

Conflict among Wants of Different Individuals. Every infant, child, or adult has many wants. Some of these cravings, like that for foods of certain tastes or for a certain amount of unhampered physical action, are native or inherited, born in the very structure of the organism. Others, like the desire for smoking, are acquired. Among both native and acquired wants of persons of all ages are some which, when satisfied in the most convenient manner by one person, tend to deprive another person of the means of satisfying one or more of his wants. If, to satisfy my hunger, I should eat all the berries in the patch, someone else may have to go hungry. If, to satisfy my urge to excel, I should follow fraudulent practices in athletics, business, or love, some more deserving person may be deprived of a satisfaction rightfully earned. If, to appease his craving for domination and power, a man should take advantage of his superiority in wealth to underpay and torment his employees, their wants will be less fully satisfied. Thus, in many cases, if one person secures the *fullest*

[1] We shall not attempt to decide what the aim of education should be for the entire universe of conscious beings; or how far man should perhaps sacrifice his wants to those of the universe as a whole.

satisfaction of his individual wants, others will be less able to satisfy their cravings.

Conflict among Wants of Different Groups. The situation is much the same when we replace the individual by the family, the local community, the members of a religious or political or social or occupational group, or even the nation or a league of nations. If one group, to satisfy its cravings for hoarding and domination, monopolizes all of a certain class of goods, such as coal, it may not only reduce the fullness with which the wants of other groups are satisfied but, in the end, it may also cause a diminution in its own satisfaction since the other group may retaliate by monopolizing some other material and the productivity of both may be thereby reduced. If the members of one nation, to enjoy the feeling of superiority, indulge in unreasonable emotional patriotism, the result is likely to be misunderstanding, distrust, rivalry in unessentials, even war, which may reduce the ability of both groups to satisfy the needs of their members. In short, by attempting solely to fulfill the needs of a particular individual, family, community, nation, or even a league of nations, we shall not achieve the fullest satisfaction of the wants of individuals on the whole. On the contrary, by attempting to satisfy the wants of all human beings, the desires of each of us will be most fully satisfied.

Education Seeks to Promote the Satisfying of the Wants of Humanity as a Whole. Education, then, aims at satisfying the wants of all people in order to give each person the fullest realization of his own desires. A fundamental principle of education, then, is that the best in life is not to be achieved by strivings for the individual aggrandizement of a person, race, nation, or any other group, but, on the contrary, by striving for the advancement of mankind as a whole.

The aim of education is international or universal in scope not for sentimental but for practical reasons; for only by considering the wants of everyone can we satisfy our own desires most fully. If we accept this aim, it will help us to appraise all types of conditions and acts that we may encounter and to evaluate changes in the physical world and in man himself which education may produce.

The chief aim of education, then, is to realize the fullest satisfaction of human wants. To this end external things and conditions and human nature must both be changed. In the last analysis, changes in human nature, to be effective, must include changes in human wants, since satisfaction and activity alike spring from cravings. In general, education aims to diminish or abolish those cravings which are futile or antagonistic to the satisfaction of other wants and to cultivate those wants which do not reduce or which actually increase the satisfaction of others.

Now that a brief statement of the ultimate aims of education has been given it may be clarified and appraised more fully by considering it in comparison with other objectives of education that have received attention. Happiness, preparation for life, growth, reorganization of experience, perfection of oneself, and culture are various terms employed to indicate other objectives of education.

Happiness as an Aim of Education

It is sometimes stated that the ultimate aim of education is to increase human happiness. If this statement takes such a form as "the greatest happiness for the most people," it is substantially equivalent to our statement of the aim of education in terms of satisfying human wants. When we inquire what occasions human happiness, we shall find that it depends upon human wants. Activity which satisfies no need, striving which results in failure or the frustration of wants will not yield the fullest happiness and often will, on the contrary, lead to unhappiness. Happiness results from the full activity of fulfilling human wants. Since the process of satisfying human wants seems to be fundamental to happiness, it is better to define the aim of education in terms of wants.

Education as Preparation for Life

To state that education should always attempt to give children happiness by the most immediate and direct means would be as unwise as to say that by satisfying any individual want the welfare of society would be fostered. Many instances of immediate happiness may reduce or deny later satisfaction; many causes of individual happiness are very dangerous to the welfare of others. Happiness for the individual and society as a whole in the long run is often best attained by denying a person some tempting opportunity of the moment. Among children, who less skillfully conceal their joys and sorrows, inconsistencies between individual immediate happiness and happiness in general for the individual and the group are often apparent. Not all happy experiences are constructively educative and not all educative activities result in immediate happiness. Overimpressed with these obvious facts, some stern souls have declared it ignoble and misleading to define the aim of education as a process of increasing happiness. Education, they claim, is the serious business of preparing children for life. Attempts to make the school add to the store of children's happiness especially are decried as unsafe, "soft pedagogy," trifling with the serious work of education.

Dewey, our leading American in the philosophy of education, has brilliantly and steadfastly opposed this false doctrine. Education, he maintains, is not preparation for life, it *is* life. It is not merely a business of getting ready to live happily and fruitfully, it is the process of living happily and fruitfully at each moment from birth to death. This view is not based on a sentimental attitude toward children but on the hard-headed realization that it represents the best method of realizing the ultimate aims of all life.

The statement that education is not preparation for later life but living here and now does not mean *mere* living but *happy* living here and now. Happiness, as stated above, results from the full process of successfully striving to fulfill our wants. To live happily, then, means not merely preparing to live later, and not merely living, in any way, now. It means living in such a way as to be striving successfully to fulfill our present wants. What Professor Dewey and other modern philosophers contend, then, apparently, is that at all stages in the process of education we must consider the individual's wants.

We should consider the child's wants not merely to make him happy—although this is desirable—but also to make his development more fruitful. If we disregard his wants, we jeopardize his physical well-being, we reduce his interests and activities, we arouse his resistance to the educative process. If, on the contrary, we relate our educational methods and materials to the wants which he experiences, we shall find the learner more vigorous, active, attentive, interested; his activity will be better motivated and longer sustained. To give due concern to the wants of children, then, is one means of making education more effective and of increasing happiness. Fundamentally the dictum *education should be living, instead of mere preparation for life* is justified by the practical results obtained by educating in conformity with, rather than in opposition to, children's wants.

Although it has the practical defense just mentioned, happiness as a guide in education may be considered from other points of view. Children have as great a claim upon happiness as do the adults which they will in time become. If the direct present happiness of children does not conflict with the ultimate ends of education, it is wholly desirable, and even if it does conflict somewhat, it has a right to be put in the balance against future goods and chosen if it outweighs them. It would be folly to deny children happiness for no purpose.

Happiness is not a fiend to be exorcised. The thwarting of every natural impulse and the deprivation of every cherished joy are not necessary means of grace. In fact, if we free ourselves from our adult tendency to think of what is good for us as adults, and consider how cheaply innocent happiness can be given to the young, and consider also that frequently (not always, of course) the childish likes and dislikes are as good guides to later welfare as our artificial prescriptions are, we shall make happiness at the time by no means a small concern of school education.

The apparent conflict between "happy living here and now" and "preparation for life" as statements of the aim of education, then, in the main, reduces itself to a conflict about the chances of attaining happiness and the relative value of present and deferred satisfaction. The greatest happiness for the most people for the most time is an end to be sought by making children's lives as happy as possible and by not denying their wants unless demonstrable good may come from it. The strongest justification of this view is the fact that happiness usually is a good guide and always a symptom of vigorous and active participation in the educative process.

Growth and Reorganization of Experiences

Education aims at change. But to define education as the process of producing change is insufficient since change may take many directions, both desirable and undesirable. It is often said that the aim of education is that growth which is brought about by a continuous reorganization of experience. The difficulty with this statement, of education as growth, is that growth may take many forms and directions—it may be wholesome or cancerous. If we express growth and reorganization of experience in terms of our previously stated aim, namely to secure the fullest gratification of wants, we have a helpful concept. Education then becomes the process of so promoting happy living that conditions in the world and our own wants are changed to increase the fullness with which our desires, as a whole, may be satisfied. The direction of growth is now defined; growth comprises changes which lead to the fuller satisfaction of human wants. As the child lives, his experiences should be constantly reorganized and reintegrated so that his wants become increasingly those which, by promoting the welfare of others, rebound to satisfy his own desires. He must grow, too, in power to fulfill his constantly improving wants. Both wants and means of satisfying them, then, are modifiable and changes in the direction of increasing their fullness constitutes growth. Such growth is the aim of education.

Perfectionism

Vague and Inadequate as a Complete Aim. A generation ago one of the most popular statements of the aim of education was "The Perfection of All One's Powers," or, in Herbert Spencer's words, "Complete Living." These statements always needed qualification. For it is not desirable that life should complete itself by having all possible varieties of envy, jealousy, and cruelty; and it is certain that some features of the life process are more desirable than others. Completeness had to be interpreted as the fulfillment of certain selected features which could work together *harmoniously*—that is, without sacrificing worthy wants. Obviously, no one would advocate perfecting the power to worry or despair. Since certain powers conflict with others, it was necessary to change the phrasing to "harmonious development" or the like.

Specialization Is Necessary. But even if the misleading character of the term *complete* and the vagueness of *perfection* are corrected by qualifying statements, the doctrine itself—that education's business is to make the best possible specimen of humanity out of each man—is faulty. The aim of life is not to stock the world as a museum with perfected specimens for man or deity to contemplate. It is to make men vital parts of an organized force for the welfare of the group. Powers are not for possession and display, but for use. This requires specialization rather than general perfection. Men have to live together and depend one upon another, not each trying to be the best possible creature in all ways, but each being taught to perform, and take pleasure in, those services in which by excelling he can do the most for the common good. Nor is it desirable, even from the point of view of individuals taken singly, that education should develop equally in every respect. Each individual, by sex, race, hereditary equipment, and the circumstances of time and place in which he is born, is more likely to meet certain situations than others during life, and it is to be competent and happy in those situations that he particularly needs to be trained. It would be wasteful to train a genius and an idiot identically. It would have been stupid to have perfected Pasteur's powers to drive a good bargain, or Darwin's powers as a public speaker, or Aristotle's powers as a gardener. Perfecting the power to shoot with bow and arrow is unimportant in America now for the very reverse of the reason that it was important four hundred years ago.

The doctrine of individual perfection is inadequate because it gives an excuse for the too common tendency of men to educate themselves for competitive display instead of coöperative work, because it opposes the specialization which is necessary for mutual aid, and because it neglects the fact that education beyond certain fundamentals should narrow itself to fit every man for a certain probable course of life, not for all life's possibilities.

Specialization Will Become Increasingly Necessary. Perfectionism of individuals, one at a time, grows less significant as an aim in proportion as more knowledge is discovered, as the world's work is more divided, and as education is for a wider group. Even today such an ideal for the education of the million children attending the public schools of New York City seems a little absurd. Many of them early show special talents to which other powers should be sacrificed for the common good and their personal happiness. Most of them have some weakness which it would be folly to try to remedy. Efficiency in service grows more significant as we see more clearly the world's needs and how to meet them. With every decade it becomes more possible for a special line of action to be chosen beforehand for an individual with a very high probability that, if he prepares himself properly, he will by that career be of greatest value to himself and to the world.

Other Narrow Aims of Education

During the long history of discussion of the aims of education, various objectives have been suggested and tested, and usually discarded as too ambiguous or too narrow to serve as the one ultimate aim. Among the objectives suggested have been knowledge, skill, mental power, culture, morality, and character. Without doubt, education does aim to assist the child to acquire character, moral and cultural traits, knowledge, skill, and mental power of some kind and for certain purposes. Merely to say, however, that the aim of education is to develop culture, information, or skill is not useful since such a statement does not suggest what kinds of culture, information, or skill, or what types of character or moral traits are to be sought. To indicate more clearly the significance of these facts, let us consider merely the cases of culture and knowledge, as representative of this list of proposed objectives.

Limitations of Culture as a General Aim

Most educated persons think they know what culture means—and usually think that they have it! But there would be a great variation in such opinions and possessions. To some, culture means a body of knowledge and habits which distinguish its possessor as a member of the leisure class, which ornament his intellect much as tailor-made clothes adorn his body, and which satisfy the craving to display his superiority to others. To others culture means knowledge of *human affairs* as contrasted with science and technology, which are taken to be knowledge of *things*. Thus history, literature, the fine arts, psychology, and government would be regarded as more cultural than physics, chemistry and geology. To others culture means primarily knowledge and skill in the *fine* arts such as music and painting as contrasted with the *practical* arts such as engineering, nursing, or cooking. According to another idea, culture is a body of knowledge, habits, and interest such as prepares a person to perform, not the special work of any trade or profession, but the general work of citizen, parent, friend, and human being. Culture is thus a name for the broad knowledge useful for being a man or woman in general, as opposed to "technical training" for being a physician, statesman, or carpenter.

The term *culture* is ambiguous. It has too many meanings to serve as a definition of the major aim of education. Culture, as defined by some persons, is an aim of education since the knowledge and skills described are means of increasing the sum of satisfaction of human wants. In so far as culture means the cultivation of impersonal pleasures, or of stainless wants, such as appreciation of beauty in nature and art, interests in human life, a sense of humor, satisfaction in knowledge, which may be satisfied without deprivations to others or, better, with benefits to the welfare of others, it is a worthy aim of education. But in so far as culture becomes synonymous with selfish display, waste, triviality, expense, or uselessness, it runs counter to the ultimate objective of education. To appraise the value of culture, then, we must apply some other criterion such as that embodied in our earlier definition of the aim of education—the increase of satisfaction of the wants of mankind as a whole.

Knowledge as an Aim of Education

Knowledge Essential to Education. There can be no doubt that to increase and diffuse knowledge constitute important aims of education. Although knowledge can be misused, it is in and of itself of utmost value. In the work of making use of the forces and laws of nature to satisfy human wants, knowledge of natural forces and laws is indispensable. In the work of improving our own wants, knowledge of the forces and laws of human nature is essential. If mean men are unwilling and stupid men unable to use knowledge for the best interests of society, the fault is not with knowledge. The cure for folly and ignorance is not less knowledge but more. And for the cure of evil intentions, knowledge is essential.

Examples of Usefulness of Knowledge. It is only by ignorance or forgetfulness of what man owes to the knowledge thus given to him that anyone can resist a holy enthusiasm in the spread of knowledge. Consider the miseries removed and satisfactions created by the spread of one small fraction of knowledge—preventive medicine—to one small group of men! Cholera, smallpox, and the plague are thereby exterminated. The end of yellow fever, malaria, and tuberculosis in a country becomes simply a matter of dollars and cents. Deaths from wounds, childbirth, and minor surgical operations dwindle to rarities. Consider the fears and suffering that have been undergone on account of purely imaginary gods and evils, whose tyranny over human happiness mere knowledge removes. Ghosts, evil spirits, witches, and demons made the life of many primitive peoples an almost incessant fear, and took tithes in labor and goods that could have added a large increment to human comfort.

Morality Based on Knowledge. Morality itself, though often contrasted with or set apart from knowledge, is, except for the good will and certain other noble and humane qualities of character and temperament, a creation of knowledge. It is chiefly knowledge that saves the mother of today from throwing her baby to an idol, the consumptive from poisoning his neighbors, or the ruler from ruining his country. Most of the greatest disasters have been due more to ignorance than to evil intent.

Thus, it appears that the development of knowledge, while not itself the supreme end of education, is nevertheless a most important means of promoting the aim of education. Knowledge is valuable because it is an essential means of promoting human welfare.

Education Requires Specialization in Pursuit of Knowledge. While the acquisition of knowledge—any knowledge—is useful it does not follow that it is desirable to teach everybody all available knowledge, even were such an achievement possible. For the teacher, a practical problem becomes: "What knowledge is of most worth for each of my pupils and how is it to be made to function?" As a general guide, we must refer to our most satisfactory general definition of the aim of education—the control of nature to increase the welfare of society at large. . . .

A detailed study of skills, habits, ideals, and attitudes, as well as of knowledge, must be made because not all of these can be given to all men, and what is most suitable for a given person at one stage in his development and in one environment and in one stage of civilization is often unsuitable at other ages or in other places and times. . . .

4 / JOHN DEWEY

Education as Reconstruction

In its contrast with the ideas both of unfolding of latent powers from within, and of the formation from without, whether by physical nature or by the cultural products of the past, the ideal of growth results in the conception that education is a constant reorganizing or reconstructing of experience. It has all the time an immediate end, and so far as activity is educative, it reaches that end—the direct transformation of the quality of experience. Infancy, youth, adult life—all stand on the same educative level in the sense that what is really *learned* at any and every stage of experience constitutes the value of that experience, and in the sense that it is the chief business of life at every point to make living thus contribute to an enrichment of its own perceptible meaning.

We thus reach a technical definition of education: It is that reconstruction or reorganization of experience which adds to the meaning of experience, and which increases ability to direct the course of subsequent experience. (1) The increment of meaning corresponds to the increased perception of the connections and continuities of the activities in which we are engaged. The activity begins in an impulsive form; that is, it is blind. It does not know what it is about; that is to say, what are its interactions with other activities. An activity which brings education or instruction with it makes one aware of some of the

John Dewey, "Education as Reconstruction," from *Democracy and Education*, pp. 89–92.

John Dewey (1859–1952) was reared in Burlington, Vermont, and took his bachelor's degree at the University of Vermont. After teaching at the high school level for two years in Oil City, Pennsylvania, he took his Ph.D. at Johns Hopkins University, where he came under the influence of Hegel's philosophy. He taught at the universities of Michigan and Minnesota, and from 1894–1904 he was director of the School of Education at the University of Chicago, where he first began to achieve renown through the implementation of his ideas in the laboratory school. From Chicago he went to Columbia University, where he remained until retirement.

Dewey was a prolific writer who addressed himself to problems in art, religion, philosophy, politics, and education. Although he was not the founder of pragmatism, he became known as its leading figure. His two most important educational works are probably *Democracy and Education* and *Experience and Education*.

connections which had been imperceptible. To recur to our simple example, a child who reaches for a bright light gets burned. Henceforth he *knows* that a certain act of touching in connection with a certain act of vision (and *vice-versa*) means heat and pain; or, a certain light means a source of heat. The acts by which a scientific man in his laboratory learns more about flame differ no whit in principle. By doing certain things, he makes perceptible certain connections of heat with other things, which had been previously ignored. Thus his acts in relation to these things get more meaning; he knows better what he is doing or "is about" when he has to do with them; he can *intend* consequences instead of just letting them happen—all synonymous ways of saying the same thing. At the same stroke, the flame has gained in meaning; all that is known about combustion, oxidation, about light and temperature, may become an intrinsic part of its intellectual content.

(2) The other side of an educative experience is an added power of subsequent direction or control. To say that one knows what he is about, or can intend certain consequences, is to say, of course, that he can better anticipate what is going to happen; that he can, therefore, get ready or prepare in advance so as to secure beneficial consequences and avert undesirable ones. A genuinely educative experience, then, one in which instruction is conveyed and ability increased, is contradistinguished from a routine activity on one hand, and a capricious activity on the other. (*a*) In the latter one "does not care what happens"; one just lets himself go and avoids connecting the consequences of one's act (the evidences of its connections with other things) with the act. It is customary to frown upon such aimless random activity, treating it as willful mischief or carelessness or lawlessness. But there is a tendency to seek the cause of such aimless activities in the youth's own disposition, isolated from everything else. But in fact such activity is explosive, and due to maladjustment with surroundings. Individuals act capriciously whenever they act under external dictation, or from being told, without having a purpose of their own or perceiving the bearing of the deed upon other acts. One may learn by doing something which he does not understand; even in the most intelligent action, we do much which we do not mean, because the largest portion of the connections of the act we consciously intend are not perceived or anticipated. But we learn only because after the act is performed we note results which we had not noted before. But much work in school consists in setting up rules by which pupils are to act of such a sort that even after pupils have acted, they are not led to see the connection between the result—say the answer—and the method pursued. So far as they are concerned, the whole thing is a trick and a kind of miracle. Such action is essentially capricious, and leads to capricious habits. (*b*) Routine action, action which is automatic, may increase skill to do a *particular* thing. In so far, it might be said to have an educative effect. But it does not lead to new perceptions of bearings and connections; it limits rather than widens the meaning-horizon. And since the

environment changes and our way of acting has to be modified in order successfully to keep a balanced connection with things, an isolated uniform way of acting becomes disastrous at some critical moment. The vaunted "skill" turns out gross ineptitude.

The essential contrast of the idea of education as continuous reconstruction with the other one-sided conceptions which have been criticized in this and the previous chapter is that it identifies the end (the result) and the process. This is verbally self-contradictory, but only verbally. It means that experience as an active process occupies time and that its later period completes its earlier portion; it brings to light connections involved, but hitherto unperceived. The later outcome thus reveals the meaning of the earlier, while the experience as a whole establishes a bent or disposition toward the things possessing this meaning. Every such continuous experience or activity is educative, and all education resides in having such experiences.

It remains only to point out (what will receive more ample attention later) that the reconstruction of experience may be social as well as personal. For purposes of simplification we have spoken in the earlier chapters somewhat as if the education of the immature which fills them with the spirit of the social group to which they belong, were a sort of catching up of the child with the aptitudes and resources of the adult group. In static societies, societies which make the maintenance of established custom their measure of value, this conception applies in the main. But not in progressive communities. They endeavor to shape the experiences of the young so that instead of reproducing current habits, better habits shall be formed, and thus the future adult society be an improvement on their own. Men have long had some intimation of the extent to which education may be consciously used to eliminate obvious social evils through starting the young on paths which shall not produce these ills, and some idea of the extent in which education may be made an instrument of realizing the better hopes of men. But we are doubtless far from realizing the potential efficacy of education as a constructive agency of improving society, from realizing that it represents not only a development of children and youth but also of the future society of which they will be the constituents. . . .

5 / RICHARD S. PETERS

Must an Educator Have an Aim?

I suppose the conviction that an educator must have aims is generated by the concept of "education" itself; for it is a concept that has a standard or norm, as it were, built into it. To speak of "education," even in contexts quite remote from that of the class-room, is to commit oneself, by implication to a judgment of value. One might say, for instance, that it was a "real education" for compilers of the Wolfenden Report to wander round Piccadilly at night-time. Some state of mind is here presupposed which is regarded as commendable, and some particular experiences are regarded as leading on to or contributing to it. There is thus a wide sense of "education" in which almost anything could be regarded as being part of one's education. Rousseau said that "education comes to us from nature, from men, and from things." And of course he was right; for the concept works in as wide a way as this. But there is a narrower and more usual sense of "education" in which *men* are very much to the fore. For we usually speak of education in contexts where we consciously put ourselves or others in such improving situations.

Given that "education" implies, first, some commendable state of mind and, secondly, some experience that is thought to lead up to or to contribute to it, and given also that people are usually deliberately put in the way of such experiences, it is only too easy to think of the whole business in terms of models like that of building a bridge or going on a journey. The commendable state of mind is thought of as an end to be aimed at, and the experiences which lead up to it are regarded as means to its attainment. For this model of adopting means to premeditated ends is one that haunts all our thinking about the promotion of what is valuable. In the educational sphere we therefore tend to look round for the equivalent of bridges to be built or ports to be

Richard S. Peters, "Must an Educator have an Aim?" from *Authority, Responsibility and Education*, pp. 84–95. Reprinted by permission of George Allen & Unwin Ltd.

Richard S. Peters (1919–) is professor of philosophy of education, Institute of Education, University of London. His books include *Authority, Responsibility and Education; Ethics and Education; Brett's History of Psychology; Hobbes; The Concept of Motivation; Perspectives on Plowden* (editor)*; Education as Initiation; The Concept of Education* (editor)*;* and *Social Principles and the Democratic State* (coauthor).

steered to. Hence the complaints of lack of direction when obvious candidates do not appear to fill the bill.

It is my conviction that this model misleads us in the sphere of education. We have got the wrong picture of the way in which values must enter into education; and this is what occasions the disillusioned muttering about the absence of agreed aims. But to bring out how we are misled we must look at the contexts where the means-end model *is* appropriate. There is, first of all, that of plans and purposes where we do things in order to put ourselves in the way of other things. We get on a bus in order to get to work; we fill up a form in order to get some spectacles. Our life is not just doing one thing after another; we impose plans and schedules on what we do by treating some as instrumental to others. Some of these we regard as more commendable than others, and what we call our scale of values bears witness to such choices. The second means-end context is that of making or producing things. We mix the flour in order to make a cake or weld steel in order to make a bridge. We speak of the end-product in a factory and of the means of production in an economic system.

In both these contexts we might well ask a person what he was aiming at, what his objective was. But in both cases the answer would usually be in terms of something pretty concrete. He might say something like "getting a better job" or "marrying the girl" in the first context; or something like "producing a soundless aeroplane" in the second. Similarly if a teacher was asked what he was aiming at, he might state a limited objective like "getting at least six children through the eleven-plus." But he might, as it were, lift his eyes a bit from the scene of battle and commit himself to one of the more general aims of education—elusive things like "the self-realization of the individual," "character," "wisdom," or "citizenship." But here the trouble starts; for going to school is not a *means* to these in the way in which getting on a bus is a means to getting to work; and they are not made or produced out of the material of the mind in the way in which a penny is produced out of copper. These very general aims are neither goals nor are they end-products. Like "happiness" they are high-sounding ways of talking about doing some things rather than others and doing them in a certain manner.

It might be objected that education is an art like medicine and that in medicine there is a commonly accepted end-product—physical health. Why should there not be a similar one for education—mental health, for instance? The answer is fairly obvious. Doctors deal mainly with the body and if they agree about what constitutes physical health it is because it can be defined in terms of physical criteria like temperature level and metabolism rate. Also there is little objection to manipulating and tinkering with the body in order to bring about the required result.

In the case of education, however, there are no agreed criteria for defining mental health; for either it designates something purely negative like the absence of unconscious conflicts, or, in so far as it is a positive concept, it has highly disputable personal and social preferences written into it. Also education is not, like medicine or psychiatry, a remedial business. When we are concerned with the minds of men there are objections to bringing about positive results in certain sorts of ways. People make moral objections to prefrontal leucotomy even as a remedial measure. How much more objectionable would it be to promote some more positive state of mind, like a love of peace, in all men by giving them drugs or operating on everyone at birth? Indeed, in my view, disputes between educationists, which take the form of disputes about aims, have largely been disputes about the desirability of a variety of principles involved in such procedures. Values are involved in education not so much as goals or end-products, but as principles implicit in different manners of proceeding or producing.

Of course there can be considerable disagreement about the value of what is to be passed on as well as about the manner of passing it on. At the moment, for instance, there is much disagreement as to whether education should be liberal, technical, or vocational. And this reflects different assessments about the value of what is to be passed on, which is a matter of governmental policies as well as of personal preferencces. An educator has an important social function in a community and, however idiosyncratic his individual aims may be, he cannot be completely indifferent to the pressing needs of the community, especially if he is paid by the state. Different weight is attached by different educators to the needs of the community as distinct from those of the individual child. Indeed those who stress "mental health" as an educational aim may well be protesting against the effects of collective pressure on the individual. Instead of trying to interpret this aim positively we might regard it as a timely warning against pushing the individual into socially approved tasks at too great a cost to his stability. It is as if a teacher was insisting that, whilst he was fulfilling his essential social function of passing on information and skills and preparing children for different jobs, it should never be forgotten that children may become unhappy and neurotic, isolates from their group, or sexually unbalanced. And the educator should not disregard these other things that go to make up "the whole man." In the old days talk of "character-training" used to serve as a corrective to undue academic or vocational pressure; or religious ideals were appealed to. But nowadays such a corrective must seem to have scientific authority. So "mental health" enters the field of education—the old Aristotelian "harmony of the soul" in respectable trappings.

But those who stress the importance of a "liberal" education are not merely voicing a protest against an academic or vocational emphasis in education which neglects the individual needs of children. Neither are they claiming merely that there should be arts subjects in the curriculum as well as science and typewriting. Their protest relates to the manner as well as to the matter of education. For both science and arts subjects can be passed on by liberal or illiberal procedures. Literature and science can both be treated as "subjects" and, as it were, stamped in to a student. Or they can be treated as living disciplines of critical thought and of the imagination, in which the student can be trained on an apprenticeship system. "Liberal" is a term used of certain types of principles and procedures such as respect for persons and facts, toleration, and deciding matters by discussion rather than by dictat. Its association with the *content* of courses is derivative from the belief that some subjects foster such principles more than others. But this is a naïve view—rather like the strange belief that technical colleges can be made more "liberal" if a certain amount of time is devoted to teaching "the humanities" to supplement science subjects. For it is surely the *manner* in which any course is presented rather than its matter which is crucial in developing a liberal attitude of mind.

To illustrate more clearly the distinction which I am drawing between "aims" and "principles of procedure," let me take a parallel from politics. A man who believes in equality, might, like Godwin, be lured by a positive picture of a society in which differences between people would be minimized. He might want to get rid of differences in wealth and rank, even to breed people in the attempt to iron out innate differences. He might even go so far as to advocate the abolition of institutions like the army or the Church in which some men were given opportunities of lording it over others. Another social reformer, however, might employ the principle of equality in a much more negative sense without any concrete picture to lure him on his journey. He might insist, merely, that whatever social changes were introduced, no one should be treated differently from anyone else unless a good reason could be produced to justify such unequal treatment. The Godwin type of man would rightly be regarded as pursuing equality as a very general aim; the more cautious Liberal would have no particular aim connected with equality. He would merely insist that whatever schemes were put forward must not be introduced in a way which would infringe his procedural principle.

I think that this is an illuminating parallel to the point I am trying to make about the aims of education. For, in my view, most disputes about the aims of education are disputes about principles of procedure rather than about "aims" in the sense of objectives to be arrived at by taking appropriate means. The so-called "aims" are ways of referring to the different valuations which are built into the different procedures like training, conditioning, the use of authority, teaching by example and rational explanation, all of which fall under the general concept of "education."

Consider, for instance, the classic dispute about the aims of education which is so often connected with an argument about the derivation of the word "education." There were those like Sir Percy Nunn who stressed the connection with *educere*—to lead out. For them the aim of education must therefore be the development or realization of individual potentialities. Others, like Sir John Adams, stressed the derivation from *educare*—to train, or mould according to some specification. They might be regarded as people who in fact believed in aims in a proper sense, in moulding boys into Christian gentlemen, for instance. The progressive who protests against this conception of education is not simply jibbing at the end-product of a Christian gentleman. He is also jibbing at the assimilation of education to an art where something is produced out of material. Rousseau, for instance, protested vociferously against treating children as little mannikins, as material to be poured into an adult mould. A child, he argued, should be treated with respect as a person. The progressive, therefore, like Dewey or Kilpatrick, presents another picture of the educational process. The child's interest must be awakened and he must be put into situations where the task rather than the man exerts the discipline. He will thus acquire habits and skills that are useful to him, and, by co-operating with others in common tasks, will develop respect for others and for himself. In the eyes of the progressive the use of authority as a principle of procedure is not only an inefficient way to pass on skills and information; it is also an immoral way to treat a child. It is made even worse in both respects by techniques like the use of reward and punishment.

So at the one end of the family tree generated by the concept of "education" there are procedures involving the use of authority in which the voice and the cane are used to produce a desirable end-product. Education is here thought of after the model of means to ends in the arts. At the other end of the model, purpose and planning is stressed; but it is the purpose and planning of the child, not of the adult. As Rousseau put it: "By attempting nothing in the beginning you would have produced an educational prodigy."

But, as any educationist must know, if he reflects on the matter, these are only a limited selection of the procedures that are in fact employed. There is, for instance, the influence exerted by one person on another in some sort of apprenticeship system, when the teacher guides rather than goads. We learn carpentry by doing it with someone who is a bit better at carpentry; we learn to think clearly by talking with someone who thinks a bit more clearly than we do. And this other person need not be a charismatic figure so beloved by the advocates of "impressionism" in the public schools or Boy Scout movement. It may be a person who is not only skilled but who has the additional ability of being able to explain and give an account of what he is up to. Progressives often object to talk and chalk and confuse the use of the voice with one way in which it is used—the authoritative way. But most good teachers use their voices to excite and to explain, not simply to instruct, command, or drill.

My guess is that most of the important things in education are passed on in this manner—by example and explanation. An attitude, a skill, is caught;

sensitivity, a critical mind, respect for people and facts develop where an articulate and intelligent exponent is on the job. Yet the model of means to ends is not remotely applicable to the transaction that is taking place. Values, of course, are involved in the transaction; if they were not it would not be called "education." Yet they are not end-products or terminating points of the process. They reside both in the skills and cultural traditions that are passed on and in the procedure for passing them on. As Aristotle put the matter long ago:

> For the things we have to learn before we can do them, we learn by doing them, e.g. men become builders by building, and lyre-players by playing the lyre; so too we become just by doing just acts, temperate by doing temperate acts . . . but it is not the man who does these that is just and temperate, but the man who does them *as* just and temperate men do them.

And how can this happen unless we learn them in the company of experienced practitioners—who understand what they are doing and who can explain it to others?

There are all sorts of things that can be passed on that are valuable. Almost anything, as I started off by saying, can be regarded as being of educational value. And, to a large extent, those who favour one type of procedure rather than another choose examples that suit themselves and advocate the practice of things that can be passed on best in accordance with their favourite model. The man who advocates authority and drill is most at home with things like Latin and arithmetic where rules have simply to be learnt defining what is right or wrong and where, in the early stages at any rate, there is little scope for rational explanation or learning by experience. The progressive is most at home with things like art, drama, and environmental studies where projects can develop without too much artificiality. And the man who believes in rational instruction is usually inclined towards things like science, history and geometry. An intelligent teacher, I suppose, will always first try to interest his pupils. As Whitehead put it, romance must proceed precision. But, given the interest, he will adapt his procedure to what he is trying to teach.

In society generally there are those who are prone to view life not as a stream of experience to be enjoyed nor as a series of predicaments to be lived through but as a chain of obstacles to be overcome in the pursuit of goals that stretch out like a chain of oases in a desert, or as recalcitrant material to be moulded into some pleasing social or personal pattern. And, of course, many of the things which we do can be regarded as ways of implementing concrete and limited objectives. But this picture of the pursuit of aims is often exalted into grandiose talk about the purpose of life or the purpose of political activity. Self-realization, the greatest happiness of the greatest number, and the classless society act as lures to provide a distant destination for the great journey of life.

Such general aims are not just harmless extravagances due to the overworking of a limited model of means to ends, a sort of metaphysical whistle in the dark. For men will do terrible things to other men in order to implement aims like racial purity which are both idiotic and illusory. The crucial question to ask, when men wax enthusiastic on the subject of their aims, is what *procedures* are to be adopted in order to implement them. We then get down to moral brass tacks. Do they in fact favour the model of implementing aims taken from the arts and from technology? There are those who favour the maximum of authoritative regulation such as is necessary in an army; there are those who use other people and mould them for their own purposes; there are those who are determined to live according to rational principles and to extend the maximum of toleration to others who disagree with them; there are those whose preoccupation is the pursuit of private good for whom hell is the other fellow.

These differences of procedure are writ large in the family, in economic affairs, and in political life. In education they are accentuated because the impact of man upon man is more conscious and because people are put into positions of authority where there is great scope for adopting their favoured procedures. My point is that arguments about the aims of education reflect these basic differences in principles of procedure. The Puritan and the Catholic both thought they were promoting God's kingdom, but they thought it had to be promoted in a different manner. And the different manner made it quite a different kingdom.

Questions for Discussion

Spencer and Hutchins offer different bases for constructing the aims of education. Compare their procedures. Overall, which approach is more defensible? Analyze each in detail, showing the steps taken and the reasons or evidence to support each step. There are a number of different functions—intellectual, moral, religious, social, and so on—that society must assume in rearing the young. Which of these functions do Spencer and Hutchins believe the schools should assume? Explain why one of the authors has a sounder position on this issue than the other. What content do they believe will bring about the aims they espouse? What is the basis for their differences on this matter?

For Thorndike and Gates, what is the determiner of good and bad, useful and useless, beautiful and ugly? Is their argument convincing? In what way does their conclusion lead to the establishment of educational aims? Notice that they begin their analysis at the level of the individual and move to a broad social level. What is the reason for this shift? Is their plan for the social level well conceived? Have the authors satisfactorily determined whether wants or cravings can ever be undesirable? In the latter part of their essay they offer criticisms of Spencer, Hutchins, and Dewey. Are their criticisms well taken?

Does Dewey present a defensible case for the reason education should not be conceived of as the unfolding of latent abilities from within or their formation from outside through nature or culture? Does he make clear what he means by his concept of experience? Is education intrinsically worthwhile, or is it also of instrumental value? On what points would Hutchins likely disagree with Dewey's conception of education?

Why is Peters skeptical of the way in which aims are customarily developed? Analyze the models he presents and determine whether they are as faulty as Peters suggests. What is wrong with very general aims? Note the solution Peters offers to the problems he has stated. Evaluate the adequacy of his solution. How do you think other authors in this chapter would evaluate Peters' approach?

Suggested Reading

The leading Thomistic philosopher, Jacques Maritain, develops educational aims and offers a critique of other positions in his *Education at the Crossroads* (New Haven, Conn.: Yale University Press, 1943). Robert M. Hutchins' much discussed and provocative position is clearly presented in *The Higher Learning in America* (New Haven, Conn.: Yale University Press, 1936). Roughly in the same tradition is a more fully developed treatment than that of Hutchins in Harry S. Broudy, *Building A Philosophy of Education*, 2d ed. (Englewood Cliffs, N.J.: Prentice-Hall, 1961), chaps. 2–4. Broudy's position is organized around the principles of self-determination, self-realization, and self-integration. In contrast to the above works, John Dewey's pragmatic approach is intended to establish criteria for educational aims. This can be found in his *Democracy and Education* (New York: Macmillan Co., 1916), chap. 8.

The analytic approach to aims is represented by several selections. D. J. O'Connor, *The Philosophy of Education* (New York: Philosophical Library, 1957), chap. 3, offers a searching critique of how aims were formulated earlier. A number of British authors examine aims in a collection edited by T. H. B. Hollins, *Aims in Education: The Philosophic Approach* (Manchester: Manchester University Press, 1964). Richard S. Peters provides a detailed, meticulous analysis in his "Aims of Education—A Conceptual Inquiry," in Willard Brehart, chrmn., *Philosophy of Education* (Toronto: Ontario Institute for Studies in Education, 1967), chap. 1.

Several diverse approaches to aims are represented by such notable figures as Whitehead, Russell, and Nunn: Alfred North Whitehead, *The Aims of Education and Other Essays* (New York: Macmillan Co., 1929), chap. 1; Bertrand Russell, *Education and the Good Life* (London: Liveright, 1926), chap. 2; and Sir Percy Nunn, *Education: Its Data and First Principles*, 3d ed. (London: Edward Arnold, 1945).

A penetrating examination of higher education is found in Huston Smith's *The Purposes of Higher Education* (New York: Harper & Row, Publishers, 1955). L. M. Brown has edited a collection of short selections on aims and cognate topics, *Aims of Education* (New York: Teachers College Press, 1970).

CHAPTER TWO /

THE QUESTION OF MAN

IT is no accident that for centuries studies of man have loomed large in metaphysics, theology, and political and educational philosophy. In religion, for example, Christianity has been influenced by the notion of original sin. Metaphysicians have had to consider the nature of *being* and man's place in the universe before they could formulate a systematic philosophy. Political philosophers of the past tended to establish the foundation of the state on their conception of human nature and the limitations they believe such conceptions impose on human relations.

Empirical and experimental studies have recently advanced on many fronts. Biochemists have sought to unlock the genetic code and thereby exercise for the first time control over man's heredity, leading eventually to determining the sex of offspring, eliminating inherited diseases and organic deficiencies, and regulating the intelligence of the newborn. Social scientists have provided greater understanding of man's social organizations and his group behavior, and the anthropologist has shown how culture shapes the lives and thoughts of its members. Psychologists are currently divided. The psychoanalysts believe that man's life is primarily motivated by unconscious forces; the behaviorists hold that man essentially is a reactive organism; and the humanistic psychologists think that man is basically a purposive, goal-directed organism.

The basic focus of education is man. Before schools can be organized and programs established, one must know something about man—what he *is*, what he *can* become, and what he *ought* to become. The purpose of this inquiry is not to make education and its aims conform to man's nature but to consider the factors that can be compatibly related to the educational process. Interpretations of man provide frameworks in which to view possibilities that one finds in different designs of the educational process.

There are, as we have seen, various interpretations of man. To assess the merits of the respective interpretations there must be criteria for determining the warrantability of evidence and the validity of arguments. Obviously not everyone uses the same criteria, otherwise disagreements would not be so widespread. The theologian employs some criteria not used by the scientist, and the metaphysician approaches his inquiry with different assumptions and evaluative criteria than does the social scientist. And, as we have noted, major disagreements exist among the behavioral scientists.

For the educator, however, the question of man is not limited exclusively to empirical findings, for he operates with a set of values and aims education is designed to fulfill. The educator is interested in the illumination provided by different interpretations and the educational consequences that accrue from acting on a particular interpretation. Even if widespread agreement existed today on what man *is* and what he *can* become, these findings would only provide the broad framework or the outer limits of man's capacities. They would not tell us which among the many possibilities man *should* choose. The establishment of educational programs constitutes a set of decisions about the possibilities that are best for man to realize. The ramifications of these decisions are not always carefully considered, although they have the utmost significance for the types of individuals a society produces.

Because numerous interpretations of man still affect the thinking of both laymen and educators, it is important to become familiar with some of the more important positions and to note the possible consequences that may result from their acceptance. In the history of education it has made a difference whether man is looked upon as basically good or inherently evil; whether his distinguishing trait is thought to be his reason or some other feature. Among the many controversies over the nature of man, one centers on whether man is nothing more than a highly complex animal or whether he is unique and discontinuous with the animal kingdom. To take the former view does not automatically commit us to Thomas Hobbes' belief that man's life in a state of nature is "solitary, poor, nasty, brutish, and short." One could hold that within the temporal backdrop of human progress, man's origin is not as important as what he is today and what he can become. Is the task of education then to shape man into what he can become? And if man has a number of possibilities, on what grounds does one choose those which are most desirable? Or should educators permit the students to make these decisions?

To hold that man is discontinuous with the animal kingdom is to advance the claim that he has characteristics found in no other form of life. Through his memory he can relive events in time, and he can profit by past experiences; through his self-consciousness he can become an object to himself from a point of detachment; and through self-transcendence the self can rise above itself.

Should schooling be a process of teaching self-transcendence? How can this be accomplished?

The claim is frequently made that the essential distinguishing trait of man is his reason and that therefore the purpose of education is to develop the intellect (the conclusion, however, does not logically follow from the premise unless other statements are added). If reason is the defining characteristic of man, could it not be held that human nature everywhere is basically the same and an education that would develop and nurture reason should also be the same everywhere? One might conclude then that the aims of education can be derived from a knowledge of man's essence, although along with man's reason is his unique ability to wreak destruction on an almost undreamed of scale. How should the schools deal with this trait? However, this discussion assumes what has yet to be proved—namely, that man has an essence; and there are those who do not accept this position (see Sartre's essay).

The character and extent of human freedom has a bearing on what man can become and the type of education he should receive. Some have believed that God has mapped out man's life for him before the individual's birth; God chooses and man obeys. For Freud, the basic personality structure, which is formed in early childhood, shapes the future direction of the individual's coping ability. He believes, moreover, that man has chosen civilization over a primitive state for the security that civilization offers. Civilization, in order to survive, must therefore repress the basic "instincts" of sexuality and aggressiveness. Hence, the price of civilization is neurosis.

Some who wish to establish a science of behavior believe that a search can be made for the causes of behavior and that for every effect there is a cause. By knowing the cause, one can predict the effects; but it is even possible to change the effects through various forms of behavioral modification. Although this position does not totally deny the individual's freedom and his ability to choose, since causes can also be due to the individual himself, the overall thrust of the position is to see the individual as a reacting organism.

A different approach, the consequences of which are similar to the behavioral position, is based on the conviction that man is totally a product of his culture. Language, laws, mores, value systems, and the like are learned by growing up in a culture, and thus the way one views the world and lives his life is determined by the culture. Each culture also has its own sanctions (rewards and punishments to get the individual to comply with the norms). There also are certain social roles deemed acceptable and unacceptable, and through its system of sanctions the institutional system of a culture attempts to induce the individual to abide by the prescribed norms. The outcome of these pressures raises the question whether the individual is no more than his social roles.

What has been overlooked in this description is that in any culture, the legal and moral systems, taken together, do not regulate all forms of behavior.

Forms not regulated include rights legally guaranteed and behavior not mentioned in legal and moral systems. The latter forms are permissible until they are regulated—and there is no assurance that they will not be. Once again, whether the individual is nothing more than what a culture has deliberately chosen to make him depends on the respective culture and its legal and moral systems. But the very fact that more and more people—especially the young and minority groups—consider their culture repressive, including systems referred to as "totalitarian" and those considered "democratic," is another reason to take seriously the enormous power of a culture to mold and shape the individual. These cultural processes are not entirely negative, however, for they teach the individual how to survive and may prepare him with the requisite skills whereby he may be able to choose more wisely when given the freedom to choose.

Another position holds that man is radically free, that the nature of human existence is freedom, and that man creates himself—what he is to become—out of his own choices. Choice can therefore become a fearful and dreaded experience because the individual recognizes that he and he alone shapes his life.

Many of the objections against this position are found in the attitudes of the other positions previously discussed. Proponents of the other positions would claim that man has no radical freedom, and they would adduce empirical evidence to show that radical freedom is not the case. They might offer evidence showing the impact of the culture—specifically religion, family, organizational life, and other areas—as it influences and shapes the individual's life. They might also attempt to show why they believe a different view of man is far more plausible.

These positions raise fundamental questions for education. If man's freedom to choose for himself is limited, it is the task of educational authorities to shape the individual to the demands of the culture (assuming that these demands can be unequivocally determined). However, if man does have a reasonable modicum of freedom, if the exercise of this freedom is essential for man to become more fully human, and if society actually values individuals of this type, it becomes incumbent upon the schools to develop human abilities and to offer viable alternatives for wise choice.

Another issue is the apparent conflict between man and society. Rousseau, for instance, believes that man is essentially good in his natural state but that society causes corruption. Others, such as Reinhold Niebuhr, find that in simpler societies where primary group relations prevailed, man had an organic relationship with his fellows, but as societies grew more complex and power expanded, the original will-to-live became transmuted into the will-to-power, leading to aggrandizement of power in the hands of a few and the consequent perpetration of injustices. According to this view, power not brought under the widest range of control becomes socially irresponsible and leads the power wielder to attempt to maintain his position at all costs. And among those who hold power there also is an inexorable lust to aggrandize more. Since it is not likely that power will ever be brought under complete control, society constitutes a mixed blessing; for as long as power is not stringently regulated, injustices will continue.

Not all thinkers view the individual as against society; some attempt to depict man *in* society. The origin of the separation sometimes originates by viewing the individual as one thing in his occupational role and another in his family role. These different roles may be viewed in watertight compartments, or the division may entail an internal conflict. Because it is possible to conceive of an individual apart from his roles, an image can be created whereby the individual is not part of any association. From this assumption the misleading question arises as to how the individual becomes part of society.

But even when we avoid the notion of the individual opposed to the social we still are left with some very real questions about man *in* society. We still need to know why societies have historically been for the most part inequitable and unjust. Does something about social life or at least about certain types of societies militate toward such outcomes? And why has education often been associated with some of the more demeaning aspects of society? If man has a nature, one that is worth preserving and developing, can society through its educational system help to destroy it? But questions such as these should not lead us to construe the problem as an illustration of the individual against society; rather, it would be more accurate to see the problem as the social interests of an individual or group of individuals conflicting with other social interests. On the other hand, it would be misleading to speak of society's demands, needs, or interests to leave the impression that society is an entity over and above and even apart from the individuals who compose it. This latter tendency has often led to the establishment of goals and programs for a society in disregard of the interests and concerns of a majority of the society's citizens.

This section contains a number of different interpretations of man. The selection by Charles Morris places man within the backdrop of nature and social life. Morris shows the importance of "interests" in human life, and he disputes the dualism of the individual pitted against society. Finally, he argues that there are three basic components in each individual's personality, differing in respective strength; from these components he attempts to develop seven personality types.

Herbert Marcuse's essay is an attack on the deleterious influences he finds in affluent societies. In the process of delineating these influences he develops a theory of human nature. Note how this theory is used to evaluate social conditions.

B. F. Skinner first reviews what he considers some misconceptions of his position; he then shows how behavior can be altered (through operant conditioning) to bring about a more desirable social order. Notice the concept of *control* that he uses, and see if he has adequately answered those who fear his plan.

Abraham Maslow, in developing his theory of human motivation, criticizes Freudian theory and prevailing learning theories. He makes a distinction between deficiency-needs and growth-needs and shows the effects of each type on motivation. He then presents the concept of the self-actualizing person and its significance for human growth.

Jean-Paul Sartre notes that although there are two types of existentialists, they do share an important conviction. Sartre presents a philosophy of man based on the starting principle that existence precedes essence. In developing his philosophy he considers such concepts as *responsibility*, *subjectivity*, *anguish*, *forlornness*, *despair*, *freedom*, and others.

6 / CHARLES MORRIS

Human Nature

. . . In terms of present-day science it seems that man is one complex type of living being operating in a world of other things with which his destiny is inextricably linked; that he is best thought of as a dynamic and hierarchically organized system of interests or desires; and that conscious intelligence is, at least in degree, the characteristic which differentiates him from other known forms of life. It is now necessary to make more explicit these features which human beings have in common.

The embeddedness of man in, and his continuity with, other processes of nature, has received overwhelming exemplification in the reinforcement which science has given to common observations. It is obvious on every hand that the life of the individual is precariously dependent upon the world into which he is born. Birth itself is an ordeal beset by countless hazards, and the individual released from the womb is confronted with endless difficulties in survival, and besieged with the constant impact of objects fulfilling their own

Charles Morris (1901–) was for many years a member of the University of Chicago faculty before assuming the position of graduate research professor, University of Florida. Among his publications are *Six Theories of Mind; Paths of Life; Varieties of Human Value; Signs, Language and Behavior;* and *Signification and Significance.*

careers. Heat, air, water—these must be present in amounts which need vary but slightly for life to be impossible; great movements of the earth or of heavenly bodies press alike upon fragile human flesh and fellow living creatures; the flow of the rivers of society constrain within narrow limits the flow of individual life.

More refined observations have made clear that the physical and chemical processes which occur in man are part and parcel of processes of much wider occurrence. The human body is a complex system of living systems delicate in its organization, dependent for its existence upon the assimilation of other living systems, invaded by similarly dependent systems of life. The human mind is no exception: moods may fluctuate with the most minute changes of the body and the environment; attitudes can be transformed by changing the conditions under which life is lived; thoughts vary with the exigencies which the living system must meet.

That man is a complex and delicate balance of animate and inanimate processes, poised in a network of similar processes which at once provide the material for his support and measure the limit of his precarious existence: this is the net impression gained from common observation and reinforced by each advance of scientific knowledge.

Yet man is not simply clay on the potter's wheel of the universe: man is everywhere a valuer, an interested center of activity, a pursuer of goals. Physical and chemical processes have in living beings taken on the urgency of desire. Activities are not mere motions: they spring from needs and impulses which direct conduct in the search for objects to meet the motivating needs. Such directed conduct is an interest; its object is a value-object. The living being is a bent bow; its arrows are directed longings; its targets are its goals.

Human interests are amazingly diverse. It is true that the apparent diversity can be seemingly reduced: men have many interests in common and many activities can be regarded as variations upon a common interest which they share. It is the task of the scientist to make what order he can out of this diversity. Yet it is significant that diversity in the concrete remains, and no attempt to reduce all interests to forms of some common interest—such as the interest in happiness, or in power, or in love, or in survival—has met with common scientific agreement. It is of the nature of an interest to be a search for an object capable of meeting a need; nothing new is added by saying that the interest seeks satisfaction, or that men seek happiness or power. The search is for objects appropriate to specific needs; and interest may extend to all the complex things which make up the human and nonhuman world: to renunciation as well as to assertion, to pain as well as to pleasure, to death as well as to survival, to the attainment of knowledge as well as to the possession of objects, to concern for other persons and things as well as to concern for oneself. Some interests are more widespread than others and some are of greater strength, but an adequate doctrine of human nature must keep all in sight, and embrace all the characteristics which human beings display under all conditions. Man is in the end best characterized as a system of interests; the range and diversity of these interests distinguish him from all other living beings known to science.

The term "system" is important here, but must not be pressed too far. A living being has many interests; but these are in dynamic interaction, and the fate of one has effects on the others; they vary in strength, and the open road which one interest has closes the road to others. What is true of the relation of the interests of an individual has an analogue in the interrelations of the interests of individuals in a society: there are social systems of interests constituted by the interrelations of individuals with each other. But the relation of interests within a system does not mean that all men have the same interests and in the same relations; or that the system of individual or social interests may not change its components or their relative strength; or that interests may not have relative degrees of independence from each other. To characterize man as a system of interests is to conceive him as a dynamically interacting set of specific interests.

Man is a system of interests—but a conscious system of interests. How is this factor of consciousness to be brought into the account? To say that man is a being with a mind is open to many ambiguities; it is better to say that man is a minded being. Yet even here caution is essential. In referring to mind we may merely call attention to the facts of feeling: to the pains, the joys, the sensed tensions which qualify the activities of a living being. All things have their qualitative aspects, and the felt qualities of the mutual impact of world and self (of the stimulation of delicate organs, of the satisfaction and frustration and shifting of interests) are incredibly variegated: they are the ways it feels to be alive.

But in referring to the mind we usually intend more than reference to the palette of feeling in which life paints itself: we refer to the processes of thought in which man extends the boundaries of his present world and lives in the light of things that have been, things distant from him, and things that may come in the future. Remarkable is this world of thought: its range is distinctive of man among the animals; it lifts the live being beyond the narrow limits of his immediate existence; it allows him to participate imaginatively in lives and processes which far outrun his own; it makes him the conscious witness of his own joy and agony; it has engendered the sciences and the arts and the religions; it has made of life and death insistent presences.

And yet if we follow the evidence, this mind of man is not a thing with a life of its own simply conjoined with the body: it is part of man's commerce with the world, born out of the aptitude of a living being to treat present things as signs of what is not present, an aptitude amplified and sustained by the fabric of communication with fellow men, and functioning in the service of the web of interests which constitute his life. It is a mode of his activity, a complicated tissue of sign processes, a quality which life has taken on; not a thing with a destiny independent of the vicissitudes of mortal existence.

It is true that science does not permit us to be dogmatic as to the finality of death: just as we cannot limit the universe to what we have encountered, so we cannot completely rule out the possibility that the processes which constitute an individual continue in some form or other beyond what we call his death. But if science prohibits dogmatism, the weight of its evidence speaks in favor of the finality of death, and of the conception of man as a complex being appearing in a wider universe, rising to consciousness and some degree of self-control, pursuing his interests by all the techniques of body and mind he can command, delicately responsive to features of the world which sustain or thwart his purposes, destined to disintegration in the larger world of which he is a concretion.

There is one feature of human nature so important that it must be brought into the focus of attention. Man is unique among living forms in the extent to which he has built social structures upon his physical and biological bases. Society, it is true, is not unique to man; animal societies are of enormous complexity. But man has evolved a distinctive type of cultural tissue in which is enmeshed nearly every feature of his activity, and it is a sea in which he does not always easily swim.

It is a common tendency of contemporary thought to stress the dependence of the most highly developed characteristics of the individual upon the social process in which he grows. The interests which he has, the types of activities in which he can engage, the tenor and direction of his thought processes, his very consciousness of himself: all these are in one way or another determined or effected by contact with the other members of the social group or groups of which a person is a member.

Of particular importance is the influence of the social matrix upon the interests which are grouped together in the term "love." In the widest sense of the term, anything that satisfies any interest is an object of love, and life, inseparable from interests, is inseparable from love. Anything may become an object of love, from the most transient object to the total cosmos. And in this wide sense of the term, love and death are the persistent features of life, inescapable for all men, influenced and molded by social structures but transcending any particular age or culture. Though the form of the religious life reflects inevitably the way in which a given society influences the interests of the members of the society and their possibilities of satisfaction, the quest for salvation has often been the search prompted by death for a stable object of love; and the universality of the quest has made it possible for particular religions to persist through diverse social changes. The process of living and dying is common to all men, even though the form of this process and the way and degree to which it is raised to awareness vary from group to group. In religion, as elsewhere, it is fatal to give priority to either the individual or society: some problems of the individual appear in any society, and no feature of the individual is free from the influence of the society in which he or she lives.

A narrower use of the term 'love' would confine love to an interest in the satisfaction of interests: to love someone is then to make the satisfaction of that person's interests one's active concern. In this sense of the term, there can be little dispute as to the existence of love, whatever may be its history and its range.

Love in this narrower usage is one interest among others, and can in principle be directed to any object which itself has interests. Morality will be regarded in this inquiry as love implemented by a concern for the fullest possible satisfaction of the interest of the loved objects; without an attempt to secure this satisfaction, love is passionate or compassionate or sentimental but not moral. The area of morality may be narrow or wide: it may extend from a concern for one's own interest to concern for specific individuals, to members of a social group, to all men, and even to all living beings. Men differ in the range of their morality, their understanding of the interests of the persons they love, and in the effectiveness in which they help the satisfaction of these interests, but the difference is one of degree, and all men have to some extent a moral phase to their activity.

The most important segment of morality is social. Indeed so true is this that common usages would deny the ascription of the term 'moral' to active concern for one's own system of interests, or to the love of nonhuman animals, or even to persons outside of a given social class or group. When lives interact, the interests of the individuals mutually influence each other. Such a group in time develops approved ways of acting, so that the conduct of one individual is regulated in terms of the effect it has, or is thought to have, upon other individuals of the social group. These approved ways of acting are the group morality; the attempts of an individual to determine by reflection the action which gives the maximum satisfaction to a set of interests in conflict may in contrast be called reflective morality. Group morality and reflective morality may not coincide: approved modes of action may not be adequate to the actual interests of the group or may not be effective in realizing these interests; the actions of the reflective individual may likewise be inadequate or ineffective, or even if both adequate and effective, may be opposed to the actions approved by other members of the group. But in either case, the moral status of an action is determined by the relation of the action to a more comprehensive system of interests, and is in that sense social.

The results of envisaging naturalistically the development of the individual within the social group in which he is born have had profound implications in the conception of human nature. The full import of the genesis of the most distinctive features of the human self within the social group has been crystallized by George H. Mead in his volume, *Mind, Self and Society*. This approach turns inside out the ancient conception of the individual as endowed at birth with a "mind" through which he enters into social relations. It has traced the appearance of that mind within the processes of social interaction, and specifically within the process of linguistic communication. It has shown that man's ability to guide his conduct by reflection requires the operation of a kind of symbol made possible only within a social community. It argues that man's ability to consciously consider himself as an object arises only in a social process in which he at the same time becomes conscious of others. It traces the phenomena of conscience to the control which society exercises upon the individual in internalizing itself into the very structure of his personality.

Seen in this light, "man as man," man as "rational animal" proves to be animal man as transformed by participation in social life. The individual is put back within society, and society itself within nature. The ancient dualism of body and mind (or soul) becomes transformed into the distinction of levels in which biologic man is complicated into social man. It no longer becomes possible to identify human nature with the particular modes of behavior characteristic of men in a particular society. The wholesale opposition of "individual" and "society" withers away at its roots, for what is characteristic of highly developed man turns out to require society for its nurture, while the highly developed societies require for their maintenance the very activities of such highly developed individuals which they have in turn made possible.

It was inevitable that Mead should even give the concept of salvation a social turn: the self, made possible by society, can envisage the outlines of a social order more congenial to its complex nature than the society in which it finds itself. The need for salvation, he writes in *The Philosophy of the Act*, is not the need for "the salvation of the individual but the salvation of the self as a social being. . . . The demand for salvation, where it swept over mankind as a whole, has gone along with the necessity of great social change." The religious need of the individual is itself generated out of the problems posed in him by participation in the society out of which he has emerged and which he no longer feels as adequate to his socially derived self.

We must, I believe, accept the results which such a social approach to the individual has obtained. We can no longer neglect in the study of individuals the social agencies by which diverse biological organisms have been given the common characteristics which they share as men and women—their minds, their morality, their consciousness of self. And yet if we stop there we have seen only one part of the story: we have neglected individual differences. To correct the emphasis it is necessary to focus our attention upon men and women as individuals.

The great interest in the social sciences in recent decades has drawn attention to the pervasive influence of a society upon its members; it has often obscured the differences between the members of a society and the effect of such individual differences upon the social structure. The one-sided emphasis, understandable historically, is now being corrected by the revival of an ancient interest in the nature of specific individuals and types of personality. This tendency is of especial importance for an investigation of the paths of life which men have followed, for the diversities of such paths are in some way correlated with the orientational problems of individuals, and the diversity of the answers is determined by the natures of various individuals, whatever may in turn be the conditions (physical, biological, and social) under which individuals with such natures have appeared.

A starting point is found in the view of man as a system of interests in which interests of greater strength control those of lesser strength. The controlling interest—if there be one—may be called the apical interest; it need not be assumed that there is any one apical interest common to all men (such as "happiness," "will to power") or that in any individual a particular apical interest is constant throughout his life. The question as to how far men at a given time, or throughout periods of time, have common interests, and how far these common interests have the same relative order of strength in different individuals, are matters for objective investigation. Such investigation, tentative though it yet is, would seem to favor the conclusion that there are a number of interests which all known men have in common (though the objects available to the satisfaction of these interests differ with various times and places), but that the relative strength of these interests differ in various individuals and are approved differently in various societies.

The existence of common interests may be elucidated by distinguishing three components of human personality: the *dionysian*, the *promethean*, the *buddhistic*. The dionysian component is made up of the tendencies to release and indulge existing desires in the presence of objects appropriate to the satisfaction of the desires. There is easy commerce of the individual with his world, and a reliance on that world, as it is, to satisfy the desires as they are. There is hunger, and one eats what will satisfy the hunger; there is sexual desire and one has sexual intercourse; there is a desire for companionship, and one seeks the company of friends. The self sinks itself in the available world and that world supports the demands of the self.

But this gracious interplay of self and world is seldom attained. Man is active even in the satisfaction of desires; for the most part he must in addition act in order to find and make secure the objects which will satisfy his interests. The promethean component of personality is the sum of these active tendencies to manipulate and remake the world in the service of the satisfaction of existing desires.

The world, physical and social, is, however, often recalcitrant. Desires may not be fully satisfied, or may be denied any satisfaction whatsoever. The wariness which is already involved in promethean activity (since desires are held in abeyance until manipulation finds or makes the appropriate objects) is transferred to the desires themselves. The buddhistic component of personality comprises those tendencies in the self to regulate itself by holding in check its desires. These are the tendencies to self-control, to solitude, to meditation, to detachment, to self-containment.

Man has at his disposal three corresponding emphases in the conduct of his life. He may merely "let himself go," relying on and utilizing the world as it presents itself; he may attempt to modify the world in which he lives so that his desires are more adequately realized; he may so modify or restrain his desires that the frustrations imposed by the world are avoided or minimized. Indulgence of his existing desires, control of the environing world, control of himself; these are the tactics open to a being whose life is commingled with the press and pull of vaster processes.

Where three weapons are available, it is not wisdom to rely on one alone, and harassed man has made the best use of the tactics of releasing, remaking, and restraining which his own nature and the conditions under which he operates permit. He has simply satisfied his desires when the objects of satisfaction were at hand; otherwise, attempts to control a stubborn world are persisted in as long as possible; the expedient of disciplining desires commends itself only when serious obstacles present themselves to the satisfaction of desire. And even when this expediency arises it may be quickly forsaken when the surrounding world presents a more inviting view. So compromise and alternation of tactics is the rule: some desires are denied expression and some are held in check until a favorable environment has been constructed; some are allowed immediate satisfaction; and a desire reined in at one moment will be given freedom at a later moment. . . .

We shall regard an individual person as characterized by a particular order of strength of dionysian, promethean, and buddhistic traits. Thus in one individual the buddhistic component may be dominant over the promethean and that in turn over the dionysian; such an individual would tend to alert self-control and detachment, would however be active and energetic, and would resist a life of sensuous comfort. There is, theoretically, a continuum of individuals differing in these respects; but, practically, it is possible to classify individuals through the degree to which the factors of personality have the same relative strength and order. And from this procedure arises the notion of a type of personality.

The number of types of personality distinguished is relative to the degree of similarity in order and strength of the components chosen as the basis of classification. For present purposes a relatively small number of types is sufficient. If we consider only the order of strengths of the dionysian, promethean, and buddhistic traits, and do not attempt to discriminate the strengths within a given order, we obtain a classification of human personalities into seven major types, to which we assign specific names:

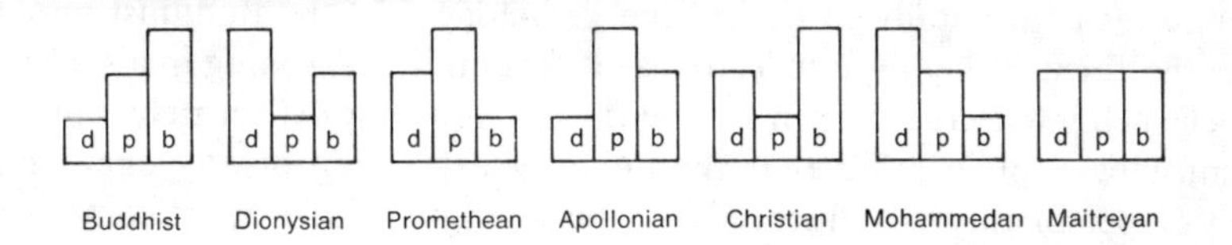

A number of comments are relevant. There may be some danger of confusion in using the same stem to designate both a component of all personalities and a specific type of personality, thus: 'dionysian' and 'Dionysian.' On the printed page, the use of small and capital letters marks the distinction; if confusion is likely, especially in speaking, it may be advisable to shift to another set of terms (or to the initial letters of the terms here used) to label the components of personality.

There is no magic virtue in the number seven; this number merely results from the method of classification employed. For other purposes, or even for a refinement of the present type of analysis, further distinctions may well prove to be convenient. Nevertheless, since the present seven types are exhaustive of the logical possibilities involved in using three basic sets of character traits (provided a convention is made to determine the classification of individuals in whom two components are of the same strength), any such further distinctions can be made within the seven types here outlined, as subtypes of Buddhists, Prometheans, or what not. The present procedure, while coarse, is nonetheless all-inclusive.

The distinctive feature of personality does not lie in the bare predominance of one component, but in its predominance in relation to the other components. Thus the Christian and Buddhist are both predominantly buddhistic (cerebrotonic), but there are marked differences in their personality: the relatively high dionysian component of the former will suffuse his detachment with a sublimated affective warmth (Christian contemplation becomes an intellectualized love of God, always near to mysticism), while the low promethean component will give to this personality a certain passivity (dependence on God's grace, upon the Church); the Buddhist in contrast, being less dionysian and more promethean, is more narrowly intellectualistic, his love is more kindly and less mystic, and he tends to take the control of himself into his own hands.

This example also makes clear that we cannot simply correlate one kind of attitude ("sociality," "rationality") with the dominance of a particular component. It is true that in general the highly buddhistic individual is inclined to abstract reasoning and to solitude in a way foreign to the highly dionysian individual, but such generality is misleading: the highly buddhistic Christian is sufficiently dionysian to seek a society in which his love can express itself, and yet sufficiently detached to be uncomfortable in the rough and ready society ("the world") in which less buddhistic individuals find themselves congenitally at home; the detachment of the Buddhist may not take the form of highly intellectualized "scientific" reasoning in a society in which such intellectuality is insufficiently developed or deliberately repressed. It must be kept in mind that the mode of expression of any one component of personality is influenced by the strength of the other components as these operate in a particular physical and social environment.

It is our conviction that the major types of personality express themselves in different philosophies, forms of art, types of society, varieties of religion. Even the features of conduct they have in common with other individuals of different types will bear their own unique imprint: the way they use symbols, the attitude to morality, the manifestation of love, the orientation of their intellectual life, the forms of insanity, the evaluation of whatever is evaluated. Some references to these differences will come into the account, but attention will center upon the general attitudes by which persons of various types have expressed themselves and given direction to their lives. We envisage the religious quest as the quest by the individual for a way of life answering to his type of personality, whether that be the type he has already attained or the type which seems to point a way out for the conflicts of his as yet unsettled and uncertain self.

7 / HERBERT MARCUSE

Aggressiveness in Advanced Industrial Society

I propose to consider here the strains and stresses in the so-called "affluent society," a phrase which has (rightly or wrongly) been coined to describe contemporary American society. Its main characteristics are: (1) an abundant industrial and technical capacity which is to a great extent spent in the production and distribution of luxury goods, gadgets, waste, planned obsolescence, military or semimilitary equipment—in short, in what economists

Herbert Marcuse, "Aggressiveness in Advanced Industrial Society," from *Negations*, pp. 248–268.

Herbert Marcuse (1898–) after serving as a lecturer at Columbia and Harvard universities and a professor of politics and philosophy at Brandeis University, joined the faculty of the University of California at San Diego. He is a leading political philosopher on the Left and is known for such books as *Reason and Revolution, Eros and Civilization, One-Dimensional Man, Negations,* and *Essays on Liberation.*

and sociologists used to call "unproductive" goods and services; (2) a rising standard of living, which also extends to previously underprivileged parts of the population; (3) a high degree of concentration of economic and political power, combined with a high degree of organization and government intervention in the economy; (4) scientific and pseudoscientific investigation, control, and manipulation of private and group behavior, both at work and at leisure (including the behavior of the psyche, the soul, the unconscious, and the subconscious) for commercial and political purposes. All these tendencies are interrelated: they make up the syndrome which expresses the normal functioning of the "affluent society." To demonstrate this interrelation is not my task here; I take its existence as the sociological basis for the thesis which I want to submit, namely, that the strains and stresses suffered by the individual in the affluent society are grounded in the normal functioning of this society (and of the individual!) rather than in its disturbances and diseases.

"Normal functioning": I think the definition presents no difficulties for the doctor. The organism functions normally if it functions, without disturbance, in accord with the biological and physiological makeup of the human body. The human faculties and capabilities are certainly very different among the members of the species, and the species itself has changed greatly in the course of its history but these changes have occurred on a biological and physiological basis which has remained largely constant. To be sure, the physician, in making his diagnosis and in proposing treatment, will take into account the patient's environment, upbringing, and occupation; these factors may limit the extent to which normal functioning can be defined and achieved, or they may even make this achievement impossible, but as criterion and goal, normality remains a clear and meaningful concept. As such, it is identical with "health,"and the various deviations from it are to various degrees of "disease."

The situation of the psychiatrist seems to be quite different. At first glance, normality seems to be defined along the same lines the physician uses. The normal functioning of the mind (psyche, psyche-soma) is that which enables the individual to perform, to function in accord with his position as child, adolescent, parent, as a single person or married, in accord with his job, profession, status. But this definition contains factors of an entirely new dimension, namely, that of society, and society is a factor of normality in a far more essential sense than that of external influence, so much so that "normal" seems to be a social and institutional rather than individual condition. It is probably easy to agree on what is the normal functioning of the digestive tract, the lungs, and the heart, but what is the normal functioning of the mind in lovemaking, in other interpersonal relations, at work and at leisure, at a meeting of a board of directors, on the golf course, in the slums, in prison, in the army? While the normal functioning of the digestive tract or the lung is likely to be the same in the case of a healthy corporation executive and of a healthy laborer, this does not hold true of their minds. In fact, the one would be very abnormal if he regularly thought, felt, and operated like the other. And what is "normal" lovemaking, a "normal" family, a "normal" occupation?

The psychiatrist might proceed like the general physician and direct therapy to making the patient function within his family, in his job or environment, while trying to influence and even change the environmental factors as much as this is in his power. The limits will soon make themselves felt, for example, if the mental strains and stresses of the patient are caused, not merely by certain bad conditions in his job, in his neighborhood, in his social status, but by the very *nature* of the job, the neighborhood, the status itself—in their normal condition. Then making him normal for this condition would mean normalizing the strains and stresses, or to put it more brutally: making him capable of being sick, of living his sickness as health, without his noticing that he is sick precisely when he sees himself and is seen as healthy and normal. This would be the case if his work is, by its very nature, "deadening," stupefying, wasteful (even though the job pays well and is "socially" necessary), or if the person belongs to a minority group which is underprivileged in the established society, traditionally poor and occupied mainly in menial and "dirty" physical labor. But this would also be the case (in very different forms) on the other side of the fence among the tycoons of business and politics, where efficient and profitable performance requires (and reproduces) the qualities of smart ruthlessness, moral indifference, and persistent aggressiveness. In such cases, "normal" functioning would be tantamount to a distortion and mutilation of a human being—no matter how modestly one may define the human qualities of a human being. Erich Fromm wrote *The Sane Society*; it deals, not with the established, but with a future, society, the implication being that the established society is *not* sane but insane. Is not the individual who functions normally, adequately, and healthily as a citizen of a sick society—is not such an individual himself sick? And would not a sick society require an antagonistic concept of mental health, a meta-concept designating (and preserving) mental qualities which are tabooed, arrested, or distorted by the "sanity" prevalent in the sick society? (For example, mental health equals the ability to live as a dissenter, to live a nonadjusted life.)

As a tentative definition of "sick society" we can say that a society is sick when its basic institutions and relations, its structure, are such that they do not permit the use of the available material and intellectual resources for the optimal development and satisfaction of individual needs. The larger the discrepancy between the potential and the actual human conditions, the greater the social need for what I term "surplus-repression," that is, repression necessitated not by the growth and preservation of civilization but by the vested interest in maintaining an established society. Such surplus-repression introduces (over and above, or rather underneath, the social conflicts) new strains and stresses in the individuals. Usually handled by the normal working of the social process, which assures adjustment and submission (fear of loss of job or status, ostracism, and so forth), no special enforcement policies with respect to the mind are required. But in the contemporary affluent society, the discrepancy between the established modes of existence, and the real possibilities of human freedom is so great that, in order to prevent an explosion, society has to insure a more effective mental coordination of individuals: in its unconscious as well as conscious dimensions, the psyche is opened up and subjected to systematic manipulation and control.

When I speak of the surplus-repression "required" for the maintenance of a society, or of the need for systematic manipulation and control, I do not refer to individually experienced social needs and consciously inaugurated policies: they may be thus experienced and inaugurated or they may not. I rather speak of *tendencies*, forces which can be identified by an analysis of the existing society and which assert themselves even if the policy makers are not aware of them. They express the requirements of the established apparatus of production, distribution, and consumption—economic, technical, political, mental requirements which have to be fulfilled in order to assure the continued functioning of the apparatus on which the population depends, and the continuing function of the social relationships derived from the organization of the apparatus. These objective tendencies become manifest in the trend of the economy, in technological change, in the domestic and foreign policy of a nation or group of nations, and they generate common, supraindividual needs and goals in the different social classes, pressure groups, and parties. Under the normal conditions of social cohesion, the objective tendencies override or absorb individual interests and goals without exploding the society; however, the particular interest is not simply determined by the universal: the former has its own range of freedom, and contributes, in accordance with its social position, to the shaping of the general interest—but short of a revolution, the particular needs and goals will remain defined by the predominant objective tendencies. Marx believed that they assert themselves "behind the back" of the individuals; in the advanced societies of today, this is true only with strong qualifications. Social engineering, scientific management of enterprise and human relations, and manipulation of instinctual needs are practiced on the policy-making level and testify to the degree of awareness within the general blindness.

As for the systematic manipulation and control of the psyche in the advanced industrial society, manipulation and control for what, and by whom? Over and above all particular manipulation in the interest of certain businesses, policies, lobbies—the general objective purpose is to reconcile the individual with the mode of existence which his society imposes on him.

Because of the high degree of surplus-repression involved in such reconciliation, it is necessary to achieve a libidinal cathexis of the merchandise the individual has to buy (or sell), the services he has to use (or perform), the fun he has to enjoy, the status symbols he has to carry—necessary, because the existence of the society depends on their uninterrupted production and consumption. In other words, social needs must become individual needs, instinctual needs. And to the degree to which the productivity of this society requires mass production and mass consumption, these needs must be standardized, coordinated, generalized. Certainly, these controls are not a conspiracy, they are not centralized in any agency or group of agencies (although the trend toward centralization is gaining momentum); they are rather diffused throughout the society, exercised by the neighbors, the community, the peer groups, mass media, corporations, and (perhaps least) by the government. But they are exercised with the help of, in fact rendered possible by, science, by the social and behavioral sciences, and especially by sociology and psychology. As industrial sociology and psychology, or, more euphemistically, as "science of human relations," these scientific efforts have become an indispensable tool in the hands of the powers that be.

These brief remarks are suggestive of the depth of society's ingression into the psyche, the extent to which mental health, normality, is not that of the individual but of his society. Such a harmony between the individual and society would be highly desirable if the society offered the individual the conditions for his development as a human being in accord with the available possibilities of freedom, peace, and happiness (that is in accord with the possible liberation of his life instincts), but it is highly destructive to the individual if these conditions do not prevail. Where they do not prevail, the healthy and normal individual is a human being equipped with all the qualities which enable him to get along with others in his society, and these very same qualities are the marks of repression, the marks of a mutilated human being, who collaborates in his own repression, in the containment of potential individual and social freedom, in the release of aggression. And this situation cannot be solved within the framework of individual psychology and therapy, nor within the framework of any psychology—a solution can be envisaged only on the political level: in the struggle against society. To be sure, therapy could demonstrate this situation and prepare the mental ground for such a struggle—but then psychiatry would be a subversive undertaking.

The question now is whether the strains in contemporary American society, in the affluent society, suggest the prevalence of conditions essentially negative to individual development in the sense just discussed. Or, to formulate the question in terms more indicative of the approach I propose to take: Do these strains vitiate the very possibility of "healthy" individual development—healthy defined in terms of optimal development of one's intellectual and emotional faculties? The question calls for an affirmative answer, that is, this society vitiates individual developments, if the prevailing strains are related to the very structure of this society and if they activate in its members instinctual needs and satisfactions which set the individuals against themselves so that they reproduce and intensify their own repression.

At first glance, the strains in our society seem to be those characteristic of any society which develops under the impact of great technological changes: they initiate new modes of work and of leisure and thereby affect all social relationships, and bring about a thorough transvaluation of values. Since physical labor tends to become increasingly unnecessary and even wasteful, since the work of salaried employees too becomes increasingly "automatic" and that of the politicians and administrators increasingly questionable, the traditional content of the struggle for existence appears more meaningless and without substance the more it appears as unnecessary necessity. But the future alternative, namely, the possible abolition of (alienated) labor seems equally meaningless, nay, frightening. And indeed, if one envisages this alternative as the progress and development of the *established* system, then the dislocation of the content of life to free time suggests the shape of a nightmare: massive self-realization, fun, sport in a steadily shrinking space.

But the threat of the "bogey of automation" is itself ideology. On the one hand it serves the perpetuation and reproduction of technically obsolete and unnecessary jobs and occupations (unemployment as normal condition, even if comfortable, seems worse than stupefying routine work); on the other hand it justifies and promotes the education and training of the managers and organization men of leisure time, that is to say, it serves to prolong and enlarge control and manipulation.

The real danger for the established system is not the abolition of labor but the possibility of nonalienated labor as the basis of the reproduction of society. Not that people are no longer compelled to work, but that they might be compelled to work for a very different life and in very different relations, that they might be given very different goals and values, that they might have to live with a very different morality—this is the "definite negation" of the established system, the liberating alternative. For example, socially necessary labor might be organized for such efforts as the rebuilding of cities and towns, the relocation of the places of work (so that people learn again how to walk), the construction of industries which produce goods without built-in obsolescence, without profitable waste and poor quality, and the subjection of the environment to the vital aesthetic needs of the organism. To be sure, to translate this possibility into reality would mean to eliminate the power of the dominant interests which, by their very function in the society, are opposed to a development that would reduce private enterprise to a minor role, that would do away with the market economy, and with the policy of military preparedness, expansion, and intervention—in other words: a development that would reverse the entire prevailing trend. There is little evidence for such a development. In the meantime, and with the new and terribly effective and total means provided by technical progress, the population is physically and mentally mobilized against this eventuality: they must continue the struggle for existence in painful, costly, and obsolete forms.

This is the real contradiction which translates itself from the social structure into the mental structure of the individuals. There, it activates and aggravates destructive tendencies which, in a hardly sublimated mode, are made socially useful in the behavior of the individuals, on the private as well as political level—in the behavior of the nation as a whole. Destructive energy becomes socially useful aggressive energy, and the aggressive behavior impels growth—growth of economic, political, and technical power. Just as in the contemporary scientific enterprise, so in the economic enterprise and in that of the nation as a whole, constructive and destructive achievements, work for life and work for death, procreating and killing are inextricably united. To restrict the exploitation of nuclear energy would mean to restrict its peaceful as well as military potential; the amelioration and protection of life appear as by-products of the scientific work on the annihilation of life; to restrict procreation would also mean to restrict potential manpower and the number of potential customers and clients. Now the (more or less sublimated) transformation of destructive into socially useful aggressive (and thereby constructive) energy is, according to Freud (on whose instinct-theory I base my interpretation) a normal and indispensable process. It is part of the same dynamic by which libido, erotic energy, is sublimated and made socially useful; the two opposite impulses are forced together and, united in this twofold transformation, they become the mental and organic vehicles of civilization. But no matter how close and effective their union, their respective quality remains unchanged and contrary: aggression activates destruction which "aims" at death, while libido seeks the preservation, protection, and amelioration of life. Therefore, it is only as long as destruction works in the service of Eros that it serves civilization and the individual; if aggression becomes stronger than its erotic counterpart, the trend is reversed. Moreover, in the Freudian conception, destructive energy cannot become stronger without reducing erotic energy: the balance between the two primary impulses is a quantitative one; the instinctual dynamic is mechanistic, distributing an available quantum of energy between the two antagonists.

I have briefly restated Freud's conception inasmuch as I shall use it to discuss the depth and character of the strains prevalent in American society. I suggest that the strains derive from the basic contradiction between the capabilities of this society, which could produce essentially new forms of freedom amounting to a subversion of the established institutions on the one hand, and the repressive use of these capabilities on the other. The contradiction explodes—and is at the same time "resolved," "contained"—in the ubiquitous aggression prevalent in this society. Its most conspicuous (but by no means isolated) manifestation is the military mobilization and its effect on the mental behavior of the individuals, but within the context of the basic contradiction, aggressiveness is fed by many sources. The following seem to be foremost:

(1) *The dehumanization of the process of production and consumption.* Technical progress is identical with the increasing elimination of personal initiative, inclination, taste, and need from the provision of goods and services. This tendency is liberating if the available resources and techniques are used for freeing the individual from labor and recreation which are required for the reproduction of the established institutions but are parasitic, wasteful, and dehumanizing in terms of the existing technical and intellectual capabilities. The same tendency often gratifies hostility.

(2) *The conditions of crowding, noise, and overtness characteristic of mass society.* As René Dubos has said, the need for "quiet, privacy, independence, initiative, and some open space" are not "frills or luxuries but constitute real biological necessities." Their lack injures the instinctual structure itself. Freud has emphasized the "asocial" character of Eros—the mass society achieves an "oversocialization" to which the individual reacts "with all sorts of frustrations, repressions, aggressions, and fears which soon develop into genuine neuroses."

I mentioned, as the most conspicuous social mobilization of aggressiveness, the militarization of the affluent society. This mobilization goes far beyond the actual draft of manpower and the buildup of the armament industry: its truly totalitarian aspects show forth in the daily mass media which feed "public opinion." The brutalization of language and image, the presentation of killing, burning, and poisoning and torture inflicted upon the victims of neocolonial slaughter is made in a common-sensible, factual, sometimes humorous style which integrates these horrors with the pranks of juvenile delinquents, football contests, accidents, stock market reports, and the weatherman. This is no longer the "classical" heroizing of killing in the national interest, but rather its reduction to the level of natural events and contingencies of daily life.

The consequence is a "psychological habituation of war" which is administered to a people protected from the actuality of war, a people who, by virtue of this habituation, easily familiarizes itself with the "kill rate" as it is already familiar with other "rates" (such as those of business or traffic or unemployment). The people are conditioned to live "with the hazards, the brutalities, and the mounting casualties of the war in Vietnam, just as one learns gradually to live with the everyday hazards and casualties of smoking, of smog, or of traffic."[1] The photos which appear in the daily newspapers and in

[1] I. Ziferstein, in the UCLA *Daily Bruin*, Los Angeles, May 24, 1966. See also M. Grotjahn, "Some Dynamics of Unconscious and Symbolic Communication in Present-Day Television," *The Psychoanalytic Study of Society*, III, pp. 356ff., and *Psychiatric Aspects of the Prevention of Nuclear War*, Group for the Advancement of Psychiatry (New York, 1964), passim.

magazines with mass circulation, often in nice and glossy color, show rows of prisoners laid out or stood up for "interrogation," little children dragged through the dust behind armored cars, mutilated women. They are nothing new ("such things happen in a war"), but it is the setting that makes the difference: their appearance in the regular program, in togetherness with the commercials, sports, local politics, and reports on the social set. And the brutality of power is further normalized by its extension to the beloved automobile: the manufacturers sell a Thunderbird, Fury, Tempest, and the oil industry puts "a tiger in your tank."

However, the administered language is rigidly discriminating: a specific vocabulary of hate, resentment, and defamation is reserved for opposition to the aggressive policies and for the enemy. The pattern constantly repeats itself. Thus, when students demonstrate against the war, it is a "mob" swelled by "bearded advocates of sexual freedom," by unwashed juveniles, and by "hoodlums and street urchins" who "tramp" the streets, while the counter-demonstrations consist of citizens who gather. In Vietnam, "typical criminal communist violence" is perpetrated against American "strategic operations." The Reds have the impertinence to launch "a sneak attack" (presumably they are supposed to announce it beforehand and to deploy in the open); they are "evading a death trap" (presumably they should have stayed in). The Vietcong attack American barracks "in the dead of night" and kill American boys (presumably, Americans only attack in broad daylight, don't disturb the sleep of the enemy, and don't kill Vietnamese boys). The massacre of hundred thousands of communists (in Indonesia) is called "impressive"—a comparable "killing rate" suffered by the other side would hardly have been honored with such an adjective. To the Chinese, the presence of American troops in East Asia is a threat to their "ideology," while presumably the presence of Chinese troops in Central or South America would be a real, and not only ideological, threat to the United States.

The loaded language proceeds according to the Orwellian recipe of the identity of opposites: in the mouth of the enemy, peace means war, and defense is attack, while on the righteous side, escalation is restraint, and saturation bombing prepares for peace. Organized in this discriminatory fashion, language designates a priori the enemy as evil in his entirety and in all his actions and intentions.

Such mobilization of aggressiveness cannot be explained by the magnitude of the communist threat: the image of the ostensible enemy is inflated out of all proportion to reality. What is at stake is rather the continued stability and growth of a system which is threatened by its own irrationality—by the narrow base on which its prosperity rests, by the dehumanization which its wasteful and parasitic affluence demands. The senseless war is itself part of this irrationality and thus of the essence of the system. What may have been a minor involvement at the beginning, almost an accident, a contingency of foreign policy, has become a test case for the productivity, competitiveness, and prestige of the whole. The billions of dollars spent for the war effort are a political as well as economic stimulus (or cure): a big way of absorbing part of the economic surplus, and of keeping the people in line. Defeat in Vietnam may well be the signal for other wars of liberation closer to home—and perhaps even for rebellion at home.

To be sure, the social utilization of aggressiveness belongs to the historical structure of civilization and has been a powerful vehicle of progress. However, here too, there is a stage where quantity may turn into quality and subvert the normal balance between the two primary instincts in favor of destruction. I mentioned the "bogey man" of automation. In fact the real spectre for the affluent society is the possible reduction of labor to a level where the human organism need no longer function as an instrument of labor. The mere quantitative decline in needed human labor power militates against the maintenance of the capitalist mode of production (as of all other exploitative modes of production). The system reacts by stepping up the production of goods and services which either do not enlarge individual consumption at all, or enlarge it with luxuries—luxuries in the face of persistent poverty, but luxuries which are necessities for occupying a labor force sufficient to reproduce the established economic and political institutions. To the degree to which this sort of work appears as superfluous, senseless, and unnecessary while necessary for earning a living, frustration is built into the very productivity of this society, and aggressiveness is activated. And to the degree to which the society in its very structure becomes aggressive, the mental structure of its citizens adjusts itself: the individual becomes at one and the same time more aggressive and more pliable and submissive, for he submits to a society which, by virtue of its affluence and power, satisfies his deepest (and otherwise greatly repressed) instinctual needs. And these instinctual needs apparently find their libidinal reflection in the representatives of the people. The chairman of the Armed Services Committee of the United States Senate, Senator Russell of Georgia, was struck by this fact. He is quoted as saying:

> There is something about preparing for destruction that causes men to be more careless in spending money than they would be if they were building for constructive purposes. Why that is, I do not know; but I have observed, over a period of almost thirty years in the Senate, that there is something about buying arms with which to kill, to destroy, to wipe out cities, and to obliterate great transportation systems which causes men not to reckon the dollar cost as closely as they do when they think about proper housing and the care of the health of human beings.[2]

[2] Quoted in *The Nation*, August 25, 1962, pp. 65–66, in an article by Senator William Proxmire.

I have argued elsewhere the question of how one can possibly gauge and historically compare the aggression prevalent in a specific society; instead of restating the case, I want now to focus on different aspects, on the specific forms in which aggression today is released and satisfied.

The most telling one, and the one which distinguishes the new from the traditional forms, is what I call *technological aggression and satisfaction*. The phenomenon is quickly described: the act of aggression is physically carried out by a mechanism with a high degree of automatism, of far greater power than the individual human being who sets it in motion, keeps it in motion, and determines its end or target. The most extreme case is the rocket or missile; the most ordinary example the automobile. This means that the energy, the power activated and consummated is the mechanical, electrical, or nuclear energy of "things" rather than the instinctual energy of a human being. Aggression is, as it were, transferred from a subject to an object, or is at least "mediated" by an object, and the target is destroyed by a thing rather than by a person. This change in the relation between human and material energy, and between the physical and mental part of aggression (man becomes the subject and agent of aggression by virtue of his mental rather than physical faculties) must also affect the mental dynamic. I submit a hypothesis which is suggested by the inner logic of the process: with the "delegation" of destruction to a more or less automated thing or group and system of things, the instinctual satisfaction of the human person is "interrupted," reduced, frustrated, "super-sublimated." And such frustration makes for repetition and escalation: increasing violence, speed, enlarged scope. At the same time, personal responsibility, conscience, and the sense of guilt is weakened, or rather diffused, displaced from the actual context in which the aggression was committed (i.e. bombing raids), and relocated in a more or less innocuous context (impoliteness, sexual inadequacy, etc.). In this reaction too, the effect is a considerable weakening of the sense of guilt, and the defense (hatred, resentment) is also redirected from the real responsible subject (the commanding officer, the government) to a substitute person: not I as a (morally and physically) acting person did it, but the thing, the machine. The machine: the word suggests that an apparatus consisting of human beings may be substituted for the mechanical apparatus: the bureaucracy, the administration, the party, or organization is the responsible agent; I, the individual person, was only the instrumentality. And an instrument cannot, in any moral sense, be responsible or be in a state of guilt. In this way, another barrier against aggression, which civilization had erected in a long and violent process of discipline is removed. And the expansion of advanced capitalism becomes involved in a fateful psychical dialectic which enters into and propels its economic and political dynamic: the more powerful and "technological" aggression becomes, the less is it apt to satisfy and pacify the primary impulse, and the more it tends toward repetition and escalation.

To be sure, the use of instruments of aggression is as old as civilization itself, but there is a decisive difference between technological aggression and the more primitive forms. The latter were not only quantitatively different (weaker): they required activation and *engagement* of the body to a much higher degree than the automated or semiautomated instruments of aggression. The knife, the "blunt instrument," even the revolver are far more "part" of the individual who uses them and they associate him more closely with his target. Moreover, and most important, their use, unless effectively sublimated and in the service of the life instincts (as in the case of the surgeon, household, etc.), is criminal—individual crime—and as such subject to severe punishment. In contrast, technological aggression is not a crime. The speeding driver of an automobile or motor boat is not called a murderer even if he is one; and certainly the missile-firing engineers are not.

Technological aggression releases a mental dynamic which aggravates the destructive, antierotic tendencies of the puritan complex. The new modes of aggression destroy without getting one's hands dirty, one's body soiled, one's mind incriminated. The killer remains clean, physically as well as mentally. The purity of his deadly work obtains added sanction if it is directed against the national enemy in the national interest.

The (anonymous) lead article in *Les Temps Modernes* (January 1966) links the war in Vietnam with the puritan tradition in the United States. The image of the enemy is that of dirt in its most repulsive forms; the unclean jungle is his natural habitat, disembowelment and beheading are his natural ways of action. Consequently, the burning of his refuge, defoliation, and the poisoning of his foodstuff are not only strategic but also moral operations: removing of contagious dirt, clearing the way for the order of political hygiene and righteousness. And the mass purging of the good conscience from all rational inhibitions leads to the atrophy of the last rebellion of sanity against the madhouse: no satire, no ridicule attends the moralists who organize and defend the crime. Thus one of them can, without becoming a laughingstock, publicly praise as the "greatest performance in our nation's history," the indeed historical achievement of the richest, most powerful, and most advanced country of the world unleashing the destructive force of its technical superiority on one of the poorest, weakest, and most helpless countries of the world.

The decline of responsibility and guilt, their absorption by the omnipotent technical and political apparatus also tends to invalidate other values which were to restrain and sublimate aggression. While the militarization of society remains the most conspicuous and destructive manifestation of this tendency, its less ostensible effects in the cultural dimension should not be minimized. One of these effects is the disintegration of the value of *truth*. The media enjoy a large dispensation from the commitment to truth, and in a very special way. The point is not that the media lie ("lie" presupposes commitment to truth), they rather mingle truth and half-truth with omission, factual reporting with commentary and evaluation, information with publicity and propaganda—all this made into an overwhelming whole through editorializing. The editorially unpleasant truths (and how many of the most decisive truths are not unpleasant?) retreat between the lines, or hide, or mingle harmoniously with nonsense, fun, and so-called human interest stories. And the consumer is readily inclined to take all this for granted—he buys it even if he knows better. Now the commitment to the truth has always been precarious, hedged with strong qualifications, suspended, or suppressed—it is only in the context of the general and democratic activation of aggressiveness that the devaluation of truth assumes special significance. For truth is a value in the strict sense inasmuch as it serves the protection and amelioration of life, as a guide in man's struggle with nature and with himself, with his own weakness and his own destructiveness. In this function, truth is indeed a matter of the sublimated life instincts, Eros, of intelligence becoming responsible and autonomous, striving to liberate life from dependence on unmastered and repressive forces. And with respect to this protective and liberating function of truth, its devaluation removes another effective barrier against destruction.

The encroachment of aggression on the domain of the life instincts also devalues the aesthetic dimension. In *Eros and Civilization* I have tried to show the erotic component in this dimension. Nonfunctional, that is to say, not committed to the functioning of a repressive society, the aesthetic values have been strong protectors of Eros in civilization. Nature is part of this dimension. Eros seeks, in polymorphous forms, its own sensuous world of fulfillment, its own "natural" environment. But only in a protected world—protected from daily business, from noise, crowds, waste, only thus can it satisfy the biological need for happiness. The aggressive business practices which turn ever more spaces of protective nature into a medium of commercial fulfillment and fun thus do not merely offend beauty—they repress biological necessities.

Once we agree to discuss the hypothesis that, in advanced industrial society surplus-aggression is released in quite unsuspected and "normal" behavior, we may see it even in areas which are far removed from the more familiar manifestations of aggression, for instance the style of publicity and information practiced by the mass media. Characteristic is the permanent repetition: the same commercial with the same text or picture broadcast or televised again and again; the same phrases and clichés poured out by the purveyors and makers of information again and again; the same programs and platforms professed by the politicians again and again. Freud arrived at his concept of the death instinct in the context of his analysis of the "repetition compulsion": he associated with it the striving for a state of complete inertia, absence of tension, return to the womb, annihilation. Hitler knew well the extreme function of repetition: the biggest lie, often enough repeated, will be acted upon and accepted as truth. Even in its less extreme use, constant repetition, imposed upon more or less captive audiences, may be destructive: destroying mental autonomy, freedom of thought, responsibility and conducive to inertia, submission, rejection of change. The established society, the master of repetition, becomes the great womb for its citizens. To be sure, this road to inertia and this reduction of tension is one of high and not very satisfactory sublimation: it does not lead to an instinctual nirvana of satisfaction. However, it may well reduce the stress of intelligence, the pain and tension which accompany autonomous mental activity—thus it may be an effective aggression against the mind in its socially disturbing, critical functions.

These are highly speculative hypotheses on the socially and mentally fateful character of aggression in our society. Aggression is (in most cases) socially useful destructiveness—and yet fateful because of its self-propelling character and scope. In this respect too, it is badly sublimated and not very satisfying. If Freud's theory is correct, and the destructive impulse strives for the annihilation of the individual's own life no matter how long the "detour" via other lives and targets, then we may indeed speak of a suicidal tendency on a truly social scale, and the national and international play with total destruction may well have found a firm basis in the instinctual structure of individuals.

8 / B. F. SKINNER

Utopia through the Control of Human Behaviour

In my first talk* I reviewed some of the outstanding utopian visions. I was not much concerned with why people would enjoy a particular good life but rather with how the authors of utopias thought a good life might be achieved. Some looked to a wise ruler, others to the word of God, some favoured law

B. F. Skinner, "Utopia through the Control of Human Behaviour," in *The Listener*, January 12, 1967. Reprinted by permission of the author.

B. F. Skinner (1904–), Edgar Pierce Professor of Psychology at Harvard University, is an internationally known behaviorist recognized for his system of operant conditioning, contributions to programmed learning, and his utopian system of controls based on positive reinforcement. His publications include *Behavior of Organisms, Walden Two, Science and Human Behavior, Schedules of Reinforcement, The Analysis of Behavior, Beyond Freedom and Dignity,* and *The Technology of Teaching*. He is also coauthor of *Verbal Behavior* and *Cumulative Record.*

* *The Listener*, January 5.

and order and the rule of reason, others would minimize civilization so that natural man might emerge in all his nobility. Economic utopias turn to the production of wealth, but in the twentieth century the relevance of a broader scientific analysis of behavior became clear. Freud, strangely enough, sparked off no utopian vision, but Pavlov and the conditioned reflex were adopted by the communists because Pavlov was Russian, and satirically by Aldous Huxley in his *Brave New World.* The account was still incomplete. The conditioned reflex is mainly concerned with the emotional responses we feel; it has little to do with action. A different branch of the science of behaviour is therefore relevant.

Abundance Leading to Inaction

When a man escapes punishment or achieves a reward, the feelings he thus generates are far less important than certain reinforcing or strengthening effects on his behaviour. Mere abundance, providing for each according to his need, leads to inaction. Whether we find it in the South Seas or in a welfare state, abundance is simply another name for a candy-mountain land or Cockaigne. It is the *Schlaraffenland* of Hans Sachs—idler's land—and idleness is the goal only of those who have been compulsively or anxiously busy. Idleness does not provide for the support of a culture, and it does not make for happiness. The wholly satisfied man is unhappy. The word "sad" is etymologically related to the word "sated". We do not need to be economic reactionaries to worry about non-productivity, nor cynics to view mere gratification with contempt. The Goncourt brothers speak of "the utopian stupidity of a phalanstery: a happiness equally divided, and a similar piece to each, like a piece of cake." Huxley's *Brave New World* was a study in the futility of simple happiness. We all make this mistake. Asked what kind of world we should like to live in, we are likely to reply by listing various things we want to find in it—food, friendship, sex, pleasant surroundings, music, and so on. Seldom, if ever, will we mention what we are to do to get these things. Yet that is the crucial issue. There is nothing wrong in pleasure *per se*, as the Protestant ethic often seemed to suggest, but the feeling of pleasure must take second place to a more important function. The things we call pleasant have an energizing or strengthening effect on our behaviour, and it is only when they have that they make us really happy.

The shortcomings of utopias which appeal to the satisfaction of needs have been made clear by what is known as the experimental analysis of behaviour. Food, sex, music, and all the other values are reinforcers. When a man behaves in such a way as to produce one of these things he is more likely to behave in that way again. By making reinforcers contingent on behaviour we can alter behaviour in a very effective way.

To make men active and happy and forward-looking, we do not need to find new reinforcers, we simply need to make better use of those we have. We must arrange effective contingencies of reinforcement. In doing so, we supplement the wise personal rule of Plato's Republic, the appeal to reason and law in More and Bacon, and particularly the economic sanctions of Adam Smith and Karl Marx. We can deal at last with a critical characteristic of human behaviour which has been overlooked in all earlier utopian designs. In doing so, we move closer to a world in which men will be happy, productive, and forward-looking.

The utopias constitute a series of essays in how human behaviour can be controlled. There are those who would rather say "influenced," "modified," or "changed," but "controlled" is the accurate term. For many good reasons, we dislike the idea of being controlled, and cherish the belief that no one is controlling us. Many methods of control are themselves objectionable—the slave-driver's whip, the punitive sanctions of governments and religions, the school-master's cane. Probably because these methods are aversive, we have slowly turned to techniques of other kinds. The control of the future will not in that sense be objectionable. Recent advances have been largely concerned with techniques of control which do not involve punishment. But that fact in itself may be particularly frightening. Punitive methods have at least the virtue that they generate revolt. We usually know that we are being controlled and who is controlling us, and rather than submit we can escape or counter-attack. The term brain-washing applies to some controlling techniques which are particularly designed so that they will not breed counter-measures.

Fear of Control

But should men always revolt when they are being controlled? The control in a utopian design is for the benefit of the controllee, and it may be unwise to fear it because it resembles control for other purposes. From a scientific point of view, we are always under control by the environment, including environments arranged by men. The control can arise from accident or design. There is no particular virtue in accident. In a design, true enough, some person must be *in* control and history has taught us to fear him just because he is—no matter why he controls, or what environmental contingencies have controlled him in turn and induced him to control.

Suppose that Mr. Krutch, or some other critic of utopias, were to discover a small, hitherto unknown culture in which people were living approximately as I described the good life in my utopian novel, *Walden Two*. There is little or no personal aggression, work is pleasant and occupies only a few hours each day, expert medical attention is available, education is advanced, the arts and sciences flourish. Would he not on that evidence alone judge it a good life? But now let him discover that it is not a stage in the accidental evolution of a culture but that, a generation or two ago, one man set forth the plan which is now being followed. In some sense that man would be in control, and that would spoil it all. It would not be the Good Life.

It does not matter to such critics that control is no longer being exerted. I tried to make that clear in my novel. In *Walden Two* there is no leader. Frazier the protagonist still lives in the community and was clearly the first mover, but he is no longer moving anyone or anything. To avoid any hint of current personal influence, I gave him what might be called negative charisma. He is not even a likable fellow. It seems rather silly to fear him just because he started it all.

"Despoiled" Citizens?

Yet there are those who would still object that the citizen of a planned community is being despoiled. The original designer can in some sense take credit for all the achievements of a culture. This has always been the case. The man who designs a better way of teaching may in some sense take credit for all the benefits which follow when people are better educated. The ruler who designs a better way of inducing people to behave well may take credit for the benefits to be found in an orderly society. The industrialist who designs a better way of producing goods may take credit for the advantage of an increased affluence.

If there is only a limited amount of credit available, then those who have been taught well, who behave well, and who produce efficiently have to some extent been robbed of a source of admiration. Good education deprives man of the chance to be admired for learning effectively when badly taught. Good government denies men the chance to get credit for behaving well when there is no reason to do so. Efficient machinery of production deprives men of the chance to be admired for handicraftmanship. A utopia, as a completely managed culture, would seem to work a wholesale despoliation of this sort. Some critics have gone so far as to say that it would rob men of their very humanity. Mr. Krutch has accused me of dehumanizing men, and C. S. Lewis entitled a book on this theme the *Abolition of Man.*

Something does happen to the notion of credit or admiration, not only when we attempt to design a more effective culture but when we simply analyse how a culture works. Let us assume for the sake of the discussion that man's behaviour is indeed traceable simply to his genetic and environmental history. In some cultures a man gets credit for good breeding (he contains his genetic endowment and is admired for it), but it is certainly not his own achievement; and the more we understand about genetics the less we are inclined to give a man credit for features of his behaviour which derive from his heredity.

A similar change follows as we begin to learn more about the contributions of environment. If we admire a man for behaving well, it is only because we are not quite sure why he does so. If we can discover reasons in the environment in which he has lived, we are likely to credit *them* with his good behaviour. In the past, we have continued to admire men for behaving well even though we were aware of religious and governmental sanctions, but this has only been because such sanctions are not directly or wholly responsible for the behaviour we observe. Men have been induced to behave well by threatening them when they behave badly, but the punishment which thus suppresses bad behaviour does not dictate what a man will do in behaving well. Something is left to be credited to the man himself. Suppose now that we design religious or governmental practices which not only suppress bad behaviour, but strengthen particular forms of good behaviour. People will now behave well automatically. Since it is obvious why they do so, they themselves cannot take credit.

The struggle for knowledge and the struggle to behave well have been such dramatic parts of man's history that we are likely to think they are an essential part of being human. A world in which one is automatically right and good is a strange and frightening prospect. Yet a long time ago Thomas Henry Huxley said that "if some great power would agree to make me always think what is true and do what is right, on condition of being turned into a sort of clock and wound up every morning before I got out of bed, I would instantly close with the offer." It does not need a covenant with some great power. We move in this direction whenever we learn something new about human behaviour and put that knowledge to work. Does anyone seriously propose that we should weaken or destroy education so that we can once again admire the autodidact, that we should destroy labour-saving devices so that we can once again admire minor Herculeses, or that we should abandon moral and ethical education and government so that we can admire the man who behaves well without them?

A rather similar objection takes this form: in the scientific view of human behaviour, man is not responsible for his own destiny. The responsibility lies in his genetic endowment and his environmental history, which are to be found outside man himself. But there is a more optimistic view. Man can and does change his environment, and in the not too distant future he may change his genetic endowment. Man may be controlled by the world in which he lives, but he himself can control that world. As science and technology grow, man becomes able as never before to alter his own history. He may not recapture any personal credit in doing so, but his development of a great culture will still rank as a most admirable human achievement.

Something very close to utopian thinking has been largely responsible for what we call western civilization. Our culture strongly encourages us to ask whether there is not a better way of doing things. Physical technology is perhaps the most dramatic example, but the same question has long been asked about practices affecting human behaviour. There is nothing new about social invention—about the refusal to accept practices as they come to us in the tradition of our culture. We try new ways of raising children, new ways of teaching them, new ways of collecting taxes, new ways of paying wages, new ways of treating neurotic and psychotic people, and so on. Utopian speculation differs from this only in the fact that many different ways of improving a culture are considered all at once.

An experimental community is like a pilot plant in industry. There are advantages in its small size, in its semi-isolation—both geographical and historical—and in the freedom to experiment, to change practices as experience dictates. The utopias of the past have been committed to a single solution—to the patchwork of a philosopher-king, to an appeal to law and order, to a single-minded concern for the production of wealth, and so on. As a science of behaviour matures, however, it is possible to take all these and other behavioural processes into consideration at once. The chances of a successful experiment are therefore improved. A change in our conception of man is no doubt required, and resistance will be felt on the part of those who want to perpetuate earlier conceptions. But the power of a behavioural technology has increased in an extraordinary way, and its application to the design of cultures is inevitable.

In the nineteenth century, particularly in America where valuable land was available for the asking, many experiments in community living were made. Many of them were much more successful than is commonly believed, and it is not difficult to explain the failures. Something of the same experimental spirit is again abroad. There is a growing disinclination on the part of young people to accept any way of life without critical examination. In some parts of the world at least, men of goodwill are still free to experiment within the framework of existing governments. In the United States several groups of people are now planning communities similar to *Walden Two*. They are not crackpots, nor escapists, they are simply demonstrating their faith that through an extension of science to human behaviour man may still be in control of his own destiny.

9 / ABRAHAM MASLOW

Deficiency Motivation and Growth Motivation

The concept "basic need" can be defined in terms of the questions which it answers and the operations which uncovered it. My original question was about psychopathogenesis. "What makes people neurotic?" My answer (a modification of and I think an improvement upon the analytic one) was, in brief, that neurosis seemed at its core, and in its beginning, to be a deficiency disease; that it was born out of being deprived of certain satisfactions which I called needs in the same sense that water and amino acids and calcium are needs, namely that their absence produces illness. Most neuroses involved, along with other complex determinants, ungratified wishes for safety, for belongingness and identification, for close love relationships and for respect and prestige. My "data" were gathered through twelve years of psychotherapeutic work and research and twenty years of personality study. One obvious control research (done at the same time and in the same operation) was on the effect of replacement therapy which showed, with many complexities, that when these deficiencies were eliminated, sicknesses tended to disappear. Still another necessary long-time control research was on the family backgrounds of both neurotic and healthy people establishing, as many others have since done, that people who are later healthy are not deprived of these essential basic-need-satisfactions, i.e., the prophylactic control.

These conclusions, which are now in effect shared by most clinicians, therapists, and child psychologists (many of them would not phrase it as I have) make it more possible year by year to define need, in a natural, easy spontaneous way, as a generalization of actual experiential data (rather

Abraham Maslow, "Deficiency Motivation and Growth Motivation," from *Nebraska Symposium on Motivation,* pp. 3–30.

Abraham H. Maslow (1908–1970) was a member of the faculty of Brooklyn College and from 1951 to 1970 was a professor of psychology at Brandeis University. A former president of the American Psychological Association, he was a leader in the humanistic psychology movement, and he contributed to studies of personality, motivation, and self-actualizing persons. He is known for his books *Motivation and Personality; Toward a Psychology of Being; Religion, Values, and Peak Experiences;* and *The Psychology of Science.*

than by fiat, arbitrarily and prematurely; *prior* to the accumulation of knowledge rather than subsequent to it (22) simply for the sake of greater objectivity).

The long-run deficiency characteristics are then the following. It is a basic or instinctoid need if:

1. its absence breeds illness,
2. its presence prevents illness,
3. its restoration cures illness,
4. under certain (very complex) free choice situations, it is preferred by the deprived person over other satisfactions,
5. it is found to be inactive, at a low ebb, or functionally absent in the healthy person.

Two additional characteristics are subjective ones, namely, conscious or unconscious yearning and desire, and feeling of lack or deficiency, as of something missing on the one hand, and, on the other, palatability ("It tastes good").

One last word on definition. Many of the problems that have plagued the writers in this series as they attempted to define and delimit motivation are a consequence of the exclusive demand for behavioral, externally observable criteria. The original criterion of motivation and the one that is still used by all human beings except behavioral psychologists is the subjective one. I am motivated when I feel desire or want or yearning or wish or lack. No objectively observable state has yet been found that correlates decently with these subjective reports, i.e., no good behavioral definition of motivation has yet been found.

Now of course we ought to keep on seeking for objective correlates of subjective states. On the day when we discover such a public and external indicator of pleasure or of anxiety or of desire, psychology will have jumped forward by a century. But *until* we find it we ought not make believe that we have. Nor ought we neglect the subjective data that we do have. It is unfortunate that we cannot ask a rat to give subjective reports. Fortunately, however, we *can* ask the human being, and I see no reason in the world why we should refrain from doing so until we have a better source of data. If the "objective" psychologists trying to define motivation sometimes seem to be staggering about in the dark, perhaps it is because they have voluntarily blindfolded themselves.

It is these needs which are essentially deficits in the organism, empty holes, so to speak, which must be filled up for health's sake, and furthermore must be filled from without by human beings *other* than the subject that I shall call deficits or deficiency needs for purposes of this exposition and to set them in contrast to another and very different kind of motivation.

There is not a person in this room to whom it would occur to question the statement that we "need" iodine or vitamin C. I remind you that the evidence that we "need" love is of exactly the same type.

In recent years more and more psychologists have found themselves compelled to postulate some tendency to growth or self-perfection to supplement the concepts of equilibrium, homeostasis, tension-reduction, defense and other conserving motivations. This was so for various reasons.

1. Psychotherapy. The pressure toward health makes therapy possible. It is an absolute *sine qua non*. If there were no such trend, therapy would be inexplicable to the extent that it goes beyond the building of defenses against pain and anxiety. (Rogers, (23), Angyal, (2), et cetera.)

2. Brain Injured Soldiers. Goldstein's work (13) is well known to all. He found it necessary to invent the concept of self-actualization to explain the reorganization of the person's capacities after injury.

3. Psychoanalysis. Some analysts, notably Fromm (12), and Horney (15), have found it impossible to understand even neuroses unless one postulates an impulse toward growth, toward perfection of development, toward the fulfillment of the person's possibilities.

4. Creativeness. Much light is being thrown on the general subject of creativeness by the study of healthy growing and grown people, especially when contrasted with sick people. Especially does the theory of art and art education call for a concept of growth and spontaneity (28).

5. Child Psychology. Observation of children shows more and more clearly that healthy children *enjoy* growing and moving forward, gaining new skills, capacities and powers. This is in flat contradiction to that version of Freudian theory which conceives of every child as hanging on desperately to each adjustment that it achieves and to each state of rest or equilibrium. According to this theory, the reluctant and conservative child has continually to be kicked upstairs, out of its comfortable, preferred state of rest *into* a new frightening situation.

While this Freudian conception is continually confirmed by clinicians as largely true for insecure and frightened children, and while it is a little bit true for all human beings, in the main it is *untrue* for healthy, happy, secure children. In these children we see clearly an eagerness to grow up, to mature, to drop the old adjustment as outworn, like an old pair of shoes. We see in them with special clarity not only the eagerness for the new skill but also the most obvious delight in repeatedly enjoying it, the so-called *Funktionslust* of Karl Buhler (8).

For the writers in these various groups, notably Fromm (12), Horney (15),

Jung (16), C. Buhler (7), Angyal (2), Rogers (23), and G. Allport (1), and recently some Catholic psychologists (3, 21), growth, individuation, autonomy self-actualization, self-development, productiveness, self-realization, are all crudely synonymous, designating a vaguely perceived area rather than a sharply defined concept. In my opinion, it is *not* possible to define this area sharply at the present time. Nor is this desirable either, since a definition which does not emerge easily and naturally from well-known facts is apt to be inhibiting and distorting rather than helpful, since it is quite likely to be wrong or mistaken if made by an act of the will on *a priori* grounds. We just don't know enough about growth yet to be able to define it well.

Its meaning can be *indicated* rather than defined, partly by positive pointing, partly by negative contrast, i.e., what it is *not*. For example, it is not equilibrium, homeostasis, tension-reduction, need-reduction, et cetera.

Its necessity has presented itself to its proponents partly because of dissatisfaction (certain newly noticed phenomena simply were not covered by extant theories); partly by positive needs for theories and concepts which would better serve the new humanistic value systems emerging from the breakdown of the older value systems.

This paper however derives mostly from a direct study of psychologically healthy individuals. This was undertaken not only for reasons of intrinsic and personal interest but also to supply a firmer foundation for the theory of therapy, of pathology and therefore of values. The true goals of education, of family training, of psychotherapy, of self-development, it seems to me, can be discovered only by such a direct attack. The end product of growth teaches us much about the processes of growth. In a recent book (19), I have described what was learned from this study and in addition theorized very freely about various possible consequences for general psychology of this kind of direct study of good rather than bad human beings, of healthy rather than sick people, of the positive as well as the negative. I must warn you that the data cannot be considered reliable until someone else repeats the study. The possibilities of projection are very real in such a study and of course are unlikely to be detected by the investigator himself. Today I should like to crystallize a little more some of the differences that I have observed to exist between the motivational lives of healthy people and of others, i.e., people motivated by growth needs contrasted with those motivated by the basic needs.

So far as motivational status is concerned, healthy people have sufficiently gratified their basic needs for safety, belongingness, love, respect and self-esteem so that they are motivated primarily by trends to self-actualization (defined as ongoing actualization of potential capacities and talents, as fulfillment of mission or call or fate or vocation, as a fuller knowledge of, and acceptance of, the person's own intrinsic nature, as an unceasing trend toward unity, integration or synergy within the person).

Much to be preferred to this generalized definition would be a descriptive and operational one which I have already published (19). These people are there defined by describing their clinically observed characteristics. These are:

1. Superior perception of reality.
2. Increased acceptance of self, of others and of nature.
3. Increased spontaneity.
4. Increase in problem-centering.
5. Increased detachment and desire for privacy.
6. Increased autonomy, and resistance to enculturation.
7. Greater freshness of appreciation, and richness of emotional reaction.
8. Higher frequency of mystic experiences.
9. Increased identification with the human species.
10. Changed (the clinician would say, improved) interpersonal relations.
11. More democratic character structure.
12. Greatly increased creativeness.
13. Certain changes in the value system.

Furthermore, in this book are described also the limitations imposed upon the definition by unavoidable shortcomings in sampling and in availability of data.

One major difficulty with this conception as so far presented is its somewhat static character.[1] Self-actualization, since I have found it only in older people, tends to be seen as an ultimate or final state of affairs, a far goal, rather than a dynamic process, active throughout life, Being rather than Becoming.

If we define growth as the various processes which bring the person toward ultimate self-actualization, then this conforms better with the observed fact that it is going on *all* the time in the life history. It discourages also the stepwise, *all* or none, saltatory conception of motivational progression toward self-actualization in which the basic needs are completely gratified, one by one, before the next higher one emerges into consciousness. Growth is seen then not only as progressive gratification of basic needs to the point where they disappear, but also in the form of specific growth motivations over and above these basic needs, e.g., talents, capacities, creative tendencies, constitutional potentialities. We are thereby helped also to realize that basic needs and self-actualization do not contradict each other any more than do childhood and maturity. One passes into the other and is a necessary prerequisite for it.

The differentiation between these growth-needs and basic needs which we

[1] I was made aware of this mostly by Frances Wilson's work with art education and Gordon Allport's new book on "The Course of Becoming," which I was privileged to read in manuscript. I profited also from discussions with my students in a graduate seminar in motivation theory.

shall explore in this paper is a consequence of the clinical perception of qualitative differences between the motivational lives of self-actualizers and of other people. These differences, listed below, are fairly well though not perfectly described by the names deficiency-needs and growth-needs. For instance, not all physiological needs are deficits, e.g., sex, elimination, sleep and rest.

At a higher level, needs for safety, belongingness, love and for respect are all clearly deficits. But the need for self-respect is a doubtful case. While the cognitive needs for curiosity-satisfaction and for a system of explanation can easily be considered deficits to be satisfied, as can also the hypothetical need for beauty, the need to create is another matter, as is also the need to express. Apparently not all basic needs are deficits but the needs whose frustration is pathogenic are deficits.

In any case, the psychological life of the person, in very many of its aspects, is lived out differently when he is deficiency-need-gratification-bent and when he is growth-dominated or "metamotivated" or growth-motivated or self-actualizing. The following differences make this clear.

1. Attitude Toward Impulse: Impulse-Rejection and Impulse-Acceptance. Practically all historical and contemporary theories of motivation unite in regarding needs, drives and motivating states in general as annoying, irritating, unpleasant, undesirable, as something to get rid of. Motivated behavior, goal seeking, consummatory responses are all techniques for reducing these discomforts. This attitude is very explicitly assumed in such widely used descriptions of motivation as need reduction, tension reduction, drive reduction, and anxiety reduction.

This approach is understandable in animal psychology and in the behaviorism which is so heavily based upon work with animals. It may be that animals have *only* deficiency needs. Whether or not this turns out to be so, in any case we have treated animals *as if* this were so for the sake of objectivity. A goal object has to be something outside the animal organism so that we can measure the effort put out by the animal in achieving this goal.

It is also understandable that the Freudian psychology should be built upon the same attitude toward motivation that impulses are dangerous and to be fought. After all this whole psychology is based upon experience with sick people, people who in fact suffer from bad experiences with their needs and with their gratifications and frustrations. It is no wonder that such people should fear or even loathe their impulses which have made so much trouble for them and which they handle so badly, and that a usual way of handling them is repression.

This derogation of desire and need has, of course, been a constant theme throughout the history of philosophy, theology and psychology. The Stoics, most hedonists, practically all theologians, many political philosophers and most economic theorists have united in affirming the fact that good or happiness or pleasure is essentially the consequence of amelioration of this unpleasant state of affairs, of wanting, of desiring, of needing.

To put it as succinctly as possible, these people all find desire or impulse to be a nuisance or even a threat and therefore will try generally to get rid of it, to deny it or to avoid it.

This contention is sometimes an accurate report of what is the case. The physiological needs, the needs for safety, for love, for respect, for information are in fact often nuisances for many people, psychic troublemakers, and problem-creators, especially for those who have had unsuccessful experiences at gratifying them and for those who cannot now count on gratification.

Even with these deficiencies, however, the case is very badly overdrawn: one can accept and enjoy one's needs and welcome them to consciousness if (a) past experience with them has been rewarding, and (b) if present and future gratification can be counted on. For example, if one has in general enjoyed food and if good food is now available, the emergence of appetite into consciousness is welcomed instead of dreaded. ("The trouble with eating is that it kills my appetite.") Something like this is true for thirst, for sleepiness, for sex, for dependency needs and for love needs. However, a far more powerful refutation of the "need-is-a-nuisance" theory is found in the recently emerging awareness of, and concern with, growth (self-actualization) motivation.

The multitude of idiosyncratic motives which come under the head of "self-actualization" can hardly be listed since each person has different talents, capacities, potentialities. But some characteristics are general to all of them. And one is that these impulses are desired and welcomed, are enjoyable and pleasant, that the person wants more of them rather than less, and that if they constitute tensions, they are *pleasurable* tensions. The creator welcomes his creative impulses, the talented person enjoys using and expanding his talents.

It is simply inaccurate to speak in such instances of tension-reduction, implying thereby the getting rid of an annoying state. For these states are not annoying.

2. Differential Effects of Gratification. Almost always associated with negative attitudes toward the need is the conception that the primary aim of the organism is to get rid of the annoying need and thereby to achieve a cessation of tension, an equilibrium, a homeostasis, a quiescence, a state of rest, a lack of pain.

The drive or need presses toward its own elimination. Its only striving is toward cessation, toward getting rid of itself, toward a state of not wanting. Pushed to its logical extreme, we wind up with Freud's Death-instinct.

Angyal, Goldstein, G. Allport, C. Buhler and others have effectively criticized this essentially circular position. If the motivational life consists essentially of a defensive removal of irritating tensions, and if the only end product of tension-reduction is a state of passive waiting for more unwelcome irritations to arise and in their turn, to be dispelled, then how does change, or development or movement or direction come about? Why do people improve? Get wiser? What does zest in living mean?

Charlotte Buhler (7) has pointed out that the theory of homeostasis is different from the theory of rest. The latter theory speaks simply of removing tension which implies that zero tension is best. Homeostasis means coming not to a zero but to an optimum level. This means sometimes reducing tension, sometimes increasing it, e.g., blood pressure may be too low as well as too high.

In either case the lack of constant direction through a lifespan is obvious. In both cases, growth of the personality, increase in wisdom, self-actualization strengthening of the character, and the planning of one's life are not and cannot be accounted for. Some long-time vector, or directional tendency, must be invoked to make any sense of development through the lifetime (7).

This theory must be put down as an inadequate description even of deficiency motivation. What is lacking here is awareness of the dynamic principle which ties together and interrelates all these separate motivational episodes. The different basic needs are related to each other in a hierarchical order such that gratification of one need and its consequent removal from the center of the stage brings about not a state of rest or Stoic apathy, but rather the emergence into consciousness of another "higher" need; wanting and desiring continues but at a "higher" level. Thus the coming-to-rest theory isn't adequate even for deficiency motivation.

However, when we examine people who are predominantly growth-motivated, the coming-to-rest conception of motivation becomes completely useless. In such people gratification breeds increased rather than decreased motivation, heightened rather than lessened excitement. The appetites become intensified and heightened. They grow upon themselves and instead of wanting less and less, such a person wants more and more of, for instance, education. The person rather than coming to rest becomes more active. The appetite for growth is whetted rather than allayed by gratification. Growth is, *in itself*, a rewarding and exciting process, e.g., the fulfilling of yearnings and ambitions, like that of being a good doctor; the acquisition of admired skills, like playing the violin or being a good carpenter; the steady increase of understanding about people or about the universe, or about oneself; the development of creativeness in whatever field, or, most important, simply the ambition to be a good human being.

Wertheimer (27) long ago stressed another aspect of this same differentiation by claiming, in a seeming paradox, that true goal-seeking activity took up less than 10% of his time. Activity can be enjoyed either intrinsically, for its own sake, or else have worth and value only because it is instrumental in bringing about a desired gratification. In the latter case it loses its value and is no longer pleasurable when it is no longer successful or efficient. More frequently, it is simply *not enjoyed at all*, but only the goal is enjoyed. This is similar to that attitude toward life which values it less for its own sake than because one goes to Heaven at the end of it. The observation upon which this generalization is based is that self-actualizing people enjoy life in general and in practically all its aspects while most other people enjoy only stray moments of triumph, of achievement or of climax.

Partly this intrinsic validity of living comes from the pleasurableness inherent in growing and in being grown. But it also comes from the ability of healthy people to transform means-activity into end-experience, so that even instrumental activity is enjoyed as if it were end activity (19). Growth motivation may be long-term in character. Most of a lifetime may be involved in becoming a good psychologist or a good artist. All equilibrium or homeostasis or rest theories deal only with short-term episodes, each of which have nothing to do with each other. Allport particularly has stressed this point. Plan-fulness and looking into the future, he points out, are of the central stuff or healthy human nature. He agrees (1) that "Deficit motives do, in fact, call for the reduction of tension and restoration of equilibrium. Growth motives, on the other hand, maintain tension in the interest of distant and often unattainable goals. As such they distinguish human from animal becoming, and adult from infant becoming."

3. Clinical Effects of Gratification. Deficit-need gratifications and growth-need gratifications have differential subjective and objective effects upon the personality. If I may phrase what I am groping for here in a very generalized way, it is this: Satisfying deficiencies avoids illness; growth satisfactions produce positive health. I must grant that this will be difficult to pin down for research purposes at this time. And yet there is a real clinical difference between fending off threat or attack and positive triumph and achievement, between protecting, defending and preserving oneself and reaching out for fulfillment, for excitement and for enlargement. I have tried to express this as a contrast between living fully and *preparing* to live fully, between growing up and being grown.

4. Different Kinds of Pleasure. Erich Fromm (12, p. 186) has made an interesting and important effort to distinguish higher from lower pleasures, as have so many others before him. This is a crucial necessity for breaking through subjective ethical relativity and is a prerequisite for a scientific value theory.

He distinguishes scarcity-pleasure from abundance-pleasure, the "lower" pleasure of satiation of a need from the "higher" pleasure of production, creation and growth of insight. The glut, the relaxation, and the loss of tension that follows deficiency-satiation can at best be called "relief" by contrast with the *Funktionslust*, the ecstasy, the serenity that one experiences when functioning easily, perfectly and at the peak of one's powers—in overdrive, so to speak.

"Relief," depending so strongly on something that disappears, is itself more likely to disappear. It must be less stable, less enduring, less constant than the pleasure accompanying growth, which can go on forever.

5. Attainable and Unattainable Goal States. Deficiency-need gratification tends to be episodic and climactic. The most frequent schema here begins with an instigating, motivating state which sets off motivated behavior designed to achieve a goal-state which, mounting gradually and steadily in desire and excitement, finally reaches a peak in a moment of success and consummation. From this peak curve of desire, excitement and pleasure fall rapidly to a plateau of quiet tension-release, and lack of motivation.

This schema, though not universally applicable, in any case contrasts very sharply with the situation in growth-motivation, for here characteristically there is no climax or consummation, no orgasmic moment, no end-state, even no goal if this be defined climactically. Growth is instead a continued, more or less steady upward or forward development. The more one gets, the more one wants so that this kind of wanting is endless and can never be attained or satisfied.

It is for this reason that the usual separation between instigation, goal-seeking behavior, the goal object and the accompanying affect breaks down completely. The behaving is itself the goal, and to differentiate the goal of growth from the instigation to growth is impossible. They too are the same.

6. Species-wide Goals and Idiosyncratic Goals. The deficit-needs are shared by all members of the human species and to some extent by other species as well. Self-actualization is idiosyncratic since every person is different. The deficits, i.e., the species requirements, must ordinarily be fairly well satisfied before real individuality can develop fully.

Just as all trees need sun, water, and foods from the environment, so do all people need safety, love and status from *their* environment. However, in both cases this is just where real development of individuality can begin, for once satiated with these elementary, species-wide necessities, each tree and each person proceeds to develop in his own style, uniquely, using these necessities for his own private purposes. In a very tangible sense, development then becomes more determined from within rather than from without.

7. Dependence and Independence of the Environment. The needs for safety, belongingness, love relations and for respect can be satisfied only by other people, i.e., only from outside the person. This means considerable dependence on the environment. A person in this dependent position cannot really be said to be governing himself, or in control of his own fate. He *must* be beholden to the sources of supply of needed gratifications. Their wishes, their whims, their rules and laws govern him and must be appeased lest he jeopardize his sources of supply. He *must* be to an extent "other-directed" and *must* be sensitive to other people's approval, affection and good will. This is the same as saying that he must adapt and adjust by being flexible and responsive and by changing himself to fit the external situation. *He* is the dependent variable; the environment is the fixed, independent variable.

Because of this, the deficiency-motivated man must be more afraid of the environment, since there is always the possibility that it may fail or disappoint him. We now know that this kind of anxious dependence breeds hostility as well. All of which adds up to a lack of freedom, more or less, depending on the good fortune or bad fortune of the individual.

In contrast, the self-actualizing individual, by definition gratified in his basic needs, is far less dependent, far less beholden, far more autonomous and self-directed. Far from needing other people, growth-motivated people may actually be hampered by them. I have already reported their special liking for privacy, for detachment and for meditativeness.

Such people become far more self-sufficient and self-contained. The determinants which govern them are now primarily inner ones, rather than social or environmental. They are the laws of their own inner nature, their potentialities and capacities, their talents, their latent resources, their creative impulses, their needs to know themselves and to become more and more integrated and unified, more and more aware of what they really are, of what they really want, of what their call or vocation or fate is to be.

Since they depend less on other people, they are less ambivalent about them, less anxious and also less hostile, less needful of their praise and their affection. They are less anxious for honors, prestige and rewards.

Autonomy or relative independence of environment means also relative independence of adverse external circumstances, such as ill fortune, hard knocks, tragedy, stress, deprivation. As Allport has stressed, the notion of the human being as essentially reactive, the S–R man we might call him, who is set into motion by external stimuli, becomes completely ridiculous and untenable for self-actualizing people. The sources of *their* actions are internal rather than external. This relative independence of the outside world and its wishes and pressures, does not mean of course lack of intercourse with it. It means only that in these contacts, the self-actualizer's wishes and plans are the primary determiners, and that the environment becomes more and more a means to his ends. This I have called psychological freedom, contrasting it with geographical freedom.

Allport's very expressive contrast (1) between "opportunistic" and "propriate" determination of behavior parallels very closely our outer-determined, inner-determined opposition. It reminds us also of the uniform agreement among biological theorists in considering increasing autonomy and independence of environmental stimuli as *the* defining characteristics of full individuality, of true freedom, of the whole evolutionary process (29).

8. Interested and Disinterested Interpersonal Relations. In essence, the deficit-motivated man is far more dependent upon other people than is the man who is predominantly growth-motivated. He is more "interested," more needful, more attached, more desirous.

This dependency colors and limits interpersonal relations. To see people primarily as need-gratifiers or as sources of supply is an abstractive act. They are seen not as wholes, as complicated, unique individuals, but rather from the point of view of usefulness. What in them is not related to the perceiver's needs is either overlooked altogether, or else bores, irritates, or threatens. This parallels our relations with cows, horses and sheep, as well as with waiters, taxicab drivers, porters, policemen or others whom we *use*.

Fully disinterested, desireless, objective and holistic perception of another human being becomes possible only when nothing is needed from him, only when *he* is not needed. Idiographic, aesthetic perception of the whole person is far more possible for self-actualizing people, and furthermore approval, admiration, and love are based less upon gratitude for usefulness and more upon the objective, intrinsic qualities of the perceived person. He is admired for objectively admirable qualities rather than because he flatters or praises. He is loved because he is love-worthy rather than because he gives out love. This is what will be discussed below as unneeded love.

One characteristic of "interested" and need-gratifying relations to other people is that to a very large extent these need-gratifying persons are interchangeable. Since, for instance, the adolescent girl needs admiration *per se*, it therefore makes little difference who supplies this admiration; one admiration-supplier is about as good as another. So also for the love-supplier or the safety-supplier.

Disinterested, unrewarded, useless, desireless perception of the other as unique, as independent, as end-in-himself, in other words as a person rather than as a tool is the more difficult, the more hungry the perceiver is for deficit satisfaction. A "high-ceiling" interpersonal psychology, i.e., an understanding of the highest possible development of human relationships, cannot base itself on deficit theory of motivation.

9. Ego-centering and Ego-transcendence. We are confronted with a difficult paradox when we attempt to describe the complex attitude toward the self or ego of the growth-oriented, self-actualized person. It is just this person, in whom ego-strength is at its height, who most easily forgets or transcends the ego, who can be most problem-centered, most self-forgetful, most spontaneous in his activities, most homonymous, to use Angyal's term (2). In such people, absorption in perceiving, in doing, in enjoying, in creating can be very complete, very integrated and very pure.

This ability to center upon the world rather than to be self-conscious, egocentric and gratification-oriented becomes the more difficult the more need-deficits the person has. The more growth-motivated the person is the more problem-centered can he be, and the more he can leave self-consciousness behind him as he deals with the objective world.

10. Interpersonal Psychotherapy and Intrapersonal Psychology. A major characteristic of people who seek psychotherapy is a former and/or present deficiency of basic-need gratification. To a larger extent than the Freudians are yet willing to admit, neurosis is a deficiency-disease. Because this is so, a basic necessity for cure is supplying what has been lacking or making it possible for the patient to do this himself. Since these supplies come from other people, ordinary therapy *must* be interpersonal.

But this fact has been very badly over-generalized. It is true that people whose deficiency needs have been gratified and who are primarily growth-motivated are by no means exempt from conflict, unhappiness, anxiety, and confusion. In such moments they too are apt to seek help and may very well turn to interpersonal therapy. And yet it is unwise to forget that *more* frequently the problems and the conflicts of the growth-motivated person are customarily solved by himself by turning inward in a meditative way, i.e., self-searching rather than seeking for help from someone. Even in principle, many of the tasks of self-actualization are largely intrapersonal, such as the making of plans, the discovery of self, the selection of potentialities to develop, the construction of a life-outlook.

In the theory of personality improvement, a place must be reserved for self-improvement and self-searching contemplation and meditation. In the later stages of growth the person is essentially alone and can rely only upon himself. This improvement of an already well person Oswald Schwarz has called psychogogy. If psychotherapy makes sick people not-sick and removes symptoms, then psychogogy takes up where therapy leaves off and tries to make not-sick people healthy. I was interested to notice in Rogers' recent book (23) that successful therapy raised the patients' average score in The Willoughby Maturity Scale from the twenty-fifth to the fiftieth percentile. Who shall then lift him to the seventy-fifth percentile? Or the one hundredth? And are we not likely to need new principles and techniques to do this with?

11. Instrumental Learning and Personality Change. So-called learning theory in this country has based itself almost entirely on deficit-motivation with goal objects usually external to the organism, i.e., learning the best way to satisfy a need. For this reason, among others, our psychology of learning is a very limited body of knowledge, useful only in small areas of life and of real interest only to other "learning theorists."

This is of very little help in solving the problems of growth and self-actualization. Here the techniques of repeatedly acquiring from the outside world satisfactions of motivational deficiencies are much less needed. Associative learning and canalizations give way more to perceptual learning (20), to the increase of insight and understanding, to knowledge of self and to the steady growth of personality, i.e., increased synergy, integration and inner consistency. Change becomes much less an acquisition of habits or associations one by one, and much more a total change of the total person, i.e., a new person rather than the same person with some habits added like new external possessions.

This kind of character-change-learning means changing a very complex, highly integrated, holistic organism, which in turn means that many impacts will make no change at all because more and more such impacts will be rejected as the person becomes more stable and more autonomous.

The most important learning experiences reported to me by my subjects were very frequently single life experiences such as tragedies, deaths, traumata, conversions, sudden insights, which forced change in the life-outlook of the person and consequently in everything that he did. (Of course the so-called "working through" of the tragedy or of the insight took place over a longer period of time but this too was not a matter of associative learning.)

To the extent that growth consists in peeling away inhibition and constraints and then permitting the person to "be himself," to emit behavior—"radioactively," as it were—rather than to repeat it, to allow his inner nature to express itself, to this extent the behavior of self-actualizers is unlearned, created and released rather than acquired, expressive rather than coping (19, p. 180.)

12. Deficiency-Motivated and Growth-Motivated Perception. What may turn out to be the most important difference of all is the greater closeness of deficit-satisfied people to the realm of Being (26). Psychologists have never yet been able to claim this vague jurisdiction of the philosophers, this area dimly seen but nevertheless having undoubted basis in reality. But it may now become feasible through the study of self-fulfilling individuals to have our eyes opened to all sorts of basic insights, old to the philosophers but new to us.

For instance, I think that our understanding of perception and therefore of the perceived world will be very much changed and enlarged if we study carefully the distinction between need-interested and need-disinterested or desireless perception. Because the latter is so much more concrete and less abstracted and selective, it is possible for such a person to see more easily the intrinsic nature of the percept. He can perceive simultaneously the opposites, the dichotomies, the polarities, the contradictions and the incompatibles (19, pp. 232–4). It is as if less developed people lived in an Aristotelian world in which classes and concepts have sharp boundaries and are mutually exclusive and incompatible, e.g. male-female, selfish-unselfish, adult-child, angel-devil, kind-cruel, good-bad. A is A and everything else is not A in the Aristotelian logic, and never the twain shall meet. But seen by self-actualizing people is the fact that A and not-A interpenetrate and are one, that any person is simultaneously good *and* bad, male *and* female, adult *and* child. One can not place a whole person on a continuum, only an abstracted aspect of a person.

We may not be aware when *we* perceive in a need-determined way. But we certainly are aware of it when *we* ourselves are perceived in this way, e.g., simply as a money-giver, a food-supplier, a safety-giver, someone to depend on, or as a waiter or other anonymous servant or means-object. When this happens we don't like it at all. We want to be taken for ourselves, as complete and whole individuals. We dislike being perceived as useful objects or as tools. We dislike being "used."

Because self-actualizing people ordinarily do not have to abstract need-gratifying qualities nor see the person as a tool, it is much more possible for them to take a non-valuing, non-judging, non-interfering, non-condemning attitude towards others, a desirelessness, a "choiceless awareness" (17). This permits much clearer and more insightful perception and understanding of what is there. This is the kind of untangled, uninvolved, detached perception that surgeons and therapists are supposed to try for and which self-actualizing people attain *without* trying for.

Especially when the structure of the person or object seen is difficult, subtle and not obvious is this difference in style of perception most important. Especially then must the perceiver have respect for the nature of the object. Perception must then be gentle, delicate, unintruding, undemanding, able to fit itself passively to the nature of things as water gently soaks into crevices. It must *not* be the need-motivated kind of perception which *shapes* things in a blustering, overriding, exploiting, purposeful fashion, in the manner of a butcher chopping apart a carcass.

The most efficient way to perceive the intrinsic nature of the world is to be more passive than active, determined as much as possible by the intrinsic organization of that which is perceived and as little as possible by the nature of the perceiver. This kind of detached, Taoist, passive, non-interfering awareness of all the simultaneously existing aspects of the concrete, has much in common with some descriptions of the aesthetic experience and of the mystic experience. The stress is the same. Do we see the real, concrete world or do we see our own system of rubrics, motives, expectations and abstractions which we have projected onto the real world? Or, to put it very bluntly, do we see or are we blind?

Needed Love and Unneeded Love

The love need as ordinarily studied, for instance by Bowlby (5), Spitz (24), and Levy (18), is a deficit need. It is a hole which has to be filled, an emptiness into which love is poured. If this healing necessity is not available, severe pathology results (5, 18); if it *is* available at the right time, in the right quantities and with proper style, then pathology is averted. Intermediate states of pathology and health follow upon intermediate states of thwarting or satiation. If the pathology is not too severe and if it is caught early enough, replacement therapy can cure. That is to say, the sickness, "love-hunger," can be cured in certain cases by making up the pathological deficiency. Love hunger is a deficiency disease exactly as is salt hunger or the avitaminoses.

The healthy person, not having this deficiency, does not need to give or to receive love except in steady, small maintenance doses and he may even do without these for periods of time. But if motivation is entirely a matter of satisfying deficits and thus getting rid of needs, then a crucial paradox results. Satisfaction of the need should cause it to disappear, which is to say that people who have stood in satisfying love relationships are precisely the people who should be *less* likely to give and to receive love! But clinical study of very healthy people, who have been love-need-satiated, shows that they are far *more*—not less—loving people than others.

This finding in itself exposes very clearly the inadequacy of ordinary (deficiency-need-centered) motivation theory and indicates how inescapable is the necessity for "metamotivation theory" (or growth-motivation, or self-actualization theory).

I have already described in a preliminary fashion (19) the contrasting dynamics of B-love (love for the Being of another person, unneeded love, unselfish love) and D-love (deficiency-love, love need, selfish love) and further findings will be set forth in detail in a future publication. At this point, I wish only to use these two contrasting groups of people to exemplify and illustrate some of the generalizations made in this paper.

1. B-Love is welcomed into consciousness, and is completely enjoyed. Since it is non-possessive, and is admiring rather than needing, it makes no trouble and is practically always gratifiable.

2. It can never be sated; it may be enjoyed without end. It usually grows greater rather than disappearing. It is intrinsically enjoyable. It is end rather than means.

3. The B-love experience is often described as being the same as and having the same effects as the aesthetic experience or the mystic experience.

4. The therapeutic and psychogogic effects of experiencing B-love are very profound and widespread. Similar are the characterological effects of the relatively pure love of a healthy mother for her baby, or the perfect love

of their God that some mystics have described. The details are too complex for description here.

5. B-love is, beyond the shadow of a doubt, a richer, "higher," more valuable subjective experience than D-love (which all B-lovers have also previously experienced.) This preference is also reported by my other older, more average subjects, many of whom experience both kinds of love simultaneously in varying combinations.

6. D-love *can* be gratified. The concept "gratification" hardly applies at all to admiration-love for another person's admiration-worthiness and love-worthiness.

7. In B-love there is a minimum of anxiety-hostility. For all practical human purposes, it may even be considered to be absent. There *can*, of course, be anxiety-for-the-other. In D-love one must always expect some degree of anxiety-hostility.

8. B-lovers are more independent of each other, more autonomous, less jealous or threatened, less needful, more individual, more disinterested, but also simultaneously more eager to help the other toward self-actualization, more proud of his triumphs, more altruistic, generous and fostering.

9. The truest, most penetrating perception of the other is made possible by B-love. It is as much a cognitive as an emotional-conative reaction, as I have already emphasized (19, pp. 257, 260). So impressive is this, and so often validated by other people's later experience, that, far from accepting the common platitude that love makes people blind, I become more and more inclined to think of the *opposite* as true, namely that non-love makes us blind.

10. Finally I may say that B-love, in a profound but testable sense, creates the partner. It gives him a self-image, it gives him self-acceptance, a feeling of love-worthiness and respect-worthiness, all of which permit him to grow. It is a real question whether the full development of the human being is possible without it.

References

1. Allport, G., *The Course of Becoming.* New Haven: Yale University Press, 1955.
2. Angyal, A., *Foundations for a Science of Personality.* New York: Commonwealth Fund, 1941.
3. Arnold, M., and Gasson, J., *The Human Person.* New York: Ronald Press, 1954.
4. Banham, K. M., The development of affectionate behavior in infancy. *J. gen. Psychol.*, 1950, *76*, 283–289.
5. Bowlby, J., *Maternal Care and Mental Health.* Geneva: World Health Organization, 1952.

6. Buber, M., *I and Thou*. Edinburgh: T. & T. Clark, 1937.
7. Buhler, C., Motivation and personality. *Dialectica*, 1951, *5*, 312–361.
8. Buhler, K., *Die geistige Entwicklung des Kindes*, 4th ed. Jena: Fischer, 1924.
9. Cannon, W. B., *Wisdom of the Body*. New York: W. W. Norton, 1932.
10. Freud, S., *An Outline of Psychoanalysis*. New York: W. W. Norton, 1949.
11. Freud, S., *Beyond the Pleasure Principle*. International Psychoanalytic Press, 1922.
12. Fromm, E., *Man For Himself*. New York: Rinehart, 1947.
13. Goldstein, K., *Human Nature from the Point of View of Psychopathology*. Cambridge: Harvard University Press, 1940.
14. Goldstein, K., *The Organism*. New York: American Book Co., 1939.
15. Horney, K., *Neurosis and Human Growth*. New York: W. W. Norton, 1950.
16. Jung, C. G., *Psychological Reflections*. (Jacobi, J., editor), New York: Pantheon Books, 1953.
17. Krishnamurti, J., *The First and Last Freedom*. New York: Harper, 1954.
18. Levy, D., *Maternal Overprotection*. New York: Columbia University Press, 1943.
19. Maslow, A. H., *Motivation and Personality*. New York: Harper, 1954.
20. Murphy, G., and Hochberg, J., Perceptual development: some tentative hypotheses, *Psychol. Rev.*, 1951, *58*, 332–349.
21. Nuttin, J., *Psychoanalysis and Personality*. New York: Sheed and Ward, 1953.
22. Ritchie, B. F., Comments on Professor Farber's paper. In Marshall R. Jones (Ed.), *Nebraska Symposium on Motivation*, 1954, 46–50.
23. Rogers, C., *Psychotherapy and Personality Change*. Chicago: University of Chicago Press, 1954.
24. Spitz, R., Anaclitic depression, *Psychoanal. Study of the Child,* 1946, *2*, 313–342.
25. Suttie, I., *Origins of Love and Hate*. London: Kegan Paul, 1935.
26. Tillich, P., *The Courage To Be*. New Haven: Yale University Press, 1952.
27. Wertheimer, M., Unpublished lectures at the New School for Social Research, 1935–6.
28. Wilson, F., Unpublished papers on art education and psychology, 1954.
29. Woodger, J., *Biological Principles*. New York: Harcourt, Brace, 1929.

10 / JEAN-PAUL SARTRE

Existentialism

Most people who use the word [existentialism] would be rather embarrassed if they had to explain it, since, now that the word is all the rage, even the work of a musician or painter is being called existentialist. A gossip columnist in *Clartés* signs himself *The Existentialist*, so that by this time the word has been so stretched and has taken on so broad a meaning, that it no longer means anything at all. It seems that for want of an advance-guard doctrine analogous to surrealism, the kind of people who are eager for scandal and flurry turn to this philosophy which in other respects does not at all serve their purposes in this sphere.

Actually, it is the least scandalous, the most austere of doctrines. It is intended strictly for specialists and philosophers. Yet it can be defined easily. What complicates matters is that there are two kinds of existentialist; first, those who are Christian, among whom I would include Jaspers and Gabriel Marcel, both Catholic; and on the other hand the atheistic existentialists, among whom I class Heidegger, and then the French existentialists and myself. What they have in common is that they think that existence precedes essence, or, if you prefer, that subjectivity must be the starting point.

Just what does that mean? Let us consider some object that is manufactured, for example, a book or a paper-cutter; here is an object which has been made by an artisan whose inspiration came from a concept. He referred to the concept of what a paper-cutter is and likewise to a known method of production, which is part of the concept, something which is, by and large, a routine. Thus, the paper-cutter is at once an object produced in a certain way and, on the other hand, one having a specific use; and one can not postulate

Jean-Paul Sartre, "Existentialism" from *Existentialism* (New York: The Philosophical Library, 1947), pp. 14, 28, 34, 35, 47, 59 and 61. Reprinted by permission of the publisher.

Jean-Paul Sartre (1905–), internationally known French existentialist and intellectual, is a philosopher, novelist, and playwright. He was one of the founders in 1948 of a small independent socialist party, and during the postwar period he has been occupied with the journal *Les Temps Moderne*. His plays express concern with problems of guilt, responsibility, and freedom. Sartre's plays include *The Flies, No Exit,* and *The Respectable Prostitute;* among his novels are *Nausea* and *Age of Reason;* and two of his chief philosophical works are *Being and Nothingness* and *Existentialism.*

a man who produces a paper-cutter but does not know what it is used for. Therefore, let us say that, for the paper-cutter, essence—that is, the ensemble of both the production routines and the properties which enable it to be both produced and defined—precedes existence. Thus, the presence of the paper-cutter or book in front of me is determined. Therefore, we have here a technical view of the world whereby it can be said that production precedes existence.

When we conceive God as the Creator, He is generally thought of as a superior sort of artisan. Whatever doctrine we may be considering, whether one like that of Descartes or that of Leibnitz, we always grant that will more or less follows understanding or, at the very least, accompanies it, and that when God creates He knows exactly what He is creating. Thus, the concept of man in the mind of God is comparable to the concept of paper-cutter in the mind of the manufacturer, and, following certain techniques and a conception, God produces man, just as the artisan, following a definition and a technique, makes a paper-cutter. Thus, the individual man is the realization of a certain concept in the divine intelligence.

In the eighteenth century, the atheism of the *philosophes* discarded the idea of God, but not so much for the notion that essence precedes existence. To a certain extent, this idea is found everywhere; we find it in Diderot, in Voltaire, and even in Kant. Man has a human nature; this human nature, which is the concept of the human, is found in all men, which means that each man is a particular example of a universal concept, man. In Kant, the result of this universality is that the wild-man, the natural man, as well as the bourgeois, are circumscribed by the same definition and have the same basic qualities. Thus, here too the essence of man precedes the historical existence that we find in nature.

Atheistic existentialism, which I represent, is more coherent. It states that if God does not exist, there is at least one being in whom existence precedes essence, a being who exists before he can be defined by any concept, and that this being is man, or, as Heidegger says, human reality. What is meant here by saying that existence precedes essence? It means that, first of all, man exists, turns up, appears on the scene, and, only afterwards, defines himself. If man, as the existentialist conceives him, is indefinable, it is because at first he is nothing. Only afterward will he be something, and he himself will have made what he will be. Thus, there is no human nature, since there is no God to conceive it. Not only is man what he conceives himself to be, but he is also only what he wills himself to be after this thrust toward existence.

Man is nothing else but what he makes of himself. Such is the first principle of existentialism. It is also what is called subjectivity, the name we are labeled with when charges are brought against us. But what do we mean by this, if not that man has a greater dignity than a stone or table? For we mean that man first exists, that is, that man first of all is the being who hurls himself toward a future and who is conscious of imagining himself as being in the future. Man is at the start a plan which is aware of itself, rather than a patch of moss, a piece of garbage, or a cauliflower; nothing exists prior to this plan; there is nothing in heaven; man will be what he will have planned to be. Not what he will want to be. Because by the word "will" we generally mean a conscious decision, which is subsequent to what we have already made of ourselves. I may want to belong to a political party, write a book, get married; but all that is only a manifestation of an earlier, more spontaneous choice that is called "will." But if existence really does precede essence, man is responsible for what he is. Thus, existentialism's first move is to make every man aware of what he is and to make the full responsibility of his existence rest on him. And when we say that a man is responsible for himself, we do not only mean that he is responsible for his own individuality, but that he is responsible for all men.

The word subjectivism has two meanings, and our opponents play on the two. Subjectivism means, on the one hand, that an individual chooses and makes himself; and, on the other, that it is impossible for man to transcend human subjectivity. The second of these is the essential meaning of existentialism. When we say that man chooses his own self, we mean that every one of us does likewise; but we also mean by that that in making this choice he also chooses all men. In fact, in creating the man that we want to be, there is not a single one of our acts which does not at the same time create an image of man as we think he ought to be. To choose to be this or that is to affirm at the same time the value of what we choose, because we can never choose evil. We always choose the good, and nothing can be good for us without being good for all.

If, on the other hand, existence precedes essence, and if we grant that we exist and fashion our image at one and the same time, the image is valid for everybody and for our whole age. Thus, our responsibility is much greater than we might have supposed, because it involves all mankind. If I am a workingman and choose to join a Christian trade-union rather than be a communist, and if by being a member I want to show that the best thing for man is resignation, that the kingdom of man is not of this world, I am not only involving my own case—I want to be resigned for everyone. As a result, my action has involved all humanity. To take a more individual matter, if I want to marry, to have children; even if this marriage depends solely on my own circumstances or passion or wish, I am involving all humanity in monogamy and not merely myself. Therefore, I am responsible for myself and for everyone else. I am creating a certain image of man of my own choosing. In choosing myself, I choose man.

This helps us understand what the actual content is of such rather grandiloquent words as anguish, forlornness, despair. As you will see, it's all quite simple.

First, what is meant by anguish? The existentialists say at once that man is anguish. What that means is this: the man who involves himself and who realizes that he is not only the person he chooses to be, but also a lawmaker who is, at the same time, choosing all mankind as well as himself, can not help escape the feeling of his total and deep responsibility. Of course, there are many people who are not anxious; but we claim that they are hiding their anxiety, that they are fleeing from it. Certainly, many people believe that when they do something, they themselves are the only ones involved, and when someone says to them, "What if everyone acted that way?" they shrug their shoulders and answer, "Everyone doesn't act that way." But really, one should always ask himself, "What would happen if everybody looked at things that way?" There is no escaping this disturbing thought except by a kind of double-dealing. A man who lies and makes excuses for himself by saying "not everybody does that," is someone with an uneasy conscience, because the act of lying implies that a universal value is conferred upon the lie.

Anguish is evident even when it conceals itself. This is the anguish that Kierkegaard called the anguish of Abraham. You know the story: an angel has ordered Abraham to sacrifice his son; if it really were an angel who has come and said, "You are Abraham, you shall sacrifice your son," everything would be all right. But everyone might first wonder, "Is it really an angel, and am I really Abraham? What proof do I have?"

There was a madwoman who had hallucinations; someone used to speak to her on the telephone and give her orders. Her doctor asked her, "Who is it who talks to you?" She answered, "He says it's God." What proof did she really have that it was God? If an angel comes to me, what proof is there that it's an angel? And if I hear voices, what proof is there that they come from heaven and not from hell, or from the subconscious, or a pathological condition? What proves that they are addressed to me? What proof is there that I have been appointed to impose my choice and my conception of man on humanity? I'll never find any proof or sign to convince me of that. If a voice addresses me, it is always for me to decide that this is the angel's voice; if I consider that such an act is a good one, it is I who will choose to say that it is good rather than bad.

Now, I'm not being singled out as an Abraham, and yet at every moment I'm obliged to perform exemplary acts. For every man, everything happens as if all mankind had its eyes fixed on him and were guiding itself by what he does. And every man ought to say to himself, "Am I really the kind of man who has the right to act in such a way that humanity might guide itself by my actions?" And if he does not say that to himself, he is masking his anguish. . . .

When we speak of forlornness, a term Heidegger was fond of, we mean only that God does not exist and that we have to face all the consequences of this. The existentialist is strongly opposed to a certain kind of secular ethics which would like to abolish God with the least possible expense. About 1880, some French teachers tried to set up a secular ethics which went something like this: God is a useless and costly hypothesis; we are discarding it; but, meanwhile, in order for there to be an ethics, a society, a civilization, it is essential that certain values be taken seriously and that they be considered as having an *a priori* existence. It must be obligatory, *a priori*, to be honest, not to lie, not to beat your wife, to have children, etc., etc. So we're going to try a little device which will make it possible to show that values exist all the same, inscribed in a heaven of ideas, though otherwise God does not exist. In other words—and this, I believe, is the tendency of everything called reformism in France—nothing will be changed if God does not exist. We shall find ourselves with the same norms of honesty, progress, and humanism, and we shall have made of God an outdated hypothesis which will peacefully die off by itself.

The existentialist, on the contrary, thinks it very distressing that God does not exist, because all possibility of finding values in a heaven of ideas disappears along with Him; there can no longer be an *a priori* Good, since there is no infinite and perfect consciousness to think it. Nowhere is it written that the Good exists, that we must be honest, that we must not lie; because the fact is we are on a plane where there are only men. Dostoievsky said, "If God didn't exist, everything would be possible." That is the very starting point of existentialism. Indeed, everything is permissible if God does not exist, and as a result man is forlorn, because neither within him nor without does he find anything to cling to. He can't start making excuses for himself.

If existence really does precede essence, there is no explaining things away by reference to a fixed and given human nature. In other words, there is no determinism, man is free, man is freedom. On the other hand, if God does not exist, we find no values or commands to turn to which legitimize our conduct. So, in the bright realm of values, we have no excuse behind us, nor justification before us. We are alone, with no excuses.

That is the idea I shall try to convey when I say that man is condemned to be free. Condemned, because he did not create himself, yet, in other respects is free; because, once thrown into the world, he is responsible for everything he does. The existentialist does not believe in the power of passion. He will never agree that a sweeping passion is a ravaging torrent which fatally leads a man to certain acts and is therefore an excuse. He thinks that man is responsible for his passion.

The existentialist does not think that man is going to help himself by finding in the world some omen by which to orient himself. Because he thinks that man will interpret the omen to suit himself. Therefore, he thinks that man, with no support and no aid, is condemned every moment to invent man. Ponge, in a very fine article, has said, "Man is the future of man." That's exactly it. But if it is taken to mean that this future is recorded in heaven, that God sees it, then it is false, because it would really no longer be a future. If it is taken to mean that, whatever a man may be, there is a future to be forged, a virgin future before him, then this remark is sound. But then we are forlorn. . . .

As for despair, the term has a very simple meaning. It means that we shall confine ourselves to reckoning only with what depends upon our will, or on the ensemble of probabilities which make our action possible. When we want something, we always have to reckon with probabilities. I may be counting on the arrival of a friend. The friend is coming by rail or street-car; this supposes that the train will arrive on schedule, or that the street-car will not jump the track. I am left in the realm of possibility; but possibilities are to be reckoned with only to the point where my action comports with the ensemble of these possibilities, and no further. The moment the possibilities I am considering are not rigorously involved by my action, I ought to disengage myself from them, because no God, no scheme, can adapt the world and its possibilities to my will. When Descartes said, "Conquer yourself rather than the world," he meant essentially the same thing. . . .

At heart, what existentialism shows is the connection between the absolute character of free involvement, by virtue of which every man realizes himself in realizing a type of mankind, an involvement always comprehensible in any age whatsoever and by any person whosoever, and the relativeness of the cultural ensemble which may result from such a choice; it must be stressed that the relativity of Cartesianism and the absolute character of Cartesian involvement go together. In this sense, you may, if you like, say that each of us performs an absolute act in breathing, eating, sleeping, or behaving in any way whatever. There is no difference between being free, like a configuration, like an existence which chooses its essence, and being absolute. There is no difference between being an absolute temporarily localized, that is, localized in history, and being universally comprehensible. . . .

Man is constantly outside of himself; in projecting himself, in losing himself outside of himself, he makes for man's existing; and, on the other hand, it is by pursuing transcendent goals that he is able to exist; man, being this state of passing-beyond, and seizing upon things only as they bear upon this passing-beyond, is at the heart, at the center of this passing-beyond. There is no universe other than a human universe, the universe of human subjectivity. This connection between transcendency, as a constituent element of man—not in the sense that God is transcendent, but in the sense of passing beyond—and subjectivity, in the sense that man is not closed in on himself but is always present in a human universe, is what we call existentialism humanism. Humanism, because we remind man that there is no law-maker other than himself, and that in his forlornness he will decide by himself; because we point out that man will fulfill himself as man, not in turning toward himself, but in seeking outside of himself a goal which is just this liberation, just this particular fulfillment.

From these few reflections it is evident that nothing is more unjust than the objections that have been raised against us. Existentialism is nothing else than an attempt to draw all the consequences of a coherent atheistic position. It isn't trying to plunge man into despair at all. But if one calls every attitude of unbelief despair, like the Christians, then the word is not being used in its original sense. Existentialism isn't so atheistic that it wears itself out showing that God doesn't exist. Rather, it declares that even if God did exist, that would change nothing. There you've got our point of view. Not that we believe that God exists, but we think that the problem of His existence is not the issue. In this sense existentialism is optimistic, a doctrine of action, and it is plain dishonesty for Christians to make no distinction between their own despair and ours and then to call us despairing.

Questions for Discussion

Morris assigns interests a central role in human life. Explain the importance he attaches to human interest. Why does he refuse to seek out one prevailing interest in human life as others have done? According to Morris, what is *mind?* He presents a unique interpretation of love. Has he construed the term too broadly? Through the ideas of George H. Mead, Morris shows the untenability of establishing a dualism between the individual and society. Has he supported his case adequately? Explain the three components of personality and the import of the seven personality types derived from them. Evaluate the importance and significance of Morris's findings for education and cross-cultural understanding.

How does Marcuse characterize the affluent society? Is his characterization accurate? Under what social conditions would "normality" be undesirable? Explain the concept *surplus-repression* and its social consequences. Does Marcuse assume certain species-wide characteristics of healthy individuals? If so, what use does he make of them? Marcuse discusses the present system of production and "nonalienated labor." Explain his interpretation. He also speaks of the "brutalization of language" and the disintegration of the value of truth. Is his analysis accurate? What grounds does Marcuse provide for his conception of human nature? What types of societal conditions are necessary before this nature can flourish?

Skinner argues that a utopia founded on abundance and resulting in idleness would not support the culture or provide happiness. Would Marcuse concur or disagree? What use would Skinner make of a system of reinforcement contingent on behavior? He believes that the control exercised in his system would be "for the benefit of the controllee." What system of control would Skinner institute, and would it actually benefit the controllee? He also points out that some may object to his system because the designer would get more of the credit for desirable behavior. Are there more serious objections to his plan than this? Evaluate the argument that because society already exercises control in various ways but not always effectively to achieve the desired results, a scientific approach to control for the purpose of securing established, desired ends should be undertaken.

Evaluate Maslow's criticism of both Freudian theory and psychologies based on homeostatic models and tension reduction. Are his criticisms sound? What does Maslow mean by *growth*, and in what way does the concept fail to fit into the two previously mentioned theories? What are the deficiency-needs and how can they be satisfied? Has Maslow established that these needs exist or that their lack of fulfillment will lead to the consequences he claims? Characterize the self-actualizing person and explain the difficulties of attaining this level. What is likely to occur if a person has many needs-deficits as compared to an individual who is more growth-motivated? Does Maslow reject the notion that needs are culturally induced and thereby are culturally relative? Assess the evidence for the cultural relativism of needs. Compare Maslow's position to Skinner's.

What is the meaning and significance of Sartre's statement that "existence precedes essence"? As a corollary, what does he mean when he states that man "defines himself"? Does he believe that man can choose evil? Explain. Give the meaning of each of the following concepts and the role they play in Sartre's philosophy: human subjectivity, anguish, forlornness, despair, and freedom. Why is man "condemned to be free"? Is there any inconsistency in Sartre's concept of responsibility (he presents a version of a categorical imperative) and the rest of his philosophy? Does he also pose incompatible concepts of transcendence and subjectivity? Are his arguments against determinism well supported?

Suggested Reading

Among a number of important historical positions are those of the political philosophers Hobbes, Locke, and Marx: Thomas Hobbes, *Leviathan*; John Locke, *Of Civil Government: Second Treatise*; and Arthur P. Mendel, ed., *Essential Works of Marxism* (New York: Bantam Books, 1965).

Man is viewed from a biological perspective in Th. Dobzhansky's *Mankind Evolving* (New Haven, Conn.: Yale University Press, 1962) and approached by Pierre Teilhard de Chardin in terms of a distinctive evolutionary position that envisions man as still evolving to a future Omega point in *The Phenomenon of Man* (New York: Harper Torchbooks, 1965). Lawrence K. Frank considers theoretical findings from the natural and social sciences in developing a social interactionist position in *Nature and Human Nature* (New Brunswick, N.J.: Rutgers University Press, 1951).

Two leading Christian theologians have developed divergent views of man. Reinhold Niebuhr has examined social and political life in terms of the problems of power and justice in his *Moral Man and Immoral Society* (New York: Charles Scribner's Sons, 1932). Paul Tillich takes an existential approach to problems such as anxiety and the sense of meaninglessness in *The Courage to Be* (New Haven, Conn.: Yale University Press, 1952). Those who desire an overview of existentialism and its import for education should consult George F. Kneller's *Existentialism and Education* (New York: Philosophical Library, 1958).

Three different psychological approaches—psychoanalysis, behaviorism, and humanistic psychology—are represented in the works that follow. Sigmund Freud, the father of psychoanalysis, has laid out his views of the conflict between man and society in *Civilization and Its Discontents*, trans. James Strachey (New York: W. W. Norton & Co., 1961). Behaviorism is represented by B. F. Skinner's *Beyond Freedom and Dignity* (New York: Alfred A. Knopf, 1971). Both Fromm and Maslow have been associated with a movement known as humanistic psychology. Erich Fromm's *Man for Himself* (New York: Rinehart, 1947) is an attempt to clarify the relation between psychology and ethics and to develop characterological types within a sociocultural backdrop. Abraham Maslow develops a concept of motivation around basic needs and self-actualization in *Motivation and Personality* (New York: Harper & Row, Publishers, 1954).

CHAPTER THREE /

EDUCATION AND THE SOCIAL ORDER

AN educational system has relationships with the larger society, and we need to determine what those relations will be. Variations in the role of the school are due in some cases to the type of political and economic systems of the society and the role that leaders in these systems expect the school to play. In some nations the school is controlled by a particular group and is used to perpetuate the values and ideologies of that group. But even in democracies power is not evenly distributed, and it is not uncommon for some groups to have a disproportionate influence on the schools. Societies are also undergoing different rates of change. Where change is rapid and has the approval of those in power, the schools can be used to accelerate and direct the changes toward preconceived ends. On the other hand, if the changes prove disruptive and threatening to those in power, they are likely to use the school to provide stability by teaching patriotism and the virtues of the old order.

The school's role is further complicated when society experiences a rapid expansion of knowledge and a concomitant multiplication of specialties and disciplines. Representatives of the new specialties and disciplines are likely to demand that the schools give ample attention to their area. The knowledge explosion places increasingly greater demands on schools, and they are unable to fulfill some of these demands. For example, when society is confronted with innovations, it may expect schools to introduce new programs for developing special skills, such as driver training or computer programming. To complicate matters further, a period of great change has an unsettling effect on people, because their cherished values and accepted ways of behavior are seriously questioned. At such times the role of the school becomes confused and ambiguous as numerous and conflicting voices express divergent goals and values. The usual conflict in such cases centers on whether education should reemphasize eternal verities and cultural traditions or concentrate on new values and behavior.

Some would argue that since the school is created by society and regulated by the legal system, it has no right to do anything other than carry out society's mandates. Under this conception the effective school is the one which best fulfills the will of the state and society; to attempt to do otherwise is to violate social trust and evade its mandate.

There are strong objections to this position. It is usually argued that to fulfill such a role is to accede to the status quo and the existing powers of a given time and place, whether they are just or unjust. The school thereby relinquishes its critical function. Moreover, it ignores the need to prepare people to change and improve society.

Others believe that the official policy should attempt to remain neutral by taking a nonpartisan stance toward social controversies of the larger society. This does not mean that the policies should prohibit the study of controversial issues. It only means that the school does not have an official position on the many disturbing matters of our time; rather, the school has the responsibility of seeing that all sides of every issue are presented fairly and impartially so that students can arrive at their own conclusions.

A corollary of this position (usually found in higher education circles) is that education should remain free of politics, that the university should not take an official position on any controversies of our time, and that its faculty should not speak on behalf of the university on these matters but only as private citizens. In addition, the faculty should desist from acts that might bring disrepute to the university or cause it to become involved in politics. Instead, the university should be a place where scholars freely search for truth and disseminate their findings to students and other interested parties.

Those who object to the neutral stance of the schools usually claim that the schools are abdicating their responsibility by failing to offer genuine criticism of the existing social order, thereby permitting social injustices and inequities to persist. Moreover, can the schools actually be neutral? As administrators make choices about the allocation of funds and resources, the curriculum, or the teaching staff, the school has decidedly taken a stand. Neutrality, its opponents argue, is merely an illusion; but it may also be a dangerous illusion because it leads to false belief in the import of one's activities and diverts attention from the social policies the schools should adopt.

As for the belief that the university should always avoid becoming enmeshed in politics, radical reformers claim that the university is already and has always been involved in politics—with state legislators and lobbyists;

through loyalty oaths; in government research contracts; in consulting work with business, government, and agriculture; in town-gown relations; in the quest for grants and subsidies from foundations, special interest groups, and private individuals; and in decisions about whether controversial political figures will speak on campus. What has happened, according to the reformers, is that the university has acceded to a multiplicity of demands from the larger society and is in danger of degenerating into mirror images of the worst practices of other institutions. The university cannot avoid politics; the problem is that it has adopted a politics that is hostile to and impedes the great changes that need to be brought about in all social institutions.

A widely accepted position is that the schools are repositories of the cultural heritage and must see to it that this heritage is imparted to the young so that they will develop into good citizens. The school's role is to provide continuity from one generation to the next and to assure that the most valuable aspects of the culture will be preserved. As they teach the heritage the schools also socialize the students by providing a system of beliefs and values that are socially acceptable. The net effect is to assure that the heritage will survive and that society will be able to maintain its stability in a period of rapid change.

But because time is short and the cultural heritage is large and diverse, a process of selection is necessary. On what basis will the selection be made and who will make it? Will a relatively impartial portrait be presented or only those features that are favorable and enhancing? Will this be a heritage of a white majority, thereby neglecting the role of minorities in the nation's history. Another objection is that teaching the heritage does not assure that students will be able to think critically about it or to make needed changes in society. Because the prevailing tendency in public education has been to teach the heritage uncritically, to make this the primary function of the school is to help perpetuate existing conditions.

Another position holds that the schools should lead in bringing about social change and helping build new ways of life to handle the enormous domestic and international problems of our time. With the world threatened by nuclear catastrophe, the population explosion, and a host of other grave problems, the schools can no longer afford the luxury of continuing their former roles. They must commit themselves to a world based on humane values and institutions committed to upholding these values and eliminating the afflictions besetting mankind. They should also be future-oriented toward educating youth to refashion the social order.

All the previous conceptions would object to this position. Among the objections would be that the schools would neglect the heritage, overstep their authority, lose public support, endorse utopian ideals not held by most people, and attempt a task doomed to failure. Moreover, teachers are incapable of carrying out a program of this type. In a democratic society the larger society, not the schools, must choose the overall direction in which that society should move. Even if educators were to seek the cooperation of other institutions in carrying out this plan, some critics would still object that the reformers have badly misunderstood the role of the school.

In the essay by Giovanni Gentile there are certain key concepts: nation, state, individual, Universal Will, and individual will. What meaning does the author assign to these concepts, and what is the relationship among them? The role of the school is explained in terms of these concepts and their interrelationships.

Isaac L. Kandel approaches the topic in terms of the historical reasons for society's establishment of schools. He shows the role of the school in relationship to social change. His position is further clarified when he offers criticisms of alternative views. Kandel presents an approach that a large number of laymen and some educators would endorse.

John Dewey analyzes social change and how the schools are caught up in it. He then offers a critique of other views and follows by posing three possible directions the schools could take, only one of which he believes to be acceptable.

Theodore Brameld states two key premises, offers evidence in their support, and then states what programs and policies education should undertake. He indicates how education can have a profound effect on the future of society.

11 / GIOVANNI GENTILE

Education and Nationality

We shall first point out the inutility of distinguishing science from culture, education from instruction. Those who insist on these distinctions maintain that though a school is never national in virtue of the content of its scientific teaching, it must nevertheless be national in that it transforms science into

From *The Reform of Education* by Giovanni Gentile, translated by Dino Bigongiari (New York: Harcourt Brace Jovanovich, Inc., 1922), pp. 7–17, 27–31. Reprinted by permission of the publisher.

Giovanni Gentile (1875–1945), an Italian educator who developed a concept of the state in Hegelian terms, was professor of history of philosophy at the University of Rome, editor of the philosophical journal *La Critica,* translator of philosophical classics, and first minister of education under Mussolini. Gentile is the author of *Summario de Pedagogia come Scienza Filosofica* and *The Reform of Education.*

culture, makes it over into an instrument with which to shape consciousness and conscience, and uses it as a tool for the making of men and for the training of citizens. Thus we have as an integral part of science a form of action directed on the character and the will of the young generations that are being nurtured and raised in accordance with national traditions and in view of the ends which the state wants to attain. Such distinctions however complicate but do not resolve the controversy. They entangle it with other questions which it were better to leave untouched at this juncture. For it might be said of questions what Manzoni said of books: one at a time is enough—if it isn't too much.

We shall therefore try to simplify matters, and begin by clarifying the two concepts of nationality and of knowledge, in order to define the concept of the "nationality of knowledge." What then, is the nation? A very intricate question, indeed, over which violent discussions are raging, and all the more passionately because the premises and conclusions of this controversy are never maintained in the peaceful seclusion of abstract speculative theories, but are dragged at every moment in the very midst of the concrete interests of the men themselves who affirm or deny the value of nationalities. So that serious difficulties are encountered every time an attempt is made to determine the specific and concrete content of this concept of the nation, which is ever present, and yet ever elusive. Proteus-like, it appears before us, but as we try to grasp it, it changes semblance and breaks away. It is visible to the immediate intuition of every national consciousness, but it slips from thought as we strive to fix its essence.

Is it common territory that constitutes nationality? or is it common language? or political life led in common? or the accumulation of memories, of traditions, and of customs by which a people looks back to *one* past where it never fails to find itself? Or is it perhaps the relationship which binds together all the individuals of a community into a strong and compact structure, assigning a mission and an apostolate to a people's faith? One or the other of these elements, or all of them together, have in turn been proposed and rejected with equally strong arguments. For in each case it may be true or it may be false that the given element constitutes the essence of a people's nationality, or of any historical association whatsoever. All these elements, whether separately or jointly, may have two different meanings, one of which makes them a mere accidental content of the national consciousness, whereas the other establishes them as necessary, essential, and unfailing constituents. For they may have a merely natural value, or they may have a moral and spiritual one. Our birth-land, which nourished us in our infancy, and now shelters the bodies of our parents, the mountains and the shores that surround it and individualise it, these are natural entities. They are not man-made; we cannot claim them, nor can we fasten our existence to them. Even our speech, our religion itself, which do indeed live in the human mind, may yet be considered as natural facts similar to the geographical accidents which give boundaries and elevation to the land of a people. We may, abstractly, look upon our language as that one which was spoken before we were born, by our departed ancestors who somehow produced this spiritual patrimony of which we now have the use and enjoyment, very much in the same way that we enjoy the sunlight showered upon us by nature. In this same way a few, perhaps many, conceive of religion: they look upon it as something bequeathed and inherited, and not therefore as the fruit of our own untiring faith and the correlate of our actual personality. All these elements in so far as they are natural are evidently extraneous to our personality. We do dwell within this peninsula cloistered by the Alps; we delight in this luminous sky, in our charming shores smiled upon by the waters of the Mediterranean. But if we emigrate from this lovely abode, if under the stress of economic motives we traverse the ocean and gather, a number of us, somewhere across the Atlantic; and there, united by the natural tie of common origin, and fastened by the identity of speech, we maintain ourselves as a special community, with common interests and peculiar moral affinities, then, in spite of the severance from our native peninsula, we have preserved our nationality: Italy has crossed the ocean in our wake. Not only can we sunder ourselves from our land, but we may even relinquish our customs, forget our language, abandon our religion; or we may, within our own fatherland, be kept separate by peculiar historical traditions, by differences of dialects or even of language, by religion, by clashing interests, and yet respond with the same sentiment and the same soul to the sound of one Name, to the colours of one flag, to the summons of common hopes, to the alarm of common dangers.

And it is then that we feel ourselves to be a people; then are we a nation. It is not what we put within this concept that gives consistency and reality to the concept itself; it is the act of spiritual energy whereby we cling to a certain element or elements in the consciousness of that collective personality to which we feel we belong. Nationality consists not in content which may vary, but in the form which a certain content of human consciousness assumes when it is felt to constitute a nation's character.

But this truth is still far from being recognised. Its existence is not even suspected by those who utilise a materially constituted nationality as a title, that is, an antecedent, and a support for political rights claimed by more or less considerable ethnical aggregates that are more or less developed and more or less prepared to take on the form of free and independent states and to secure recognition of a *de facto* political personality on the strength of an assumed *de jure* existence.

This truth, however, was grasped by the profound intuition of Mazzini, the apostle of nationalities, the man who roused our national energies, and whose irresistible call awakened Italy and powerfully impelled her to affirm her national being. Even from the first years of the *Giovine Italia* he insisted that Italy, when still merely an idea, prior to her taking on a concrete and actual political reality, was not a people and was not a nation. For a nation, he maintained, is not something existing in nature, but a great spiritual reality. Therefore like all that is in and for the spirit, it is never a fact ready to be ascertained, but always a mission, a purpose, something that has to be realised—an action.

The Italians to whom Mazzini spoke were not the people around him. He was addressing that future people which the Italians themselves had to create. And they would create it by fixing their souls on one idea—the idea of a fatherland to be conquered—a sacred idea, so noble that people would live and die for it, as for that sovereign and ultimate Good for which all sacrifices are gladly borne, without which man can not live, outside of which he finds nothing that satisfies him, nothing that is conducive to a life's work. For Mazzini nationality is not inherited wealth, but it is man's own conquest. A people can not faint-heartedly claim from others recognition of their nation, but must themselves demonstrate its existence, realise it by their willingness to fight and die for its independence: independence which is freedom and unity and constitutes the nation. It is not true that first comes the nation and then follows the state; the nation is the state when it has triumphed over the enemy, and has overcome the oppression, which till then were hindering its formation. It is not therefore a vague aspiration or a faint wish, but an active faith, an energetic volition which creates, in the freed political Power, the reality of its own moral personality and of its collective consciousness. Hence the lofty aim of Mazzini in insisting that Italy should not be made with the help of foreigners but should be a product of the revolution, that is, of its own will.

And truly the nation is, substantially, as Mazzini saw and firmly believed, the common will of a people which affirms itself and thus secures self-realization. A nation is a nation only when it wills to be one. I said, when it really wills, not when it merely says it does. It must therefore act in such a manner as to realise its own personality in the form of the State beyond which there is no collective will, no common personality of the people. And it must act seriously, sacrificing the individual to the collective whole, and welcoming martyrdom, which in every case is but the sacrifice of the individual to the universal, the lavishing of our own self to the ideal for which we toil.

From this we are not, however, to infer that a nation can under no circumstances exist prior to the formation of its State. For if this formation means the formal proclamation or the recognition by other States, it surely does pre-exist. But it does not if we consider that the proclamation of sovereignty is a moment in a previously initiated process, and the effect of pre-existing forces already at work; which effect is never definite because a State, even after it has been constituted, continues to develop in virtue of those very forces which produce it; so that it is constantly renewing and continually reconstituting itself. Hence a State is always a future. It is that state which this very day we must set up, or rather at this very instant, and with all our future efforts bent to that political ideal which gleams before us, not only in the light of a beautiful thought, but as the irresistible need of our own personality.

The nation therefore is as intimately pertinent and native to our own being as the State, considered as Universal Will, is one with our concrete and actual ethical personality. Italy for us is the fatherland which lives in our souls as that complex and lofty moral idea which we are realising. We realise it in every instant of our lives, by our feelings, and by our thoughts, by our speech and by our imagination, indeed, by our whole life which concretely flows into that Will which is the State and which thus makes itself felt in the world. And this Will, this State is Italy, which has fought and won; which has struggled for a long time amid errors and sorrows, hopes and dejection, manifestations of strength and confessions of weakness, but always with a secret thought, with a deep-seated aspiration which sustained her throughout her entire ordeal, now exalting her in the flush of action, now, in the critical moment of resistance, confirming and fortifying her by the undying faith in ultimate triumph. This nation, which we all wish to raise to an ever loftier station of honour and of beauty, even though we differ as to the means of attaining this end, is it not the substance of our personality—of that personality which we possess not as individuals who drift with the current, but as men who have a powerful self-consciousness and who look upward for their destiny?

If we thus understand the nation, it follows that not only every man must bear the imprint of his nationality, but that also there is no true science, no man's science, which is not national. The ancients believed, in conformity with the teachings of the Greeks, that science soars outside of the human life, above the vicissitudes of mortals, beyond the current of history, which is troubled by the fatal conflicts of error, by falterings and doubts, and by the unsatisfied thirst for knowledge. Truth, lofty, pure, motionless, and unchangeable, was to them the fixed goal toward which the human mind moved but completely severed from it and transcendent. This concept, after two thousand years of speculation, was to reveal itself as abstract and therefore fallacious,—abstract from the human mind, which at every given instance mirrors itself in such an image of truth, ever gazing upon an eternal ideal but always intent on reshaping it in a new and more adequate form. The modern world, at first with dim consciousness, and guided rather by a fortunate intuition than by a clear concept of its own real orientation, then with an ever clearer, ever more critical conviction, has elaborated a concept which is directly antithetical to the classical idea of a celestial truth removed from the turmoil of earthly things. It has accordingly and by many ways reached the conclusion that reality, lofty though it be, and truth itself, which nourishes the mind and alone gives validity to human thought, are in life itself, in the development of the mind, in the growth of the human personality, and that this personality, though ideally beyond our grasp, is yet in the concrete always historical and actual, and realises itself in its immanent value. It therefore creates its truth and its world. Modern philosophy and modern consciousness no longer point to values which, transcending history, determine its movement and its direction by external finalities: they show to man that the lofty aim which is his law is within himself; that it is in his ever unsatisfied personality as it unceasingly strains upward towards its own ideal.

Science is no longer conceived today as the indifferent pure matter of the intellect. It is an interest which invests the entire person, extols it and with it moves onward in the eternal rhythm of an infinite development. Science is not for us the abstract contemplation of yore; it is self-consciousness that man acquires, and by means of which he actuates his own humanity. And therefore science is no longer an adornment or an equipment of the mind considered as diverse to its content; it is culture, and the formation of this very mind. So that whenever science is as yet so abstract that it seems not to touch the person and fails to form it or transform it, it is an indication that it is not as yet true science.

So we conclude thus: he who distinguishes his person from his knowledge is ignorant of the nature of knowledge. The modern teacher knows of no science which is not an act of a personality. It knows no personality which admits of being sequestered from its ideas, from its ways of thinking and of feeling, from that greater life which is the nation. Concrete personality then is nationality, and therefore neither the school nor science possesses a learning which is not national.

And for this reason therefore our educational reforms which are inspired by the teachings of modern idealistic philosophy demand that the school be animated and vivified by the spiritual breath of the fatherland.

. . . But, then, when is it that my will really is effective, really *wills?* I am a citizen of a state which has power; this power, this will of the state expresses itself to me in laws which I must obey. The transgression of laws, if the state is in existence, bears with it the inevitable punishment of the transgressor, that is, the application of that law which the offender has refused to recognise. The state is supported by the inviolability of laws, of those sacred laws of the land which Socrates, as Plato tells us, taught his pupils to revere. I, then, as a citizen of my country, am bound by its Law in such a manner that to will its transgression is to aim at the impossible. If I did so, I should be indulging in vain velleities, in which my personality, far from realising itself, would on the contrary be disintegrated and scattered. I then want what the law wants me to will.

It makes no difference that, from a material and explicit point of view, a system of positive law does not coincide throughout with the sphere of my activity, and that therefore the major part of the standards of my conduct must be determined by the inner dictates of my particular conscience. For it is the Will of the State that determines the limits between the moral and the juridical, between what is imposed by the law of the land and what is demanded by the ethical conscience of the individual. And there is no limit which pre-exists to the line by which the constituent and legislative power of the State delimits the sphere subject to its sanctions. So that positively or negatively, either by command or by permission, our whole conduct is subject to that will by which the State establishes its reality.

But the Will of the State does not manifest itself solely by the enactments of positive legislation. It opens to private initiative such courses of action as may presumably be carried on satisfactorily without the impulse and the direct control of the sovereign power. But this concession has a temporary character, and the State is ever ready to intervene as soon as the private management ceases to be effective. So that even in the exercise of what seems the untrammelled will of the individual we discern the power of the State; and the individual is free to will something only because the sovereign power wants him to. So that in reality this apparently autonomous particular will is the will of the state not expressed in terms of positive legislation, there being no need of such an expression. But since the essence of law is not in the expression of it, but in the will which dictates it, or observes it, or enforces the observance of it, in the will, in short, that wills it, it follows that the law exists even though unwritten.

In the way of conclusion, then, it may be said that I, as a citizen, have indeed a will of my own; but that upon further investigation my will is found to coincide exactly with the will of the State, and I want anything only in so far as the State wants me to want it.

Could it possibly be otherwise? Such an hypothesis overwhelms me at the very thought of it. For it would come to this,—that I exist and my state does not:—the state in which I was born, which sustained and protected me before I saw the light of day, which formed and guaranteed to me this communion of life; the state in which I have always lived, which has constituted this spiritual substance, this world in which I support myself, and which I trust will never fail me even though it does change constantly. I could, it is true, ignore this close bond by which I am tied and united to that great will which is the will of my country. I might balk and refuse to obey its laws. But acting thus, I would be indulging in what I have called velleities. My personality, unable to transform the will of the state, would be overcome and suppressed by it.

Let us however assume for a moment that I might in the innermost depths of my being segregate myself. Averse to the common will and to the law of the land, I decide to proclaim over the boundless expanse of my thought the proud independence of my ego, as a lone, inaccessible summit rising out of the solitude. Up to a certain point this hypothesis is verified constantly by the manner in which my personality freely becomes actual. But even then I do not act as a particular being: it is the universal power that acts through my personal will.

For when we effectively observe the law, with true moral adhesion and in thorough sincerity, the law becomes part of ourselves, and our actions are the direct results of our convictions—of the necessity of our convictions. For every time we act, inwardly we see that such must be our course; we must have a clear intuition of this necessity. The Saint who has no will but the will of God intuitively sees necessity in his norm. So does the sinner in his own way: but his norm is erroneous and therefore destined to fail. Every criminal in transgressing the law obeys a precept of his own making which is in opposition to the enactments of the state. And in so doing he creates almost a state of his own, different from the one which historically exists and must exist because of certain good reasons, the excellence of which the criminal himself will subsequently realise. From the unfortunate point of view which he has taken, the transgressor is justified in acting as he does, and to such an extent that no one in his position, as he thinks, could possibly take exception to it. His will is also universal; if he were allowed to, if it were possible for him, he would establish new laws in place of the old ones: he would set up another state over the ruins of the one which he undermines. And what else does the tyrant when he destroys the freedom of the land and substitutes a new state for the crushed Commonwealth? In the same manner the rebel does away with the despot, starts a revolution and establishes liberty if he is successful; if not, he is overcome and must again conform his will to the will of that state which he has not been able to overthrow. So then, I exercise my true volition whenever the will of my state acts in my personal will, or rather when my will is the realisation of the will of a super-national group in which my state co-exists with other states, acting upon them, and being re-acted upon in reciprocal determinations. Or perhaps better still, when the entire world wills in me. For my will, I shall say it once again, is not individual but universal, and in the political community by which individuals are united into a higher individuality, historically distinct from other similar ones, we must see a form of universality.

12 / ISAAC L. KANDEL

Education and Social Change

The general social and cultural unrest which can be traced back to the beginnings of the modern scientific movement and the consequent technological changes, an unrest which has grown in intensity, since the War, has had its repercussions on educational thought. This has, indeed, been the history of education, for education has been most vigorous and vital in periods of great social changes, as, for example, in Athens, during the Renaissance and the Reformation, at the time of the early scientific movement of the seventeenth century, and at the beginning of the nineteenth century following the Industrial Revolution and the consolidation of nation-states. The period through which the world is passing in the present era is probably one of those nodal periods in which old ideas and ideals, standards and loyalties, are being questioned and modified, if not revolutionized. Science is remaking the world and bringing an economic upheaval in its train; political institutions are being questioned or overturned; a war of ideas is going on in every field that concerns human relationships. The conflicts are more profound and more widespread than those which have always existed between the older and younger generations.

Under these conditions unrest in education is inevitable, but in the discussions on education and social change it is not clear whether a formula is being sought whereby the rising generation shall be acquainted with the social changes going on about it or whether it is proposed that the school itself should be made an instrument for the reconstruction of society. These alternatives can be answered only in the light of the purposes for which society establishes schools.

The earliest and most persistent reason for the establishment of schools as formal agencies of education is the desire on the part of a group, society, or state to conserve and transmit its culture and heritage to the younger

Isaac L. Kandel, "Education and Social Change," in *Conflicting Theories of Education* (New York: The Macmillan Company, 1938), pp. 77–88.

Isaac L. Kandel (1881–1965), an early leader in the essentialist movement and comparative studies of education, served as a faculty member at Teachers College, Columbia University. He is the author of *Comparative Education* and *Conflicting Theories of Education*.

generation and to equip this generation with those habits, skills, knowledges, and ideals that will enable it to take its place in a society and contribute to the stability and perpetuation of that society. This purpose is based on faith in the possibilities of formal education during the formative and plastic period of childhood and adolescence. This is the principle in Plato's statement that the effectual functioning of the state depends upon the proper training of the young, and in Aristotle's insistence that the stability of systems of government has its basis in the adaptation of education to the form of government.

Education does not proceed in a vacuum; its character is determined by the group culture, and schools are institutions created by society to attain certain specific ends. These ends began to be defined when the national states at the beginning of the nineteenth century undertook to establish systems of education to initiate their future citizens into the national culture. Stability was to be secured by instructing the pupils in the schools in a common language, common history, common government and political ideals, common economic and social ideas and ideals, and common objects of social allegiance in order that there might emerge a common group, or national, self-consciousness. If the younger generation is to enter into meaningful partnership in and responsibility for its heritage the first function of the school is to initiate it into its common culture. Society is, in fact, prior to the individual, and the school is an agency for promoting stability and adapting the individual to the environment in which he lives. Without entering into other considerations which justify the transmission of the social heritage or the experiences of the race as a basis for understanding the present, it will be generally agreed that the function here described has received wide acceptance from the days of Plato down to modern times.

If, however, the school stops with the performance of this function, then a society either stagnates, as was the case in China, or its progress is determined by the will of the few who lead the rest, trained through the school to habits of duty, discipline, quiescent obedience, and uncritical acceptance of authority. The method of such a school is that of direct indoctrination and education becomes indistinguishable from propaganda. This was already the trend in authoritarian states of the last century; it is the principle definitely accepted in the totalitarian states of the present, in which education is directed by and to a common ideology. The social changes wrought by revolutions have produced patterns which know no compromise and are not open to question or criticism. Education has become adjustment to a fixed and unchanging environment, and national culture is something that is colored by a particular ideology and controlled by organizations created to prevent changes in it.

The situation is different in those countries in which culture is accepted as the spontaneous expression of individuals and the free interplay among individuals or groups. It is at this point that education and social change begin to be clothed with meaning and to challenge traditional practices. The procedure in the past was to impart a body of content, knowledge, and information representing selections from the group culture designed primarily to "train the mind." It tended to become stereotyped and formal and rarely came to grips with the present. The school was a cloistered institution which eschewed any contact with the environment into which the pupil was soon to pass. It must be remembered, however, that even this type of procedure did not ignore the changing environment and was not designed to maintain a static society, but it was conducted with the conviction that a mind trained by "academic" or "scholastic" material would have no difficulty in dealing with the realities of life. Nor was the procedure in the education of the masses differentiated from the procedure in the education of the potential leaders.

These practices were not accepted without protest. Since the days of Seneca educators have urged that education must be for life and not for the school, but it was not until the beginning of the present century that widespread efforts began to be made to bring school and society together. A better understanding of the process of child growth, a new interpretation of the concept of interest, a clearer realization of the meaning of democracy and the part to be played by the individual in it, and the rapid changes in the culture, due in the main to the progress of science—all these forces and many others contributed to the spread of the theory that if education is a social process, it must contribute to an understanding of the society which it serves. The influence of John Dewey's philosophy in bringing about the change of outlook not only in the United States but in other parts of the world is too well known to need further discussion. The vast body of educational literature which has grown up in the United States in the past three decades speaks eloquently of this influence. The educational trend in Germany during the period of the short-lived Republic was rooted in *Bodenständigkeit*, the relation of education to the environment. In England the latest edition of the *Handbook of Suggestions for Teachers* is inspired by the same principle, as is illustrated by a statement in the general introduction that "we feel more deeply the need of relating what is taught in the schools to what is happening in the world outside."

The new theory of education, in insisting that the work of the school must be related to the environment in which and for which its pupils are being educated, contains in its definition the suggestion that discussions of social change are implicit in the curriculum. It means that pupils should be taught to understand the world in which they live. Up to this point the problem is fairly simple. Difficulties arise, however, when it is suggested that change is the characteristic note of the present world—and change not merely in its material but in its ideational aspects. To what extent should or can the school concern itself with political and economic conflicts, with changes in the attitudes to authority, or with the general atmosphere that questions all traditions?

Changes in the material world are facts; political and economic theories are matters of opinion. If the teacher is an agent of the state, to what extent is he free to introduce controversial issues into the classroom? It is not necessary here to state that the issues should be relevant to the stage of development and the maturity of the pupils concerned and to the subject of instruction. But if the function of education is to develop an understanding of the problems of the environment in which the learner lives, the opportunity of discussing controversial issues in the school cannot be ignored. Indeed, one may argue that it is essential to train the pupil in recognizing the importance of accurate knowledge before reaching an opinion.

If the doors of the school are to be closed to the discussion of controversial issues, it might well be asked what the alternative would be; in a period of change the schools would be guilty of turning pupils out into the world ignorant of the problems that will confront them. There is, in fact, no choice but to bring those elements of conflict into the classroom. To adopt an ostrichlike attitude and ignore the existence of such issues, to deny the right to mention even the existence of what may be regarded as subversive ideas, is to follow the old practice of ignoring the existence of sex. Carried to its logical conclusion, such a policy could be used to justify the suppression of a free press and of freedom of opinion, and the arrest of anyone suspected of "harboring dangerous thoughts."

Any reference to the introduction of controversial issues in politics and economics arouses the fear that pupils will be exposed to the bias of the teachers. It may be true that no teacher can successfully conduct a discussion of controversial issues without the pupils' detecting his bias. Nevertheless, pupils pass through the hands of a large number of teachers during their school careers; to suspect that all teachers have the same bias has no justification in fact; nor are teachers the only educational influences that play upon the growing youth. The choice is whether the rising generation is to receive its political and economic education through informal agencies or through methods that are truly educative; whether the young are to be enlightened and trained through the scientific study of facts or whether they are to be exposed to deliberate propaganda without the support of accurate information on both sides of an issue. If the relationship between school and society or education and the environment means anything, then the schools must, at the appropriate stage, impart the realities of society. And if that society is in process of change, then all that the school can do is to place the pupils in possession of full knowledge of the facts in the issues involved and to give them that training which will enable them to make up their own minds on the basis of that knowledge.

The emphasis in this argument is on training in methods of thinking through issues that are real. There is some truth in the objection that solutions cannot be given to contemporary controversial issues; this objection is, however, not a valid argument for their exclusion from the schools. Neither the issues nor the solutions are likely to be the same when pupils now in school take their places in life as adult citizens; the detailed facts of an issue and the knowledge requisite to its solution will inevitably be different, but unless some training is given in the schools in the patterns of thinking with which a problem is to be approached, the intellectual equipment necessary to recognize even the existence of problems will have been withheld. If democracy depends for its survival upon the intelligence and understanding of the ordinary man, it is the function of the school to equip him in advance with the necessary knowledge and powers of clear thinking to discharge his duties as a citizen.

It is only in this sense that education and social change can be discussed. Education must go beyond its task of imparting a knowledge and appreciation of the common interests, or what Dewey has called the objects of that social allegiance which makes common social understanding and consciousness of group membership possible. It must help men and women to think for themselves, unless they are to succumb to the will of an authority which claims omniscience and infallibility.

There has, however, been injected into discussions of education and social change the suggestion that schools should, in a period of change, educate for a new social order, and that teachers should ally themselves with some political group and use their classrooms to propagate certain doctrines. Schools and teachers should, in other words, participate more directly and vitally in projecting particular ideas or patterns of social change and in their execution. The whole history of education emphasizes the impossibility of this idea, for society establishes schools to provide a firm basis for itself and to sustain the common interest. Schools are a part of the environment which they serve; they are not autonomous or insulated against the social forces and influences around them; nor can teachers on the basis of a guess as to the active forces of the day help to build a new social order. Society changes first and schools follow.

It is, however, becoming increasingly important that teachers should be more alive than they have been in the past and better informed about the environment in and for which they are educating their pupils. Only in this way can they give meaning to the subjects for which they are responsible, for subjects, if they are to have any significance, must be saturated with social meaning. To attempt to instill ready-made ideas on controversial issues or to influence pupils to accept one doctrine rather than another is to adopt the methods of totalitarian states and to confuse education with propaganda.

In a democracy the only acceptable aim in bringing the school and society more closely together is to develop the knowledge and understanding that make for enlightened citizenship. But the acquisition of knowledge, facts, and information about the environment in all those aspects that concern the conduct of the citizen is not the sole end of education; such an acquisition must be made the vehicle for training in scientific methods of thinking and for cultivating free and disciplined minds. To educate for a new social order is to close the minds of the pupils, for, in a society in transition, no one can have a final answer concerning the issues that are involved. True education would help to put the pupils in a position to appreciate the urgent necessity of acquiring knowledge, to discriminate between facts and prejudices, to weigh and judge evidence, to reach conclusions warranted by the information secured, and to recognize the issues involved in a period of social transition or crisis. If this end is to be achieved, if the aim of education is to develop free and enlightened citizens, then the teachers who are to be entrusted with carrying out this aim must themselves be enlightened and free. The problem, like all other problems in education, becomes one of teacher preparation and of the status of teachers. In the words of a former president of the English Board of Education, "The standards of the teaching profession itself are the only sure protection" against the abuse of the teachers' positions in discussing educational and social change.

The problem of education and social change solves itself if education is defined as the process of bringing pupils to an understanding of the environment in and for which they are being educated. That environment is a constantly expanding one; to concentrate on change alone is to deal only with the immediate present and to avoid the development of an understanding of the rich heritage which the environment carries with it. But understanding must lead to conduct, and if democracy is to survive, the schools must cultivate in their pupils ideals of freedom, tolerance, and open-mindedness, a critical attitude and intellectual sensitiveness based on ascertained facts and knowledge, a spirit of inquiry and insight, and those emotional qualities in addition which make for a sense of responsibility and co-operation. For democracy, in the words of Santayana, is a blind, groping adventure which implies open-mindedness and sensitiveness to the need of flexibility and adaptation of social institutions. These are the qualities which education can cultivate as the basis of social change.

13 / JOHN DEWEY

Education and Social Change

Attention has been continually called of late to the fact that society is in process of change, and that the schools tend to lag behind. We are all familiar with the pleas that are urged to bring education in the schools into closer relation with the forces that are producing social change and with the needs that arise from these changes. Probably no question has received so much attention in educational discussion during the past few years as the problem of integration of the schools with social life. Upon these general matters, I could hardly do more than reiterate what has often been said.

Nevertheless, there is as yet little consensus of opinion as to what the schools can do in relation to the forces of social change and how they should do it. There are those who assert in effect that the schools must simply reflect social changes that have already occurred, as best they may. Some would go so far as to make the work of schools virtually parasitic. Others hold that the schools should take an active part in *directing* social change, and share in the construction of a new social order. Even among the latter there is, however, marked difference of attitude. Some think the schools should assume this directive role by means of indoctrination; others oppose this method. Even if there were more unity of thought than exists there would still be the practical problem of overcoming institutional inertia so as to realize in fact an agreed-upon program.

There is, accordingly, no need to justify further discussion of the problem of the relation of education to social change. I shall do what I can, then, to indicate the factors that seem to me to enter into the problem, together with some of the reasons that prove that the schools do have a role—and an important one—in *production* of social change.

One factor inherent in the situation is that schools *do* follow and reflect the social "order" that exists. I do not make this statement as a grudging admission, nor yet in order to argue that they should *not* do so. I make it rather as a statement of a *conditioning* factor which supports the conclusion that the schools thereby do take part in the determination of a future social

John Dewey, "Education and Social Change," *The Social Frontier*, III, No. 26 (May 1937), 235–238. Reprinted by permission of the publisher.

order; and that, accordingly, the problem is not whether the schools *should* participate in the production of a future society (since they do so anyway) but whether they should do it blindly and irresponsibly or with the maximum possible of courageous intelligence and responsibility.

The grounds that lead me to make this statement are as follows: The existing state of society, which the schools reflect, is not something fixed and uniform. The idea that such is the case is a self-imposed hallucination. Social conditions are not only in process of change, but the changes going on are in different directions, so different as to produce social confusion and conflict. There is no single and clear-cut pattern that pervades and holds together in a unified way the social conditions and forces that operate. It requires a good deal of either ignorance or intellectual naivete to suppose that these changes have all been tending to one coherent social outcome. The plaint of the conservative about the imperiling of old and time-tried values and truths, and the efforts of reactionaries to stem the tide of changes that occur, are sufficient evidence, if evidence be needed to the contrary.

Of course the schools have mirrored the social changes that take place. The notion that the educational system has been static is too absurd for notice; it has been and still is in a state of flux.

The fact that it is possible to argue about the desirability of many of the changes that have occurred, and to give valid reasons for deploring aspects of the flux, is not relevant to the main point. For the stronger the arguments brought forth on these points, and the greater the amount of evidence produced to show that the educational system is in a state of disorder and confusion, the greater is the proof that the schools have responded to, and have reflected, social conditions which are themselves in a state of confusion and conflict.

Do those who hold the idea that the schools should not attempt to give direction to social change accept complacently the confusion that exists, because the schools *have* followed in the track of one social change after another? They certainly do not, although the logic of their position demands it. For the most part they are severe critics of the existing state of education. They are as a rule opposed to the studies called modern and the methods called progressive. They tend to favor return to older types of studies and to strenuous "disciplinary" methods. What does this attitude mean? Does it not show that its advocates in reality adopt the position that the schools can do something to affect positively and constructively social conditions? For they hold in effect that the school should discriminate with respect to the social forces that play upon it; that instead of accepting the latter *in toto*, education should select and organize in a given direction. The adherents of this view can hardly believe that the effect of selection and organization will stop at the doors of school rooms. They must expect some ordering and healing influence to be exerted sooner or later upon the structure and movement of life outside.

What they are really doing when they deny directive social effect to education is to express their opposition to some of the directions social change is actually taking, and their choice of other social forces as those with which education should throw in its lot so as to promote as far as may be their victory in the strife of forces. They are conservatives in education because they are socially conservative and vice-versa.

This is as it should be in the interest of clearness and consistency of thought and action. If these conservatives in education were more aware of what is involved in their position, and franker in stating its implications, they would help bring out the real issue. It is not whether the schools shall or shall not influence the course of future social life, but in what direction they shall do so and how. In some fashion or other, the schools will influence social life anyway. But they can exercise such influence in different ways and to different ends, and the important thing is to become conscious of these different ways and ends, so that an intelligent choice may be made, and so that if opposed choices are made, the further conflict may at least be carried on with understanding of what is at stake, and not in the dark.

There are three possible directions of choice. Educators may act so as to perpetuate the present confusion and possibly increase it. That will be the result of drift, and under present conditions to drift is in the end to make a choice. Or they may select the newer scientific, technological, and cultural forces that are producing change in the old order; may estimate the direction in which they are moving and their outcome if they are given freer play, and see what can be done to make the schools their ally. Or, educators may become intelligently conservative and strive to make the schools a force in maintaining the old order intact against the impact of new forces.

If the second course is chosen—as of course I believe it should be—the problem will be other than merely that of accelerating the rate of the change that is going on. The problem will be to develop the insight and understanding that will enable the youth who go forth from the schools to take part in the great work of construction and organization that will have to be done, and to equip them with the attitudes and habits of action that will make their understanding and insight practically effective.

There is much that can be said for an intelligent conservatism. I do not know anything that can be said for perpetuation of a wavering, uncertain, confused condition of social life and education. Nevertheless, the easiest thing is to refrain from fundamental thinking and let things go on drifting. Upon the basis of any other policy than drift—which after all is a policy, though a blind one—every special issue and problem, whether that of selection and organization of subject-matter of study, of methods of teaching, of school buildings and equipment, of school administration, is a special phase of the inclusive and fundamental problem: What movement of social forces, economic, political, religious, cultural, shall the school take to be controlling in its aims and methods, and with which forces shall the school align itself?

Failure to discuss educational problems from this point of view but intensifies the existing confusion. Apart from this background, and outside of this perspective, educational questions have to be settled *ad hoc* and are speedily unsettled. What is suggested does not mean that the schools shall throw themselves into the political and economic arena and take sides with some party there. I am not talking about parties; I am talking about social forces and their movement. In spite of absolute claims that are made for this party or that, it is altogether probable that existing parties and sects themselves suffer from existing confusions and conflicts, so that the understanding, the ideas, and attitudes that control their policies, need re-education and re-orientation. I know that there are some who think that the implications of what I have said point to abstinence and futility; that they negate the stand first taken. But I am surprised when educators adopt this position, for it shows a profound lack of faith in their own calling. It assumes that education as education has nothing or next to nothing to contribute; that formation of understanding and disposition counts for nothing; that only immediate overt action counts and that it can count equally whether or not it has been modified by education.

Before leaving this aspect of the subject, I wish to recur to the utopian nature of the idea that the schools can be completely neutral. This idea sets up an end incapable of accomplishment. So far as it is acted upon, it has a definite social effect, but that effect is, as I have said, perpetuation of disorder and increase of blind because unintelligent conflict. Practically, moreover, the weight of such action falls upon the reactionary side. Perhaps the most effective way of re-inforcing reaction under the name of neutrality, consists in keeping the oncoming generation ignorant of the conditions in which they live and the issues they have to face. This effect is the more pronounced because it is subtle and indirect; because neither teachers nor those taught are aware of what they are doing and what is being done to them. Clarity can develop only in the extent to which there is frank acknowledgment of the basic issue: Where shall the social emphasis of school life and work fall, and what are the educational policies which correspond to this emphasis?

14 / THEODORE BRAMELD

Imperatives for a Reconstructed Philosophy of Education

Recently an invitation came to me, as it did to others, that was unusual not only in itself but because of its signers. I was asked to comment for the impending 10th Anniversary Conference of the New Lincoln School on this kind of question: "What should American education become in the next ten years?" The signers were William H. Kilpatrick, Jerrold Zacharias, Arthur Bestor, and Robert M. Hutchins. Almost anyone would be intrigued by such an invitation: could it mean that leaders representing such extremely diverse educational views as Kilpatrick and Hutchins were actually going to listen carefully to one another? My reply provides the framework for this article.

Addressing myself to Dr. Kilpatrick, I wrote as follows:

> Your desire to include the views of people of very different educational outlooks is most commendable and surely much needed in a time of extraordinary concern. . . . As you know, my own philosophic position in education is quite unorthodox and differs at rather crucial points not only from your own but particularly from that of Dr. Bestor and Dr. Hutchins whose names accompany your own. . . . I assume that, since you have written me, you wish to have my viewpoint heard along with others.
>
> . . . The challenge of the sputnik has not only aroused the American people from their educational lethargy as few if any events have done, but it has since demonstrated the appalling confusion among us as to the functions and purposes of education in our democracy. Even more appalling, if that is possible, is the evidence that exceedingly

Theodore Brameld, "Imperatives for a Reconstructed Philosophy of Education," from *School and Society*, Vol. 87, No. 2145 (January 17, 1959), pp. 18–20. Reprinted by permission of the publisher and the author.

Theodore Brameld (1904–), formerly a member of the Boston University faculty, is presently a visiting professor at the University of Hawaii. Brameld is known as the leading reconstructionist, and his educational ideas have been presented in such works as *Patterns of Educational Philosophy, Toward a Reconstructed Philosophy of Education, Cultural Foundations of Education, Education as Power, Education for the Emerging Age,* and *The Climactic Decades.*

powerful voices in America—exemplified by *Life* and *Time*—oversimplify and prejudge the issues. The editorial in the March 31st [1958] issue of *Life*, reprinted in *Time, The New York Times,* and elsewhere, so outrageously falsified these issues that the Philosophy of Education Society in its annual meeting, Indianapolis, April 2, 1958, unanimously went on record in condemnation of such "irresponsible" journalism. The President of the Society, incidentally, was Father R. J. Henle, S.J., and many members are in disagreement with the philosophy of John Dewey, which was especially under attack in the editorial.

And yet, in one respect, the thesis of the *Life* editorial represents the attitudes of millions of so-called, self-appointed "authorities" on American education. This thesis is, of course, that education must ultimately choose between two points of view—the one, represented by the progressivism of Dewey and his disciples; the other, represented by the kind of neoconservatism which *Life* itself espouses and which, typified by the writings of such earnest persons as Professor Bestor, has the support of all those forces in the culture that identify education with traditional forms of learning and classical subject matters.

. . . This kind of either-or choice is quite as false as is the kind of pseudosyntheses and patchwork proposals exemplified in the equally earnest writings of Professor Paul Woodring. There is, I submit, a radically different approach to the problem which we shall have to give consideration if we are not to be deluded indefinitely by oversimplifications and fuzzy or nostalgic thinking. This approach is based upon at least two fundamental premises.

The first premise is that we live today in one of the greatest periods of crisis in human history. Granting that all history consists of recurrent crises, this one is unprecedented in several ways, the most monstrous of which is the fact that man has achieved the capacity to destroy civilization over night. America, living as it does in an aura of deceptive prosperity and complacency, refuses thus far to admit this fact with any real conviction. In many other parts of the world, however, the masses of people are very deeply concerned—so deeply that, as anyone knows who follows world events, our own country is looked upon with more and more skepticism, less and less as the great democratic vanguard which it once was.

The second premise is that, just as the physical sciences have recently passed through a revolution which was, indeed, partly responsible for the crisis itself, so today the behavioral sciences . . . are rapidly entering upon a revolution of their own. This revolution is already awakening those familiar with it to the realization that mankind is now approaching the opportunity to achieve a world civilization of abundance, health, and humane capacity that is as life-affirming and promising as the crisis symbolized by sputniks and hydrogen bombs is life-denying and dreadful.

The kind of education needed in America must, I submit, be reconstructed upon these two premises. It can become an education that inspires young people to adventure and creation and yet is at diametrically opposite poles from its one real opponent—the totalitarian education of the communist orbit. Instead of being based upon outmoded conceptions of learning and discipline, such as are at bottom

> endorsed by the neoconservative forces, it can utilize the richest resources of the behavioral sciences and a theory of unified man which those resources elucidate. The superficial arguments of the pro-science versus the pro-humanities groups are overarched in the same way as are those between the so-called educationists and academicians.
>
> Teacher training, for example, would of course be reorganized once such a conception took hold. Of course it is cluttered with busy work, with overemphasis upon method, and with all sorts of absurdities. But so, too, would the liberal-arts program of the typical high school and college require reorganization—characterized as it often is with a chaos of unrelated courses, bad teaching, and unmotivated learning. Neither teacher training nor liberal arts can be called satisfactory because neither is governed by a philosophy of education and culture suitable to a world in crisis. And neither is satisfactory because neither is aware (except vaguely at most) that a revolution in the behavioral sciences, which is breaking down old classifications and opening new vistas of human potentiality, is already well under way.
>
> I cannot now indicate in any detail what this conception would mean for the curriculum, for standards of scholarship, for school administration, or for the profession of teaching; I can only suggest that it does mean a completely new look at all of them. The question of how to move from the high level of generalization to the concrete level of practice is, however, answerable in one way here. There is pressing need for new forms of educational experimentation—new designs in the form of testable hypotheses. . . . The time has come to initiate audacious, imaginative pilot projects based upon the conception I have tried to indicate. Teachers and students alike would enter into them with an excitement that could be contagious, and that could affect education not only throughout America but throughout other countries that are attuned to the crisis of our time and await our leadership again.

The remaining paragraphs spell out a little further the implications of the above statement.

The first premise—that we live in an age of crisis—is supportable in a great many ways besides the one selected for mention. Granting that destruction by nuclear war is the most horrifying fear of our time, only a little less horrifying are the insidious disintegrations threatened by radioactive fallouts. Add to these the record of two bloody intercontinental wars within a quarter-century, the rise of a mighty totalitarian system that already jeopardizes America's position as the foremost industrial power, and now the looming conquest of space with its portents of evil as well as good. For any educational system not to give these events priority, for it not to provide every possible opportunity to diagnose their causes and to consider how the growing generation may cope with them while time remains, is for that system to shirk its most urgent responsibility.

Although certain other viewpoints besides the one I support would agree on the fact of major crisis, no other derives from it similar educational imperatives. The most crucial of these rest upon the second major premise—the revolution occurring in the behavioral sciences. This revolution requires education to re-examine its whole conventional structure and to consider new ways of (1) ordering its subject matters, (2) engaging in the processes by which they are taught and learned, and (3) formulating the purposes of school and society.

None of these imperatives would have been practicably realizable before the emergence of such young sciences as cultural anthropology and psychiatry, or the interrelating of these with such older ones as economics, sociology, and history. None of them depends upon metaphysical or otherwise speculative doctrines of the classical philosophies. All of them, while open to a great deal of further clarification and verification, are potentially demonstrable and defensible in the same way that all science is demonstrable and defensible.

Let me try now to illustrate each of the three imperatives in educational terms.

1. Up to this time, the structure of the typical school and college curriculum has been largely a jumble of discrete subject matters that, for the average student, have little or no meaningful relations to one another—languages, mathematics, social science, natural science, and others—each of which is often again subdivided into further discrete units. The behavioral sciences are now demonstrating that, as far at least as all the areas having to do with biopsychological experience are concerned, these divisions and subdivisions are less and less tenable. Concepts such as organism, connoting relationships between parts as much as the parts related, are replacing the older atomistic concepts. Human life, individually and culturally, is increasingly seen in terms of patterns and configurations.

Programs of general or integrated education, recognizing that something must be done to give meaningful unity to the curriculum structure, have sometimes been tangentially affected by this interdisciplinary view of human behavior. Unfortunately, however, they also have been plagued by the same confusions in theory and practice that are chronic to other educational programs. Some general educationists, for example, take their cue from the physical sciences; others, from neo-scholasticism or like doctrines. Few as yet regard the tasks and goals of human beings as the first and most important concern of vital education in an age such as our, or, for that matter, in any age.

This is not to say that the physical sciences, any more than the humanities, should be neglected by the needed new framework. It does mean that they are encompassed by it. A theory of unified man, both derived from and contributing to our experimental knowledge of human behavior in its multiple perspectives, not only should integrate all other fields of knowledge; it should provide them with a fresh and potent significance.

2. The required rebuilding of teaching and learning processes is heralded by a great body of recent behavioral research, only a fraction of which has begun to permeate educational practice. Perhaps the one point where

permeation has occurred at all fruitfully thus far is in the methodology of "group dynamics." Yet, even here, as so commonly happens in educational circles, it has acquired more often the earmarks of a superficial fad than of a profound process dependent upon a widening range of discoveries about the "fields of force" that constitute the interactions of human beings in their multiple roles.

Even more promising is the "culture-and-personality" frontier. Here anthropologists and psychologists are joining hands. And they are demonstrating that learning, for example, involves polaristic dimensions of inner and outer experience, some of it quite unconscious, that have been almost totally neglected by the orthodox formulations still underlying classroom routines.

Again, the problem of how to enlist education in the processes of institutional change so that it functions, not merely to transmit but to modify and reconstruct outmoded arrangements, can now be attacked with the aid of substantial knowledge. The concept of crisis itself exemplifies this opportunity. Citing outstanding authorities in the behavioral sciences, I have pointed out elsewhere that

> There is no good reason, except timidity or irresponsibility, that prevents high schools and colleges from encouraging young people to analyze both the meaning of crisis theoretically and its manifestations overtly. Leaders ought accordingly to clarify their orientation here: they ought to face the issue of whether education is to be regarded as capable of sharing importantly in the control and resolution of crises, or as a pawn of overpowering material or spiritual forces beyond control and resolution.[1]

3. The shaping of new purposes for education and culture is also becoming feasible in a way that could hardly have been conceived even three or four decades ago. In other words, the behavioral sciences are beginning to prove, really for the first time in history, that it is possible to formulate human goals not for sentimental, romantic, mystical, or similarly arbitrary reasons, but on the basis of what we are learning about cross-cultural and even universal values. Though studies in this difficult field have moved only a little way, they have moved far enough so that it is already becoming plausible both to describe these values objectively and to demonstrate that most human beings prefer them to alternative values.

Freedom is an example. By analyzing drives and motivations, by determining what human beings in many different cultures most deeply need and want, freedom both as fact and norm undergoes something of a

[1] "Cultural Foundations of Education—An Interdisciplinary Exploration" (New York: Harper, 1957), p. 153.

metamorphosis of meaning. Yet it preserves the rich kernel of significance intuited by Jefferson and other geniuses of a pre-scientific age.

This way of constructing educational purposes rests, too, upon an expanding inventory of research evidence. Human resources for a happy life on earth are infinitely greater than we have ever dreamed possible—resources that we have hardly begun to tap because we are so often blinded by conflict, ignorance, and fear. A truly goal-centered education could contribute more than any other agency to displacing these destructive forces by scientifically ascertainable and testable hopes for the future of mankind.

To what extent is educational theory presently concerned with the kind of imperatives that I have indicated? I regret to say: very little, indeed. The only recent books that, in my judgment, help (each in a different way) are three: *The Ideal and the Community—A Philosophy of Education*, by I. B. Berkson;[2] *Philosophy of Education for Our Time*, by Frederick Mayer;[3] and *Philosophy and Education*, edited by Israel Scheffler.[4]

It is difficult, however, to feel that the dominant neo-conservative mood of the moment is anything more than passing. The single most encouraging fact about the behavioral sciences as they are now swiftly developing (I have been able, of course, to reveal only a few glimpses) is that they offer so little comfort to those of such a timid if not defeatist mood and so much support to those who continue deeply to believe in the need of a philosophy and program appropriate to our revolutionary age.

Questions for Discussion

Compare the positions of Gentile and Kandel, noting their similarities and differences. Do they differ in their interpretations of the individual and his responsibilities to society or the state? Does Gentile support his basic concepts adequately? What would be the social consequences of his position? Why do you believe Gentile's position has been accepted by many nations of the past and present? Kandel's views, on the other hand, are developed by looking at what schools were expected to do in the past, and what he considers feasible and proper for them today. Are his arguments sound? Why do you believe his views still enjoy wide popularity, especially among laymen?

What is Dewey's interpretation of social change and its impact on education? What role does he envision for the schools in relation to widespread social change? Notice his criticism of other positions. What are his principal

[2] (New York: Harper, 1958.)
[3] (New York: Odyssey, 1958.)
[4] (Boston: Allyn and Bacon, 1958.)

objections to these positions, and are his arguments cogent? Could Dewey be charged with partisanship for urging the alliance of the school with certain social forces?

What are Brameld's two key premises and the policies and recommendations he believes are needed in light of these premises? Do you believe he has analyzed today's social conditions accurately and has offered a defensible plan of action? Compare and evaluate Dewey's and Brameld's positions in terms of their attitudes toward social change and the consequent role they believe education should pursue.

In light of these four essays, develop your own position and defend it. Show in what respects it is similar to one or more of the essays.

Suggested Reading

Two of the most influential books ever written on education exhibit highly divergent and original views of the relation of education and the larger society: *The Republic of Plato*, trans. F. M. Cornford (New York: Oxford, 1945); and *The Emile of Jean Jacques Rousseau*, ed. and trans. William Boyd (New York: Teachers College Press, 1962). Plato shows how a selective educational system can build an ideal state crowned by the philosopher-king, whereas Rousseau relates the need to remove the child from the corruptions of urban life and educate him close to nature.

The need to provide stability and unity, thereby welding a nation from disparate and warring factions, has prompted Giovanni Gentile to ascribe preeminence to the state in relation to education and the individual in his *The Reform of Education*, trans. Dino Bigorgiari (New York: Harcourt Brace Jovanovich, 1922). Isaac Kandel's *Conflicting Theories of Education* (New York: Macmillan Co., 1939) contends that it is society's role to lead and the school's role to follow. In *Education and the New America* (New York: Random House, 1962), Solon T. Kimball and James E. McClellan, Jr., after conducting an historical and contemporary analysis of American society and education, conclude that the technological society of today is desirable and will be perpetuated.

Several works are sympathetic to Dewey's position. John L. Childs provides an intensive analysis of some of the problems education faces in a democracy in his *Education and Morals* (New York: Appleton-Century-Crofts, 1950). This approach is complimented by Ephraim Vern Sayers and Ward Madden, *Education and the Democratic Faith* (New York: Appleton-Century-Crofts, 1959); and V. T. Thayer and Martin Levit, *The Role of the School in American Society* (New York: Dodd, Mead & Co., 1966). The Thayer and Levit work also considers many underlying assumptions and critical educational issues in American society.

Moving toward a reconstruction position is William O. Stanley's *Education and Social Integration* (New York: Teachers College, Columbia University, 1953). George S. Counts' monograph *Dare the Schools Build a New Social Order?* (New York: John Day, 1932) created much attention and aroused controversy by its clash with the child-centered educators of the 1930s. More panoramic and interdisciplinary than Counts' monograph is Harold Rugg's *Foundations for American Education* (New York: World, 1947). The reconstructionist philosophy has been carried forward by Theodore Brameld in a number of works, including *Toward a Reconstructed Philosophy of Education* (New York: Dryden Press, 1956).

CHAPTER FOUR /

VALUES IN EDUCATION

VALUES are inescapably woven into the process of education. Implicit in the teaching act is that the teacher wants to effect one set of outcomes rather than another. The outcomes are chosen because they are considered desirable; if undesirable or far less desirable outcomes occur, the teacher may consider his efforts unsuccessful. Teachers may also have in mind the type of individual—or at least some general qualities and abilities—that schools should produce. This model is based on a value system. When teachers see the teaching process as moving students from one state or condition to another (whether it is an improvement of reading, computation, reflective thinking, aesthetic appreciation, or other changes), they are projecting outcomes on the basis of what they consider desirable in the situation. Thus all statements about aims are expressions of values. The difficulty is not so much drawing up a list of aims (as there are numerous ones available should none come to mind); rather, the difficulty lies in finding adequate grounds on which to base value decisions.

It would be a mistake, however, to consider values as pertaining only to ends and outcomes. Values are also involved in the means chosen to realize the ends selected. The teacher's choice of instructional materials, teaching methods, classroom arrangements, and evaluation procedures involves a significant value component. Some may argue that the choice of means is sometimes based on expediency. In this case expediency is given preference to other values. If expediency is considered by observers as an undesirable value, but the goal itself is thought worthwhile, perhaps there should be greater consistency between ends and means and a value other than expediency should be chosen.

A professional code of ethics, consisting of value statements which prescribe conduct and impose obligations, is one of the many forms values take in education. The development and use of standards, which help determine to what extent an educational program is fulfilling its aims, is another example. Educational policy also bears a relation to values. Policy takes the form of rule-like statements; a set of policies enables the school system to attain its goals effectively and efficiently.

There are three general types of values: moral, aesthetic, and utility. Moral values relate to right conduct, moral obligation, the "good life," and metaethical statements. Statements that prescribe conduct in relation to others (for example, "Be honest in your dealings") concern right conduct.

Moral obligatory statements record an individual's responsibilities toward others or toward society in one's citizenship role, the violation of which is considered morally wrong or immoral. For instance, parents are thought to have not only legal but moral obligations to their offspring; one is thought to have certain moral obligations to his spouse and to his aged parents, especially when they are infirm or impoverished; a citizen is generally thought to have an obligation to his country by refusing to spy for another nation. Matters of obligation, as with other moral values, are undergoing considerable change today; traditional obligations may no longer be as strong and compelling as they once were, and new ones command greater consideration.

Moral statements about the "good life" are concerned with an overall way to live. These usually take the form of normative systems, such as Epicureanism, Stoicism, utilitarianism, Christianity, Buddhism, and others, which may be religious or secular. Each system attempts to provide a coherent way to live and to carry out one's moral responsibilities. The system may offer supporting reasons why the way of life should be favored above others and may also state the weaknesses of opposing ways.

Metaethics is concerned with the meaning of ethical concepts and the rules for using these terms. It also addresses itself to the difference between moral and nonmoral terms. The grounds for justifying value statements is one of its principal areas of inquiry. In contrast with normative ethics, metaethics is not concerned with formulating a system that would show people how to live their lives. It is interested in refining ethical discoveries and finding a more adequate basis for the analysis and support of ethical arguments.

There have been various interpretations of the possible grounds for justifying ethical statements. One school of thought contends that ethical statements are expressions of the speaker's emotions and feelings. Such statements are not true or false, and rational justification cannot be offered in their behalf. A modification of this view holds that value judgments are expressions of the speaker's attitudes and are designed to evoke similar attitudes in the hearer. A second school of thought believes that ethics can either be studied scientifically, or ethical statements can be converted into nonethical, factual statements. A third school believes that such ethical terms as *good* and *ought* are indefinable. Although they agree with the second school that ethical statements can be true or false, they do not believe that ethical statements can be studied empirically; rather, they can be known through intuition. A fourth school contends that there are absolute ethical statements, such as those God commands, and that these are revealed through sacred scriptures, acts of revelation, church teachings, or other sources.

Aesthetic statements—statements about art and the standards by which art is judged—are a second type of value statement. Aesthetics studies works of art and determines standards for their evaluation; it is concerned with aesthetic experiences and the process of creating art objects; and it focuses on nature and society to capture elements of beauty, human emotion, and other sensory qualities. Among the numerous aesthetic qualities and standards in art are symmetry, harmony, balance, perspective, coherence, texture, and others, depending on the type of art and whether it is found in music, literature, painting, sculpture, or some other field. Aesthetic values are not limited to the fine arts but can be found by the student in the conceptualization of problems and their resolution and in the devising of an elegant hypothesis.

Aesthetic education involves cognitive, affective, and psychomotor domains, but it especially emphasizes the affective side—an often neglected dimension of education which recently has received greater attention. The affective domain—sensitivity to feelings, emotions, and value attributes—is a significant aspect of aesthetic education; judging, appraising, and applying standards to works of art involves the cognitive domain; and the actual creation of art involves the psychomotor domain as well as the others. It would seem that education should widen the range of aesthetic appreciation and develop defensible standards of aesthetic judgment.

Utility values which concern the quality or appropriateness of a means-ends relationship and the value of a product or object, are the third type of value statement. When efficiency and the conservation of resources are prime considerations, it is necessary to choose which procedure is best under the circumstances. Utility values are also concerned with the value of a product or object. In the process of purchasing a new car, for instance, one must establish standards by which the various makes and models can be compared. These standards might include: initial costs, resale value, safety, speed, horsepower, smoothness of the ride, warranty, upkeep costs, gasoline mileage, size of tail fins, and antipollution devices. These standards are weighed in terms of their importance to the individual, so that for one individual the size of tail fins may be three times as important as gasoline mileage, whereas for another individual, the converse may be true. Utility values of this type are also used in selecting plans for new school buildings, in choosing instructional hardware and software, and equipment, and so forth. At times moral and aesthetic values and utility values may overlap, but the important point is that utility values have characteristics by which they can be distinguished from the other two.

A basic value question is whether education should be considered of intrinsic or extrinsic worth. That which is intrinsically valuable is good in itself or for its own sake; that which is extrinsically valuable can be used as an instrument for the attainment of something else. It is often argued that to become an educated person is desirable for its own sake; the liberal arts tradition generally tends to view education as of intrinsic worth. However, it is more common today to hear education extolled for its extrinsic worth—to enable the individual to obtain a good job, to secure a promotion, to rise in the socioeconomic scale, to make useful "social contacts," to meet an eligible mate, to participate in fun and games, to establish a revolutionary base within academia, and other reasons.

The following selections provide further clarification on these and other matters. Richard S. Peters attempts to distinguish moral from legal and religious considerations by emphasizing basic moral concepts and the reasoning process used in their support. He touches on a number of important matters but tends to concentrate on how a child learns a moral code, the stages of moral development, and the importance of initiation into the code of the community through instruction and explanation. Peters distinguishes morality from a body of beliefs and a system of skills and shows why certain methods, such as discovery, are not appropriate for learning moral codes.

Richard M. Hare shows different forms of moral arguments as illustrations of decisions of principle. He then discusses how students can be taught to make intelligent decisions based on principles and how such principles may be justified.

The point made earlier that values pervade and undergird the educational process is brought out more fully by Stafford Clayton. He also discusses the competences necessary to making value judgments and the general role of value judgments in human affairs. These outcomes are accomplished by distinguishing different general senses of value and their respective functions, different types of judgments, the use of rules and standards, and the verification and validation of norms.

James Perry and Philip Smith attempt to elucidate four levels of valuational discourse by showing their distinctive features, their interrelationships, and their educational import.

15 / RICHARD S. PETERS

The Bases of Moral Education

To the question—why do problems of moral education loom so large nowadays?—an obvious answer is that standards are no longer stable. A moral code cannot be taken for granted as it could, say, fifty years ago. Not that people now tend to fall short more frequently of the standards which they set themselves; rather there is much more dispute about what such standards should be. Older people are often shocked, not because the young have no standards but because they seem to have different ones.

There is something to this thesis, but not, I would suggest, quite as much as is often claimed. Perhaps in more settled and stable times parents were able to pass on a code, the details of which could be adequate for their children. When such conditions no longer obtained, after World War I, it is true that some of the younger generation did revolt on certain matters, proclaiming defiantly that morals were merely a matter of private feeling or of individual decision. But both their subjective stance and the reliance of the older generation on a tradition seem equally inadequate at this time. For, on the one hand, it sounds pretty thin to suggest that telling lies and being cruel are wrong just because of one's private feelings or personal decisions; and on the other hand, established traditions palpably cannot deal adequately with such an issue as sexual morality. The task of this generation is to work out a morality that does justice both to the "Victorian" view and to the progressive protest against it. My present purpose is to mark out such a middle road.

The first task is to identify what we are talking about when we speak of morals. What *is* a moral matter as distinct from a legal or religious one? The question is not as simple as it sounds, for moral rules cannot be identified simply by their content. Theft, murder and incest, for instance, are against the law; they are also religious sins and defy custom. And they are thought immoral. On the other hand there are some rules like those against lying and the breaking of promises that are generally matters of morality, and matters of law only under very special circumstances. Still other practices, like spitting, are highly indeterminate. Is it immoral to spit in the street? It is against the

Richard Peters, "The Bases of Moral Education," from *The Nation*, Vol. 208 (January 13, 1969), pp. 49–52. Reprinted by permission of the publisher and the author.

law in the subway, but in some homes it is quite customary when near a fire. What makes some say that it is an immoral practice and not just a filthy habit? What lies behind the conviction that some rules are matters of morality and others not?

It is surely the suggestion that *reasons* support such concepts as *good, right, wrong* and *ought* which gives them the status of moral rules. Such reasons mark out their importance. A rule is a rule of law if, roughly speaking, it has issued from a determinate source such as a king, a parliament or a judge. It may or may not be backed by what we would deem a sufficient reason, or deal with a matter of moral importance. If, on the other hand, we call something like shaking hands a matter of *custom*, we suggest that there's no such determinate source. Heaven knows where it came from and there may or may not be some point to it. If we were to speak of it as a moral rule, however, that would imply a reason, however limited.

To say that moral rules are those which have some backing in reasons does not, of course, go far enough; for reasons may be very peculiar. Imagine, for instance, a discussion about corporal punishment in which one person is against it because it gives rise to bruises. "What is wrong with a few bruises?" asks the other. "They turn blue," replies the opponent of such drastic measures, "and our bounden duty is to minimize the amount of blueness in the world. It's such a horrible color." We would think such a man morally mad, even though he gave reasons for his policies. And this would be because his fundamental principle, which made reasons relevant to him, was "Minimize the blueness in the world" instead of our commonly accepted principle of "Minimize suffering."

I've introduced this rather grotesque example merely to indicate the crucial point that fundamental principles are needed to make reasons relevant, and to confer *importance* on the moral rules which they support. The task of the moral philosopher is to show why a principle such as "Minimize suffering" is defensible, whereas a principle such as "Maximize suffering" or "Minimize blueness" is not. I cannot pursue the crucial task of justifying fundamental principles any further in this article.[1] I shall have to assume a general agreement that some fundamental principles—such as those of fairness, freedom, respect for persons and the like—are justifiable and that others are not. Such abstract higher order principles lie behind the conviction that matters like theft and the breaking of promises are wrong, and other things like holding a fork in the left hand, rather than in the right, are merely conventions. When, too, we wonder about the morality of such acts as spitting or extramarital sex relations we are looking at them through peepholes provided by such principles. The principles make us take account of some aspects of these practices rather than others.

[1] See my *Ethics and Education* (Allen and Unwin, 1966).

My example, too, brings out the further point that there are different *levels* of morality. A small number of fundamental higher order principles are appealed to for justification of other lower order moral rules. Our duty, for instance, to obey the government obviously derives from more abstract principles such as the protection of the general welfare. But these lower-order rules are not all of a piece. Some rules, like those relating to spitting, depend very much on time and place; others, like those concerned with contracts or with noninjury to the person, are not as relative. Indeed it is difficult to conceive of a society of men in which some such rules did not obtain.

This, I think, is where one of the widespread muddles about morality creeps in; people do not distinguish among the different types of rules within a moral system. They will think that because some rules, say about gambling or sex, are relative and depend very much on time, place and circumstances, *all* moral rules are similarly relative. In parts of Africa, it is said, men are encouraged to have more than one wife; in Europe only one; in the United States only one at a time. Therefore, all morals as to marriage are relative. And fraud, murder, rape and theft are then presumably just as "culture-bound" as spitting in the street!

It should not be thought, either, that any simple appeal to a lack of consensus about moral rules necessarily establishes anything of ultimate significance about their validity. If consensus were the acid test of validity, science would also be in an insecure position; for the scientific view of the world is accepted by only a minority of the human race. If there are good reasons for moral or scientific beliefs, the fact that many cannot grasp them is irrelevant. There are probably many in the Trobriand Islands—or in England—who cannot grasp Newton's laws. Is our estimate of their truth affected by this deficiency?

Those who attack "absolute" moral principles often develop another type of argument. They say that such principles cannot be absolute because there are circumstances in which they must be bent a bit. What about "white lies"? What about breaking a promise to save someone's life? This is really a very feeble objection, because most people who believe that there are fundamental principles of morality also claim that these principles are subject to an "other things being equal" clause. If there is more than one fundamental principle, it must sometimes be the case that there is a conflict of principle. A person must nevertheless act in such cases, and whatever he does, *one* of his principles is infringed. A "white lie" is not told out of inclination or for gain or glory. It is told when the truth might cause needless suffering. In such a case other things are *not* equal. But because there are *some* cases where a principle must be infringed, nothing follows about the general duties involved. The general duty to tell the truth is not undermined by the fact that on rare occasions other duties are more urgent.

I have spent so much time on the refinements of morality before mentioning anything about moral *education* because I believe that efforts at moral education on the part of well-meaning parents and teachers are often hamstrung by confusions of the sort that I have indicated. The realization that some moral matters are far from straightforward leads to a generalized agnosticism about morality and to a lack of firmness in handing on rules to children. Children, it is proclaimed, must decide such issues for themselves. As if anyone—let alone a child—ever decided for himself that lying and cruelty are wrong!

Actually a child is well along to maturity before he can assess the rules which structure his life, can work out a code "of his own." This parallels the history of the race; for morality, as a code distinct from religion, custom and law, took a very long time to emerge. A small child lacks the subtlety of discrimination required to distinguish matters of morality from matters of law and custom, let alone to decide "for himself" on his moral principles.

How then can this process get started? Obviously this child must learn to use concepts such as "right," "wrong," and "ought." How can he do so except by being initiated into the code of a community, into a tradition? Much is picked up by imitation and identification—especially in the sphere of attitudes to others. But morality is not a skill like swimming, to be learned purely by imitation; it involves learning a whole family of concepts, which cannot be acquired without a great deal of instruction and explanation. Parents often think that they are teaching children not to steal by scolding or punishing them when they take what belongs to somebody else. They do not ask themselves whether the child has yet the concept of property, of people having rights to things, and of distinctions like that between lending and giving. Without a grasp of this family of concepts, a child cannot properly understand what stealing is. Moral education must always take account of where children are, and that requires considerable imagination. Because of his limited conceptual apparatus, a child's actions look quite different to him and to the adults who are judging him.

But learning to be moral is not just a matter of learning to apply concepts correctly to certain situations; it is also a matter of learning to behave consistently in the required way. Rules must regulate something and what they regulate are human inclinations. Children must develop early the habit of regulating their inclinations. They will usually learn to do this gradually if there is a steady and predictable pressure from their parents; for one of the most valid generalizations about human behavior is that people behave overwhelmingly in accordance with their understanding of what is expected and approved. That is why *consistency* on the part of parents is so important. If a child is brought up within a firm framework of rules, and is consistently approved of when he conforms to them, he will gradually take the rules into his own mind. In this way a firm basis of habits can be laid down. Without that start, a later development of an autonomous code is most unlikely. For how can children learn to adopt rules of their own and also learn to apply them intelligently to varying situations if they have not learned from the inside what constitutes a moral rule?

Very young children do not properly understand moral concepts. By that I mean that, though they can learn to regulate their inclinations with the consciousness that certain things are right and wrong, their grasp of the *grounds* for such judgments is very hazy. They regard rules, so Piaget argues, as more or less transcendentally laid down. The notion of the validity of rules, and that they are grounded in principles, takes much longer to dawn. So it is pointless to expect very young children to do what they should because they see the reasons for it. That will come later as their understanding increases and their sympathies and loyalties begin to extend to their contemporaries. In the early stages they have to learn to do what is right without properly understanding why.

Many readers may be shocked by such a suggestion. If so, it is perhaps because their view of learning is modeled too much on "discovery methods" in, say, mathematics whereby children can be induced, through appropriate questioning, to grasp principles, to have "insight," etc. That is one very important way of learning, but it obviously has little application to such things as mechanical skills or historical facts. The beginning of wisdom in understanding human learning is to realize that there are many ways of learning and many different *types* of things that have to be learned. And one of the palpable facts is that most things in life must be learned *before* they are properly understood. In any case, understanding is usually a matter of degree. Young children learn that bodies fall to the ground if you drop them; but they cannot possibly understand why. Indeed, how many educated adults can explain gravity? In the learning of skills, such as golf or cooking, great proficiency can be attained by a mixture of practice and imitation, without the slightest understanding of the underlying principles. Morality is not just a body of beliefs; nor is it merely a system of skills. But it is like both in that during the early stages traditions must be accepted on trust from those with more experience and wisdom. Trust is essential, for without that relationship between parent or teacher and child the basic body of rules cannot be imparted with firmness and without fear.

What should form the content of a basic body of rules to provide the substance for a tradition? It would obviously include either fundamental principles themselves, such as the consideration of people's interests; or such rules as those relating to respect for persons, for property and for the keeping of contracts, that fall under the fundamental principles. A few such rules can be insisted on, without constantly correcting children over trivialities. Many conscientious parents seem to me to lack discrimination in this respect. They make as much fuss over table manners and tidiness as they do over lying and stealing. If children are hemmed in by rules, they have trouble developing a sense of what is morally important and what is not. I often doubt that parents are clear about this themselves!

Children vary greatly in the pace of their development, and no hard and fast rules can be laid down as to when the giving of reasons will begin to bite on a child's behavior. But one thing is apparent—reasons will be ineffective until the child's psychological development has reached the point where they awaken some response in him. A good reason for keeping a promise is the inconvenience caused to others if it is broken. But what does that mean to a boy who cares nothing about others? How can he even be moved by respect for persons if he has not gained the sympathy out of which such an attitude arises? How the psychological underpinning for morality emerges is a matter for psychologists, but I suspect that children largely learn to care if they are brought up by those whose own sympathy spreads like a contagion.

If all goes well, as the child begins to develop interests and companions outside the home, his capacity for moral reasoning will also develop—that is, if he is *encouraged* to discuss different points of view. In our highly differentiated society he will find that he has much need for such a capacity, because on many matters he will find that standards conflict. He may find, too, that social changes make some of his parents' views seem a bit old-fashioned—at least on matters that do not fall under basic moral rules. At that point there is some justification for saying that he must decide for himself where he stands. He will, however, be able to do so only if his early training has given him the necessary equipment. It is most unlikely that he will find that his parents have been mistaken on basic rules such as those relating to injury to the person and to property and to the keeping of contracts. On more relative matters, such as thrift, business ethics or sex relations, he may come to think that they are mistaken. It would be surprising nowadays if an adolescent of any spirit accepted all his parents' standards! But at least he should learn to accept or reject elements in the tradition into which he has been initiated by seeing how they square with fundamental principles. A solid basis of rules has to be passed on in such a way that a sane and sensitive morality can grow out of it. Reason must have an inheritance of traditions to work upon.

The view of morality I have here advanced assigns a crucial role to the authority of parents and teachers, both in laying down a foundation of moral rules and in encouraging children, as they develop, to strike out on their own. So I must end by saying a bit about authority, for I think that on this matter, also, there are many muddles. Our society has staged a successful revolt against the *traditional* concept of authority which gave unlimited prerogatives to men over women, to parents over children, to employers over employees. But in overthrowing this patriarchal type of authority we have tended to go too far, concluding that there is no place at all for authority—save, of course, in the sphere of law and state action. This all-or-none reaction overlooks the fact that in school and home, as well as in the state, there is a paramount need for authority—provided that it is *rationalized* and carefully related to the tasks at hand and the individuals concerned.

Authority is what bridges the gap between the generations, for unless authority figures are identified and accepted, knowledge and skill can be handed on only by coercion or bribery. In the old days children were often driven to learning things that were difficult. Progressive teachers in revolt against this approach appealed to the methods of the supermarket, where a premium is placed on appetite. The treatment of children fell in with the tendency of modern industrial societies to gear everything to consumer wants. Progressive therapists tended to forget the extreme plasticity of children's desires and the enormous part played by identification with others. This oversight is relevant both to the formation of wants and to the taking in of rules to control and channel them. Authority enters here as an intermediary between bribery and coercion. It should not be used, of course, to keep children in subservience but to bring about identification with the elements of a society that must be transmitted. A child may become interested in learning something like metal work because he admires his teacher; he may take into himself the code of a beloved parent. But unless he comes to sense what there is of value in the cherished pursuit, unless he comes to feel subjectively the rightness of a course of action, the teacher and parent have failed. Their task is to use their authority so that another generation will eventually grasp what there is of merit for itself in a style of life. They must work hard, in other words, to do themselves out of a job.

As children get older, self-discipline should take the place of imposed discipline. Constraints become internalized and children begin to weigh from within the validity of their promptings. But their tendency to be self-critical, to develop a code of their own, depends on the extent to which they must have kept critical company. The dialogue within reflects the dialogue without; that is why discussion is so important during adolescence. Those in authority over children will, therefore, attempt to get children to do what is sensible by appealing to their common sense instead of ordering them around or appealing to their own status. They will not say, "I'm your father and I'm telling you not to smoke," but will point out the dangers involved. It is a further question, however, whether a child's acceptance of good reasons should be the final criterion for his action. If a parent explains to a child why it is stupid and wrong to put objects on railway lines, and yet sees him doing so, will he stand aside and reflect that the boy is learning to choose? Parents must weigh their own fundamental principles against what is instructive for their children.

Example, of course, is crucial. Parents and others must provide a pattern out of which the child can eventually develop his own style of self-regulation. This is not likely to happen unless exercise of authority is rationalized and sensitively adapted to age, to persons, and to the tasks in hand. For the young will rightly rebel against the irrational expression of a traditional status. In brief, teachers and parents must learn to be in authority without being authoritarian.

16 / RICHARD M. HARE

Decisions of Principle

There are two factors which may be involved in the making of any decision to do something. Of these, the first may at any rate theoretically be absent, the second is always present to some degree. They correspond to the major and minor premisses of the Aristotelian practical syllogism. The major premiss is a principle of conduct; the minor premiss is a statement, more or less full, of what we should in fact be doing if we did one or other of the alternatives open to us. Thus if I decide not to say something, because it is false, I am acting on a principle, "Never (or never under certain conditions) say what is false", and I must know that this, which I am wondering whether to say, is false.

Let us take the minor premiss first, since it presents less difficulty. We plainly cannot decide what to do unless we know at least something about what we should be doing if we did this or that. For example, suppose that I am an employer, and am wondering whether or not to sack a clerk who habitually turns up at the office after the hour at which he has undertaken to turn up. If I sack him I shall be depriving his family of the money on which they live, perhaps giving my firm a reputation which will lead clerks to avoid it when other jobs are available, and so on; if I keep him, I shall be causing the other clerks to do work which otherwise would be done by this clerk; and the affairs of the office will not be transacted so quickly as they would if all the clerks were punctual. These would be the sorts of consideration that I should take into account in making my decision. They would be the effects on the total situation of the alternative actions, sacking him or not sacking him. It is the effects which determine what I should be doing; it is between the two sets of

Richard M. Hare, "Decisions of Principle," from *The Language of Morals* (New York: Oxford University Press, 1952), pp. 56–78. Reprinted by permission of The Clarendon Press.

Richard Mervyn Hare (1919–), one of England's leading authorities in ethics, is White's Professor of Moral Philosophy, Corpus Christi College, Oxford University. He is the author of *The Language of Morals* and *Freedom and Reason*.

effects that I am deciding. The whole point about a decision is that it makes a difference to what happens; and this difference is the difference between the effects of deciding one way, and the effects of deciding the other.

It sometimes seems to be implied by writers on ethics that it is immoral, on certain sorts of occasion, to consider the effects of doing something. We ought, it is said, to do our duty no matter what the effects of doing it. As I am using the word "effects," this cannot be maintained. I am not making a claim for "expediency" (in the bad sense) as against "duty". Even to do our duty—in so far as it is *doing* something—is effecting certain changes in the total situation. It is quite true that, of the changes that it is possible to effect in the total situation, most people would agree that we ought to consider certain kinds more relevant than others (which than which, it is the purpose of moral principles to tell us). I do not think that the immediacy or remoteness of the effects makes any difference, though their certainty or uncertainty does. The reason why it is considered immoral to fail to right an injustice whose effects will maximize pleasure, is not that in such a choice the effects are considered when they should not have been; it is that certain of the effects—namely, the maximization of pleasure—are given a relevance which they should not have, in view of the prior claim of those other effects which should have consisted in the righting of the injustice.

For reasons which will become apparent when we have examined the logic of value-words, it is most important, in a verbal exposition of an argument about what to do, not to allow value-words in the minor premiss. In setting out the facts of the case, we should be as factual as we can. Those versed in the logic of these words, and therefore forewarned against its pitfalls, may in the interests of brevity neglect this precaution; but for the inexperienced it is very much better to keep value-expressions where they belong, in the major premiss. This will prevent the inadvertent admission of an ambiguous middle term, as in the example in 3. 3 *sub fine*. I do not mean that in discussing the facts of the case we should not admit any words which could possibly have an evaluative meaning; for this, in view of the way in which evaluative meaning pervades our language, would be well-nigh impossible. I only mean that we must be sure that, as we are using the words in the minor premiss, there are definite tests (not themselves involving evaluation) for ascertaining its truth or falsity. In the last paragraph I was using the word "pleasure" in such a sense, though it is not always so used.

The relation between the two premisses may perhaps be made clearer by considering an artificial example. Let us suppose that a man has a peculiar kind of clairvoyance such that he can know everything about the effects of all the alternative actions open to him. But let us suppose that he has so far formed for himself, or been taught, no principles of conduct. In deciding between alternative courses of action, such a man would know, fully and exactly, between what he was deciding. We have to ask to what extent, if any, such a man would be handicapped, in coming to a decision, by not having any formed principles. It would seem beyond doubt that he could choose between two courses; it would be strange, even, to call such a choice necessarily arbitrary or ungrounded; for if a man knows to the last detail exactly what he is doing, and what he might otherwise have done, his choice is not arbitrary in the sense in which a choice would be arbitrary if made by the toss of a coin without any consideration of the effects. But suppose that we were to ask such a man "Why did you choose this set of effects rather than that? Which of the many effects were they that led you to decide the way you did?" His answer to this question might be of two kinds. He might say "I can't give any reasons; I just felt like deciding that way; another time, faced with the same choice, I might decide differently." On the other hand, he might say "It was this and this that made me decide; I was deliberately avoiding such and such effects, and seeking such and such." If he gave the first of these two answers, we might in a certain sense of that word call his decision arbitrary (though even in that case he had *some* reason for his choice, namely, that he felt that way); but if he gave the second, we should not.

Let us see what is involved in this second type of answer. Although we have assumed that the man has no formed principles, he shows, if he gives the second answer, that he has started to form principles for himself; for to choose effects *because* they are such and such is to begin to act on a principle that such and such effects are to be chosen. We see in this example that in order to act on principle it is not necessary in some sense to have a principle already, before you act; it may be that the decision to act in a certain way, because of something about the effects of acting in that way, *is* to subscribe to a principle of action—though it is not necessarily to adopt it in any permanent sense.

Ordinary men are not so fortunate as the man in our artificial example. They start, indeed, without any knowledge of the future at all; and when they acquire knowledge it is not of this intuitive kind. The kind of knowledge that we have of the future—unless we are clairvoyant—is based upon principles of prediction which we are taught, or form for ourselves. Principles of prediction are one kind of principle of action; for to predict is to act in a certain way. Thus, although there is nothing logically to prevent someone doing entirely without principles, and making all his choices in the arbitrary manner exhibited in the first kind of answer, this never in fact occurs. Moreover, our knowledge of the future is fragmentary and only probable; and therefore in many cases the principles which we are taught or form for ourselves say, not "Choose this kind of effect rather than that," but "You do not know for certain what will be the effects; but do this rather than that, and the effects are most likely to be such as you would have chosen, if you had known them." It is important to remember, in this connexion, that "likely" and "probable" are value-words; in many contexts "It is probable (or likely) that P' is adequately rendered by "There is *good* reason (or evidence) for holding that P."

We may distinguish, so far, two reasons why we have principles. The first reason applies to anyone, even a man with complete insight into the future, who decides to choose something because it is of a certain character. The second reason applies to us because we do not in fact have complete knowledge of the future, and because such knowledge as we do have involves principles. To these reasons a third must now be added. Without principles, most kinds of teaching are impossible, for what is taught is in most cases a principle. In particular, when we learn *to do* something, what we learn is always a principle. Even to learn or be taught a fact (like the names of the five rivers of the Punjab) is to learn how to answer a question; it is to learn the principle "When asked 'What are the names of the five rivers of the Punjab?' answer 'The Jhelum, the Chenab, &c.'." By this I do not of course mean, that to learn to do anything is to learn to recite by rote some universal imperative sentence. This would involve us in a vicious regress; for learning to recite is a kind of learning, and must have its principles; but in that case we should have to learn to recite the principles of reciting. The point is rather this, that to learn to do anything is never to learn to do an individual act; it is always to learn to do acts of a certain kind in a certain kind of situation; and this is to learn a principle. Thus, in learning to drive, I learn, not to change gear *now*, but to change gear when the engine makes a certain kind of noise. If this were not so, instruction would be of no use at all; for if all an instructor could do were to tell us to change gear *now*, he would have to sit beside us for the rest of our lives in order to tell us just when, on each occasion, to change gear.

Thus without principles we could not learn anything whatever from our elders. This would mean that every generation would have to start from scratch and teach itself. But even if each generation were able to teach itself, it could not do so without principles; for self-teaching, like all other teaching, is the teaching of principles. This may be seen by recurring to our artificial example. Let us suppose that our clairvoyant made all his choices on some principle, but always forgot, as soon as he had made the choice, what the principle had been. He would have, accordingly, each time he made a decision, to go over all the effects of the alternative actions. This would be so time-consuming that he would not have the leisure to make many decisions in the course of his life. He would spend his whole time deciding matters like whether to step off with the right or the left foot, and would never reach what we should call the more important decisions. But if he could remember the principles on which he acted, he would be in a much better position; he could *learn* how to act in certain kinds of circumstances; he could learn to single out quickly the relevant aspects of a situation, including the effects of the various possible actions, and so choose quickly, and in many cases habitually. Thus his powers of considered decision would be set free for more momentous decisions. When the cabinet-maker has learnt how to make a dovetail without thinking much about it, he will have time to think about such things as the proportions and aesthetic appearance of the finished product. And it is the same with our conduct in the moral sphere; when the performance of the lesser duties has become a matter of habit, we have time to think about the greater.

There is a limit in practice to the amount that can be taught to someone by someone else. Beyond this point, self-teaching is necessary. The limit is set by the variety of conditions which may be met with in doing whatever is being taught; and this variety is greater in some cases than in others. A sergeant can teach a recruit almost all there is to be known about fixing bayonets on parade, because one occasion of fixing bayonets on parade is much like another; but a driving instructor cannot do more than begin to teach his pupil the art of driving, because the conditions to be met with in driving are so various. In most cases, teaching cannot consist in getting the learner to perform faultlessly a fixed drill. One of the things that has to be included in any but the most elementary kinds of instruction is the opportunity for the learner to make decisions for himself, and in so doing to examine, and even modify to suit particular types of case, the principles which are being taught. The principles that are taught us initially are of a provisional kind (very like the principle "Never say what is false" which I discussed in the last chapter). One training, after the initial stages, consists in taking these principles, and making them less provisional; we do this by using them continually in our own decisions, and sometimes making exceptions to them; some of the exceptions are made because our instructor points out to us that certain cases are instances of classes of exceptions to the principle; and some of the exceptions we decide on for ourselves. This presents no more difficulty than our clairvoyant had in deciding between two sets of effects. If we learn from experiment that to follow a certain principle would have certain effects, whereas to modify it in a certain way would have certain other effects, we adopt whichever form of the principle leads to the effects which we choose to pursue.

We may illustrate this process of modifying principles from the example already used, that of learning to drive. I am told, for instance, always to draw into the side of the road when I stop the car; but later I am told that this does not apply when I stop before turning into a sideroad to the off-side—for then I must stop near the middle of the road until it is possible for me to turn. Still later I learn that in this manoeuvre it is not necessary to stop at all if it is an uncontrolled junction and I can see that there is no traffic which I should obstruct by turning. When I have picked up all these modifications to the rule, and the similar modifications to all the other rules, and practice them habitually as so modified, then I am said to be a good driver, because my car is always in the right place on the road, travelling at the right speed, and so on. The good driver is, among other things, one whose actions are so exactly governed by principles which have become a habit with him, that he normally does not have to *think* just what to do. But road conditions are exceedingly various, and therefore it is unwise to let all one's driving become a matter of habit. One can never be certain that one's principles of driving are perfect—indeed, one can be very sure that they are not; and therefore the good driver not only drives well from habit, but constantly attends to his driving habits, to see whether they might not be improved; he never stops learning.

It is hardly necessary to point out that principles of driving, like other principles, are normally not inculcated by their verbal repetition, but by example, demonstration, and other practical means. We learn to drive, not by precept, but by being shown how to do particular bits of driving; the precepts are usually only explanatory or mnemonic of what we are being shown. Thereafter, we try to do the particular manoeuvres ourselves, and are criticized for failures, commended when we do them well, and so gradually get the hang of the various principles of good driving. For although our instruction is far from being purely verbal, nevertheless what we are being taught are principles. The fact that the derivation of particular acts (or commands to do them) from principles is normally done non-verbally does not show that it is not a logical process, any more than the inference:

> The clock has just struck seven times
> The clock strikes seven times at seven o'clock only
> ∴ It is just after seven o'clock

is shown to be non-logical because it is never made explicitly in words.

Drivers often know just what to do in a certain situation without being able to enunciate in words the principle on which they act. This is a very common state of affairs with all kinds of principles. Trappers know just where to set their traps, but often cannot explain just why they have put a trap in a particular place. We all know how to use words to convey our meaning; but if a logician presses us for the exact definition of a word we have used, or the exact rules for its use, we are often at a loss. This does not mean that the setting of traps or the use of words or the driving of cars does not proceed according to principles. One may know how, without being able to say how—though if a skill is to be taught, it is easier if we *can* say how.

We must not think that, if we can decide between one course and another without further thought (it seems self-evident to us, which we should do), this necessarily implies that we have some mysterious intuitive faculty which tells us what to do. A driver does not know when to change gear by intuition; he knows it because he has learnt and not forgotten; what he knows is a principle, though he cannot formulate the principle in words. The same is true of moral decisions which are sometimes called "intuitive." We have moral "intuitions" because we have learnt how to behave, and have different ones according to how we have learnt to behave.

It would be a mistake to say that all that had to be done to a man to make him into a good driver was to tell him, or otherwise inculcate into him, a lot of general principles. This would be to leave out the factor of decision. Very soon after he begins to learn, he will be faced with situations to deal with which the provisional principles so far taught him require modification; and he will then have to decide what to do. He will very soon discover which decisions were right and which wrong, partly because his instructor tells him, and partly because having seen the effects of the decisions he determines in future not to bring about such effects. On no account must we commit the mistake of supposing that decisions and principles occupy two separate spheres and do not meet at any point. All decisions except those, if any, that are completely arbitrary are to some extent decisions of principle. We are always setting precedents for ourselves. It is not a case of the principle settling everything down to a certain point, and decision dealing with everything below that point. Rather, decision and principles interact throughout the whole field. Suppose that we have a principle to act in a certain way in certain circumstances. Suppose then that we find ourselves in circumstances which fall under the principle, but which have certain other peculiar features, not met before, which make us ask "Is the principle really intended to cover cases like this, or is it incompletely specified—is there here a case belonging to a class which should be treated as exceptional?" Our answer to this question will be a decision, but a decision of principle, as is shown by the use of the value-word "should." If we decide that this should be an exception, we thereby modify the principle by laying down an exception to it.

Suppose, for example, that in learning to drive I have been taught always to signal before I slow down or stop, but have not yet been taught what to do when stopping in an emergency; if a child leaps in front of my car, I do not signal, but keep both hands on the steering-wheel; and thereafter I accept the former principle with this exception, that in cases of emergency it is better to steer than to signal. I have, even on the spur of the moment, made a decision of principle. To understand what happens in cases like this is to understand a great deal about the making of value-judgements.

I do not wish to seem to be pressing too far my comparison, in respect of the way in which they are learnt, between principles of driving and principles of conduct. It is necessary also to bear in mind some distinctions. In the first place, the expression "good driver" is itself ambiguous in that it is not immediately clear what standard is being applied. It might be simply a standard of expertness; we might call a person a good driver if he were able to do just what he wanted with his car; we might say 'Although a very good driver, he is most inconsiderate to other road users." On the other hand, we sometimes expect a good driver to have moral qualities as well; we do not, according to this criterion, call a man a good driver if he drives expertly, but without the slightest heed for the convenience or safety of other people. The line between these two standards of good driving is not easy to draw in practice. There is also a third standard, according to which a driver is said to be good if he conforms to the accepted principles of good driving as laid down, for example, in the *Highway Code*. Since the *Highway Code* is compiled with a definite purpose in view, this standard coincides to a great extent with the second.

Secondly, there are two ways of looking at driving instruction:

1. We establish at the beginning certain ends, for example the avoidance of collisions, and instruction consists in teaching what practices are conducive to those ends. According to this way of looking at them, the principles of good driving are hypothetical imperatives.
2. We teach at first simple rules of thumb, and the learner only gradually comes to see what the ends are, at which the instruction is aimed.

It must not be thought that either (1) or (2) by itself gives a complete account of our procedure. Which method we adopt depends to a great extent on the maturity and intelligence of the learner. In teaching African soldiers to drive, we might incline more to the second method; if I had to teach my two-year-old son to drive, I should have to adopt the same methods as I now adopt for teaching him to refrain from interfering with the controls when I am driving myself. With a highly intelligent learner, on the other hand, we may adopt a method which has more of (1) in it than of (2).

It must not be thought, however, that method (2) is ever entirely without a place even in the case of the most rational of learners. It may be that the desirability of avoiding collisions is at once understood and accepted even by comparatively stupid learners; but there are a great many more ends than this which a good driver has to aim at. He has to avoid causing many kinds of avoidable inconvenience both to himself and to others; he has to learn not to do things which result in damage to his vehicle, and so on. It is of no use to establish at the beginning a general end, "the avoidance of avoidable inconvenience"; for "inconvenience" is a value-word, and until he has had experience of driving, the learner will not know what sorts of situation are to count as avoidable inconvenience. The general end or principle is vacuous until by our detailed instruction we have given it content. Therefore it is always necessary to start, to some extent, by teaching our learner *what* to do, and leaving it for him to find out later *why*. We may therefore say that although moral principles, which are normally taught us when we are immature, are taught largely by method (2), and principles of driving preponderantly by method (1), there is not an absolute division between the two sorts of principle in this respect. What I have just said about first learning *what* to do, and about the initial vacuity of the general end, is borrowed from Aristotle.[1] The one fundamental distinction between principles of driving and principles of conduct is that the latter are, in Aristotle's term, "architectonic" of the former; for the ends of good driving (safety, the avoidance of inconvenience to others, the preservation of property, and so on) are justified ultimately, if justification is sought, by appeal to moral considerations.[2]

It would be folly, however, to say that there is only one way of learning a skill or any other body of principles, or of justifying a particular decision made in the practice of it. There are many ways, and I have tried to make the above account sufficiently general to cover all of them. It is sometimes said by writers on morals that we have to justify an act by reference to its effects, and that we tell which effects are to be sought, which avoided, by reference to some principle. Such a theory is that of the utilitarians, who bid us look at the effects, and examine these in the light of the principle of utility, to see which effects would maximize pleasure. Sometimes, on the other hand, it is said (as by Mr. Toulmin)[3] that an act is justified directly by reference to the principles which it observes, and these principles in their turn by reference to the effects of always observing them. Sometimes it is said that we should observe principles and ignore the effects—though for the reasons given above "effects" cannot be here intended in the sense in which I have been using it. What is wrong with these theories is not what they say, but their assumption that they are telling us the only way to justify actions, or decide what actions to do. We do, indeed, justify and decide on actions in all these ways; for example, sometimes, if asked why we did *A*, we say, "Because it was a case falling under principle *P*," and if asked to justify *P* in turn, we go into the effects of observing it and of not observing it. But sometimes, when asked the same question "Why did you do *A*?" we say "Because if I hadn't, *E* would have happened," and if asked what was wrong about *E* happening, we appeal to some principle.

The truth is that, if asked to justify as completely as possible any decision, we have to bring in both effects—to give content to the decision—and principles, and the effects in general of observing those principles, and so on, until we have satisfied our inquirer. Thus a complete justification of a decision would consist of a complete account of its effects, together with a complete account of the principles which it observed, and the effects of observing those principles—for, of course, it is the effects (what obeying them in fact consists in) which give content to the principles too. Thus, if pressed to justify a decision completely, we have to give a complete specification of the way of life

[1] *Nicomachean Ethics,* i. 4.
[2] *Op. cit.*, i. 1, 2.
[3] *Reason in Ethics,* pp. 144ff.

of which it is a part. This complete specification it is impossible in practice to give; the nearest attempts are those given by the great religions, especially those which can point to historical persons who carried out the way of life in practice. Suppose, however, that we can give it. If the inquirer still goes on asking "But why *should* I live like that?" then there is no further answer to give him, because we have already, *ex hypothesi*, said everything that could be included in this further answer. We can only ask him to make up his own mind which way he ought to live; for in the end everything rests upon such a decision of principle. He has to decide whether to accept that way of life or not; if he accepts it, then we can proceed to justify the decisions that are based upon it; if he does not accept it, then let him accept some other, and try to live by it. The sting is in the last clause. To describe such ultimate decisions as arbitrary, because *ex hypothesi* everything which could be used to justify them has already been included in the decision, would be like saying that a complete description of the universe was utterly unfounded, because no further fact could be called upon in corroboration of it. This is not how we use the words "arbitrary" and "unfounded." Far from being arbitrary, such a decision would be the most well-founded of decisions, because it would be based upon a consideration of everything upon which it could possibly be founded.

It will be noticed how, in talking of decisions of principle, I have inevitably started talking value-language. Thus we decide that the principle *should* be modified, or that it is *better* to steer than to signal. This illustrates the very close relevance of what I have been saying in the first part of this book to the problems of the second part; for to make a value-judgement is to make a decision of principle. To ask whether I ought to do *A* in these circumstances is (to borrow Kantian language with a small though important modification) to ask whether or not I will that doing *A* in such circumstances should become a universal law.[4] It may seem a far cry from Kant to Professor Stevenson; but the same question could be put in other words by asking "What attitude shall I adopt and recommend towards doing *A* in such circumstances?"; for "attitude," if it means anything, means a principle of action. Unfortunately Stevenson, unlike Kant, devotes very little space to the examination of this first-person question; had he paid due attention to it, and avoided the dangers of the word "persuasive," he might have reached a position not unlike that of Kant.

As Kant points out in the important passage on the Autonomy of the Will, to which I referred earlier, we have to make our own decisions of principle.[5] Other people cannot make them for us unless we have first decided to take their advice or obey their orders. There is an interesting

[4] Cf. *Groundwork of the Metaphysic of Morals*, tr. H. J. Paton, p. 88.
[5] *Op. cit.*, pp. 108ff.

analogy here with the position of the scientist, who also has to rely on his own observations. It might be said that there is a difference here between decisions and observations, to the detriment of the former, in that an observation, once made, is public property, whereas decisions have to be made by the agent himself on each occasion. But the difference is only apparent. A scientist would not have become a scientist unless he had convinced himself that the observations of other scientists were in general reliable. He did this by making some observations of his own. When we learnt elementary chemistry at school, we had some theoretical periods and some practical. In the theoretical periods we studied books; in the practical periods we made experiments, and found, if we were lucky, that the results tallied with what the books said. This showed us that what the books said was not all nonsense; so that even if, by reason of disturbing factors ignored by us, our experiments came out wrong, we were inclined to trust the books and acknowledge that we had made a mistake. We were confirmed in this assumption by the fact that we often discovered later what the mistake had been. If our observations, however carefully we did them, were always at variance with the textbooks, we should not be tempted to make science our profession. Thus the confidence of the scientist in other people's observations is ultimately based, among other things, on his own observations and his own judgements about what is reliable. He has in the end to rely on himself.

The case of the moral agent is not dissimilar. When in our early days we are given our elementary moral instruction, there are some things that we are told, and some things that we do. If, when we did as we were told, the total effects of our so doing, when they happened, were always such as we would not have chosen, had we known, then we should seek better advice, or, if prevented from so doing, either work out our own salvation or become moral defectives. If we are in general given what we subsequently come to see to have been good advice, we decide in general to follow the advice and adopt the principles of those who have given us this good advice in the past. This is what happens to any child who is well brought up. Just as the scientist does not try to rewrite all that is in the textbooks, but takes that for granted and sticks to his own particular researches, so this fortunate child will take over bodily the principles of his elders and adapt them in detail, by his own decisions, to suit his own circumstances from time to time. This is how in a well-ordered society morality remains stable, and at the same time gets adapted to changing circumstances.

There are, however, many ways in which this happy state of affairs can deteriorate. Let us consider a process that seems to occur quite often in history; it occurred in Greece during the fifth and fourth centuries, and it has occurred in our own time. Suppose that the people of a certain generation—I will call it the first generation—have got very settled principles, inherited from their fathers. Suppose that they have become so settled as to be second nature, so that generally speaking people act on the principle without thinking, and their power of making considered decisions of principle becomes atrophied. They act always by the book, and come to no harm, because the state of the world in their time remains much the same as that for which the principles were thought out. But their sons, the second generation, as they grow up, find that conditions have changed (e.g. through a protracted war or an industrial revolution), and that the principles in which they have been brought up are no longer adequate. Since, in their education, much stress has been laid on observing principles, and very little on making the decisions on which these principles are ultimately based, their morality has no roots, and becomes completely unstable. Books on "The Whole Duty of Man" are no longer written or read. Often, when they do what it says in such books, they subsequently find cause to regret their decisions; and there are too many cases of this kind for any confidence in the old principles, as a body, to remain. No doubt there are among these old principles certain very general ones, which will remain acceptable unless human nature and the state of the world undergo a most fundamental change; but the second generation, not having been brought up to make decisions of principle, but to do what it says in the book, will not, most of them, be able to make those crucial decisions which would determine which principles to keep, which to modify, and which to abandon. Some people, the Polemarchuses of the second generation, will have been so steeped in the old principles that they just follow them come what may; and these will on the whole be more fortunate than the others, for it is better to have some principles, even if they sometimes lead to decisions which we regret, than to be morally adrift. The bulk of the second generation, and still more perhaps of the third, will not know which of the principles to keep and which to reject; and so they will come more and more to live from day to day—not a bad thing, because it trains their powers of decision, but it is an unpleasant and dangerous state to be in. A few among them, the rebels, will shout from the house-tops that some or all of the old moral principles are worthless; some of these rebels will advocate new principles of their own; some will have nothing to offer. Though they increase the confusion, these rebels perform the useful function of making people decide between their rival principles; and if they not only advocate new principles, but sincerely try to live by them, they are conducting a moral experiment which may be of the utmost value to man (in which case they go down in history as great moral teachers), or may, on the other hand, prove disastrous both to them and to their disciples.

It may take several generations for this disease to play itself out. Morality regains its vigour when ordinary people have learnt afresh to decide for themselves what principles to live by, and more especially what principles to teach their children. Since the world, though subject to vast material changes, changes only very slowly in matters that are fundamental from the moral point of view, the principles which win the acceptance of the mass of people are not likely to differ enormously from those which their fathers came to distrust. The moral principles of Aristotle resemble those of Aeschylus more than they differ from them, and we ourselves shall perhaps come back to something recognizably like the morality of our grandfathers But there will be some changes; some of the principles advocated by the rebels will have been adopted. That is how morality progresses—or retrogresses. The process is, as we shall see, reflected by very subtle changes in the uses of value-words; the impossibility of translating Aristotle's catalogue of virtues into modern English may serve as an example, and the disappearance without trace of the word "righteous" may serve as another.

The question "How shall I bring up my children?" which we have mentioned, is one to the logic of which, since ancient times, few philosophers have given much attention. A child's moral upbringing has an effect upon him which will remain largely untouched by anything that happens to him thereafter. If he has had a stable upbringing, whether on good principles or on bad ones, it will be extremely difficult for him to abandon those principles in later life—difficult but not impossible. They will have for him the force of an objective moral law; and his behavior will seem to give much evidence in support of intuitionist ethical theories, provided that it is not compared with the behavior of those who stick just as firmly to quite different principles. But nevertheless, unless our education has been so thorough as to transform us into automata, we can come to doubt or even reject these principles; that is what makes human beings, whose moral systems change, different from ants, whose "moral system" does not. Therefore, even if for me the question "What shall I do in such and such a situation?" is almost invariably answered without ambiguity by the moral intuition which my upbringing has given me, I may, if I ask myself "How shall I bring up my children?", pause before giving an answer. It is here that the most fundamental moral decisions of all arise; and it is here, if only moral philosophers would pay attention to them, that the most characteristic uses of moral words are to be found. Shall I bring up my children *exactly* as I was brought up, so that they have the same intuitions about morals as I have? Or have circumstances altered, so that the moral character of the father will not provide a suitable equipment for the children? Perhaps I shall try to bring them up like their father, and shall fail; perhaps their new environment will be too strong for me, and they will come to repudiate my principles. Or I may have become so bewildered by the strange new world that, although I still act from force of habit on the principles that I have learnt, I simply do not know what principles to impart to my children, if, indeed, one in my condition can impart any settled principles at all. On all these questions, I have to make up my mind; only the most hide-bound father will try to bring up his children, without thinking, in exactly the way that he himself was brought up; and even he will usually fail disastrously.

Many of the dark places of ethics become clearer when we consider this dilemma in which parents are liable to find themselves. We have already noticed that, although principles have in the end to rest upon decisions of principle, decisions as such cannot be taught; only principles can be taught. It is the powerlessness of the parent to make for his son those many decisions of principle which the son during his future career will make, that gives moral language its characteristic shape. The only instrument which the parent possesses is moral education—the teaching of principles by example and precept, backed up by chastisement and other more up-to-date psychological methods. Shall he use these means, and to what extent? Certain generations of parents have had no doubts about this question. They have used them to the full; and the result has been to turn their children into good intuitionists, able to cling to the rails, but bad at steering round corners. At other times parents—and who shall blame them?—suffer from lack of confidence; they are not sure enough what they themselves think, to be ready to impart to their children a stable way of life. The children of such a generation are likely to grow up opportunists, well able to make individual decisions, but without the settled body of principles which is the most priceless heritage that any generation can leave to its successors. For, though principles are in the end built upon decisions of principle, the building is the work of many generations, and the man who has to start from the beginning is to be pitied; he will not be likely, unless he is a genius, to achieve many conclusions of importance, any more than the average boy, turned loose without instruction upon a desert island, or even in a laboratory, would be likely to make any of the major scientific discoveries.

The dilemma between these two extreme courses in education is plainly a false one. Why it is a false one is apparent, if we recall what was said earlier about the dynamic relation between decisions and principles. It is very like learning to drive. It would be foolish, in teaching someone to drive, to try to inculcate into him such fixed and comprehensive principles that he would never have to make an independent decision. It would be equally foolish to go to the other extreme and leave it to him to find his own way of driving. What we do, if we are sensible, is to give him a solid basis of principles, but at the same time ample opportunity of making the decisions upon which these principles are based, and by which they are modified, improved, adapted to changed circumstances, or even abandoned if they become entirely unsuited to a new environment. To teach only the principles, without giving the opportunity of subjecting them to the learner's own decisions of principle, is like teaching science exclusively from textbooks without entering a laboratory. On the other hand, to abandon one's child or one's driving-pupil to his own self-expression is like putting a boy into a laboratory and saying "Get on with it." The boy may enjoy himself or kill himself, but will probably not learn much science.

The moral words, of which we may take "ought" as an example, reflect in their logical behaviour this double nature of moral instruction—as well they may, for it is in moral instruction that they are most typically used. The sentences in which they appear are normally the expression of decisions of principle—and it is easy to let the decisions get separated, in our discussion of the subject, from the principles. This is the source of the controversy between the "objectivists," as intuitionists sometimes call themselves, and the "subjectivists," as they often call their opponents. The former lay stress on the fixed principles that are handed down by the father, the latter on the new decisions which have to be made by the son. The objectivist says "Of course you know what you ought to do; look at what your conscience tells you, and if in doubt go by the consciences of the vast majority of men." He is able to say this, because our consciences are the product of the principles which our early training has indelibly planted in us, and in one society these principles do not differ much from one person to another. The subjectivist, on the other hand, says "But surely, when it comes to the point—when I have listened to what other people say, and given due weight to my own intuitions, the legacy of my upbringing—I have in the end to decide for myself what I ought to do. To deny this is to be a conventionalist; for both common moral notions and my own intuitions are the legacy of tradition, and— apart from the fact that there are so many different traditions in the world—traditions cannot be started without someone doing what I now feel called upon to do, decide. If I refuse to make my own decisions, I am, in merely copying my fathers, showing myself a lesser man than they; for whereas they must have initiated, I shall be merely accepting." This plea of the subjectivist is quite justified. It is the plea of the adolescent who wants to be adult. To become morally adult is to reconcile these two apparently conflicting positions by learning to make decisions of principle; it is to learn to use "ought"-sentences in the realization that they can only be verified by reference to a standard or set of principles which we have by our own decision accepted and made our own. This is what our present generation is so painfully trying to do.

17 / A. STAFFORD CLAYTON

Education and Some Moves Toward a Value Methodology

That teaching is pervaded by value choices and judgments has been clearly pointed out by John L. Childs.[1]

> Judgments about life values inescapably pervade and undergird the whole process of providing and guiding experience. More than many teachers realize, a scheme of values—a structure of things considered significant, worthful, and right—operates in their endless responses to the daily behavings of their pupils.

Furthermore, these educational value judgments cut to the core of human concerns, and teachers inevitably encourage dispositions and habits about fundamental matters. Educational values "have to do with such elemental things as the rights, the responsibilities, the beliefs, the tastes, the appreciations, the faiths and the allegiances of human beings." The fullness of the teacher's involvement with values is part and parcel of his role as an agent of choice.

> In order to encourage, we must also discourage; in order to foster, we must also hinder; in order to emphasize the significant, we must identify the non-significant; and finally, in order to select and focus attention on certain subject-matters of life, we have to reject and ignore other subject-matters. Were our values different our selections and our rejections would also be different. The process of selecting and rejecting, of fostering and hindering, of distinguishing the lovely from the unlovely, and of discriminating the important from the unimportant is unending in education.

A. Stafford Clayton, "Education and Some Moves Toward a Value Methodology," from *Educational Theory*, Vol. 19, No. 2 (Spring 1969), pp. 198–210. Reprinted by permission of the publisher and the author.

A. Stafford Clayton (1911–) is professor of philosophy of education at Indiana University. In addition to articles on educational policy, he is the author of *Religion and Schooling*.

[1]John L. Childs, *Education and Morals* (New York: Appleton-Century-Crofts, 1950), pp. 19–20.

It is readily apparent that contemporary conditions have not invalidated the thrust of these remarks. The growth of knowledge, the acceleration in the means of communicating it, the centrality of educational concerns in the national effort have underscored rather than vitiated the significance of Professor Childs' words.

It should also be recognized that what Professor Childs said of acts of teaching also holds for the study of education. When one puts his mind to the consideration of educational problems, acts of valuing may be identified throughout one's endeavors. In designing the content of teacher education, in organizing it into programs of teacher education, and in appraising the outcomes, judgments about criteria are central. In systematic inquiry and research into educational problems, questions of selection, focus, and relevance are frequently decisive. A paraphrase of Professor Childs' words may be appropriate. More than many inquirers recognize, "a scheme of values—a structure of things considered significant, worthful, and right"—operates in the selection and design of what in education is studied. Since questions about selection, interpretation, explanation, and evaluation characterize the study of education, as well as acts of teaching, critical attention needs to be given to the norms upon which judgments are based.

The recognition of the central and pervasive role of value judgments in teaching and in the study of education does not, however, take us very far in the direction of what we need to know. To tell us that values pervade education is not to reveal in what way we ought to proceed with normative processes in educational study and discourse. We have yet to inquire into what constitutes competence in judgments of value. One of the distinctive tasks of philosophy of education is to provide disciplined guidance about the evaluation of value judgments and to recommend methods and procedures to reduce the arbitrary character of value claims.

Before mapping out some ways in which normative judgments may be more adequately controlled and evaluated, several clarifications are in order.

In the first place, we propose to talk about the normative in the full range of educational concerns. Our discourse is not limited to moral, aesthetic, religious, political or other specified contexts. We are talking about the general role of value judgments in the widest range of human affairs.

Some hold, contrary to the view here taken, that only vague and imprecise moves can result from so general a concern with the normative. In their view, only specific detailed study of the fields of the ethical, the moral, the aesthetic, and the like can yield determinate recommendations of an adequate kind about normative judgments. Thus one must turn to specific moral, aesthetic, or political theorists to inquire with meaningful precision into valuative matters. As distinct from this view, it is here proposed as a heuristic notion that the study of value judgments may profitably center in a more general concern with the normative. This is particularly appropriate in the field of education. In the practice and in the study of education the normative appears not already refined into academic disciplines but in the matrix of complex human conditions and efforts. If we center exclusively upon the substantive contributions of the established divisions of academic thought, we may very well overlook the features of methodology which in education are most needed. Furthermore, what we want to look at cuts across academic fields and is common to value choice in different contexts.

Second, our attention to the normative will focus upon the intellectual moves that justify normative claims. We shall not be trying to settle the question, "What are the right values to be used in teaching or in the study of education?" Rather we are asking, "What are we to do in judging values?" Additionally, we shall not be concerned with the sociology of norms, with the community as the locus of value consensus, or with the social dimensions of value inquiry, and our concern is clearly more restricted than a complete theory of valuation. It is limited to what might be called the informal logic of normative discourse. In this sense we might also talk of applied logic or logic as it is put to use in argument. We seek to be methodologically clear about the recommended moves one should make in dealing with "norms" when we use that term in the sense of criteria involving commitments.

Third, the concern with the moves that are made in normative discourse is not narrowly restricted to the value theory of a particular philosophic school or position. We are concerned with defensible moves in normative discourse, not a theory of values in the sense of argument about the status or source of values as ontological entities. For example, although we shall make use of Dewey's distinction between prizing and appraising, this does not entail the espousal of some particular interpretation of a pragmatic theory of value. We want to map out what educators should attend to in their general management of value claims rather than discuss the absolutist-relativist positions in value theory and the like.

Although these stipulations concerning the present treatment of the normative may merit more extensive discussion, it may be sufficient to have indicated the general sense of their meaning in order to clear the ground for the moves we are about to indicate.

We begin by distinguishing three general senses of "value" and shall call these the mathematical, the descriptive, and the normative uses of the term. We make this distinction in order to see that when we speak of teaching and the study of education as pervaded and undergirded by value judgments, we need to distinguish the normative or prescriptive sense of "value" from other uses.

The mathematical sense of "value" will not detain us long for this use does not entail any sense of *ought* or *should* but simply ascribes a function to some variable in an equation. "As the value of *A* increases, *B* decreases" exemplifies a non-prescriptive sense of "value." This use is also exemplified in the logician's talk of the truth-value of propositions.

By the descriptive use of "value" we mean those statements which assert a value-fact. To say that someone values something or that something has value asserts a fact of prizing or pricing. Something is as a matter of fact prized or deplored. Something has a price that one is willing to pay for it; it may be an economic matter, expressed in terms of a medium of exchange or a matter of relative importance with reference to time and energy, that one is willing to expend for it. This use is not different from a report of any other fact.

In the purely descriptive sense of "value" we talk about what we like or what we want but we are not concerned with the appraisal of the criteria used to rate what is regarded as valuable. The value is simply had; its character as valuable is immediately present. The scrutiny of the criteria by which it is appraised as valuable is not at stake. There may be questions as to whether people really prize what they seem to. There may be investigation as to how many people make the same prizing. Inquiry into the factors which lead to certain prizings may be undertaken. When we center narrowly upon the description of valuables or upon exposing the causes that lead to prizings we have not penetrated to appraisive questions about the criteria involved in moral choice.

In teaching and in the study of education much of this descriptive sense of valuing occurs. Teachers expound on the values of a group of people or of a thing valued. Values in this sense of existing social norms are taught to the child. There is even much talk about "the value-centered humanities" which has only this sense of a concern with value-facts in literature and works of art. In the social studies one may be told that teaching concerns not only the acquiring of facts about political-civil life but also the acquiring of the values that are expressed in it. In these and other instances of the kind, when the school is said to teach values, it is to teach prizings. The educational task is seen as one concerned with the replication of assessments; questions concerning the criteria premised in the assessments are submerged.

If the act of prizing is all that is meant by "making value judgments" then the root job of considering the weighing and appraising of normative judgments is unsensed and minimized. All we can do is to study values as though they were facts. In this use one does not probe the reasoned grounds for value commitment. Furthermore, the common equating of value with desire, with subjective feelings, leads to notions that value matters are arbitrary opinions. When values are simply prizings, all that we can do about them is to exhort and extol; we feel secure in "selling" our values to others. There is no discipline for the adjudication of conflicts between values. The source of these consequences is found in the fallacy of the reduction of values to the status of facts.

If we are to understand more fully the observation that teaching is pervasively and fundamentally colored by choices concerning life values, we shall want to distinguish between prizing and appraising, between discussions about prizings and arguments justifying normative judgments. In contrast with assertions that something is valued, a normative claim asserts a valuation with reference to non-arbitrary norms. Something is valuable by virtue of its characteristics that fulfill some requirements posted by a standard. We know not only that something is prized but that the grounds for the prizing are specified by criteria that tell us exactly what is worthy of being prized. In the normative sense of "value" attention focuses upon the appraisal and justification of the norm and this sense conveys the prescriptive sense of "ought."

We should be clear that this prescriptive sense of "normative" is distinguished from other uses which may be encountered in educational discourse. The judgment expressing *should* or *ought* is distinguished from a statistical sense of "normative" deriving from "the norm of a distribution" or the norm as the group of subjects upon which a test has been standardized. To say "we are interested in the accumulation of normative data that are predictive of learning disabilities" is to use the term "normative" with reference to data which adequately sample a population and are distributed about some measure of central tendency. If the words *should* or *ought* are used with reference to this context, they have the force of prediction, not prescription. "Normative data" are data which tell us what we should expect from normal cases.

The maintenance of this distinction is important if we are to avoid reading off "average" as "desirable." Average, normal, or typical performance of any kind makes no moral claim, nor are deviations from the statistical norm abnormal in a pejorative sense. The central tendency of a distribution has nothing to recommend morally; the typical is frequently not the morally preferable. If the tyranny of the norm is to be avoided, we must avoid this variety of deriving an "ought" from an "is."

Normative valuing, distinguished from prizing and from statistical normalizing, involves an assessment of worth. If it is not arbitrary, it involves a judgment open to others in which one thing or quality is graded or ranked with reference to a criterion. In grading one judges an instance with reference to a general standard identifying what is graded and how well the instance fulfills the criterion. Ranking is a matter of judging whether something is better or worse than, or equivalent with, another thing with reference to a criterion identifying what is relevant to and what counts in the ranking.

If our rankings and gradings are to be non-arbitrary, i.e., justified by some ordered and scrutinized process, normative judgments need to be looked at in two dimensions. One concerns whether the thing or quality declared to be valuable has, with reference to the criterion, the characteristics assigned to it. We inquire into whether the valuable has the good-making or the bad-making characteristics indicated by the norm. The other is whether the norm is an appropriate one. We inquire into the justification of the norm. A fully normative judgment makes a two-fold claim. One is that whatever is ranked or graded fulfills or fails to fulfill the norms. The other is that the norms are valid ones to apply to what is being considered.

It will be helpful to illustrate with reference to a common task in teaching. Consider the teacher evaluating the discursive writing of his students, in short, grading papers. If his grading is non-arbitrary, he has certain norms in mind. Grammatical errors should be avoided; the paper should take account of certain facts; sentences should be clearly worded; paragraphs should have internal coherence; reasoning should be cogent; the paper should have something significant to say. The teacher assesses the good-making and the bad-making characteristics of the paper as they are posted by the norms. His responsibility is to determine not only that the paper has the characteristics but also that the norms being used are appropriate ones.

In a similar way we could see more clearly what is involved in a wide variety of tasks in the study of education if we took care to identify the two-fold responsibility in normative judgment. The teacher in his role as curriculum designer not only contrives whatever enters the school experience by ranking or grading alternative possibilities, but he justifies these moves with reference to norms that specify what is to be entered as valuable. The items of the content of the curriculum become valuable, as distinct from "are prized" or "are usually there," to the extent that the norms guiding his selection are clearly reasoned.

In research concerning the characteristics of good teachers, the criteria establishing "good teachers" in some sufficiently operational sense are essential to determining whether teachers have these characteristics. Inquiry which is not sensitive to what counts as worth-making in delineating criteria will not be helpful in telling us something that we can count on concerning the characteristics of good teachers.

The educator as participant in the forming and implementing of educational policy is similarly responsible for defensible norms as well as for actions in their behalf. In instances where questions of academic freedom arise, he grades or ranks the behaviors of agents in the situation with respect to norms concerning due process, the freedom of thought and of inquiry, the educational responsibility of authorized autonomy, and the like. Without clear and good reasons about the norms and spirited use of them, the situation is likely to degenerate to manipulation of power by groups guided only by their own prizings.

The point is that critical reasoning about the justification of the norm is an indispensable aspect of the educator's concern with values. Declarations of valuables without adequate defense of the norm by which the valuable is established fail to offer their credentials.

But we can go further than this in sorting out the moves that characterize adequacy in normative judgment. Educators make many kinds of judgments which involve values but in which the norm is not directly inquired into or justified. These judgments are not simply prizings because they are reasoned about with reference to criteria. But the criteria themselves are assumed to be valid rather than being made at that point the focus of study. In these instances we say something like this; we have sufficient reasons to take it for granted that these norms are appropriate. They are assigned a *prima facie* validity. Good reasons would have to be offered for an exception to them. This does not mean that the question of their appropriateness and adequacy may not be raised; rather they are judged to be sufficiently warranted to proceed with their use in finding good-making characteristics.

In grading papers the teacher judges that a paragraph does not have internal consistency. He judges that the norm is sufficiently clear and appropriate to determine whether the student's writing has good-making qualities. The teacher does not have to stop and entertain an argument about the relation of one sentence to another and the introduction of unrelated considerations that obscure the integrity of paragraphs. He uses the norm in making a characterizing judgment. On another occasion he will, if he is a good teacher, explain the norm in a host of ways so that its use in a variety of characterizing judgments may be shared.

In making characterizing judgments one is selecting and interpreting particular instances as falling within those of an agreed upon worth-making category. The category itself is not under scrutiny. It becomes so only if the characterizing judgment is challenged. The judgment is normative in the sense that it is a norm-using, but not a norm-defending, judgment. Characterizing judgments are made with reference to norms and involve appraisal of valuables but since appraisal of the norm itself is not undertaken, they fall short of fully appraisive normative judgments.

In the characterizing judgment the norm is used as a criterion to determine whether the particular event or instance falls within the class of those things marked off by the criterion. The judgment is public in the sense that the criterion is shared and open to inspection. Such a judgment, since it is persuasive, differs from the immediacy of the act of prizing. It expresses a commonly agreed upon way of assessing an incident; on *prima facie* grounds knowledgeable people assume that the criterion is valid and effective.

The characterizing judgment merits more attention in making judgments than it is commonly given. In selecting and interpreting what is taught it is used time and again where a fully appraisive judgment is not demanded. Its use is analogous to that of an adjustive habit in that continuity in plan and action is not interrupted. Yet, like a flexible habit, it may be guided by cognitive processes and is open to reconstruction as conditions vary. It economizes by reserving the moral thrust of the fully persuasive "ought" for instances meriting that deeper justification. It enables us to distinguish situations where the full moral stance of the "ought" is not needed in order to get on with the processes of education.

Consider the norm rejecting plagiarism. Its most frequent use is on *prima facie* grounds: "You ought to say it in your own words rather than crib another's." The teacher can then get on with the job of promoting original expression. The more fully moral "ought," typically called for in the conflict between conflicting moral claims, involves looking into the competing worth-making features of norms. In such situations one is dealing not with a predictive "ought" but with an obligatory "ought." The full significance of the moral "ought" involves a critically conscious appeal to obligative norms used to persuade agents in a shared act of their common concern for others by means of arguments that justify norms. Here the teacher guides, leads, and demonstrates in a full capacity as moral agent.

Yet the characterizing judgment needs to be monitored—reserving the stronger term "discipline" for the more fully appraisive judgment—so that characterizing value judgments may be adequately public. Here we can call attention to the need to characterize the valuable clearly so that what merits consideration is identified. The categories serving to place the valuable in some domain receiving attention need to be sufficiently clear so that they can serve *prima facie* requirements. Characterizing judgments are rule-governed in that, for example, exceptional conditions need to be entered and weighed by a process that is open to inspection. Since characterizing judgments occur within some matrix of purpose, sufficient clarity of purpose is called for in order to determine what abets and what hinders or denies the end-in-view. We are not here trying to exhaust the consideration of what monitors the characterizing value judgment. Rather, it is suggested that in marking it off as an area of concern we open the door to fuller consideration of conditions promoting clarity and effectiveness in judgments serving this function.

At this point we pause to recapitulate. We have argued that making value judgments is not one undifferentiated act. It is analyzable. We can distinguish the sense of "ought" in characterizing judgments where the norm or standard is taken for granted. When evidences concerning the valuable are obtained, the judgment concerns the extent to which they fulfill the requirements of the standard. The good-making and bad-making characteristics of the valuable are judged with reference to the *prima facie* norm. The norm itself is not justified; its worth-making characteristics are accepted; they are not inquired into. On the other hand, in the fully appraisive, typically moral judgment, to which we now turn, the responsibility is not only to weigh the good-and-bad making features of the valuable but also to defend the norm itself. By what processes shall the worth-making aspects of the norm be justified? We shall be concerned with questions about relevance in norm-making, questions about priority or precedence of norms, and questions about the validation of norms.

Questions of Relevance in Norm-Making

The worth-making characteristics of norm, if norms are to be justified, are not just vaguely related in some wholesale way to a process of appraising. There is a difference between saying that two things are related and saying that something is relevant to something else. Relevance is a specific kind of relationship, one in which bearing or pertinence is shown. To speak of questions of relevance in norm-making is to speak of so stating the norm that it reveals as clearly as possible what counts as worth-making. What is included and what is excluded as contributing to the fulfillment of the norm is to be made public. If we are to judge the appropriateness of the norm for the instance in which something is evaluated, we need to know that what counts as worth-making is relevant to the case at hand and that the reasons urged in support of the norm are good ones, i.e., are relevant to it.

Consider again the teacher who is evaluating the student's essay. Some of the norms are taken for granted. The paper should show correct grammatical form. The standards are supplied in the rules: avoid comma faults, incomplete sentences, split infinitives, and the like. However, other norms are also involved. The essay should have something to say; it should be organized; it should have a certain completeness so that it stands on its own. It should have a cogency of reasoning. It should make its case in view of readers who may hold different points of view. The point is that if the teacher is fulfilling his normative responsibilities, the evaluation of the paper involves clarity about the relevance of the worth-making characteristics of the norm. Presumably, if the teaching is good, the student can build into his essay that which is called for by the relevant norms. He becomes self-critical through considered use of the relevant criteria in his writing.

Questions of relevance in norm-building are not exhausted by making clear what counts as worth-making. That which counts can be shown to bear at certain key points in the appraisive judgment. The relevance can be pinpointed. In the student's writing at certain places cogency of argument may be more relevant than suggestion through the use of metaphor or analogy. At other places the reverse may be the case. The teacher can point out what counts in his ranking or grading of the paper by specifying the pertinent worth-making features looked for in a good paper.

Requirements of relevance not only demand precision about what counts as worth-making. They also express a concern that the maximum range of considerations has not been overlooked. In evaluating the student's paper richness of detail, smoothness of style, and the like may be relevant. Whether they are or not depends upon the purposes centered upon in the instruction.

Furthermore, considerations of relevance are supported by reasoned argument. Reasons are offered in support of the relevancy of the worth-making characteristics of the norm. The defense of the norm is not arbitrary.

The evaluator can offer reasons which support or deny the relevance of the norm to the particular aspect of the student's writing.

Additionally, the function of rules in regard to considerations of relevance ranges beyond their use in making characterizing judgments. In the case of the latter, as we have seen, existing rules provide a framework for identifying good- or bad-making characteristics. Rules of usage are taken for granted; the teacher's function is to teach communication through observance of the rules. The teacher interprets the rules; is concerned with their balanced application. In this sense he is explaining the rule to the learner, but he is not making new rules or justifying them to his colleagues.

In making judgments about the relevance of worth-making characteristics of norms we could say that rules of relevance should be followed. However it is not clear that rules of relevance are commonly known in the sense pertaining to rules of usage. Relevance is a matter, as we have suggested, of pin-pointing the particular bearings or pertinence of worth-making features of norms to conditions of situations. This indicates rule-making as well as rule-obeying, and rule-making should be argued rather than imposed by decree.

Furthermore, attention to rule-making in judgments of relevance involves care about another distinction in the class of things called rules. Some rules are primarily definitional; they state the way words are used in the communication of meaning or in a common endeavor. Adverbs modify verbs, adjectives, or other adverbs; in chess pawns move only one block forward save for the initial move which may be two. Such rules specify how the game is to be played. Other rules, however, are not analytic with respect to the game; they are contingent as to the strategy of achieving the ends-in-view of the game. They are "if . . . then" rules to be interpreted with respect to the conditions one is in and the consequences that typically follow in situations of a similar kind. While definitional rules are central in characterizing judgments, strategic rules are more focal in matters of relevance. When one claims that an aspect of a norm is relevant, he is not merely appealing to a known rule; he is offering an argument that conditions and consequences call for attention to the bearing of something that has been overlooked.

The significance of this attention to rule-making as well as to rule-obeying is that justification of the norm does not consist simply in rationalizing a received norm. It involves building the norm—clearly not *de novo*, for norm-building may be communicated and shared—by giving the norm such attention that its worth-making characteristics are vitalized and high-lighted in the situation one faces. Such attention enables the norm-using agent to scrutinize and assess the norm rather than accept it as complete and final, already present and waiting to be replicated upon demand. In arguments about the relevance of the worth-making features of the norm one contributes to the norm those features which give it compelling, yet non-arbitrary, impact on the quality of our judgments.

Questions of Priority in Appraisal Judgments

If one has determined the relevance of the worth-making characteristics of norms, he then faces the question of which of two or more of these characteristics takes precedence over the others. Of two competing relevant worth-making features, which has priority?

Here the logic of norm-making suggests that the judgment focuses in the reasons advanced for the relevance of the worth-making considerations. One judges the cogency of the reasons and the consequences in the situation at hand of arranging the various criteria in some order of priority. Although not every worth-making feature competes with or excludes others, yet in normative judgments not everything can be had at once. Some aspects of norm fulfillment may reasonably be assigned precedence, relative to and conditional upon, others.

Consider again the teacher's need for normative clarity in assessing students' papers. The teacher may reason that the norm of having something to say takes priority over avoiding split infinitives. He may reason that the worth-making characteristics of innovative thinking weighs more heavily than cogency of argument. If the student's paper is to be critically appraised in this fashion, not only must the paper have the property, but the teacher must be able to reason critically about the weight to be assigned to the various criteria used in his teaching. The normatively sensitive teacher knows what he is looking for in his students' papers because he has clarified the relative priorities of his worth-making standards. Perhaps the teacher says to himself something like this: "It is more important that my students have something original to say than that they say it perfectly. Although they should avoid gross grammatical errors, it is a higher good that they express their own ideas. Thus they will be encouraged to think creatively and avoid simply cribbing the ideas and expressions of others." Judgments of priorities in the worth-making features of norms pervade the many different things that are done in teaching, and since being clear about the centrality of some clear purpose frequently involves removing some other purpose from the center of attention, ordering the worth-making features of norms promotes constancy and clarity in pursuit of purposes.

Care in these matters is indicated by the teacher who notes that he ought not to push Johnny beyond a certain point in the mastery of a particular learning for fear of alienating his later learnings about the matter. The teacher assigns priority to what he judges to be of higher worth. The teacher says in effect, "The continued concern of the student with something that challenges him surpasses the worth of pushing through to complete mastery at this time." The teacher arranges his priorities with good reasons for assigning priorities in his standards. Of course at another time the teacher may reassign priorities differently, judging that more complete mastery takes precedence over the student's sense of present achievement.

It should be clear that I am not talking about a general hierarchical system of values. Questions of priority of the worth-making components of norms are judgments made in the context of situations. Though some priorities are held to endure, they do so by virtue of a recurrent appraisal of their worth in concrete situations.

It should also be clear that this does not mean a general softness and looseness about the teacher's sense of values. It recommends against the rootless assigning of good-making characteristics of what is valued in favor of reasoned argument about competing worth-making features of norms. Reasons, rather than clichés, should be appealed to in this process.

Questions about the Validation of Norms

Questions of relevance and of priority in the worth-making features of norms do not exhaust the logical moves in the justification of norms. There remain questions about what we appeal to in the criticism and appraisal of norms. Granted that we support worth-making characteristics with relevant reasons, that we have not overlooked relevant considerations, and that these good reasons help in justifying priorities among worth-making characteristics, we still need to know that the selected standards are the right ones, that they ought to be used. Moves of this kind concern the validation of norms. In general, we validate norms by appealing to higher ones.

With reference to the grading of papers again, the teacher says: "Having something significant to say is a relevant norm. Further, it out-weighs the rigid observance of rules of grammar." The teacher validates this having something significant to say by appeal to the higher norm that he ought to encourage the student to think creatively for himself. It is a higher norm in the sense that it subsumes the worth-making standard of "having something significant to say."

What do we mean by saying that a higher norm subsumes a lower one? Part of what we mean is that the higher norm has *prima facie* appropriateness as a universal. The case for an exception to it has to be made. There are sufficient reasons and evidences to warrant the desirability of creative thinking on the part of the student. If there were to be an exception to this norm or qualification of it, one would have to argue the point by using good reasons.

One could, however, push the question of the validation of the norm a step further. He could ask what validates the norm expressing the desirability of creative thinking. Here the justification might take either of at least two forms. One might argue that he deduced this norm from a still more general normative principle or set of normative generalizations. By continuing this process one could, in principle, arrive at that norm which is not validated on *prima facie* grounds or on grounds of its relations with the other norms but which is self-evidently good for all men at all times everywhere. The final norm is in this sense absolute. Some philosophers hold that only as one pushes the justifications of norms back to the absolute has one any solid basis for his middle-range norms.

The other avenue of justification of more ultimate norms takes the form of the appraisal of consequences. One looks to the consequences in social practice of the more general normative principle. One may push the justification of norms back to an ultimate principle—say, the principle of moral equality—but in this view the justification of the most ultimate normative principle is not exempt from the total consequences that it produces in the way of life of a people.

The issue between these two avenues of justification of ultimate norms continues to be basic in modern philosophy. Without further elaboration of it, it seems fruitful to mark off moves of this kind from other moves in the justification of norms. Here one is not only reasoning about questions of relevance, priority, and subsumptive relations in norm making. He is reasoning about the status and security of ultimate norms. Such reasoning involves a position or point of view on philosophic issues in value theory.

Without seeking anything approaching a full dissection of this matter, it might be said that there are several alternatives at this point. One could push the justification in the direction of search for an uncompromising absolutism of ultimate norms. Or one could search for the security of norms in the mutually supporting pattern of values found to be expressions of the qualities of a good life—a kind of relational absolutism—which may transcend the value pattern of a given society. A third avenue might be suggested by speaking of the vindication of norms. This might take the form of arguing that our highest values are confirmable as reasonable and just, defended against denial or disbelief, on the grounds of their producing consequences that bear maximum goods for the human situation as it is perceived. Although philosophers of education may properly pursue the grounds of commitment at various levels of ultimacy, the concern of this paper has a focus in the middle range of normative moves on the assumption that teachers and students of education can profitably explore mid-range problems in the justification of norms without settling some of philosophy's larger questions.

Let us put the matter again in terms of the teacher's evaluation of the student's paper. The teacher validates the norm of "having something significant to say" by giving good reasons for bringing it under a universal about encouraging creative thinking. He reasons about exceptions to this presumptive norm. What aspects of creativity take precedence over rules of good grammar and rhetoric? He further justifies the norm of promoting creative thinking by reasoning about it in relation to other universal norms such as the moral principle of equality of treatment. He may pursue a course searching for final values, unequivocal for all men everywhere, or his reasoning may pursue a more relational and contextual basis for the security of ultimate value. At a minimum, the teacher sees whether his norms are mutually supporting, whether they add up to a consistent pattern of direction in grading papers and in other teaching acts. He may go further to vindicate his total framework of values as reasonable and just in the context of the human situation. In short, in the validation of norms it is fruitful to pay attention to what I have called the middle-range moves in the justification of norms.

We now review the major distinctions and moves involved in making value judgments and in the general field of normative discourse.

Following Dewey's distinction between primary values and evaluated values, we mark off primary value judgments in the sense that when something is said to have value, the value is simply had. Reasons or justifications, to the extent that they are present, are descriptive; questions about standards have narrative or factual import. It is only as one moves into considerations about evaluated values that considerations of the normative in a qualitative sense arise.

We then noted that a normative judgment involves a two-fold claim: on the one hand, something evaluated has good-making or bad-making characteristics or may be neutral with reference to a standard, and, on the other hand, the standard is specified by delineating its worth-making features.

We then distinguished characterizing from appraising aspects of normative judgments. In characterizing value judgments norms are commonly agreed upon or taken for granted. In appraisive value judgments they are to be justified. Rules are involved in both characterizing and appraisive judgments, but the more fully normative judgment involves rule-making. In the logic of appraisive judgment, since norms are to be justified, questions about relevance, priority, and validation of norms are focal.

Philosophers of education are concerned not only with the making and recommending of value judgments; everyone does that. They are not alone in pushing valuables. They do rise to the occasion of justifying the norms whereby valuables acquire their value. They do this not only by clarifying rules of normative discourse, but they also go beyond the rules by justifying them and scrutinizing the appraisive judgments involved in rule-making. In the final analysis this pushes them back to questions of the ultimate security of values, but questions of relevance, precedence and vindication of norms indicate a middle-range set of concerns of such focal importance in educational thought and talk that philosophers would be well advised to devote more attention to them.

18 / JAMES F. PERRY and PHILIP G. SMITH

Levels of Valuational Discourse in Education

A useful proposal for structuring valuational discourse is found in H. D. Aiken's "Levels of Moral Discourse."[1]. According to Aiken, we can distinguish four levels of discourse which he calls (1) "expressive-evocative," (2) "moral," (3) "ethical," and (4) "postethical" or "human." These levels are to be distinguished primarily by the different functions performed by the same valuational terms when used at each of the levels. Because of different functions there are different kinds of arguments, objections, and "good reasons" appropriate or relevant at each level.

Without examining all of the meta-ethical questions involved in the Aiken article, we shall suggest first, that his analysis can be generalized to apply to any kind of valuational discourse (rather than just moral discourse) and second, that such a generalized analysis may be useful in a consideration of the bewildering maze of valuational problems that run through the theory and practice of education. While fully acknowledging our indebtedness to Professor Aiken we make no claim to having expressed *his* point of view. Especially in connection with the fourth level we have deliberately departed from what we take to be some of his presuppositions.

James F. Perry and Philip G. Smith, "Levels of Valuational Discourse in Education," from *Philosophy of Education 1969*, Proceedings of the Twenty-fifth Annual Meeting, Philosophy of Education Society, 1969, pp. 105–112. Reprinted by permission of the publisher and the authors.

James F. Perry is completing his doctorate in philosophy of education at Indiana University. His papers have appeared in *Philosophy of Education*, Proceedings of the Philosophy of Education Society.

Philip G. Smith (1917–) is professor and chairman of the Department of History and Philosophy of Education at Indiana University. His publications include *Reflective Thinking: The Method of Education* (coauthor), *Philosophy of Education: Introductory Studies,* and *Theories of Value and Problems of Education* (editor).

[1] H. D. Aiken, "Levels of Moral Discourse," *Ethics*, LXII, no. 4 (July, 1952); also in *Reason and Conduct* (New York: Alfred A. Knopf, 1962), Chapter 4.

The Expressive-Evocative Level

Whether heatedly or dispassionately, and whether by using gestures and facial expressions or by using words such as "good" and "bad," most of us express our feelings countless times each day. In the classroom we sometimes express our feelings by assigning rewards and punishments or by offering or denying opportunities. When this sort of thing is done at what Aiken calls the expressive level, we do not expect to be called upon to defend our expressions with good reasons. An expression of a feeling merely indicates that the feeling is actual; it does not imply a claim about the value of the object or event toward which the feeling is directed.

This is not to say that we may not have reasons *for expressing* our feelings. In addition merely to venting our emotions, we sometimes express our feelings in order to influence someone's decisions or behavior, or in order to enable others to understand us and thus to enable them to predict our own future behavior. But unless there is something rather obviously unstable or problematic about the situation, we tend to use valuational language at this level in an unreflective manner. In most situations we do not have to stop and think about it in order to know how we feel, and to the extent that we tend to be open and frank and not given to dissembling, we tend to express our feelings without giving much thought to the effects of such use of valuational terms.

In the classroom this may present serious problems. Involved here is the practice of using expressive valuational language for the purpose of valuational structuring.[2] Teachers use valuational language to exhort, to express empathy, and to encourage empathy, and they promote "valuational sets" by the use of valuational terms more or less disguised as factual descriptions. Some of this practice is probably inevitable in any complex teaching situation and it may be that under certain circumstances it is an essential and desirable means toward important educational objectives. Our concern at this point is merely to note how the use of a generalized version of Aiken's analysis quickly enables one to spot this comparatively unstudied aspect of classroom teaching and to recognize that the pedagogical problems connected with this use of valuational language are not reducible to the problems of the logic of evaluations. The question "Was it pedagogically appropriate for the teacher to express a certain valuation in a certain way at a certain time?" is quite different from the question "Could the expressed valuation be defended as a

[2] Philip G. Smith, "Verbal Operations in Classroom Instruction," Chapter IV in David W. Ecker, *Improving the Teaching of Art Appreciation* (U.S. Department of Health, Education, and Welfare, Cooperative Research Project #V-006, Ohio State University Research Foundation, November, 1966).

value claim or proposition?" The second question is really an invitation to escalate the discourse to a higher level.

The Moral Level, or, the Level of Case Evaluations

Aiken points out that two kinds of considerations are acknowledged to be relevant at the moral level: factual means-ends claims, and moral rules or standards. If I claim that *X* is good, I am operating at the moral level if I point out that *X* is a means for achieving *Y* (where *Y* is conceded to be good) and/or if I point out that *X* is a kind of *Z* (where *Z* is conceded to be good). My claim can then be challenged by arguments or evidence to show that *X* is not a means for achieving *Y*, or that *X* is not a kind of *Z*, or that there are other overriding considerations.

In practice, as Aiken points out, valuational discourse at this level frequently contains ellipses and elisions. When only conclusions are stated they may appear to be merely first-level expressions of personal preference: "Caesar was a great general," "This is an 'A' paper." Differentiation between levels depends upon function, and function is related to intention, point, and context. For example, the statement "Caesar was a great general" made by an elementary school teacher may be seen, in context, to be nothing more than an attempt at valuational structuring (however questionable this may be from an instructional standpoint). The same statement made as an aside during a lecture by an accomplished historian of military affairs has a significantly different function. From the standpoint of intent, the distinction is a matter of whether or not the assertion is a conclusion from good reasons either stated or held in mind.

In the studies of teaching conducted by B. Othanel Smith, it was found that it is very common for teachers to call upon students to make what we have called "case evaluations." Professor Smith reports, "But all too often, when the student makes a decision in these cases, the teacher either accepts or rejects it without regard for the facts and criteria involved." From this, Professor Smith concludes that "this practice of disregarding facts and criteria is probably the chief defect of teaching in the domain of valuation."[3]

Certainly when what is at issue is a case evaluation, a lack of regard for the relevant facts and criteria is a mark of poor or confused teaching. But the Aiken analysis should enable us to see that "teaching in the domain of valuation" involves much more than case evaluations. And this is, perhaps, especially true in teaching in the arts, the topic to which Professor Smith was addressing his remarks. The domain of valuation includes affective and conative aspects that are not necessarily reducible to the cognitive operations

[3] B. Othanel Smith, "The Logic of Teaching in the Arts," *Teachers College Record,* LXIII, no. 3 (1961).

involved in case evaluations, and case evaluations do not exhaust even the cognitive aspects of the domain of valuations.

Nevertheless, failure to make explicit the facts and criteria involved in case evaluations is a serious fault not only with respect to teaching in the domain of valuations but also with respect to the complex web of evaluations involved in the selecting, organizing, and presenting of any content of instruction and in evaluating and reporting student progress. Too many ellipses and elisions here give teaching the appearance of being either highly arbitrary or else based on some artful mystique to be learned only by an extended apprenticeship. This, in turn, is fatal to any program of teacher preparation that strives to lift teaching to the level of a professional practice.

It is almost axiomatic that education is permeated with values; less well understood is the corollary that the various tasks and procedures that constitute *teaching* are laced together into actual teaching methods or strategies by a series of evaluative decisions. It follows that the logic of teaching (in contrast to logical structures within the context of instruction) is the logic of evaluative judgments. Our analysis of levels of valuational discourse in education uncovered, at the expressive level, the need for psychological and other scientific study of the pedagogical effects of valuational language; we now suggest that it is an understanding of the case evaluation level that is at the heart of the logic of teaching.

The Ethical Level, or, Norm Evaluations

When valuational discourse proceeds at the case evaluation level, the soundness of the rules and standards used to justify value claims is taken for granted. When we question such rules or standards, asking whether they are based on good reasons, we shift the discourse to the ethical level in Aiken's analysis or, when the analysis is generalized, to the level of norm evaluations.

To the extent that any domain of valuation (e.g., moral, aesthetic, educational) is well structured with clear and widely accepted rules and standards, valuational discourse tends to remain on the first two levels. But there are occasions for further escalation of the discourse. Changing conditions or increased knowledge of consequences may bring to light a conflict between two or more rules, or it may be found that the consistent application of certain standards has results that were unintended. There may also be crossovers from one domain to another. For example, the application of some educational rule or standard that appears appropriate from a pedagogical point of view may become unacceptable when viewed from a moral point of view.

Regardless of the conditions or causes that animate valuational discourse, at the level of norm evaluation the essential characteristic is an impersonal criticism of standards or rules. They and/or their consequences are judged in the light of higher-order norms or principles. For example, at the second level of discourse the moral question is "What ought I to do in this situation?" but at the third level the ethical question is "What moral standards ought one to follow in a situation such as this?" In order to answer the moral question the appeal is to moral rules or standards; in order to answer the ethical question the appeal is to ethical criteria.

Principles in any valuational domain or "point of view"[4] may exist at various levels of generality but principles of the highest order always appear empty (i.e., abstract and not prescribing any particular concrete act) at the level of case evaluations. Consider, for example, the golden rule or Kant's maxim. This "emptiness" is an essential characteristic, for such criteria function as a base for criticism of the more specific standards and rules. The function of principles of the highest order is to define a domain or point of view. This is to say that the highest-order ethical principles show what it means to be moral, or to take the moral point of view.

In the context of education, "objectives" perform a similar function and in the language of education, this term covers a very wide range of levels of generality. On the one hand we speak of the objectives of American schooling and on the other of the objectives of the instruction planned for tomorrow's eighth grade general science class. Nevertheless, it is "objectives" that provide a base for criticism of educational standards and rules. For example, the statement "This is an 'A' paper" may be viewed as a conclusion in a case evaluation when such a judgment was arrived at in the light of standards or rules established for the assignment. But the appropriateness of the assignment and its standards may be criticized in the light of the instructional objectives. These in turn may be criticized in terms of higher-order objectives until finally we arrive at a consideration of what are sometimes called the aims of education. At this level of generality what is needed, as John Dewey clearly recognized, is some "empty" principle that will define the domain or point of view—for example, the principle of "growth", or the definition of an educative experience as one that adds to the meaning of experience and increases control over the course of subsequent experience. To criticize this principle as, for example, Boyd Bode did,[5] because it does not specify what one ought to do in any particular case, is simply to misunderstand its point and function. A proper criticism of such a principle would more likely take the form (à la Peters)[6] of a conceptual mapping of "education" in relation to both subordinate concepts (e.g., "teaching" and "learning") and superordinate concepts (e.g., "man," "rationality," etc.) in order to explicate and assess the scope and thrust of the principle.

[4] Paul W. Taylor, *Normative Discourse* (Englewood Cliffs, N.J.: Prentice-Hall, 1961).

[5] Boyd H. Bode, *Progressive Education at the Crossroads* (New York: Newson, 1938).

[6] Richard S. Peters, *Ethics and Education* (Chicago: Scott, Foresman, 1967).

It follows that the moves involved at the level of norm evaluations ought to be mastered by those engaged in the justification of objectives or the development of prescriptive theories within the field of education. At the highest level of generality such prescriptive theories are usually known as normative philosophies of education.

The Postethical or Human Level, or, The Level of Existential Commitment

Consider now the question "Why ought *I* to do what one ought to do?" That is, "Why ought I be moral?" Or, at the more generalized level, "Why should I be responsible about valuational decisions?" Or, in the context of education, "Why should I be educated?" When such a question is asked *within* the levels of discourse so far discussed, it is in a sense quite meaningless, for it says, in effect, "I now know what I ought to do but I still don't know whether or not I ought to do it!"

Nevertheless, as Aiken points out, the fact that we recognize that there are some occasions on which asking such questions is not meaningless suggests a fourth level of valuational discourse. According to Aiken, "There is a sense in which man transcends all his works and is 'free,' albeit at his peril, to junk any and all of them at any time. I am bound to the rules of morality so long as I am responsive to the demands of a 'rational' moral being. But nothing can give them authority over my conduct unless I, in virtue of my attitudes and wants, am moved by them."

Aiken asserts that, at the fourth level, once again "decision is king." But one might add that "reason may still be parliament," and decision at this level should not be confused with the more or less spontaneous expression of personal preference by valuational language at the first level. Consider the persuasive and evocative function of valuational terms: At the first level the appeal is to desires and attitudes that dance on the surface of personality; at the fourth level the call is to the very roots of man's humanness and rationality. At this level an appropriate response to the question "Why should I be reasonable?" might be, "Come, join with me in the life of striving to be reasonable and see if you don't find it good."

In the context of education it is the human level of valuational discourse that provides the arena for doing philosophy of education in the traditional grand manner—a literary account of a "life style" (in education and elsewhere), an attempt to "tell it like it is" when seen from the inside. In such an account valuational terms are invitations to empathetic understanding and identification—they are ways of saying "Come, join with me." They point toward the virtues of universal coherence—the absence of working "at cross purposes," the solving of all problems at once (without generating new, and possibly greater, problems). At this level it doesn't make much sense to ask for justification (in the form of a second- or third-level argument) of the key or intrinsic values. But it is also a confusion of levels to suppose that nothing more is involved in such systematic invitations to existential commitment than a sophisticated form of the emotive language used in the first level of valuational discourse.

Now, of course, it is possible to view the schools in a purely instrumental sense, as educational planners sometimes do, abdicating all responsibility for deep philosophic commitment. Final decision concerning the role of the school may be viewed as a political decision quite beyond the responsibility of professional educators who are properly concerned only with accomplishing the mission assigned to the schools by society or by the state. It may be that some who take this position are victims of a confusion of the fourth and first levels and, desiring to remain within the domain of "orderly objective decisions," see no way of entering the dialogue concerning commitments that seem to them doomed to be "subjective," "arbitrary," or "hopelessly relativistic." But we take it that in a free, democratic society, there is really no such escape from freedom. Unless responsibility is accepted for the personal, existential commitment appropriate at the fourth level of valuational discourse, the ideal of both moral autonomy and truly "liberal" education is shattered on the rocks of legalistic and heteronomous standards of value.

Concerning "teaching in the domain of valuations," until students have developed some of the habits involved in being reasonable, formal study of the logic and structure of evaluative judgments is not likely to result in much more than some form of "knowing that"—that is, a formal knowledge of the structure of such judgments. It is only after a person is already disposed (that is, feels obligated) to do what ever it is that *one ought to do* that a study of rules and standards becomes meaningful in a personal sense. And, unfortunately, it is only after the two are put together—that is, only after a person feels that he ought to be reasonable about oughts—that ethical or other forms of valuational education (in contrast to moral or other forms of training) are likely to be efficacious.

Finally, concerning the study of philosophy of education, since one does not empathize or identify with what is strange or alien, to an "outsider" a view from the inside is generally not very convincing. It appears, therefore, that until a student is already striving to order his understandings and commitments concerning education into a comprehensive view or philosophy, a systematic study of the attempts of others to do so is not likely to have much real point or bearing in his life.

Hopefully, this analysis of four levels of valuational discourse in education should prove helpful in understanding: (1) the various kinds of valuational problems encountered in the conduct of schooling; (2) some problems encountered in the teaching of valuations; (3) the importance of differentiating: the empirical study of the pedagogical effects of the use of valuational language, the study of the logic and structure of evaluative judgments as the key to the logic of teaching, the study of the logical structure of the content of instruction, and the study of philosophies of education as persuasive accounts of what it means to be committed to some systematic conception of education.

Questions for Discussion

Peters discussed a large and diverse number of points on moral education. What does he mean by different levels of morality, and how do high-order principles and lower-order rules operate at these levels? Why cannot moral rules be defended on the basis of a consensus? Peters believes that the child learns morality by a process of initiation. What does initiation involve? What connection, if any, do imitation, consistency, learning of skills, a body of beliefs, and "discovery methods" have with moral education? According to Peters, "Reason must have an inheritance of tradition to work upon." Is such a basis for reason actually necessary? Peters also develops a conception of authority. Does he make any provision for youth to develop moral codes which are relatively autonomous from those of persons in authority?

Hare shows the *form* reasoning takes in moral decisions. What does he mean by "decisions of principle"? Why does he believe that many forms of teaching are impossible without the teaching of principles? Why does he believe it necessary to teach the student *what* he should do before we teach him to analyze *why* he should do it? What role do correct habits play in enabling the individual to make decisions of principle?

Clayton states three general senses of value: mathematical, descriptive, and normative. Why does he focus attention on one of the three? He discusses ranking, grading, the act of prizing, and appraisive judgment. How does each function in the process of valuation? He discusses *relevance*, a term frequently on the lips of students. Evaluate the adequacy of his conception. How are norms validated?

Four levels of valuational discourse are delineated by Perry and Smith. What are the distinguishing characteristics of each level and the relationships, if any, among the levels? What specific types of valuational activity in education would you expect at each level? Give examples. At what level do aims of education fit into their schema? Personal commitment?

Suggested Reading

Plato's dialogues, *Protagoras* and *Meno*, trans. W. K. C. Guthrie (Baltimore: Penguin Books, 1964), are two of the most influential works on values, raising questions about the sources of values, the nature of virtue and whether it can be taught, the relation of knowing and doing, and other vital questions. Emile Durkheim develops from his sociology the relation of morality to society, social cohesion, and moral education in *Moral Education* (New York: Free Press, 1961). One of Dewey's earlier works, *Moral Principles in Education* (Boston: Houghton Mifflin Co., 1909), charts the outline of his principles of moral education. Within the Deweyan tradition, John L. Childs places moral values within a broad democratic framework in *Education and Morals,* (New York: Appleton-Century-Crofts, 1950).

A systematic and detailed analysis from the perspective of analytic philosophy is found in Richard S. Peters' *Ethics and Education* (Atlanta: Scott, Foresman and Co., 1967). A philosopher, a psychologist, and a sociologist have combined efforts in John Wilson et al., *Introducton to Moral Education* (Baltimore: Penguin Books, 1967). Cultural, organizational, moral, and aesthetic values are examined in John Martin Rich's *Education and Human Values* (Reading, Mass.: Addison-Wesley Publishing Co., 1968). Jean Piaget reports the findings of his studies on the child's development of moral reasoning in *The Moral Judgment of the Child* (New York: Free Press, 1965).

The collection of essays edited by W. R. Niblett, *Moral Education in a Changing Society* (London: Faber and Faber, 1963), is drawn from a British series of lectures on facets of moral education. A far-ranging series of topics is discussed by American writers in Theodore Brameld and Stanley Elam, eds., *Values in American Education* (Bloomington, Ind.: Phi Delta Kappa, 1964). Those interested in a useful collection of readings on relation of value theory and education should see Philip G. Smith, ed., *Theories of Value and Problems of Education* (Urbana, Ill.: University of Illinois Press, 1970).

PART TWO /

KNOWLEDGE AND CONCEPTS IN EDUCATION

CHAPTER FIVE /

KNOWLEDGE AND EDUCATION

THE tasks of schooling include not only transmitting knowledge but teaching students to act intelligently on the basis of knowledge. Some educators also encourage students to develop the ability to discover knowledge for themselves. Additionally, educators must determine what knowledge is of greatest worth and how this knowledge should be organized. Each of these tasks raises a series of important problems.

Schools have always been in the business of transmitting knowledge. Historically the fundamental reason for transmitting a body of knowledge was to preserve and to perpetuate the cultural heritage. In relatively stable societies where change was much slower than today, there was usually less difficulty in gaining consensus on the content of the curriculum. Determining what should be taught in today's schools is a highly complex affair.

Some have argued that even if agreement could be reached on which elements were most essential, other critical problems would still remain. Knowing that something is the case does not mean that the individual will be able to act on the basis of this knowledge. Education is a process not only of gaining knowledge but of becoming a certain type of person. This problem is analogous to the problem of knowing what is good or the right thing to do but not exemplifying it in one's conduct. Of course not all knowledge takes propositional form—that is, knowing that something is the case; there is also knowing how to do something, which generally is associated in schooling with the learning of skills. This form of knowledge would seem to obviate the discrepancy between knowing and acting because it is a form of action. The problem that one may be able to act successfully in a school situation but not outside a school setting still remains, however. Here it is a case of being unable to transfer what one has learned in one situation to similar situations. This disability may be rectified by pointing out the similarities and differences in situations outside the classroom and also by offering students an opportunity to practice their abilities in the actual situations or at least under simulated conditions. Thus when an individual claims he knows something he implies that he has the ability to give a successful performance. The criteria of performance may not be limited to classroom situations but may extend to many everyday situations.

There is also a personal element in the process of gaining knowledge. When knowledge does not take on meaning and significance for the learner, it becomes knowledge passively received, and it will not likely be acted upon. In other words, commitment is a factor. For commitment to occur, knowledge must first be meaningful to the learner; it must find a place in his value system in the sense that the knowledge is prized for the meaning it gives one's life. When these conditions are met, knowledge is likely to play a significant role in an individual's life.

Educators also want to develop independent learners who can discover knowledge for themselves. Because traditional approaches to transmitting knowledge are generally thought to be inadequate in effecting such ends, new methods have been proposed to correct these deficiencies. Teaching students how scholars conduct investigations is one approach; emphasizing the discovery method and problem-solving methods are other approaches.

Since life is short and organized knowledge is vast, selection is necessary, and one selects what is considered to be of greatest worth. Some educators believe that there is a body of knowledge—a set of great books, religious teachings, a series of courses known as "liberal arts," or what have you—which is desirable for everyone to study, irrespective of individual differences, and time, place, or circumstances. Other educators believe that the worth of knowledge is relative to the students, the school system, and the culture; the chosen body of knowledge may be changed when the situation warrants.

Whether one chooses an absolute or a relative position, the decision of the worth of a body of knowledge is usually based on a value system, a set of educational aims, or a philosophy of education. Because schools frequently are not clear on what knowledge has primacy and because the curriculum often expands as a result of public pressures rather than a well-conceived plan, it is likely that educators are not always clear about the values and aims that guide educational decision-making.

The knowledge considered of greatest worth also influences the way in which knowledge is organized, because not all knowledge in a curriculum is of equal importance. This means that in the organization of a curriculum, the structure will reflect the relative importance of the different elements. In addition, curriculum organization is based on beliefs about which arrangements will most successfully promote the desired learning outcomes.

One solution to the problem of what knowledge is of greatest worth is the belief that exact knowledge equips future leaders with the ability to make careful inquiries in all lines of endeavor. Mathematics epitomizes exact knowledge, with some arrangement of the natural sciences following in descending order. This then is the beginning of a classification scheme for the curriculum in which priorities can be assigned and undesirable material eliminated. Much depends, however, on one's system of classification and the criteria on which it is based, for if the criteria are too limited the curriculum may become one-sided.

Another approach to selecting knowledge of greatest worth is to determine the tasks youth will be expected to fulfill as citizens, and by making systematic, empirical studies of the nature and demands of these tasks, the requisite skills can be developed in school. This approach would eliminate courses of study with no bearing on the tasks individual students face. Some argue, however, that what *is* done in society and the manner in which it is done is not necessarily what *ought* to be done, and thus such an approach is unsuitable as a criterion for determining the basis of the curriculum.

Instead of seeking a classification for knowledge or cataloging the tasks youth will face as adults, one could look at the nature of man to determine what should be taught. If, as some argue, man's distinguishing traits (features that distinguish man from animals) are his most important traits, then education should concentrate on cultivating these traits. Disagreement exists over which traits are the distinguishing ones—whether it is man's reason, language, opposable thumb, tool-making ability, or some other trait. Others argue that man is continuous with the animal kingdom and his alleged distinguishing traits differ from animals only in degree rather than in kind. However, even assuming agreement that man has a distinctive nature was reached and that observers concurred on distinguishing traits, no direct inferences could logically be drawn as to what should be done and what the role of the school should be. The reason for this difficulty is that there is no one-to-one correspondence between statements about human nature and a set of policies or prescriptions. Philosophy is not a deductive system like geometry. Additionally, some proponents of different theories of human nature may overlap in their support of educational policies or programs.

Attempts have been made to determine the structure of the disciplines and organized knowledge and to clarify the methodological procedures that each discipline uses in gaining new knowledge. Some believe that if students can grasp the structure of a discipline and can gain some experience in using the modes of inquiry that have proved fruitful in research, the student will be in a position to interpret new knowledge, to think with sophistication, and to see relationships and situations in which he can use his new learning.

Others object that this may not be the manner in which young minds operate best and that there is merit in maintaining and extending interdisciplinary curriculum patterns that build carefully on the learner's interests and recognize his developmental characteristics.

The following selections treat in greater depth a number of concerns we have raised. Aristotle attempts to distinguish different forms of knowledge and their respective characteristics. He delineates theoretical, practical, and productive forms of knowledge and shows their relationships. Note what Aristotle believes to be the highest form of knowledge and how this form differs from the others. Consider how the curriculum should be organized by following Aristotle's system.

Another approach to organizing the curriculum by determining the relative importance of different forms of knowledge is found in Auguste Comte's essay. He surveys and orders the disciplines of his time by developing and applying to them certain criteria. In this manner he is able to develop a hierarchical arrangement of the disciplines and to prescribe the order in which they should be taught.

Joseph Schwab reviews a number of approaches to organizing the disciplines, including those of Aristotle and Comte, and offers several observations and criticisms. He states and explains three basic problems that confront the structure of the disciplines approach. Out of this analysis he is able to consider how the disciplines can best be organized and taught.

On the other hand, Arno Bellack points up some of the limitations of the structure of the disciplines approach. He offers instead proposals he believes will effect better connections between curriculum components. He believes that acting on these proposals will produce greater curriculum unity and a more sensitive recognition of the way students learn best.

The selection by Harry Broudy, Othanel Smith, and Joe Burnett differs from the preceding ones in that it addresses itself to the uses of knowledge rather than to how the forms and structures of knowledge can best be organized and taught. The authors delineate four uses of knowledge and indicate the distinctive features and operations of each. They also show the connections among the uses and which ones are involved in critical thinking.

19 / ARISTOTLE

Metaphysics

All men by nature desire to know. An indication of this is the delight we take in our senses; for even apart from their usefulness they are loved for themselves; and above all others the sense of sight. For not only with a view to action, but even when we are not going to do anything, we prefer seeing (one might say) to everything else. The reason is that this, most of all the senses, makes us know and brings to light many differences between things.

By nature animals are born with the faculty of sensation, and from sensation memory is produced in some of them, though not in others. And therefore the former are more intelligent and apt at learning than those which cannot remember; those which are incapable of hearing sounds are intelligent though they cannot be taught, e.g. the bee, and any other race of animals that may be like it; and those which besides memory have this sense of hearing can be taught.

The animals other than man live by appearances and memories, and have but little of connected experience; but the human race lives also by art and reasonings. Now from memory experience is produced in men; for the several memories of the same thing produce finally the capacity for a single experience. And experience seems pretty much like science and art, but really science and art come to men *through* experience; for "experience made art," as Polus says, "but inexperience luck." Now art arises when from many notions gained

Aristotle, from *Metaphysics*, Book A, Chaps. 1 and 2, and *Nicomachean Ethics*, Book VI, Chaps. 3–7, in the *Works of Aristotle*. Translation by W. D. Ross (Oxford: The Clarendon Press, 1910–1952). Reprinted by permission of the publisher.

Aristotle (384–322 B.C.) was born in the Greek colony of Stagira, the son of Nicomachus, the physician of King Amyntas of Macedon. Aristotle was a student of Plato and remained for nearly twenty years at the Academy. He later tutored Alexander the Great and founded the Peripatetic school in the Lyceum at Athens. Aristotle's extant works cover almost all the sciences known in his time. He was the founder of deductive logic and was a systematic scientific researcher who gained a wide mastery of empirical facts. Aristotle had great influence among Arabian and Jewish philosophers after the ninth century and was the single most important philosophical authority during the later Christian Middle Ages. He is generally thought to be one of the two or three most influential philosophers in the history of Western thought. A complete English translation of his works has been published (Oxford: Clarendon Press, 1910–1952) under the editorship of W. D. Ross.

by experience one universal judgement about a class of objects is produced. For to have a judgement that when Callias was ill of this disease this did him good, and similarly in the case of Socrates and in many individual cases, is a matter of experience; but to judge that it has done good to all persons of a certain constitution, marked off in one class, when they were ill of this disease, e.g. to phlegmatic or bilious people when burning with fever,—this is a matter of art.

With a view to action experience seems in no respect inferior to art, and men of experience succeed even better than those who have theory without experience. (The reason is that experience is knowledge of individuals, art of universals, and actions and productions are all concerned with the individual; for the physician does not cure *man*, except in an incidental way, but Callias or Socrates or some other called by some such individual name, who happens to be a man. If, then, a man has the theory without the experience, and recognizes the universal but does not know the individual included in this, he will often fail to cure; for it is the individual that is to be cured.) But yet we think that *knowledge* and *understanding* belong to art rather than to experience, and we suppose artists to be wiser than men of experience (which implies that Wisdom depends in all cases rather on knowledge); and this because the former know the cause, but the latter do not. For men of experience know that the thing is so, but do not know why, while the others know the 'why' and the cause. Hence we think also that the master-workers in each craft are more honourable and know in a truer sense and are wiser than the manual workers, because they know the causes of the things that are done (we think the manual workers are like certain lifeless things which act indeed, but act without knowing what they do, as fire burns,—but while the lifeless things perform each of their functions by a natural tendency, the labourers perform them through habit); thus we view them as being wiser not in virtue of being able to act, but of having the theory for themselves and knowing the causes. And in general it is a sign of the man who knows and of the man who does not know, that the former can teach, and therefore we think art more truly knowledge than experience is; for artists can teach, and men of mere experience cannot.

Again, we do not regard any of the senses as Wisdom; yet surely these give the most authoritative knowledge of particulars. But they do not tell us the 'why' of anything—e.g. why fire is hot; they only say *that* it is hot.

At first he who invented any art whatever that went beyond the common perceptions of man was naturally admired by men, not only because there was something useful in the inventions, but because he was thought wise and superior to the rest. But as more arts were invented, and some were directed to the necessities of life, others to recreation, the inventors of the latter were naturally always regarded as wiser than the inventors of the former, because their branches of knowledge did not aim at utility. Hence when all such inventions were already established, the sciences which do not aim at giving pleasure or at the necessities of life were discovered, and first in the places where men first began to have leisure. This is why the mathematical arts were founded in Egypt; for there the priestly caste was allowed to be at leisure.

We have said in the *Ethics* what the difference is between art and science and the other kindred faculties; but the point of our present discussion is this, that all men suppose what is called Wisdom to deal with the first causes and the principles of things; so that, as has been said before, the man of experience is thought to be wiser than the possessors of any sense-perception whatever, the artist wiser than the men of experience, the master-worker than the mechanic, and the theoretical kinds of knowledge to be more of the nature of Wisdom than the productive. Clearly then Wisdom is knowledge about certain principles and causes.

Since we are seeking this knowledge, we must inquire of what kind are the causes and the principles, the knowledge of which is Wisdom. If one were to take the notions we have about the wise man, this might perhaps make the answer more evident. We suppose first, then, that the wise man knows all things, as far as possible, although he has not knowledge of each of them in detail; secondly, that he who can learn things that are difficult, and not easy for man to know, is wise (sense-perception is common to all, and therefore easy and no mark of Wisdom); again, that he who is more exact and more capable of teaching the causes is wiser, in every branch of knowledge; and that of the sciences, also, that which is desirable on its own account and for the sake of knowing it is more of the nature of Wisdom than that which is desirable on account of its results, and the superior science is more of the nature of Wisdom than the ancillary; for the wise man must not be ordered but must order, and he must not obey another, but the less wise must obey *him*.

Such and so many are the notions, then, which we have about Wisdom and the wise. Now of these characteristics that of knowing all things must belong to him who has in the highest degree universal knowledge; for he knows in a sense all the instances that fall under the universal. And these things, the most universal, are on the whole the hardest for men to know; for they are farthest from the senses. And the most exact of the sciences are those which deal most with first principles; for those which involve fewer principles are more exact than those which involve additional principles, e.g. arithmetic than geometry. But the science which investigates causes is also *instructive*, in a higher degree, for the people who instruct us are those who tell the causes of each thing. And understanding and knowledge pursued for their own sake are found most in the knowledge of that which is most knowable (for he who chooses to know for the sake of knowing will choose most readily that which is most truly knowledge, and such is the knowledge of that which is most knowable); and the first principles and the causes are most knowable; for by reason of these, and from these, all other things come to be known, and not these by means of the things subordinate to them. And the science which knows to what end each thing must be done is the most authoritative of the sciences, and more authoritative than any ancillary science; and this end is the good of that thing, and in general the supreme good in the whole of nature. Judged by all the tests we have mentioned, then, the name in question falls to the same science; this must be a science that investigates the first principles and causes; for the good, i.e. the end, is one of the causes.

That it is not a science of production is clear even from the history of the earliest philosophers. For it is owing to their wonder that men both now begin and at first began to philosophize; they wondered originally at the obvious difficulties, then advanced little by little and stated difficulties about the greater matters, e.g. about the phenomena of the moon and those of the sun and of the stars, and about the genesis of the universe. And a man who is puzzled and wonders thinks himself ignorant (whence even the lover of myth is in a sense a lover of Wisdom, for the myth is composed of wonders); therefore since they philosophized in order to escape from ignorance, evidently they were pursuing science in order to know, and not for any utilitarian end. And this is confirmed by the facts; for it was when almost all the necessities of life and the things that make for comfort and recreation had been secured, that such knowledge began to be sought. Evidently then we do not seek it for the sake of any other advantage; but as the man is free, we say, who exists for his own sake and not for another's, so we pursue this as the only free science, for it alone exists for its own sake. . . .

Let us begin, then, from the beginning, and discuss these states once more. Let it be assumed that the states by virtue of which the soul possesses truth by way of affirmation or denial are five in number, i.e. art, scientific knowledge, practical wisdom, philosophic wisdom, intuitive reason; we do not include judgement and opinion because in these we may be mistaken.

Now what *scientific knowledge* is, if we are to speak exactly and not follow mere similarities, is plain from what follows. We all suppose that what we know is not even capable of being otherwise; of things capable of being otherwise we do not know, when they have passed outside our observation, whether they exist or not. Therefore the object of scientific knowledge is of necessity. Therefore it is eternal; for things that are of necessity in the unqualified sense are all eternal; and things that are eternal are ungenerated and imperishable. Again, every science is thought to be capable of being taught, and its object of being learned. And all teaching starts from what is already known, as we maintain in the *Analytics* also; for it proceeds sometimes through induction and sometimes by syllogism. Now induction is the starting-point which knowledge even of the universal presupposes, while syllogism proceeds *from* universals. There are therefore starting-points from which syllogism proceeds, which are not reached by syllogism; it is therefore by induction that they are acquired. Scientific knowledge is, then, a state of capacity to demonstrate, and has the other limiting characteristics which we specify in the *Analytics*; for it is when a man believes in a certain way and the starting-points are known to him that he has scientific knowledge, since if they are not better known to him than the conclusion, he will have his knowledge only incidentally.

Let this, then, be taken as our account of scientific knowledge.

In the variable are included both things made and things done; making and acting are different (for their nature we treat even the discussions outside our school as reliable); so that the reasoned state of capacity to act is different from the reasoned state of capacity to make. Hence too they are not included one in the other; for neither is acting making nor is making acting. Now since architecture is an art and is essentially a reasoned state of capacity to make, and there is neither any art that is not such a state nor any such state that is not an art, *art* is identical with a state of capacity to make, involving a true course of reasoning. All art is concerned with coming into being, i.e. with contriving and considering how something may come into being which is capable of either being or not being, and whose origin is in the maker and not in the thing made; for art is concerned neither with things that are, or come into being, by necessity, nor with things that do so in accordance with nature (since these have their origin in themselves). Making and acting being different, art must be a matter of making, not of acting. And in a sense chance and art are concerned with the same objects; as Agathon says, "art loves chance and chance loves art." Art, then, as has been said, is a state concerned with making, involving a true course of reasoning, and lack of art on the contrary is a state concerned with making, involving a false course of reasoning; both are concerned with the variable.

Regarding *practical wisdom* we shall get at the truth by considering who are the persons we credit with it. Now it is thought to be the mark of a man of practical wisdom to be able to deliberate well about what is good and expedient for himself, not in some particular respect, e.g. about what sorts of thing conduce to health or to strength, but about what sorts of thing conduce to the good life in general. This is shown by the fact that we credit men with practical wisdom in some particular respect when they have calculated well with a view to some good end which is one of those that are not the object of any art. It follows that in the general sense also the man who is capable of deliberating has practical wisdom. Now no one deliberates about things that are invariable, nor about things that it is impossible for him to do. Therefore, since scientific knowledge involves demonstration, but there is no demonstration of things whose first principles are variable (for all such things might actually be otherwise), and since it is impossible to deliberate about things that are of necessity, practical wisdom cannot be scientific knowledge nor art; not science because that which can be done is capable of being otherwise, not art because action and making are different kinds of thing. The remaining alternative, then, is that it is a true and reasoned state of capacity to act with regard to the things that are good or bad for man. For while making has an end other than itself, action cannot; for good action itself is its end. It is for this reason that we think Pericles and men like him have practical wisdom, viz. because they can see what is good for themselves and what is good for men in general; we consider that those can do this who are good at managing households or states. (This is why we call temperance (*σωφροσύνη*) by this name; we imply that it preserves one's practical wisdom (*σῶζουσα τὴν φρόνησιν*). Now what it preserves is a judgement of the kind we have described. For it is not any and every judgement that pleasant and painful objects destroy and pervert, e.g. the judgement that the triangle has or has not its angles equal to two right angles, but only judgements about what is to be done. For the originating causes of the things that are done consist in the end at which they are aimed; but the man who has been ruined by pleasure or pain forthwith fails to see any such originating cause—to see that for the sake of this or because of this he ought to choose and do whatever he chooses and does; for vice is destructive of the originating cause of action.)

Practical wisdom, then, must be a reasoned and true state of capacity to act with regard to human goods. But further, while there is such a thing as excellence in art, there is no such thing as excellence in practical wisdom; and in art he who errs willingly is preferable, but in practical wisdom, as in the virtues, he is the reverse. Plainly, then, practical wisdom is a virtue and not an art. There being two parts of the soul that can follow a course of reasoning, it must be the virtue of one of the two, i.e. of that part which forms opinions; for opinion is about the variable and so is practical wisdom. But yet it is not only a reasoned state; this is shown by the fact that a state of that sort may be forgotten but practical wisdom cannot.

Scientific knowledge is judgement about things that are universal and necessary, and the conclusions of demonstration, and all scientific knowledge, follow from first principles (for scientific knowledge involves apprehension of a rational ground). This being so, the first principle from which what is scientifically known follows cannot be an object of scientific knowledge, of art, or of practical wisdom; for that which can be scientifically known can be demonstrated, and art and practical wisdom deal with things that are variable. Nor are these first principles the objects of philosophic wisdom, for it is a mark of the philosopher to have *demonstration* about some things. If, then, the states of mind by which we have truth and are never deceived about things invariable or even variable are scientific knowledge, practical wisdom, philosophic wisdom, and intuitive reason, and it cannot be any of the three (i.e. practical wisdom, scientific knowledge, or philosophic wisdom), the remaining alternative is that it is *intuitive reason* that grasps the first principles.

Wisdom[1] (1) in the arts we ascribe to their most finished exponents, e.g. to Phidias as a sculptor and to Polyclitus as a maker of portrait-statues, and here we mean nothing by wisdom except excellence in art; but (2) we think that some people are wise in general, not in some particular field or in any other limited respect, as Homer says in the *Margites*,

> Him did the gods make neither a digger nor yet a ploughman
> Nor wise in anything else.

Therefore wisdom must plainly be the most finished of the forms of knowledge. It follows that the wise man must not only know what follows from the first principles, but must also possess truth about the first principles. Therefore wisdom must be intuitive reason combined with scientific knowledge—scientific knowledge of the highest objects which has received as it were its proper completion.

Of the highest objects, we say; for it would be strange to think that the art of politics, or practical wisdom, is the best knowledge, since man is not the best thing in the world. Now if what is healthy or good is different for men and for fishes, but what is white or straight is always the same, any one would say that what is wise is the same but what is practically wise is different; for it is to that which observes well the various matters concerning itself that one ascribes practical wisdom, and it is to this that one will entrust such matters. This is why we say that some even of the lower animals have practical wisdom,[2] viz. those which are found to have a power of foresight with regard to their own life. It is evident also that philosophic wisdom and the art of politics cannot be the same; for if the state of mind concerned with a man's own interests is to be called philosophic wisdom, there will be many philosophic wisdoms; there will not be one concerned with the good of all animals (any more than there is one art of medicine for all existing things), but a different philosophic wisdom about the good of each species.

But if the argument be that man is the best of the animals, this makes no difference; for there are other things much more divine in their nature even than man, e.g., most conspicuously, the bodies of which the heavens are framed. From what has been said it is plain, then, that philosophic wisdom is scientific knowledge, combined with intuitive reason, of the things that are highest by nature. This is why we say Anaxagoras, Thales, and men like them have philosophic but not practical wisdom, when we see them ignorant of what is to their own advantage, and why we say that they know things

[1] In this chapter Aristotle restricts to a very definite meaning the word σοφία, which in ordinary Greek, as the beginning of the chapter points out, was used both of skill in a particular art or craft, and of wisdom in general.

[2] We do not say this in English; but we call them "intelligent" or "sagacious," which comes to the same thing.

that are remarkable, admirable, difficult, and divine, but useless; viz., because it is not human goods that they seek.

Practical wisdom on the other hand is concerned with things human and things about which it is possible to deliberate; for we say this is above all the work of the man of practical wisdom, to deliberate well, but no one deliberates about things invariable, nor about things which have not an end, and that a good that can be brought about by action. The man who is without qualification good at deliberating is the man who is capable of aiming in accordance with calculation at the best for man of things attainable by action. Nor is practical wisdom concerned with universals only—it must also recognize the particulars; for it is practical, and practice is concerned with particulars. This is why some who do not know, and especially those who have experience, are more practical than others who know; for if a man knew that light meats are digestible and wholesome, but did not know which sorts of meat are light, he would not produce health, but the man who knows that chicken is wholesome is more likely to produce health.

Now practical wisdom is concerned with action; therefore one should have both forms of it, or the latter in preference to the former. But of practical as of philosophic wisdom there must be a controlling kind.

20 / AUGUSTE COMTE

Hierarchy of the Positive Sciences

In proceeding to offer a Classification of the Sciences, we must leave on one side all others that have as yet been attempted. Such scales as those of

From Auguste Comte, *Course on the Positive Philosophy*. Translation by Harriet Martineau (London: Trubner and Co., 1875), Chap. 2, pp. 15–27.

August Comte (1798–1857), the founding father of sociology, was born in Montpellier, France. Early in his life the improvement of society became his main preoccupation, but in order to improve society he believed a theoretical science was needed, which he promptly set out to develop. From 1817 to 1823 Comte collaborated with Henri de Saint-Simon, the French social philosopher whose writings foreshadowed socialism; thereafter their partnership dissolved in bitterness. Comte never again found a stable, remunerative position. A small group of admirers asked him to give a series of lectures; his lecture notes were published between 1830 and 1842, forming his masterwork, *Course of Positive Philosophy*, in six volumes. Between 1851 and 1854 he wrote *System of Positive Politics*, in four volumes, in which findings of theoretical sociology were applied to social problems. Herein he deviated from his earlier work by attempting to construct a religion of humanity.

Bacon and D'Alembert are constructed upon an arbitrary division of the faculties of the mind; whereas, our principal faculties are often engaged at the same time in any scientific pursuit. As for other classifications, they have failed, through one fault or another, to command assent: so that there are almost as many schemes as there are individuals to propose them. The failure has been so conspicuous, that the best minds feel a prejudice against this kind of enterprise, in any shape.

Now, what is the reason of this?—For one reason, the distribution of the sciences, having become a somewhat discredited task, has of late been undertaken chiefly by persons who have no sound knowledge of any science at all. A more important and less personal reason, however, is the want of homogeneousness in the different parts of the intellectual system,—some having successively become positive, while others remain theological or metaphysical. Among such incoherent materials, classification is of course impossible. Every attempt at a distribution has failed from this cause, without the distributor being able to see why;—without his discovering that a radical contrariety existed between the materials he was endeavouring to combine. The fact was clear enough; if it had but been understood, that the enterprise was premature; and that it was useless to undertake it till our principal scientific conceptions should all have become positive. The preceding chapter seems to show that this indispensable condition may now be considered fulfilled: and thus the time has arrived for laying down a sound and durable system of scientific order.

We may derive encouragement from the example set by recent botanists and zoologists, whose philosophical labours have exhibited the true principle of classification; viz., that the classification must proceed from the study of the things to be classified, and must by no means be determined by *a priori* considerations. The real affinities and natural connections presented by objects being allowed to determine their order, the classification itself becomes the expression of the most general fact. And thus does the positive method apply to the question of classification itself, as well as to the objects included under it. It follows that the mutual dependence of the sciences,—a dependence resulting from that of the corresponding phenomena,—must determine the arrangement of the system of human knowledge. Before proceeding to investigate this mutual dependence, we have only to ascertain the real bounds of the classification proposed: in other words, to settle what we mean by human knowledge, as the subject of this work.

The field of human labour is either speculation or action: and thus, we are accustomed to divide our knowledge into the theoretical and the practical. It is obvious that, in this inquiry, we have to do only with the theoretical. We are not going to treat of all human notions whatever, but of those fundamental conceptions of the different orders of phenomena which furnish a solid basis to all combinations, and are not founded on any antecedent intellectual system. In such a study, speculation is our material, and not the application of it,—except where the application may happen to throw back light on its speculative origin. This is probably what Bacon meant by that First Philosophy which he declared to be an extract from the whole of Science, and which has been so differently and so strangely interpreted by his metaphysical commentators.

There can be no doubt that Man's study of nature must furnish the only basis of his action upon nature; for it is only by knowing the laws of phenomena, and thus being able to foresee them, that we can, in active life, set them to modify one another for our advantage. Our direct natural power over everything about us is extremely weak, and altogether disproportioned to our needs. Whenever we effect anything great it is through a knowledge of natural laws, by which we can set one agent to work upon another,—even very weak modifying elements producing a change in the results of a large aggregate of causes. The relation of science to art may be summed up in a brief expression:

From Science comes Prevision: from Prevision comes Action.

We must not, however, fall into the error of our time, of regarding Science chiefly as a basis of Art. However great may be the services rendered to Industry by science, however true may be the saying that Knowledge is Power, we must never forget that the sciences have a higher destination still;—and not only higher but more direct;—that of satisfying the craving of our understanding to know the laws of phenomena. To feel how deep and urgent this need is, we have only to consider for a moment the physiological effects of *consternation*, and to remember that the most terrible sensation we are capable of, is that which we experience when any phenomenon seems to arise in violation of the familiar laws of nature. This need of disposing facts in a comprehensible order (which is the proper object of all scientific theories) is so inherent in our organization, that if we could not satisfy it by positive conceptions, we must inevitably return to those theological and metaphysical explanations which had their origin in this very fact of human nature.—It is this original tendency which acts as a preservative, in the minds of men of science, against the narrowness and incompleteness which the practical habits of our age are apt to produce. It is through this that we are able to maintain just and noble ideas of the importance and destination of the sciences; and if it were not thus, the human understanding would soon, as Condorcet has observed, come to a stand, even as to the practical applications for the sake of which higher things had been sacrificed; for, if the arts flow from science, the neglect of science must destroy the consequent arts. Some of the most important arts are derived from speculations pursued during long ages with a purely scientific intention. For instance, the ancient Greek geometers delighted themselves with beautiful speculations of Conic Sections; those speculations wrought, after a long series of generations, the renovation of astronomy; and out of this has the art of navigation attained a perfection which it never could have reached otherwise than through the speculative labours of Archimedes and Apollonius: so that, to use Condorcet's illustration, "the sailor who is preserved from shipwreck by the exact observation of the longitude, owes his life to a theory conceived two thousand years before by men of genius who had in view simply geometrical speculations."

Our business, it is clear, is with theoretical researches, letting alone their practical application altogether. Though we may conceive of a course of study which should unite the generalities of speculation and application, the time is not come for it. To say nothing of its vast extent, it would require preliminary achievements which have not yet been attempted. We must first be in possession of appropriate Special conceptions, formed according to scientific theories; and for these we have yet to wait. Meantime, an intermediate class is rising up, whose particular destination is to organize the relations of theory and practice; such as the engineers, who do not labour in the advancement of science, but who study it in its existing state, to apply it to practical purposes. Such classes are furnishing us with the elements of a future body of doctrine on the theories of the different arts. Already, Monge, in his view of descriptive geometry, has given us a general theory of the arts of construction. But we have as yet only a few scattered instances of this nature. The time will come when out of such results, a department of Positive philosophy may arise: but it will be in a distant future. If we remember that several sciences are implicated in every important art,—that, for instance, a true theory of Agriculture requires a combination of physiological, chemical, mechanical, and even astronomical and mathematical science,—it will be evident that true theories of the arts must wait for a large and equable development of these constituent sciences.

One more preliminary remark occurs, before we finish the prescription of our limits,—the ascertainment of our field of inquiry. We must distinguish between the two classes of Natural science;—the abstract or general, which have for their object the discovery of the laws which regulate phenomena in all conceivable cases: and the concrete, particular, or descriptive, which are sometimes called Natural sciences in a restricted sense, whose function it is to apply these laws to the actual history of existing beings. The first are fundamental; and our business is with them alone, as the second are derived, and however important, not rising into the rank of our subjects of contemplation. We shall treat of physiology, but not of botany and zoology, which are derived from it. We shall treat of chemistry, but not of mineralogy, which is secondary to it.—We may say of Concrete Physics, as these secondary sciences are called, the same thing that we said of theories of the arts,—that they require a preliminary knowledge of several sciences, and an advance of those sciences not yet achieved; so that, if there were no other reason, we must leave these secondary classes alone. At a future time Concrete Physics will have made progress, according to the development of Abstract Physics, and will afford a mass of less incoherent materials than those which it now presents. At present, too few of the students of these secondary sciences appear to be even aware that a due acquaintance with the primary sciences is requisite to all successful prosecution of their own.

We have now considered,

First, that science being composed of speculative knowledge and of practical knowledge, we have to deal only with the first; and

Second, that theoretical knowledge, or science properly so called, being divided into general and particular, or abstract and concrete science, we have again to deal only with the first.

Being thus in possession of our proper subject, duly prescribed, we may proceed to the ascertainment of the true order of the fundamental sciences.

This classification of the sciences is not so easy a matter as it may appear. However natural it may be, it will always involve something, if not arbitrary, at least artificial; and in so far, it will always involve imperfection. It is impossible to fulfil, quite rigorously, the object of presenting the sciences in their natural connection, and according to their mutual dependence, so as to avoid the smallest danger of being involved in a vicious circle. It is easy to show why.

Every science may be exhibited under two methods or procedures, the Historical and the Dogmatic. These are wholly distinct from each other, and any other method can be nothing but some combination of these two. By the first method knowledge is presented in the same order in which it was actually obtained by the human mind, together with the way in which it was obtained. By the second, the system of ideas is presented as it might be conceived of at this day, by a mind which, duly prepared and placed at the right point of view, should begin to reconstitute the science as a whole. A new science must be pursued historically, the only thing to be done being to study in chronological order the different works which have contributed to the progress of the science. But when such materials have become recast to form a general system, to meet the demand for a more natural logical order, it is because the science is too far advanced for the historical order to be practicable or suitable. The more discoveries are made, the greater becomes the labour of the historical method of study, and the more effectual the dogmatic, because the new conceptions bring forward the earlier ones in a fresh light. Thus, the education of an ancient geometer consisted simply in the study, in their due order, of the very small number of original treatises then existing on the different parts of geometry. The writings of Archimedes and Apollonius were, in fact, about all. On the contrary, a modern geometer commonly finishes his education without having read a single original work dating further back than the most recent discoveries, which cannot be known by any other means. Thus the Dogmatic Method is for ever superseding the Historical, as we advance to a higher position in science. If every mind had to pass through all the stages that every predecessor in the study had gone through, it is clear that, however easy it is to learn rather than invent, it would be impossible to effect the purpose of education—to place the student on the vantage-ground gained by the labours of all the men who have gone before. By the dogmatic method this is done, even though the living student may have only an ordinary intellect, and the dead may have been men of lofty genius. By the dogmatic method therefore must every advanced science be attained, with so much of the historical combined with it as is rendered necessary by discoveries too recent to be studied elsewhere than in their own records. The only objection to the preference of the Dogmatic method is that it does not show how the science was attained; but a moment's reflection will show that this is the case also with the Historical method. To pursue a science historically is quite a different thing from learning the history of its progress. This last pertains to the study of human history, as we shall see when we reach the final division of this work. It is true that a science cannot be completely understood without a knowledge of how it arose; and again, a dogmatic knowledge of any science is necessary to an understanding of its history; and therefore we shall notice, in treating of the fundamental sciences, the incidents of their origin, when distinct and illustrative; and we shall use their history, in a scientific sense, in our treatment of Social Physics; but the historical study, important, even essential, as it is, remains entirely distinct from the proper dogmatic study of science. These considerations in this place, tend to define more precisely the spirit of our course of inquiry, while they more exactly determine the conditions under which we may hope to succeed in the construction of a true scale of the aggregate fundamental sciences. Great confusion would arise from any attempt to adhere strictly to historical order in our exposition of the sciences, for they have not all advanced at the same rate; and we must be for ever borrowing from each some fact to illustrate another, without regard to priority of origin. Thus, it is clear that, in the system of the sciences, astronomy must come before physics, properly so called: and yet, several branches of physics, above all, optics, are indispensable to the complete exposition of astronomy. Minor defects, if inevitable, cannot invalidate a classification which, on the whole, fulfils the principal conditions of the case. They belong to what is essentially artificial in our division of intellectual labour. In the main, however, our classification agrees with the history of science; the more general and simple sciences actually occurring first and advancing best in human history, and being followed by the more complex and restricted, though all were, since the earliest times, enlarging simultaneously.

A simple mathematical illustration will precisely represent the difficulty of the question we have to resolve, while it will sum up the preliminary considerations we have just concluded.

We propose to classify the fundamental sciences. They are six, as we shall soon see. We cannot make them less; and most scientific men would reckon them as more. Six objects admit of 720 different dispositions, or, in popular language, changes. Thus we have to choose the one right order (and there can be but one right) out of 720 possible ones. Very few of these have ever been proposed; yet we might venture to say that there is probably not one in favour of which some plausible reason might not be assigned; for we see the wildest divergences among the schemes which have been proposed,—the sciences which are placed by some at the head of the scale being sent by others to the further extremity. Our problem is, then, to find the one rational order, among a host of possible systems.

Now we must remember that we have to look for the principle of classification in the comparison of the different orders of phenomena, through which science discovers the laws which are her object. What we have to determine is the real dependence of scientific studies. Now, this dependence can result only from that of the corresponding phenomena. All observable phenomena may be included within a very few natural categories, so arranged as that the study of each category may be grounded on the principal laws of the preceding, and serve as the basis of the next ensuing. This order is determined by the degree of simplicity, or, what comes to the same thing, of generality of their phenomena. Hence results their successive dependence, and the greater or lesser facility for being studied.

It is clear, *a priori*, that the most simple phenomena must be the most general; for whatever is observed in the greatest number of cases is of course the most disengaged from the incidents of particular cases. We must begin then with the study of the most general or simple phenomena, going on successively to the more particular or complex. This must be the most methodical way, for this order of generality or simplicity fixes the degree of facility in the study of phenomena, while it determines the necessary connection of the sciences by the successive dependence of their phenomena. It is worthy of remark in this place that the most general and simple phenomena are the furthest removed from Man's ordinary sphere, and must thereby be studied in a calmer and more rational frame of mind than those in which he is more nearly implicated; and this constitutes a new ground for the corresponding sciences being developed more rapidly.

We have now obtained our rule. Next we proceed to our classification.

We are first struck by the clear division of all natural phenomena into two classes—of inorganic and of organic bodies. The organized are evidently, in fact, more complex and less general than the inorganic, and depend upon them, instead of being depended on by them. Therefore it is that physiological study should begin with inorganic phenomena; since the organic include all the qualities belonging to them, with a special order added, viz., the vital phenomena, which belong to organization. We have not to investigate the nature of either; for the positive philosophy does not inquire into natures. Whether their nature be supposed different or the same, it is evidently necessary to separate the two studies of inorganic matter and of living bodies. Our classification will stand through any future decision as to the way in which living bodies are to be regarded; for, on any supposition, the general laws of inorganic physics must be established before we can proceed with success to the examination of a dependent class of phenomena.

Each of these great halves of natural philosophy has subdivisions. Inorganic physics must, in accordance with our rule of generality and the order of dependence of phenomena, be divided into two sections—of celestial and terrestrial phenomena. Thus we have Astronomy, geometrical and mechanical, and Terrestrial Physics. The necessity of this division is exactly the same as in the former case.

Astronomical phenomena are the most general, simple, and abstract of all; and therefore the study of natural philosophy must clearly begin with them. They are themselves independent, while the laws to which they are subject influence all others whatsoever. The general effects of gravitation preponderate, in all terrestrial phenomena, over all effects which may be peculiar to them, and modify the original ones. It follows that the analysis of the simplest terrestrial phenomenon, not only chemical, but even purely mechanical, presents a greater complication than the most compound astronomical phenomenon. The most difficult astronomical question involves less intricacy than the simple movement of even a solid body, when the determining circumstances are to be computed. Thus we see that we must separate these two studies, and proceed to the second only through the first, from which it is derived.

In the same manner, we find a natural division of Terrestrial Physics into two, according as we regard bodies in their mechanical or their chemical character. Hence we have Physics, properly so called, and Chemistry. Again, the second class must be studied through the first. Chemical phenomena are more complicated than mechanical, and depend upon them, without influencing them in return. Every one knows that all chemical action is first submitted to the influence of weight, heat, electricity, etc., and presents moreover something which modifies all these. Thus, while it follows Physics, it presents itself as a distinct science.

Such are the divisions of the sciences relating to inorganic matter. An analogous division arises in the other half of Natural Philosophy—the science of organized bodies.

Here we find ourselves presented with two orders of phenomena; those which relate to the individual, and those which relate to the species, especially when it is gregarious. With regard to Man, especially, this distinction is fundamental. The last order of phenomena is evidently dependent on the first, and is more complex. Hence we have two great sections in organic physics—Physiology, properly so called, and Social Physics, which is dependent on it. In all Social phenomena we perceive the working of the physiological laws of the individual; and moreover something which modifies their effects, and which belongs to the influence of individuals over each other—singularly complicated in the case of the human race by the influence of generations on their successors. Thus it is clear that our social science must issue from that which relates to the life of the individual. On the other hand, there is no occasion to suppose, as some eminent physiologists have done, that Social Physics is only an appendage to physiology. The phenomena of the two are not identical, though they are homogeneous; and it is of high importance to hold the two sciences separate. As social conditions modify the operation of physiological laws, Social Physics must have a set of observations of its own.

It would be easy to make the divisions of the Organic half of Science correspond with those of the Inorganic, by dividing physiology into vegetable and animal, according to popular custom. But this distinction, however important in Concrete Physics (in that secondary and special class of studies before declared to be inappropriate to this work), hardly extends into those Abstract Physics with which we have to do. Vegetables and animals come alike under our notice, when our object is to learn the general laws of life —that is, to study physiology. To say nothing of the fact that the distinction grows ever fainter and more dubious with new discoveries, it bears no relation to our plan of research; and we shall therefore consider that there is only one division in the science of organized bodies.

Thus we have before us Five fundamental Sciences in successive dependence,—Astronomy, Physics, Chemistry, Physiology, and finally Social Physics. The first considers the most general, simple, abstract, and remote phenomena known to us, and those which affect all others without being affected by them. The last considers the most particular, compound, concrete phenomena, and those which are the most interesting to Man. Between these two, the degrees of speciality, of complexity, and individuality, are in regular proportion to the place of the respective sciences in the scale exhibited. This—casting out everything arbitrary—we must regard as the true filiation of the sciences; and in it we find the plan of this work.

As we proceed, we shall find that the same principle which gives this order to the whole body of science arranges the parts of each science; and its soundness will therefore be freshly attested as often as it presents itself afresh. There is no refusing a principle which distributes the interior of each science after the same method with the aggregate sciences. But this is not the place in which to do more than indicate what we shall contemplate more closely hereafter. We must now rapidly review some of the leading properties of the hierarchy of science that has been disclosed.

This gradation is in essential conformity with the order which has spontaneously taken place among the branches of natural philosophy, when pursued separately, and without any purpose of establishing such order. Such an accordance is a strong presumption that the arrangement is natural. Again, it coincides with the actual development of natural philosophy. If no leading science can be effectually pursued otherwise than through those which precede it in the scale, it is evident that no vast development of any science could take place prior to the great astronomical discoveries to which we owe the impulse given to the whole. The progression may since have been simultaneous; but it has taken place in the order we have recognized.

This consideration is so important that it is difficult to understand without it the history of the human mind. The general law which governs this history, as we have already seen, cannot be verified, unless we combine it with the scientific gradation just laid down: for it is according to this gradation that the different human theories have attained in succession the theological state, the metaphysical, and finally the positive. If we do not bear in mind the law which governs progression, we shall encounter insurmountable difficulties: for it is clear that the theological or metaphysical state of some fundamental theories must have temporarily coincided with the positive state of others which precede them in our established gradation, and actually have at times coincided with them; and this must involve the law itself in an obscurity which can be cleared up only by the classification we have proposed.

Again, this classification marks, with precision, the relative perfection of the different sciences, which consists in the degree of precision of knowledge, and in the relation of its different branches. It is easy to see that the more general, simple, and abstract any phenomena are, the less they depend on others, and the more precise they are in themselves, and the more clear in their relations with each other. Thus, organic phenomena are less exact and systematic than inorganic; and of these again terrestrial are less exact and systematic than those of astronomy. This fact is completely accounted for by the gradation we have laid down; and we shall see as we proceed, that the possibility of applying mathematical analysis to the study of phenomena is exactly in proportion to the rank which they hold in the scale of the whole.

There is one liability to be guarded against, which we may mention here. We must beware of confounding the degree of precision which we are able to attain in regard to any science, with the certainty of the science itself. The certainty of science, and our precision in the knowledge of it, are two very different things, which have been too often confounded; and are so still, though less than formerly. A very absurd proposition may be very precise; as if we should say, for instance, that the sum of the angles of a triangle is equal to three right angles; and a very certain proposition may be wanting in precision in our statement of it; as, for instance, when we assert that every man will die. If the different sciences offer to us a varying degree of precision, it is from no want of certainty in themselves, but of our mastery of their phenomena.

The most interesting property of our formula of gradation is its effect on education, both general and scientific. This is its direct and unquestionable result. It will be more and more evident as we proceed, that no science can be effectually pursued without the preparation of a competent knowledge of the anterior sciences on which it depends. Physical philosophers cannot understand Physics without at least a general knowledge of Astronomy; nor Chemists, without Physics and Astronomy; nor Physiologists, without Chemistry, Physics, and Astronomy; nor, above all, the students of Social philosophy, without a general knowledge of all the anterior sciences. As such conditions are, as yet, rarely fulfilled, and as no organization exists for their fulfillment, there is amongst us, in fact, no rational scientific education. To this may be attributed, in great part, the imperfection of even the most important sciences at this day. If the fact is so in regard to scientific education, it is no less striking in regard to general education. Our intellectual system cannot be renovated till the natural sciences are studied in their proper order. Even the highest understandings are apt to associate their ideas according to the order in which they were received: and it is only an intellect here and there, in any age, which in its utmost vigour can, like Bacon, Descartes, and Leibnitz, make a clearance in their field of knowledge, so as to reconstruct from the foundation their system of ideas.

Such is the operation of our great law upon scientific education through its effect on Doctrine. We cannot appreciate it duly without seeing how it affects Method.

As the phenomena which are homogeneous have been classed under one science, while those which belong to other sciences are heterogeneous, it follows that the Positive Method must be constantly modified in an uniform manner in the range of the same fundamental science, and will undergo modifications, different and more and more compound, in passing from one science to another. Thus, under the scale laid down, we shall meet with it in all its varieties; which could not happen if we were to adopt a scale which should not fulfil the conditions we have admitted. This is an all-important consideration; for if, as we have already seen, we cannot understand the positive method in the abstract, but only by its application, it is clear that we can have no adequate conception of it but by studying it in its varieties of application. No one science, however well chosen, could exhibit it. Though the Method is always the same, its procedure is varied. For instance, it should be Observation with regard to one kind of phenomena, and Experiment with regard to another; and different kinds of experiment, according to the case. In the same way, a general precept, derived from one fundamental science, however applicable to another, must have its spirit preserved by a reference to its origin; as in the case of the theory of Classifications. The best idea of the Positive Method would, of course, be obtained by the study of the most primitive and exalted of the sciences, if we were confined to one;

but this isolated view would give no idea of its capacity of application to others in a modified form. Each science has its own proper advantages; and without some knowledge of them all, no conception can be formed of the power of the Method.

One more consideration must be briefly adverted to. It is necessary not only to have a general knowledge of all the sciences, but to study them in their order. What can come of a study of complicated phenomena, if the student have not learned, by the contemplation of the simpler, what a Law is, what it is to Observe; what a Positive conception is; and even what a chain of reasoning is? Yet this is the way our young physiologists proceed every day,—plunging into the study of living bodies, without any other preparation than a knowledge of a dead language or two, or at most a superficial acquaintance with Physics and Chemistry, acquired without any philosophical method, or reference to any true point of departure in Natural philosophy. In the same way, with regard to Social phenomena, which are yet more complicated, what can be effected but by the rectification of the intellectual instrument, through an adequate study of the range of anterior phenomena? There are many who admit this: but they do not see how to set about the work, nor understand the Method itself for want of the preparatory study; and thus, the admission remains barren, and social theories abide in the theological or metaphysical state, in spite of the efforts of those who believe themselves positive reformers.

These, then, are the four points of view under which we have recognized the importance of a Rational and Positive Classification.

It cannot but have been observed that in our enumeration of the sciences there is a prodigious omission. We have said nothing of Mathematical science. The omission was intentional; and the reason is no other than the vast importance of mathematics. This science will be the first of which we shall treat. Meantime, in order not to omit from our sketch a department so prominent, we may indicate here the general results of the study we are about to enter upon.

In the present state of our knowledge we must regard Mathematics less as a constituent part of natural philosophy than as having been, since the time of Descartes and Newton, the true basis of the whole of natural philosophy; though it is, exactly speaking, both the one and the other. To us it is of less value for the knowledge of which it consists, substantial and valuable as that knowledge is, than as being the most powerful instrument that the human mind can employ in the investigation of the laws of natural phenomena.

In due precision, Mathematics must be divided into two great sciences, quite distinct from each other—Abstract Mathematics, or the Calculus (taking the word in its most extended sense), and Concrete Mathematics, which is composed of General Geometry and of Rational Mechanics. The Concrete part is necessarily founded on the Abstract, and it becomes in its turn the basis of all natural philosophy; all the phenomena of the universe being regarded, as far as possible, as geometrical or mechanical.

The Abstract portion is the only one which is purely instrumental, it being simply an immense extension of natural logic to a certain order of deductions. Geometry and mechanics must, on the contrary, be regarded as true natural sciences, founded, like all others, on observation, though, by the extreme simplicity of their phenomena, they can be systematized to much greater perfection. It is this capacity which has caused the experimental character of their first principles to be too much lost sight of. But these two physical sciences have this peculiarity, that they are now, and will be more and more, employed rather as method than as doctrine.

It need scarcely be pointed out that in placing Mathematics at the head of Positive Philosophy, we are only extending the application of the principle which has governed our whole Classification. We are simply carrying back our principle to its first manifestation. Geometrical and Mechanical phenomena are the most general, the most simple, the most abstract of all,—the most irreducible to others, the most independent of them; serving, in fact, as a basis to all others. It follows that the study of them is an indispensable preliminary to that of all others. Therefore must Mathematics hold the first place in the hierarchy of the sciences, and be the point of departure of all Education, whether general or special. In an empirical way, this has hitherto been the custom,—a custom which arose from the great antiquity of mathematical science. We now see why it must be renewed on a rational foundation.

We have now considered, in the form of a philosophical problem, the rational plan of the study of the Positive Philosophy. The order that result is this; an order which of all possible arrangements is the only one that accords with the natural manifestation of all phenomena. MATHEMATICS, ASTRONOMY, PHYSICS, CHEMISTRY, PHYSIOLOGY, SOCIAL PHYSICS.

21 / JOSEPH J. SCHWAB

Structure of the Disciplines: Meanings and Significances

We embark here on an exploration of one of the most difficult of terrains: investigation of the nature, variety, and extent of human knowledge; and the attempt to determine what that nature, variety, and extent have to tell us about teaching and learning. My share of this task is a specialized one and a preliminary one. It is simply to map that terrain. Later papers will explore the land itself.

What is meant by the structure of the disciplines? It means three things, three distinct but related sets of problems. Let us take a foretaste of all three together without discriminating them by name.

It has been widely supposed that there are indubitable grounds for recognizing basically different orders of phenomena, each requiring a different discipline for its investigation because of the differences in the character of the phenomena.

There are many different views based on such a premise. For example, many philosophers have insisted on a fundamental distinction between living phenomena and non-living, thus generating the notion that there are two fundamentally different sciences, the biological and the physiochemical. These two sciences were supposed to differ in method, in guiding conceptions, in the kind of knowledge produced, and in degree of certainty, differing to precisely the same extent that their subject matters were supposed to differ.

Another such view is generated by a distinction between man and nature, a distinction in which nature is conceived as bound by inexorable laws while men are in some sense and in some degree free. In this view, two major areas of investigation are again discriminated: on the one hand, science, concerned

Joseph J. Schwab, "Structures of the Disciplines: Meanings and Significances," in G. W. Ford and L. Pugno (eds.), *The Structure of Knowledge and the Curriculum* (Chicago: Rand McNally and Company, 1964), pp. 6–30. Reprinted by permission of Joseph J. Schwab.

Joseph J. Schwab (1909–) is William Rainey Harper Professor of Natural Sciences and professor of education at the University of Chicago. He has written widely on science education, curriculum, and higher education. His works include *The Teaching of Science as Inquiry* (coauthor) and *College Curriculum and Student Protest*.

with the inexorable laws that nature presumably obeys; and on the other hand, a discipline in the neighborhood of ethics and politics, which would investigate the freedom that man has and the ways in which men make their choices.

There is also a view that emphasizes the vast difference between the generality of "natural" phenomena (i.e., their predictability, the tendency of "natural" things to behave or be the same in instance after instance) and the particularity of human events (the essentially unique and nonrepeating character of acts notable in the behavior of man). Again, two widely different bodies of investigation and study are generated: science on the one hand and history on the other. Science, in this view, would seek the general laws that characterize the repeating behavior of natural things, while history would seek to determine the precise, unique events that characterized each life, each era, each civilization or culture that it studied. Hence, again, there would be two basically different curriculum components, differing in method, principle, and warrantability.

There have been similar separations of other disciplines, notably mathematics and logic. Mathematics was long ago seen to differ radically from other disciplines, including the sciences, in that its subject matter appeared to have no material existence. The objects of physical or biological enquiry could be seen, touched, smelled, tasted. The objects of mathematics could not. The plane, the line, the point, unity, number, etc. existed in some way which was not material or did not exist at all. This peculiarity of mathematical objects continues to be a puzzle. No one view of the nature of mathematics has been developed which is satisfactory to all concerned, though most moderns are agreed that mathematics differs radically from the other sciences.

Logic has been set apart because of its unique relationship to other disciplines rather than because of something peculiar about its subject matter To one degree or another, all other disciplines test the reliability of their conclusions by appealing to canons of reasoning and of evidence which are developed in the first place by the discipline of logic. Since logic is responsible for developing these canons, it cannot itself use them to check its own work. Logic thus stands as a sort of "queen of the sciences," dictating their rules but having for itself rules of some other and puzzling sort. Unlike the case of mathematics, this peculiarity of logic is no longer universally recognized. In some quarters, for example, it is held that logic does no more than formulate the methods and the canons of reasoning and of evidence which other sciences have developed, used, and bear witness to by their effectiveness. In this view, logic is not so much the queen of the sciences as their handmaiden.

Let us continue our foretaste of the problems of the structures of the disciplines by noting a peculiarity of the distinctions we have described. The peculiarity is that the differences among phenomena which appear at one period in the history of the disciplines to be radical and self-evident may at a later date disappear or become inconsequential as bases for differentiating disciplines. Take, for example, the differentiation of biology from the physical-chemical sciences. In early times and through the eighteenth century, fundamental differences between the living and the non-living could not be evaded. The living thing was "self-moving"; no other object was. The living thing reproduced itself; the living thing developed, had a personal history which no non-living thing could duplicate. Then, in the middle to late nineteenth century, some of these differences ceased to be notable, others disappeared entirely from human recognition. In this altered climate, the physiologist Claude Bernard pleaded for a study of living things strictly in terms of physics and chemistry. Since then, such an approach to living things has been so fruitful that it is now safe to say that it will be only a brief time before we shall synthesize living molecules in the laboratory. In recent years a still further shift in outlook has taken place: we now hear pleas from some physicists that certain physical phenomena be treated in much the way that living things were investigated *before* Bernard.

A similar shift is visible on a smaller scale in the history of the science of mechanics. Three hundred years ago the behavior of celestial bodies (the planets and the stars) and the behavior of terrestrial bodies in motion (things rolling on the surface of the earth and things thrown or propelled through the air) appeared to be radically different. Terrestrial bodies inevitably came to rest and fell to earth; celestial bodies inevitably continued in their regular motion without stop. Then, with Newton, these differences, though still visible, became entirely unimportant.

In brief, what we see of and in things changes from epoch to epoch. Differences that once appeared to be radical are seen later to be illusory or trivial; then, at another period, some of these differences reappear in a new guise. What can account for such changes in what appears to be objectively perceived? The answer is most easily exemplified in the case of mechanics, where in our own day the once radical difference between terrestrial and celestial bodies continues to be treated as illusory.

Granted that this difference was an illusion, what made the illusion disappear? The answer is this: Newton conceived an idea called universal gravitation. In the light of this idea, it became desirable and possible to examine the motion of the celestial bodies (in Newton's case, the moon) in a new way. Specifically, it became desirable and possible to measure the changing directions and changing velocities of the moon in such a fashion that it could be described as continually falling toward earth, while, at the same time, continually moving in a straight line at an angle to its fall. Thus its continuous orbit of the earth could be understood as the resultant of these two motions. In the same way it became possible to conceive of a terrestrial missile as falling to earth and coming to rest there only because its initial velocity in a straight line was not great enough to carry it straight forward beyond the bend of the earth before its fall brought it into contact with the earth. One could then see that as the initial velocity of a missile became greater and greater, it would not only go farther before it fell to earth, but at some point the increased velocity would be so great that the fall of the missile would be compensated by the falling away of the spherical surface of the earth. Such a missile would then become a satellite of the earth precisely like the moon. In brief, a new conception dictating new studies and a new way to interpret the data exhibited the movement of celestial bodies as nothing more than an extreme case of the motions of familiar terrestrial bodies moving at lower velocities.

In general, two collections of phenomena appear to be vastly different because we have used separate and distinct bodies of conceptions in studying them and discovering knowledge about them. Each such body of conceptions dictates what data we think we should seek, what experiments to perform, and what to make of our data by way of knowledge. If widely different conceptions are used to guide enquiries on two different collections of phenomena, we end inevitably with bodies of knowledge which exhibit few similarities and many differences. It is through the limiting or distorting lenses of these bodies of knowledge that we look at things. Hence, if the lenses distort or limit in different ways, we see things as different. The differences we see disappear if, but only if, a new conception is given birth which permits the study of both collections of phenomena in one set of terms and therefore makes for unity where diversity existed before.

Before we discriminate the problems of the structure of the disciplines, let us take note of a *caveat*. It is this: the integration of previously separate bodies of knowledge by new and unifying conceptions should not blind us to the possibility that some of the differences we recognize among phenomena may be genuine; some differentiation of disciplines may be perennial. There really may be joints in nature, a forearm, then an elbow, and then an upper arm. Science, ethics, and aesthetics may indeed represent three widely variant objects of enquiry. The doctrine of the unity of science, which insists on a unification of all knowledge, is either a dogma or a hope but not a fact. There are no data from which to conclude decisively that eventually all the disciplines will become or should become one.

Now let us step back and identify in this foretaste of knowledge and knowledge-seeking the three major but related sets of problems which define the area called structure of the disciplines.

Recall first our brief review of efforts to discriminate life from non-life, science from history, and so on. These efforts illustrate the first problem of the structure of the disciplines. It is the problem of determining the membership and organization of the disciplines, of identifying the significantly different disciplines, and of locating their relations to one another.

This set of problems is illustrated by the following questions. *Is* mathematical knowledge significantly different from knowledge of physical things?

If so, how are the behaviors of mathematical objects related to the behaviors of physical objects? That is, how must we account for the extraordinary usefulness of mathematics to the sciences? Is it because we impose mathematical forms on our observation of physical things, or is it because, in some mysterious way, the objects of the external world behave according to patterns that we discover through mathematical enquiry into our own intellects? Similarly, we might raise questions about practical knowledge and scientific or theoretical knowledge. Are they much the same or truly different? Is practical knowledge merely the application of science? Or does science take hold of ideal objects extrapolated from experience of things while practical knowledge must supply the bridge for return from scientific knowledge of such ideal objects to the actual and practicable? This set of problems may properly be called a problem of the structure of the disciplines, if we keep in mind that by the plural "disciplines" we refer to them collectively rather than distributively, while "structure" is singular and refers to the organization of the disciplines *inter se*.

The significance of this set of problems to education is obvious enough. To identify the disciplines that constitute contemporary knowledge and mastery of the world, is to identify the subject matter of education, the material that constitutes both its resources and its obligations. To locate the relations of these disciplines to one another is to determine what may be joined together for purposes of instruction and what should be held apart; these same relations will also weigh heavily in determining our decisions about the sequence of instruction, for it will tell us what must come before what, or what is most desirably placed first, or second, or third.

The second set of problems of the structure of the disciplines is exemplified by the tremendous role of the concept of universal gravitation in supplying us with a more nearly universal mechanics. A similar role is played by other conceptions in the attainment and formulation of all scientific knowledge. Embedded in the knowledge we have of the workings of the human body lies one or another concept of the nature of an organism, of the character of the parts of such an organism and how they relate to one another. Back of our knowledge of heredity lies a conception of particles behaving as do the terms in the expansion of a binomial to the second or higher powers. Back of our ability to make decisions in playing games lie similar conceptions. Again, the conceptions happen to be mathematical: the expansion of the binomial or a more complex mathematical structure derived by taking the expansion of the binomial to its limit. These mathematical conceptions provide us with a body of probability theory with which we play poker, determine tactics in battle, plan the production and sale of the products of our industries. Similarly, knowledge of human behavior, both individual and social, has arisen only as the men concerned with enquiry in psychology, sociology, and anthropology have developed conceptions that have enabled them to plan their researches.

In general then, enquiry has its origin in a conceptual structure, often mathematical, but not necessarily so. It is this conceptual structure through which we are able to formulate a telling question. It is through the telling question that we know what data to seek and what experiments to perform to get those data. Once the data are in hand, the same conceptual structure tells us how to interpret them, what to make of them by way of knowledge. Finally, the knowledge itself is formulated in the terms provided by the same conception. Thus we formulate and convey some of the knowledge we discover about the body in terms of organs and functions; we formulate and communicate our knowledge of atomic structure in terms of a concept of particles and waves; we formulate some of our knowledge of human personality in terms of psychic organs and their functions and other portions of it in terms of interpersonal relations.

In each science and in many arts such conceptual structures prevail. The second problem of the structure of the disciplines is to identify these structures and understand the powers and limits of the enquiries that take place under their guidance. Let us call this set of problems the problem of the *substantive* structures of each discipline.

Again, the significance of this problem of the structure of the disciplines to education is obvious enough—or at least one part of it is. For to know what structures underlie a given body of knowledge is to know what problems we shall face in imparting this knowledge. Perhaps the conceptual structure is no more complex than that involved in the discrimination of two classes of things by a single criterion, such as color or shape. In that case, we may suppose that little difficulty would be encountered in teaching this body of knowledge even to the very young. Perhaps the conceptual structure is more complex but so firmly embedded in common-sense knowledge of things that the child at some early, given age will already have encountered it and become familiar with it. In that case, we should, again, have little difficulty in imparting our knowledge, provided that we impart it at the right time in the development of the child in our culture. However, suppose the conceptual structure is both complex and largely unused in common-sense knowledge? This would be the case at the moment for the physical conception of a wave-like particle. In such a case, to locate and identify the conception is to locate and identify a difficult problem of instruction requiring much experiment and study.

A second curricular significance of the problem of the substantive structures of each discipline is less obvious. It concerns a peculiar consequence of the role of conceptual structures on our knowledge, a consequence little noted until recently. The dependence of knowledge on a conceptual structure means that any body of knowledge is likely to be of only temporary significance. For the knowledge which develops from the use of a given concept usually discloses new complexities of the subject matter which call forth new concepts. These new concepts in turn give rise to new bodies of enquiry and therefore, to new and more complete bodies of knowledge stated in new terms. The significance of this ephemeral character of knowledge to education consists in the fact that it exhibits the desirability if not the necessity for so teaching what we teach that students understand that the knowledge we possess is not mere literal, factual truth but a kind of knowledge which is true in a more complex sense. This in turn means that we must clarify for students the role of concepts in making knowledge possible (and limiting its validity) and impart to them some idea of the particular concepts that underlie present knowledge of each subject matter, together with the reasons for the appropriateness of these concepts and some hint of their limitations.[1]

The third problem of the structure of the disciplines we shall call the problem of the *syntactical* structure of the disciplines. This problem is hidden in the fact that if different sciences pursue knowledge of their respective subject matters by means of different conceptual frames, it is very likely that there will be major differences between one discipline and another in the way and in the extent to which it can verify its knowledge. There is, then, the problem of determining for each discipline what it does by way of discovery and proof, what criteria it uses for measuring the quality of its data, how strictly it can apply canons of evidence, and in general, of determining the route or pathway by which the discipline moves from its raw data through a longer or shorter process of interpretation to its conclusion.

Again, certain obvious consequences to education accrue from such a study. For, unless we intend to treat all knowledge as literal, true dogma, and thereby treat students as mere passive, obedient servants of our current culture, we want our students to know, concerning each body of knowledge learned, how sound, how dependable it is.

In summary then, three different sets of problems constitute the general problem of the structure of the disciplines. First there is the problem of the organization of the disciplines: how many there are; what they are; and how they relate to one another. Second, there is the problem of the substantive conceptual structures used by each discipline. Third, there is the problem of the syntax of each discipline: what its canons of evidence and proof are and how well they can be applied. Let us turn now to a brief investigation of each of these problems.

The Problem of the Organization of the Disciplines

With the problem of the organization of the disciplines we must face at once one of the inevitable complexities of this terrain, the fact that it does

[1] See Joseph J. Schwab, "Enquiry, the Science Teacher, and the Educator," *School Review*, LXVIII (Summer 1960), for an elaboration of this point.

not and cannot supply a single, authoritative answer to the question of what disciplines there are, how many there are and how they are related to one another. The reason for this complexity is fairly obvious. The problem of organization is a problem of classification primarily. If we classify any group of complex things, we are faced with a wide choice of bases of classification. (Even with postage stamps, we could classify by country of origin, by color, by shape or size, or by some combination of two or more of these.) Disciplines are very complex, hence the diversity and variety of available modes of classification are great. Consequently, depending on what one emphasizes about the disciplines, one or another or still a third or a fifth or a tenth classification of them is generated.

Four bases of classification of disciplines have always demanded attention: (1) their subject matter, what they aim to investigate, or work upon; (2) their practitioners, what competences and habits are required to carry on their work; (3) their methods (syntax), and modes of enquiry by which the enquirer brings himself to bear on the subject matter; (4) their ends, the kinds of knowledge or other outcomes at which they aim. Let us, then, examine a few organizations of the disciplines which use one or more of these, choosing them for the light they may throw on current curriculum problems.

The basic organization of the sciences proposed by Aristotle is worth taking a brief look at nowadays because we have tended to forget what it emphasizes. In this organization, Aristotle made most use of the end or aim of the disciplines together with the character of the materials they work on, the subject matter. Using these two as bases of classification, Aristotle distinguished three major groups of disciplines, the names of which have survived even in our current common-sense knowledge of the disciplines—though the significance assigned them has altered or been lost. The three basic divisions are the *Theoretical*, the *Practical*, and the *Productive*.

The theoretical disciplines are those whose aim is to know. For Aristotle, "to know" meant to know indubitably. Therefore, the theoretical disciplines included only those whose subject matters exhibited such inexorable regularity that they could be considered proper objects of "knowing" enquiry. Aristotle thought there were three such "knowing" or theoretical disciplines: physics, mathematics, and metaphysics. Today, though we would be very doubtful about the possibility of indubitable knowledge, we would, nevertheless, recognize a group of "theoretical" disciplines whose aim was to know and whose subject matters were such that the knowledge these disciplines sought was as nearly stable as knowledge can be. We would include the physical and biological sciences in this group. We would include substantial portions of the social sciences. We would exclude metaphysics as doubtful indeed. We would exclude mathematics, not because it is doubtful, but because we would consider it very special.

The practical disciplines, for Aristotle, included those concerned with choice, decision, and action based on deliberate decision. Precisely because its aim was to do, and therefore to alter the course of things, its subject matter had to have the property that was exactly opposite to the property required for the theoretical sciences. The subject matters of the practical sciences by necessity, must be not inexorable in their behavior, but capable of alteration, not fixed and stable but changeable.

It is exceedingly important, if we are to appreciate the bearing of this Aristotelian classification on modern problems, that we realize that "deliberate action" meant for Aristotle actions undertaken for their *own sakes* and not actions undertaken merely as the necessary preliminaries to some other end. Such actions, undertaken for their own sakes, constitute, then, what we mean by "a good life." They are the activities that stem from and express the best of which each man is capable. The practical sciences were (and are) therefore, ethics and politics. For us in modern times, ethics and politics would include not only each individual effort to lead and examine a deliberate life and the governing and policymaking in high places, but also the difficult and terrifying business of being parents, of being teachers *deliberately* and not as automatons, and the responsible work of administration and policymaking at all levels, together with those parts of the social sciences which contribute to such activities. I need not add that of all the things the schools might do, they do least of this. A few nursery schools, a very few teachers at the elementary level, and some few men and women at the college level give thought and time and energy toward evoking in their students the competencies and habits that lead to the making of good choices and good decisions and help the person to act in ways commensurate with his decisions. But by and large, the time, the energy, and the resources of our public schools ignore the very existence of practical disciplines in the Aristotelian sense.

The productive disciplines in the Aristotelian scheme are what the work "productive" suggests. They are the disciplines devoted to *making*: the fine arts, the applied arts; engineering. In connection with the significance of the Aristotelian productive disciplines for modern curriculum problems, let us note a principal characteristic of the entire Aristotelian organization: it emphasizes the sharp differences among the three groups of disciplines. The theoretical disciplines, devoted to knowing, concern themselves with those aspects of things which are fixed, stable, enduring. Hence, the theoretical disciplines are concerned with precisely these aspects of things which we cannot alter by making or make use of by doing. The productive disciplines are concerned with what is malleable, capable of being changed. The practical disciplines are concerned with another sort of malleability of human character, its ability to deliberate on its future and (within limits) to do as it sees fit.

We, on the other hand, have tended to fall into the habit of treating all disciplines proper to the schools as if they were theoretical. We manage to maintain this preoccupation in the case of the practical disciplines by ignoring them. In the case of the productive disciplines, we ignore them in some cases and in others resort to the trick of treating them as if they were theoretical. Music appreciation is taught as if its purpose were to recognize obvious themes of symphonies or concertos and proudly announce the opus number and the composer's name. Performing music is taught as if the aim were merely to follow the notes and obey the teacher's instructions about the score. Literature is taught as if dramas and novels were windows looking out on life, or worse, as if, as in the case of music appreciation, the object of the game were to know choice tidbits about the character, the life, or the times of the author. Art is taught, like literature, as if its aim were to provide a true, a faithful photograph of life. Happily, the exceptions to these strictures are increasing. Music appreciation is more and more being taught as a mastery of those arts by which the ear and the mind creatively take in the form and content of music. Performing music is more and more being taught in such a way that the students learn the grounds by which to discover and select from alternative interpretations of the score. Poetry, literature, and drama are more and more the objects of the kind of scrutiny which permits their appreciation as works of art rather than as sources of vicarious experience. More and more teachers of art permit their students the freedom for creation which society has long since accorded the professional artist. Nevertheless, the theorizing of the productive disciplines is still prevalent enough to render this warning relevant.

Let us turn to another organization of the sciences, notable in that one version of it is reborn with every undergraduate generation. This is Auguste Comte's positive hierarchy of the sciences. This scheme is based on the view that subject matter, and only subject matter, should provide the basis for classification. It takes the further view that subject matters should be ordered in terms of *their* subject matters; that is, Comte maintains that orders of phenomena can be discerned, each order consisting of members of the next lower order organized into more complex structures. Using this Chinese box conception of the world, Comte locates physical things as the simplest of all orders (presumably something like our modern fundamental particles). Chemicals come next, as consisting of physicals organized in a new way. Then come biologicals as still higher organizations of chemicals. Finally, at the top, come socials as organizations of biologicals. Thus the Comtian hierarchy of the sciences runs: physics, chemistry, biology, the social sciences. Then Comte adds one last factor. At the bottom of the entire structure he places another "science"—mathematics, mathematics conceived as a kind of natural logic governing the study of all the sciences above it.

Perhaps because of its simplicity and its tendency to be reborn in every generation, this particular organization of the disciplines has been one of the most tyrannical and unexamined curriculum principles in our time. It has dictated, I suspect, at least thirty-five per cent of all the sequences and orders of study of the sciences at the high school and college level in the country. The biologist tries to make his task easier by insisting that chemistry precede his subject field. In turn, the chemist demands that physics precede his. The physicist demands that mathematics precede physics. And each appeals to the Comtian hierarchy as the principal reason for his demand.

There is some justice in this view but there is injustice too. For it is quite possible to read the Comtian hierarchy the other way around. The inverted reading can indeed, be done without departing from Comte's own principles, as Comte himself well knew. The principle in question requires that each science in the hierarchy shall be well developed before the one above it can be developed. Thus an adequate sociology must wait upon thoroughly adequate biology; biology, in turn, cannot become complete until chemistry is complete, and so on. This *seems* to suggest that physics ought to be developed by a study simply of physical things, postponing chemistry until the study of physicals is complete; in the same way chemistry would be developed by a study of chemicals, postponing biology until the chemistry is complete. However, if we look closely at the basic Comtian principles, we realize that a complete, positive knowledge of the constituents and the organization of chemicals can be developed only if we have sought out and identified all the behaviors of which chemicals are capable. At this point arises the startling corollary that leads to an inverted reading of the Comtian hierarchy. For, clearly, if biologicals are organizations of chemicals, biologicals constitute the place in which some large array of chemical potentialities becomes real and can be seen. It follows, then, that a study of biologicals must precede any completion of chemistry; a study of socials must, in the same way, precede complete knowledge of biologicals, and so on.

The developments of science since the days of Comte most certainly bear out this reading of his hierarchy. Organic chemistry has developed only as we have studied the complex chemistry of the living organism. The behavior of the human individual has become better understood as we have studied culture and society. The development by physicists of adequate theories of atomic structure rests upon knowledge of chemicals. Thus we see that it is just as plausible to read the Comtian hierarchy downward from sociology through biology, chemistry, and physics to mathematics, as it is to read it upward from mathematics to physics, to chemistry, to biology, and finally to social science.

We cannot, then, rest our arguments for mathematics as prerequisite to physics, physics prerequisite to chemistry, and so on, on the assumption that the upward reading of the Comtian hierarchy constitutes an unequivocal curriculum principle. Rather, we might well argue that bits and portions of each of these alleged prerequisites should be taught as the need arises during the study of the higher sciences. For example, physics might well be taught by examining the obvious behaviors of physical things up to the point where it becomes clear to student and teacher alike that further progress in the physics requires mastery of certain mathematical conceptions or operations. At this point, the class would turn to the mastery of the mathematics required by the physics under study. In the same way, the complex study of the microchemistry of the living cell would not be taught as a prerequisite to study of the organism and its larger parts and functions; rather, the visible behaviors of the organism, of its organ systems and gross organs might well come first, with the biochemical materials so placed as to be meaningful to the students as the physio-chemical basis for the behaviors already known.

The curriculum sequence of prerequisites based on the upward reading of the Comtian hierarchy (i.e., mathematics to physics to chemistry, etc.) is often referred to as the "logical order" of instruction. The fact that the Comtian hierarchy can be read plausibly in either direction requires us to realize, however, that the phrase "logical order" applied only to one of them is a special pleading. Either order is "logical." The upward order from mathematics to the social sciences we might well call the dogmatic order, i.e., the order that runs from the current explanation to that which is explained. The downward order from, say, biology to chemistry, we might call the order of enquiry, i.e., the order that runs from a display of phenomena calling for explanation to the explanation the science has developed. A curriculum choice between the order of enquiry and the dogmatic order cannot be made on subject-matter criteria alone. Rather, we must look to the capacities of our students, to knowledge of ways in which learning takes place, and to our objectives, what we hope our students will achieve, in order to make our decision.

The Problem of the Syntax of the Disciplines

If all disciplines sought only to know and if the knowledge they sought were merely the simple facts, the syntax of the disciplines would be no problem. As we have seen, the disciplines are not this simple. Many are not, in the Aristotelian sense, theoretical at all: they seek ends that are not knowledge but something else—making, the appreciation of what is made, the arts and habits of deliberation, choice, and action. Those that are theoretical seek knowledge of different kinds (commensurate to their subject matters), hence use different methods and different canons of evidence and warrantability. For example, science seeks very general or even universal knowledge, while much history seeks the most detailed and particular knowledge. Each of these objects of enquiry poses problems peculiar to itself. Hence knowledge of each of them is sought in different ways. Even within the sciences there is much variability. Biologists find it necessary or desirable to seek knowledge in bits and pieces while physicists, at the other extreme, work hard to develop broad, comprehensive theories which embrace vast ranges of subject matter. The evidence that justifies the acceptance of an isolated bit of knowledge and the evidence that justifies the acceptance of a broad, comprehensive theory are of different sorts. There is a problem, therefore, of determining for each discipline or for small groups of disciplines what pathway of enquiry they use, what they mean by verified knowledge and how they go about this verification.

To illustrate this diversity, let us take three "things" that are asserted to exist and to have certain defining properties and behaviors. Let us take, first, an automobile, second, an electron, third, a neutrino. Let the three statements read as follows:

The automobile in front of the house is black.

The electron is a particle with a small mass and a negative electrical charge.

The neutrino is a particle with neither charge nor rest mass.

All three statements, let us suppose, are "true." That they are "true" in different senses becomes plain when we consider the following points. We say that the car in front of the house is black and say it with confidence on two bases. First, we look at the car and its neighborhood and report what we see. Second, we invite a colleague to look at the car and its neighborhood; we repeat the statement that reports what we saw; our colleague nods agreement. This, then, is a very simple syntax of discovery, requiring only a naive, private experience of the objects we propose to make statements about plus a transaction between ourself, another enquirer, and the same objects.

By contrast, the syntax that leads us to assert that the electron is a particle with a small mass and a negative electrical charge is far more complex. The statement most certainly does not rest on the fact that I have looked at an electron and that my colleague has also looked and nodded agreement. It cannot arise from such a syntax because the electron is not visible. It rests rather, on a syntax that involves looking at quite different things, seeking agreement about them, and then adding two further steps. We note certain phenomena; others note the same; then we seek an *explanation* for what we have seen. For explanation we conceive the existence of a minute particle. To it, we assign precisely the mass and precisely the magnitude and kind of charge which would permit this particle—if it existed—to give rise to the phenomena we have observed. The two additional steps are hidden in the additional process of seeking explanation. First, we conceive of something that would account for the phenomena we are concerned about. However, we are not satisfied to use just any conception that will account for it. Rather, we demand that the conception fulfill a second condition: that it fit in with, be coherent with, the rest of the body of knowledge that constitutes our science. In the case of our electron we meet this condition by choosing a particular mass and a particular charge as its important properties. The choice of a particular mass ties our electron to the entire body of physical knowledge called gravitational dynamics. The assignment of a certain electrical charge ties our particle to our knowledge of electricity and its dynamical laws.

The assertion about the neutrino rests on still a third kind of syntactical structure. For not only are neutrinos invisible by definition but they have been assigned a *lack* of such properties as charge and rest mass which characterize the electron. The assigned lack of such properties means that in the ordinary course of events the behavior of neutrinos would have no detectable consequences, would give rise to no phenomena such as we observed and accounted for by positing the existence of the electron. Instead, the ground for positing the existence of the neutrino was roughly as follows: certain effects were found in a phenomenon called beta decay which appeared to be exceptions to certain of the so-called conservation laws, laws that formed part of the very foundation of the body of physical knowledge. One way to account for these beta decay phenomena would be to treat them as "disproofs" of these conservation laws. Another way would have been to treat the decay phenomena as exceptions to the conservation laws and then to dream up an ad hoc explanation for the exception. Physicists preferred, however (for reasons I shall not go into now), to keep the conservation laws intact and universal, and the only conceived alternative enabling them to retain these laws was to suppose the existence of a well-nigh undetectable particle that carried off the quantities whose disappearance would otherwise have called the conservation laws into question.

We have here, then, three different senses in which statements are said to be "true" or warranted, differences of sense not revealed by the statements themselves. The statements are all of the same form—the automobile is black, the neutrino is such and such, the electron is something else. Only the context, the structure of problem, evidence, inference, and interpretation which constitutes the syntax of discovery behind each statement, would reveal to us the different senses in which each is true.

The significance of this variety of modes of enquiry, of patterns of discovery and verification, lies in this: most statements of most disciplines are like the single words of a sentence. They take their most telling meanings, not from their dictionary sense, not from their sense in isolation, but from their context, their place in the syntax. The meaning of $F = MA$ or of free fall, of electron or neutrino, is understood properly only in the context of the enquiry that produced them.

This need for context of enquiry wherewith to make teaching and learning clear has been almost universally overlooked because of a singular failure in the subject-matter preparation of teachers. They have been permitted to assume, or, indeed, have been flatly told, that "induction" or "scientific method" stands for something simple, single, and well defined. Quite the contrary is true: "induction" is not the name for some single, definite process but merely an honorific word attached by various philosophers to whatever mode of enquiry they favor. To a few philosophers, "induction" means the process of simple enumeration of a large number of instances of something or other by which we try to discern what is common among them. In this view, the outcome of "induction" is "generalization." To other philosophers, "induction" means the analysis of phenomena into unit events and the attempt to find out which events invariably precede which others. To still others, "induction" means the attempt to conceive ideas, however remote they may be from the possibility of direct verification, which will "explain," "account for," "embrace," the largest possible variety of phenomena with the greatest economy.

The Problem of the Substantive Structures of the Disciplines

Let us first redevelop the idea of substantive structures and their role in enquiry as sketched in our introduction.

The fact that we propose to investigate a given subject is to admit that we are, in large part, ignorant of it. We may have some superficial knowledge: we may have dealt with the subject matter as part of our round of practical problems; but the very fact that we propose to investigate the subject means that we mistrust our knowledge or consider it entirely inadequate. Thus, enquiry begins in virtual ignorance. Ignorance however, cannot originate an enquiry. Subjects complex enough to demand enquiry are subjects that confound us by the great variety of characteristics, qualities, behaviors, and interactions they present to our view. This richness paralyzes enquiry, for it is far too much to handle all at once and, in our ignorance, we have no way of discerning the greater from the lesser fact; we cannot discriminate the facts that are most "telling" about our subject matter from those that are trivial. In short, if data are to be collected, we must have some sort of guide to relevance and irrelevance, importance and unimportance.

This role of guide to the enquiry is played by a conception borrowed or invented by the enquirer. These conceptions constitute the substantive structures of a discipline.

Let us take, as an example of a primitive beginning of enquiry, the situation that prevailed in the study of animal behavior some sixty years ago. Our knowledge of the behavior of small aquatic animals at that time was no greater than might have been possessed by an alert, small boy who had watched the darting of fish, the play of tadpoles, and the movements of insect larvae in the ponds and streams of his farm. What, then, should we investigate about these dartings, movements, and plays? Should we ask what needs they serve? Perhaps. Yet we do not even know that needs are involved. Shall we ask what purposes the animals have in mind? We do not know whether they have purposes or not. Shall we then try to discover the patterns of these motions, the order in which they occur? The trouble with this is that when a vast number of movements are involved, we must suppose, by analogy to ourselves, that they do not all belong together. Hence the over-all order of them would be meaningless. Yet we cannot discern each coherent sub-group of motions because we do not yet know either the beginnings ("wants," "needs," "stimuli") or their terminations ("goals," "needs satisfied," "terminal response").

This frustration of enquiry was resolved by appealing to the then popular view that all things, including living things, were no more than simple machines, the pattern of which was simple the one known to nineteenth-century physics. This idea of a simple machine was applied to the study of behavior by supposing that every movement through space of an animal was a response to some single, specific stimulating factor in the environment. It was further supposed that each such stimulated response could be one of only two possible kinds—a movement toward the stimulus or a movement away from it. Such a movement was dubbed a "tropism," "taxis"; movements toward the stimulus being called positive, those away from the stimulus, negative.

This naive and now obsolete conception removed the frustration of enquiry by giving us questions to ask. We were to determine for each organism what stimuli it responded to and whether it responded in the positive or negative sense. These identified questions in turn determined the pattern of experiment. We were to place our aquatic organism in a tank of water, make sure that all physical stimuli but one were uniform throughout the tank, let one stimulus, light, for example, be of high intensity at one end of the tank and low intensity at the other, and then note, as our important datum, which way the animal went. Then our knowledge of animal behavior was to be summed up in a catalogue of negative and positive tropisms characteristic of each species investigated.

Similar naive conceptions enabled us to begin enquiry in other complex fields. Chemistry was able to make great advances in the study of the array of substances of the world by imposing on them the notion of "element." By "element" was meant a substance of ultimate simplicity, a substance made only of itself and incapable of being changed into another such simple substance. This conception dictated the questions to be asked of matter by chemists and the patterns of experiment. The fundamental question was: into what simpler substance can this substance be decomposed? Hence the patterns of experiment were analysis and synthesis. Similar "elements" were devised to guide our earliest enquiries into human personality. We conceived of each human person as consisting of a greater or lesser quantity of each of a number of "traits." Like the chemical elements, each such "trait" (such as courage, imagination, logical reasoning, assiduity) was supposed to be simple (made of no further sub-traits) and independent of all other traits.

The substantive principles chosen to guide enquiry are controlled by two opposing criteria. One of these I shall call reliability. Reliability requires that the guiding principle be free of vagueness and ambiguity, that the referents of its terms have unequivocal location and limit, and that the measurements or manipulations of these referents can be made precisely and can be repeated with uniform results. The substantive structures cited as examples above meet this criterion as well as could be expected.

They do not, however, satisfactorily fulfill the second criterion, which I shall call validity. Note the failure in each case which illustrates the lack of adequate validity. Animal behavior is reduced to a catalogue of independent responses to independently acting stimuli. Yet our knowledge of ourselves and of higher animals makes it highly unlikely that any animal's behavior will be a repertory of separate and independent responses to stimuli. It is much more likely (we suspect) that previous responses modify later ones and that the responses to two stimuli presented simultaneously will *not* be the algebraic sum of the responses to each when presented separately. The idea of simple and independent traits, which enable us to make a start on a study of human personality, is similarly questionable. It is entirely likely that traits are not independent at all but, rather, affect one another. Further, traits may not be fixed quantities but products of experience, changing as our experience grows and changes. Indeed, it may be that a much richer and more complete understanding of human personality could be achieved by doing away entirely with a notion of traits in any form. The notion of chemical element and compound in its most primitive form we may also suspect to be highly incomplete. It supposes that the properties of a compound arise simply by juxtaposition or union of two or more elements. Yet our experience in art, architecture, and engineering tells us that it is not only the constituents of a compound which confer properties on the compound but the organization of these constituents as well.

In short, the criterion of validity asks that the data we use be not only reliable but representative. It asks that the substantive structure that points to these data as the appropriate data of enquiry reflect as much as possible of the richness and complexity of the subject matter to which it is applied.

The existence of these two criteria is important to us because they lead to two characteristics of knowledge which, in turn, have important implications for curriculum. In the first place, the play of these two criteria confer on scientific knowledge a distinctly revisionary character. In the second place, in some sciences the same interplay leads to the concurrent development of a number of bodies of knowledge of the same subject matter.

The revisionary character of scientific knowledge accrues from the continuing assessment and modification of substantive structures. As investigations proceed under the guidance of an early, naive structure, we begin to detect inconsistencies in our data and disparities between our conclusions and the behavior of our subject. These inconsistencies and disparities help us identify the invalidities in our conception. Meanwhile, the naive structure has enabled us nevertheless to gain some knowledge of our subject and to sharpen our techniques for study. Our new knowledge of the subject, our improved techniques, and our sharpened awareness of inadequacies in our substantive structures enable us to conceive new structures more complex than the old, more adequate to the richness of the subject matter. With the advent of a new structure, the knowledge contained in the older conceptions, though "right" enough in its own terms, is rendered obsolete and replaced by a new formulation which puts old facts and new ones together in more revealing ways.

While different substantive structures tend to succeed one another in physics, chemistry, and biology, other disciplines are characterized by the concurrent utilization of several sets of structures. In the recent study of human personality, for example, two bodies of knowledge competed in the market place at the same time. One body of knowledge had been developed by conceiving personality, after the analogy of the body, as consisting of psychic organs. The other body of knowledge had been developed by conceiving of personalities as arising from the need of persons for one another, as developing, for better or for worse, out of the experience of self and of others. Personality, this body of knowledge held, is best described in terms of the various relations the self can establish with others.

Such a pluralism of substantive structures and of bodies of knowledge is characteristic of the social sciences generally and of many humane studies. There is more than one body of economic knowledge; different anthropologists and different sociologists tackle their problems in different terms and in different ways; different critics use widely different conceptions of the art object in the analysis and evaluation of drama, poetry, music, and painting.

The curricular significances of the revisionary character of knowledge and the plural character of knowledge are too numerous to develop fully here. Let us be satisfied with three.

In the first place, both characteristics point to the danger of a purely dogmatic, inculcative curriculum. If we dogmatically select one of several bodies of theory in a given field and dogmatically teach this as the truth about its subject matter, we shall create division and failure of communication among our citizens. Students of different school systems in different regions who are dogmatically taught different histories of crucial moments in our nation's development are an obvious case in point. It is no less divisive, however, if our future citizens are barred from sharing enjoyment of literature and the arts by having been the victims of different dogmas, or barred from understanding each other by having been inculcated with different dogmatic views of the roots of human action or the origins of culture and civilization. The alternative is to avoid indoctrination. We may, if we like, choose but one of several pluralities of bodies of knowledge. But if we do, let it be taught in such a way that the student learns what substantive structures gave rise to the chosen body of knowledge, what the strengths and limitations of these structures are, and what some of the alternative structures are which give rise to alternative bodies of knowledge.

The revisionary character of knowledge assumes curriculum significance because revisions now take place so rapidly that they will probably occur not once but several times in the lives of our students. If they have been taught their physics, chemistry, or biology dogmatically, their discovery that revision has occurred can lead only to bewilderment and disaffection. Again, the alternative is the teaching of scientific knowledge in the light of the enquiry that produced it. If students discover how one body of knowledge succeeds another, if they are aware of the substantive structures that underlie our current knowledge, if they are given a little freedom to speculate on the possible changes in structures which the future may bring, they will not only be prepared to meet future revisions with intelligence but will better understand the knowledge they are currently being taught.

22 / ARNO A. BELLACK

The Structure of Knowledge and the Structure of the Curriculum

During the current period of curriculum reform, most of the debate hinges on an old and familiar question: "What shall the schools teach?" This is a perennial question, one that apparently every generation has to solve over again for itself in the light of changing conditions and changing needs. And it is a question that can be answered only by reference to one's view of the nature of knowledge, for by universal agreement knowledge is the stock-in-trade of the school. Few would deny that the fields of organized inquiry are significant aspects of our culture that the school is uniquely equipped to introduce to students.

Arno A. Bellack, "The Structure of Knowledge and the Structure of the Curriculum," in *A Reassessment of the Curriculum* (New York: Bureau of Publications, Teachers College, Columbia University, 1964), pp. 25–40. Reprinted by permission.

Arno A. Bellack (1919–) is professor of education at Teachers College, Columbia University. He has written extensively in the field of curriculum and is coauthor of *The Language of the Classroom.*

But there is also general agreement that the school's responsibility extends beyond teaching the organized fields of learning and inquiry; the school must also serve a multitude of ends and needs created by our society and our culture. At different times in the history of our schools widely different views have been held regarding the way in which knowledge should be organized and taught to meet these ends and needs. The traditionalists, for example, taught the time-honored subjects as anthologies of separate topics, with the hope that the bits and pieces of information would somehow or other turn out to be useful in the lives of their students. History became a recital of "one damned thing after another" (the phrase is Toynbee's), civics turned out to be a collection of miscellaneous information about government, and geography was nothing more than a catalogue of facts about places scattered over the globe.

Convinced that this kind of teaching would not prepare students to face the increasingly complex problems of their society, the progressive reformers of the 1930's and '40's proposed a new curriculum—one centered on the personal and social problems of youth and drawing on the academic disciplines as they became relevant to the problems under study. The disciplines were viewed as reservoirs from which facts and ideas could be drawn as needed; emphasis was on the *practical* ordering of knowledge with reference to problems to be solved.

Contemporary efforts to redefine the role of knowledge in the curriculum place emphasis on the *logical* order inherent in knowledge itself, on the structure of concepts and principles of inquiry that characterize the various fields of learning. Whereas formerly factual and descriptive content was stressed, now the emphasis is on basic concepts and methods which scholars use as intellectual tools to analyze and order their data.

Several claims are made for teaching the fundamental structures of the disciplines, two of which are of central importance and are worth considering here. The first is that understanding of fundamental ideas is the main road to adequate transfer of training. Professor Bruner, who is largely responsible for introducing the concept of structure into educational discourse, observes that

> knowledge is a model we construct to give meaning and structure to regularities in experience. The organizing ideas of any body of knowledge are inventions for rendering experience economical and connected. We invent concepts such as force in physics, the bond in chemistry, motives in psychology, style in literature as means to the end of comprehension. . . . The power of great organizing concepts is in large part that they permit us to understand and sometimes to predict or change the world in which we live. But their power lies also in the fact that ideas provide instruments for experience.

Therefore, he contends, "the structure of knowledge—its connectedness and its derivations that make one idea follow another—is the proper emphasis in education."[1]

The second important claim for emphasis on structure is that by constantly re-examining material taught in the schools for its fundamental patterns of organization, the schools will be able to narrow the gap between "advanced" knowledge and "elementary" knowledge. Since scholars at the forefront of their disciplines are able to make the greatest contribution to the substantive reorganization of their fields, current curriculum projects place great emphasis on the participation of university researchers in continuing revision of the program of studies. Scholars in the various disciplines and their professional organizations have in recent years made proposals for revamping the curriculum in elementary and secondary schools—first in mathematics, physics, chemistry, and biology; then in English; and recently and belatedly in economics, geography, anthropology, and history.

The focus of attention in each of these projects is an individual discipline. Little or no attention is given to the relationships of the individual fields to each other or to the program of studies within which they must find their place. National committees in the fields of chemistry, physics, and biology have proceeded independently of each other. The projects in economics, geography, and anthropology are unrelated to one another or to the other social sciences. Only in mathematics has there been a disposition to view the field as a whole, but this is a reflection of developments within the discipline of mathematics at the highest levels of scholarship.

The situation developing in the elementary and secondary schools thus begins to reflect, at least to some degree, the state of affairs in the universities with respect to the development and organization of knowledge, which Professor John Randall has described in this way:

As reflected in the microcosm of the modern university, the world of knowledge has today become radically plural. It is a world of many different knowledges, pursued in varied ways to diverse ends. These many inquiries are normally carried on with little thought for their relation to each other. The student of John Donne's poetry, the student of the structure of the atom—each gives little enough attention to what the others are doing, and none at all to any total picture of anything. Each has his own goals, his own methods, his own language for talking about what he is doing and what he has discovered. Each seems happiest when left to his own devices, glad indeed if he can keep others from treading on his toes. Each is convinced that what he himself is doing is worth while. But none has too much respect for the

[1] Jerome Bruner, *On Knowing* (Cambridge, Mass., Harvard University Press, 1962), p. 120.

others, though he is willing enough to tolerate them. They have all little understanding of each other's pursuits—what they are trying to do, how they are doing it, and what they really mean when they talk about it.[2]

I emphasize this pluralism in the academic world not to deplore it but to call attention to the problem that it presents for those who are concerned with the organization of the entire curriculum. For the curriculum builder is concerned not only with the structures of the individual disciplines, but also with the structure of the instructional program within which the fields of knowledge find their place. The problem can be very simply stated, if not easily solved: What general structure of the curriculum can be developed so that autonomy of the parts does not result in anarchy in the program as a whole? This is the question I propose to discuss briefly here.

When one looks beyond the structure of the individual disciplines and asks about the structure of the curriculum, attention is focused on *relationships* among the various fields that comprise the program of studies. For just as relationships among ideas is at the heart of the concept of structure as applied to the individual disciplines, so relationships among the disciplines is at the heart of the notion of structure as applied to the curriculum as a whole.

The mathematics teacher, the science teacher, the music teacher, and so on through the list of specialized functionaries in the school—each tends typically to interpret the entire program of the school through his own specialized teaching field. This is probably inevitable, and it would not be undesirable except for one stubborn fact: each of the specialized aspects of the program deals with human beings, and since human beings are not infinitely plastic in adapting to particular situations, it follows that what goes on at one place in the system sets limiting conditions for the accomplishments of purposes elsewhere in the system. Hence the importance of giving attention not only to connections between ideas in an individual field, but also to relationships among the fields of knowledge included in the curriculum.

There are many ways in which one can conceive of these interconnections. I should like to focus attention on three types of relationships that obtain (or *ought* to obtain) among the teaching fields that comprise the curriculum:

(1) *Relationships among cognate or allied disciplines that deal with similar problems or phenomena.* Here I have in mind, for example, relations among the social sciences, whose common objective is to describe and explain the social and cultural behavior of man; and connections among the natural sciences, whose common aim is to describe and explain physical and biological phenomena.

(2) *Relationships among the broad areas of knowledge—the sciences and mathematics on the one hand, and the humanities on the other.* Call to mind

[2] John H. Randall, Jr., "The World to be Unified," in Lewis Leary, ed., *The Unity of Knowledge* (Garden City, N.Y., Doubleday and Company, 1955), p. 63.

the problem raised by C. P. Snow in his *The Two Cultures and the Scientific Revolution*, the great gulf that lies between the literary world and the scientific world. Snow insists that the only way to close the gap between the two cultures is by rethinking our education.

(3) *Relationships of knowledge to human affairs.* Given the current emphasis on the role of organized knowledge in the curriculum, we do well to remind ourselves that the goal of general education is not to train students as specialists in mathematics, geography, biology, or whatever other subjects they might study. Rather, the goal is to make available to students the intellectual and aesthetic resources of their culture in such a way that they become guides for intelligent action and help students create meaning and order out of the complex world in which they find themselves.

Let us briefly examine these three types of relationships.

I. Relationships Among Allied Disciplines

According to long and honorable tradition, knowledge is grouped for pedagogical purposes in four major categories—the natural sciences, the social sciences, mathematics, and the humanities (the latter an omnibus term that includes art, literature, philosophy, and music). These broad groupings of organized disciplines are generally recognized as basic cultural interests of our society which constitute both the resources and the obligations of the schools. Each major field represents distinctive methods and conceptual schemes in which the world and man are viewed from quite different vantage points. Instruction in these areas has as its primary goal equipping students with key concepts and methods that inform and sustain intelligent choice in human affairs.

Although the four major areas of knowledge are generally recognized as important components of the curriculum, they are not currently used as the context or framework for curriculum building. Instead, as we have already noted, recent curriculum projects have focused attention on individual disciplines without concern for their relationships to allied fields. Thus the economists, the geographers, and the anthropologists have proceeded independently of each other, as have the biologists, chemists, and physicists. To be sure, economists suggest ways in which economic ideas can be taught in history; and anthropologists show how some of their generalizations can be woven into courses in geography. This is all to the good; it even seems to suggest that integration of a limited variety might be appropriate for teaching purposes. But scant attention is given to building a curriculum design within which the individual fields might find their place.

It is my contention that this approach has certain inherent shortcomings and that we would do well to shift the context for curriculum planning from the individual disciplines, as is now the vogue, to the broad groupings of knowledge represented by the natural sciences, the social sciences, mathematics, and the humanities. Let us briefly consider some of the problems involved in curriculum building in the social sciences to show why this proposed shift is desirable and necessary.

The social sciences—economics, social psychology, political science, sociology, anthropology, geography, and history—are all seeking explanations of the same phenomenon, man's social life. This common goal is what makes it reasonable to group them together as the *social* sciences. All of them have grown out of man's attempt to interpret, understand, and control the social environment. But each field formulates its own questions about this subject matter and develops its own system of concepts to guide its research. The economist is preoccupied with the concept of scarcity, the political scientist with the concepts of power and authority, the anthropologist with the notion of culture, and the sociologist with social functions and social systems. Each science is thus abstract, dealing with only certain facets of actual social relationships and institutions—facets that do not permit of physical separation but only of analytical separation.

Man's social life as it is actually lived is therefore far more complex than the limited image of it reflected in the concepts and generalizations of any one of the social disciplines. It follows then, as Professor Kingsley Davis has suggested, that "in so far as the prediction of actual events is concerned, the various social sciences are mutually interdependent, because only by combining their various points of view can anything approaching a complete anticipation of future occurrences be achieved."[3] Policies that are proposed and actions that are taken to deal with problems in social affairs are of necessity interdisciplinary, for concrete social reality is not mirrored in the findings of any one discipline.

Now this is a matter of central importance to those whose job it is to plan and organize the social studies curriculum. To focus exclusive attention on certain aspects of the social world as seen through the eyes of one or two of the social sciences is to give students a myopic vision of man's social behavior and his institutions. To shape children's conceptions of the social world through exclusive emphasis on the language of the economist, for example, to the exclusion of the language of the sociologist, political scientist, anthropologist, and historian is to determine that they shall interpret human affairs principally in terms which the economist uses to view reality—in terms of supply, demand, scarcity, production, and consumption.

Students must be helped to see the limitations as well as the uses of a single discipline in interpreting events as they actually occur. And for anything approaching a comprehensive view of man's functioning in society, the

[3] *Human Society* (New York, The Macmillan Company, 1948), p. 8.

specialized perspectives of all the social sciences are needed. Curriculum builders in the social studies have the enormously difficult job of providing a place in their programs for all the social sciences, each of which contributes its distinctive perspective on human institutions and human behavior.

It is clear that such a program can be developed only on the basis of collaboration among the various social sciences. Such collaboration does not presuppose a "unified social science" as the basis for planning the elementary and secondary school curriculum. Quite the opposite is the case. For the social disciplines today are characterized by a plurality of methods and conceptual schemes developed by social scientists to deal with problems within their individual spheres. Instead of a unity of method or a single universe of discourse, we find a vast confederation of separate areas of study. Modes of thinking and analysis differ from field to field, and even from problem to problem within the same field. In time, a Bacon of the sciences that bear on the social and cultural behavior of man may emerge, but that time is not yet.

At the same time, in spite of increasing specialization and internal differentiation, there are interconnections among the social sciences that curriculum planning for the schools should take into account. For example, the various social sciences borrow rather handily from each other when it comes to both concepts and methods. Historians make use of concepts from all the other social sciences. Political scientists interested in political socialization get their methods from behavioral scientists and seem in many respects more closely related to sociologists and social psychologists than to fellow political scientists. Certain anthropologists have utilized the Freudian view of human development in analyzing patterns of various cultures. Geographers make extensive use of the perspectives of history and concepts developed by all the behavioral sciences.

Furthermore, we find not only interchange of concepts and methods but growing collaboration among specialists. For example, studies of the nature and function of "authority" are now undertaken jointly by political scientists and sociologists, and there have been recent studies conducted by economists in collaboration with anthropologists to determine whether certain economic theories hold for different types of economic systems. The convergence of social scientists upon the same problems has given rise to what Professor Robert Merton calls "interdisciplines," such as social biology, political sociology, and sociological history.

The picture that emerges from this cursory review of the current state of affairs in the social sciences is one of great diversity. Given this mosaic of disciplines and interdisciplines, each characterized by multiple conceptual schemes and methods, the curriculum builder is faced with the problem of developing structures for teaching that relate the social sciences to each other in meaningful ways and avoid undue fragmentation of knowledge.

What has been said about the social sciences applies in principle to the natural sciences, mathematics, and the humanities. The significant point is that there is a need for a broader context for curriculum planning than the separate disciplines, and the broad fields of knowledge furnish a useful framework for this purpose. I am not calling for indiscriminate scrambling of superficial knowledge. Indeed, at this point we would do well to suspend judgment as to when in the school program teaching should be organized around the individual disciplines, and when around the broad groupings of the disciplines. In all likelihood, different patterns or organization will be found to be appropriate for different levels of the school program. Dewey's notion of the "progressive organization of knowledge," long ignored by most of his interpreters, might serve as a guiding hypothesis in planning the sequence of the program through the elementary and secondary school years.

In sum, scholars in the natural sciences, the social sciences, mathematics, and the humanities should now be invited to join in the search for new structures for teaching—structures that respect the integrity of the individual fields and at the same time help these fields find their place in a pattern of studies that provides a substantial measure of coherence and relatedness for the program as a whole.

II. Relationships among Broad Fields of Knowledge

There is not only the question of relationships among disciplines that deal with similar problems or phenomena, but also the question of the relationships among the broad areas of knowledge—the sciences and mathematics on the one hand, and the humanities on the other. The growing separation and lack of effective communication between the arts and sciences have been widely noted and greatly deplored. C. P. Snow's analysis of this situation in terms of the two cultures of the literary intellectuals and the scientists is well known to all of us. That this state of affairs should somehow be remedied is the theme of many earnest discussions. The upshot of the discussion is usually that there is one way out of all this: it is, as Snow suggests, by rethinking our education.

But how shall the school go about bridging the gulf between the literary and aesthetic and the scientific studies? It seems reasonable to inquire first of all if human knowledge in its many dimensions forms a recognized unity within which the fields of inquiry and creativity fall neatly into place. Is there a sense in which all knowledge is one, with the arts and the sciences having a place in a unity of fundamental principles or basic methods of inquiry?

The progressives, taking their cue from Dewey, found for themselves such a unity in the "scientific method" (or the "method of intelligence," as it was frequently labeled) that was assumed to characterize all types of rational, intelligent activity in academic pursuits and in artistic and practical affairs as well. The problem-solving method came to be viewed as the basic ingredient in programs of general education.

But by no means is there agreement among scientists that there is a single all-encompassing set of procedures, even in the natural sciences, as assumed by those who talk about *the* scientific method. There seems to be little warrant for assuming that there is one overarching method sufficiently flexible and inclusive to deal with problems in the various scientific fields, to say nothing of the arts, crafts, and applied areas. Indeed, as we have already noted, the intellectual world today is characterized by a plurality of methods and conceptual schemes developed by the disciplines to deal with problems within their individual spheres. Analysis of the various disciplines reveals a wide range of organizations and intellectual methods associated with them. Instead of a unity of method or a single universe of discourse, we are confronted with a vast confederation of separate areas of study. Modes of analysis differ from field to field, and even from problem to problem within the same field.

The heterogeneous character of the intellectual resources that are a part of the culture is a fact of major significance for the curriculum builder. We would do well frankly to recognize this and make a place in our programs for the variety of logical orders that characterize the fields of knowledge on which we draw in building the curriculum.

But what then of the relationships among the various fields of creativity and inquiry? Is it perhaps possible, in spite of the variety of logical orders characteristic of knowledge in its various branches, to identify the principal kinds of cognitive operations or modes of thinking that characterize man's intellectual activities?

A proposal to facilitate students' insight into relationships among the various fields of knowledge by introducing them to the "principal modes of intellectual activity" comes from Professor Peterson of Oxford University. In making suggestions for the reform of secondary education in Britain, Peterson urges educators to stop thinking of general education in terms of "general knowledge":

"It is not a sign that a man lacks general education if he does not know the date of The Treaty of Utrecht, the latitude of Singapore, the formula for nitro-glycerine or the author of the *Four Quartets*. It does denote a lack of general education if he cares nothing for any of the arts, confuses a moral judgment with an aesthetic judgment, interprets the actions of Asian political leaders in terms of nineteenth-century English parliamentarianism or believes that the existence of God has been scientifically disproved."[4]

Peterson urges therefore that the British secondary schools devise programs

[4] Oxford University Department of Education, *Arts and Sciences Sides in the Sixth Form* (Abingdon-Berkshire, The Abbey Press, 1960), p. 13.

of general education not in terms of wide general knowledge, but in terms of development in the main modes of intellectual activity, of which he identifies four: the logical (or the analytic), the empirical, the moral, the aesthetic. These different modes of thought are associated with different uses of language. For example, the empirical mode has to do with statements about the world based on our experience of it. The analytic mode has to do with statements that do not describe the world of fact, but rather tell us how the meanings of symbols are related to one another logically. (A definition is a special case of analytic sentences.) The moral and the aesthetic modes are concerned with statements of preferences, evaluations, and judgments of the good and the evil, the beautiful and the ugly, the desirable and the undesirable.

Any one discipline gives opportunity for the development of more than one mode of thought, and each mode can be developed through more than one of the disciplines. For example, literature can contribute to the development of both moral and aesthetic judgment. Mathematics and philosophy both contribute to the development of the analytic mode. History has probably the widest range of any discipline, for the historian employs all four modes in constructing his comprehensive interpretation of what happened in the past.

If the students are to gain understanding of the similarities and differences among the fields of knowledge, the different modes of mental activity must be made explicit to them:

"They must have time and guidance in which to see that what is a proof in the Mathematics they pursue on Tuesday is not the same kind of thing as a proof in History, which follows on Wednesday; that the truth of George Eliot or Joseph Conrad is not the same thing as the truths of Mendel or Max Planck; and yet that there are similarities as well as differences."[5]

Peterson accordingly suggests that in addition to giving attention to these varying modes of thought in the subject fields, the secondary program include a special course in which these ways of thinking are the object of study. One important aspect of such teaching has to do with ways in which these modes of thought are verified. Verification is particularly significant in that it is the guide to meaning of the various types of thought. For example, empirical statements are verified by tests conducted in terms of experience, whereas moral statements are verified by reference to criteria or principles of judgment. On the other hand, analytic statements depend for their truth on an agreed upon set of rules, and follow logically from accepted definitions.

Thus far I have suggested that in structuring the curriculum with due regard for the relationships among the fields of knowledge we view knowledge from two complementary perspectives. In the first, emphasis is on the conceptual schemes and methods of inquiry associated with the broad fields

[5] *Ibid.*, p. 18.

of knowledge, the natural sciences, the social sciences, mathematics, and the humanities. In the second, attention is focused on modes of thought—the analytic, the empirical, the aesthetic, and the moral—that transcend the boundaries of the individual fields. These two views thus present mutually reinforcing conceptions of knowledge that serve well as the basis for curriculum planning.

Professor Toulmin has coined two terms that might be helpful in clarifying the relationships between these two views of knowledge. He distinguishes between "participant's language" and "onlooker's language."[6] Participant's language is the language used by members of a professional group or discipline as they carry on their work in their specialized field. Hence we talk today about the language of science, the language of psychology, the language of mathematics, and even the language of education. In the context of our discussion, participant's language has to do with the language systems that are the distinguishing characteristics of the various disciplined areas of study such as the sciences, mathematics, and the humanities.

Now if we want to examine or talk about the language we use in any one of these fields, we must use another level of discourse. We must, in Toulmin's terms, use onlooker's language. For example, it was suggested that students need help in understanding that a proof in mathematics is not the same as a proof in science or that the "truth" of a scientist is not the same as the "truth" of the poet or novelist. To make these comparisons and contrasts we need a language system that enables us to look at these various areas of study from the outside, as it were. The principal modes of thought—the analytic, the empirical, the moral, and the aesthetic—furnish us with language tools that are useful for this purpose. Hence their importance in teaching.

III. Relationships of Knowledge to Human Affairs

That the schools ought to provide students with the means for intelligent action is not a new or controversial idea. When, however, it comes to deciding what to teach and how to teach to accomplish this goal, we find marked differences of opinion.

Is it sufficient in general education, for example, to have students learn how to think like physicists, historians, or economists? I think not. For the economist *as* economist (to mention just one field) is in no position to prescribe courses of action regarding the host of public policy issues we face, and questions of public policy and decision loom large in general education. To be sure, economics does provide us with a body of theory that is essential in examining the probable consequences of alternative economic policies, and a

[6] S. Toulmin, *Philosophy of Science* (London, Hutchinson University Library, 1953), p. 13.

good many of these analytical tools ought to become part of the intellectual equipment of all students. Economists are able to tell us what the probable consequences will be if the supply of money is increased, or if the interest rates are lowered; but they cannot *as* economists tell us whether or not we ought to take either of these two courses of action. Decisions regarding these alternative courses of action involve technical economic analysis *and* weighing of values.

It is therefore clear that both values and economic theory are involved in deciding courses of action in economic affairs, and both must find their place in social studies teaching. Here the different modes of thought come prominently into play. Technical economic analysis involves the empirical mode of thinking (that is, it is concerned with matters of fact and theory), while considering alternative values involves the moral mode (that is, it is concerned with criteria of what is desirable or undesirable). The teacher's job is to help students learn to make these necessary distinctions, so that they recognize when questions of fact and analysis are under consideration and when questions of value are at stake.[7] This would of course hold as well for instruction in fields of study other than economics.

Thus far we have been talking about problems associated with a single field. But problems in the world of human affairs do not come neatly labeled "historical," "economic," or "political." They come as decisions to be made and force us to call upon all we know and make us wish we knew more. It was concern for broad cultural and moral questions that go beyond the boundaries of any one discipline that led the progressives to urge that students have the opportunity to deal with them in all their complexity. They proposed a new curriculum, one centered on the problems of youth and broad social issues and drawing upon the academic disciplines as they become relevant to the problems under study. This idea became the hallmark of progressivism in curriculum building. It gained wide acceptance among educators and found expression in many influential statements of policy and opinion during the 1920's, '30's, and '40's. Attempted applications of this viewpoint were made in courses labeled core, common learnings, and the like.

Difficulties in this approach soon became apparent, not the least of which was the students' lack of first-hand acquaintance with the disciplines that were the source of the concepts and ideas essential to structuring problems under study. Without adequate understanding of the various fields of knowledge, students had no way of knowing which fields were relevant to problems of concern to them. Indeed, without knowledge of the organized fields it was difficult for them to ask the kinds of questions about their problems that the various disciplines could help them answer.

[7] See *Economic Education in the Schools,* Report of the National Task Force on Economic Education, 1961.

Giving students an opportunity to grapple with broad social and cultural problems was basically a promising innovation. But at the same time one is forced to recognize that problem solving on such a broad base cannot be pursued successfully without growing understanding of the fields of knowledge on which the problem solver must draw.

Recognizing then the value in systematic study of the fields of knowledge and the importance of developing competence in dealing with problems and issues that are broader than those of any one field, the question arises of why opportunities for both types of activities should not be included in the program for all students. One might envision a general education program that would include basic instruction in the major fields defined earlier in this paper (the natural sciences, the physical sciences, mathematics, and the humanities), together with a coordinating seminar in which students deal with problems "in the round" and in which special effort is made to show the intimate relationships between the fields of study as concepts from those fields are brought to bear on these problems. Such a seminar would also furnish excellent opportunities to help students become aware of the different modes of thought and various types of language usage involved in dealing with problematic situations and the necessity for making clear distinctions among them.

This is not a new proposal. I am here dusting off an old idea first set forth in the 1956 ASCD Yearbook, *What Shall the High Schools Teach?* In making this suggestion, we were much influenced by Dewey's contention that

> The aim of education should be to secure a balanced interaction of the two types of mental attitude (the practical and the theoretical), having sufficient regard to the disposition of the individual not to hamper and cripple whatever powers are naturally strong in him. The narrowness of individuals of strong concrete bent needs to be liberalized. Every opportunity that occurs within practical activities for developing curiosity and susceptibility to intellectual problems should be seized. Violence is not done to natural disposition; rather, the latter is broadened. Otherwise, the concrete becomes narrowing and deadening. As regards the smaller number of those who have a taste for abstract, purely intellectual topics, pains should be taken to multiply opportunities and demands for the application of ideas, for translating symbolic truths into terms of everyday and social life. Every human being has both capabilities, and every individual will be more effective and happier if both powers are developed in easy and close interaction with each other.[8]

Let it be recognized that the difficulties in building a curriculum that takes account of the relationships among the various fields of inquiry and creativity are overwhelming. The greatest difficulty is that the job involves the

[8] *How We Think* (Boston, D. C. Heath and Co., 1933), pp. 228–229.

collaboration of specialists—in the various disciplines, in curriculum development, and in teaching. In such collaborative efforts it would seem that curriculum specialists, concerned as they are with the instructional program as a whole, have a crucial role to play. But in all frankness it must be recognized that they do not play a central crucial role in curriculum revision projects now underway. Whether they will be able to do so in the future is another matter. And I suspect that whether they will indeed make the contribution one might reasonably expect them to make will depend, first of all, on their ability to work effectively with representatives of the various fields of knowledge to identify important relationships among these fields and to fashion programs of instruction that take due account of these relationships and connections; and secondly, on their ability to build curricula that help students see the relevance of the intellectual resources of the culture for their own lives as productive workers, as citizens, and as individuals. For as Professor Bestor, who scarcely qualifies as an advocate of education for life adjustment, has reminded us, "The basic argument of the intellectual disciplines in education is not that they lift a man's spirits above the world, but that they equip his mind to enter the world and perform its tasks."[9]

[9] *Educational Wastelands* (Urbana, Ill., University of Illinois Press, 1953), p. 15.

23 / HARRY S. BROUDY, B. OTHANEL SMITH, and JOE R. BURNETT

Reassessment of the Uses of Schooling

The writers have distinguished four typical uses of knowledge or school learnings and have called them replicative, associative, applicative, and interpretive. The point of making such distinctions is not to multiply terms or to make the obvious seem esoteric and learned. The justification for distinctions among concepts and terms is that they denote processes that are more or less independent of each other or that cannot be substituted for each other. If such differences exist, the curriculum designer should be alerted, lest his efforts produce effects he did not anticipate and fail to produce those he had a right to expect.

We use school learnings in nonschool situations in ways that range from the apparently unconscious to the most deliberatively explicit use. There is the report of an experiment concerning the effect of reading Greek poetry to an infant on the child's ability to learn Greek peotry many years later. In the same vein, subliminal advertising on television has been banned, presumably because it effectively uses stimuli of which the viewer is not conscious. One can only speculate on the potency of "forgotten" learnings to affect adult behavior. Who knows how much of what we call "individuality,"

Harry S. Broudy, B. Othanel Smith, and Joe R. Burnett, "Reassessment of the Uses of Schooling," from *Democracy and Excellence in American Secondary Education*, pp. 45–59. Reprinted by permission of the authors.

Harry S. Broudy (1905–) is professor of philosophy of education at the University of Illinois and is a prominent philosophical realist. He is the author of *Building A Philosophy of Education, Paradox and Promise, Psychology for General Education,* and *Democracy and Excellence in American Secondary Education* (coauthor).

B. Othanel Smith (1903–) is professor emeritus of education at the University of Illinois. He has published *Logical Aspects of Educational Measurement* and is coauthor of *Fundamentals of Curriculum Development, The Improvement of Practical Intelligence,* and *A Study of the Logic of Teaching,* and coeditor of *Social Foundations of Education* and *Language and Concepts in Education.*

Joe R. Burnett (1928–) is professor of philosophy of education at the University of Illinois, editor of the journal *Educational Theory*, and coauthor of *Democracy and Excellence in American Secondary Education.*

"creativeness," and "charm" is caused by learnings that operate at the unconscious or preconscious level? Various schools of psychiatric thought have capitalized on "forgotten" learnings and their role in neurotic behavior. The schools have not capitalized on them, partly because students of schooling have not taken the trouble to perfect methods for studying their effects.

Associative Use of Schooling

Many learnings, while not subliminal or unconscious, have an air of the accidental about them, as when something we have learned comes to mind because it has something in common with what is before us. For example, we read the word "Greek" in the newspaper, and the thought of Achilles or Homer occurs to us, to be followed, perhaps, by the thought of rubber heels.

This is an example of the associative use of learning. When we are asked to respond to a question, we resurrect from memory something or other that the cue suggests. The laws of association—resemblance, contiguity, and satisfaction—purport to tell us what learnings the given cue is most likely to elicit.

Resemblance, contiguity, satisfaction, and vividness can determine what is associated with what, but these are not logical relations. "Red Square" and "redhead" are not related logically, although they have the word "red" in common. We cannot say logically that, given the stimulus "Red Square," the subject must respond with "redhead" or red-anything-else, but psychologically one might have expected something like this on the basis of what is known about people's speech patterns and the law of resemblance in association of ideas.

Nevertheless, the subliminal and associative modes of using what is learned in school are important, partly because many students and perhaps even some teachers mistake an associative response for a logical one. For example, if the teacher asks, "Why is the sun hot?" the pupil may reply, "Because it is round and bright." This is not a logical answer, although it is understandable as an associative use of learning, because the sun *is* round and it *is* bright.

Unfortunately, neither students nor teachers display adequate sensitivity to this distinction, as is made clear in subsequent chapters. Here, it may be remarked that many a conscientious student has passed high school courses by using learnings associatively in answering questions on essay examinations. In other words, students learn to respond with everything they can recall that is in any way related to some word or phrase in the examination question. Such an answer may contain nothing that is false and nothing that was not in the textbook and yet be completely irrelevant to the point of the question. If this answer is written in legible hand and with due respect for grammar and spelling, chances are better than even that the student will get a passing grade.

Indeed, if there is anything that might qualify as a universal learning pattern in American schooling, it is precisely the method of using the instructor's questions as cues for the recall and statement of any and all associated materials. The valiant attempts of the Progressive critics to change this pattern unfortunately were in vain. The discovery that such responses will not earn passing grades for the student in college—although in many colleges they will—must be traumatic. Every time, therefore, an instructor accepts a psychologically relevant answer in place of a logically relevant one, he is an accessory after a pedagogical crime, and if in his teaching he ignores this distinction, he is an accessory to the crime.

Another reason for the importance of the associative use of school learnings is that it constitutes an important matrix of meaning for the appreciation of the arts. Much of the imagery in the reading of poetry, fiction, and drama depends on learned materials that cannot be recalled exactly as learned. Much of the effectiveness of figures of speech rests on comparisons once noted, now forgotten, yet still amenable to partial recall.[1] We perhaps have overlooked the importance of this use of school learnings because, as has been pointed out, we cannot trace their origins to particular school experiences.

Much of what has been called concomitant learnings by William H. Kilpatrick and others illustrates what is here meant by the associative use of schooling. The stress on this type of learning is justified both by the fact that it probably does occur and by its important effects. The difficulty in using it as a basis for curriculum theory arises because it makes too much depend on what, in the nature of the case, is highly idiosyncratic and uncontrollable. It should also be noted that associative uses of schooling do not all originate in the interpersonal relationships of pupils and teachers. Content, if rightly chosen, also teaches more than meets the eye or the test.

Replicative Use of Schooling

At almost the opposite pole of the unconscious and randomly associative use of learnings is the replicative use. When we read a newspaper, compute a

[1] See William York Tindall, *The Literary Symbol* (New York: Columbia University Press, 1955). Beginning the section called "Burial of the Dead," T. S. Eliot wrote in *The Waste Land* (*Collected Poems of T. S. Eliot, 1909–1935* [New York: Harcourt, Brace & World, Inc., 1936]):

> April is the cruelest month, breeding
> Lilacs out of the dead land, mixing
> Memory and desire, stirring
> Dull roots with spring rain.

What can we recall explicitly that gives these lines their haunting appropriateness? Grover Smith devoted twenty-six pages, in his *T. S. Eliot's Poetry and Plays* (Chicago: University of Chicago Press, 1950), to the sources of meaning of this section of the poem.

sum, look up a word in the dictionary, read a map, or recite a poem, we repeat an operation performed many times in our school days and pretty much as we performed it in those days. The replicative use of schooling is most noticeable in the practice of the skills. Ordinarily we do not say that we "apply" our skills of reading and writing in nonschool situations; rather we repeat the school performance in writing and reading situations, and such situations are virtually self-announcing in school and out. When does one write? When paper and pen are before him and when the situation says, "Write it down."

Attitudes presumably are instances of the same use, except that the triggering situations vary over a wider range. That neatness in school will transfer to tasks outside of the classroom is not so certain as that writing will take place in writing situations. Yet when the neatness attitude is instated in an unpracticed task, it is a repetition of much the same sort of experience that the learner underwent at the times when the attitude was formed.

We rely on the replicative use of schooling for those operations and contents that are used very much as learned in a wide range of frequently occurring situations. They are the most reliable type of school learnings precisely because life affords opportunities to overlearn them to the point of virtually faultless performance. Because the school can anticipate only a small portion of the behavior that is demanded by life, the replicative use of schooling is limited less in importance than in range.

The traditional emphasis on reading, writing, and arithmetic placed great reliance on the replicative use of schooling. Life was to make repeated demands on the individual to use these symbolic skills; hence, to overlearn them was the primary task of elementary schooling, whatever else might be added to garnish the education menu.

There is another ingredient of schooling that is sometimes used replicatively, the use of "facts" or, more precisely, statements of fact. If one is asked, "When did Columbus discover America?" the replicative response is "1492," a repetition of an oft-repeated response made in similar situations.

How many of the facts learned in school are used in this way is impossible to estimate. A repertory of facts is assuredly indispensable to life and thought. The building of such a repertory has been belittled first, because compared to the total stock of knowledge, any individual's stock is bound to be minuscule and second, because fact-storing is generally regarded as being of a lower order of mentation than thinking and reasoning. Yet all thinking requires facts as well as meanings and relations. Even in purely formal logical thinking one cannot wholly dispense with facts, for example, that certain symbols stand for certain logical meanings and operations, that there are logical rules, and the like. So in every thinking situation some elements are regarded as fact and when so taken they are used replicatively, that is, as given or as learned.

Thus, while it is admittedly futile to attempt to store all the facts one will need, the replicative use of facts is such that schooling should give attention to the strategy of fact-storage and retrieval, to use the language of the computer. Such strategy concerns itself, on the one hand, with selection of key facts to be stored, and, on the other, with conceptual nets or maps that facilitate both the storage of facts and their recall. These are the direct objective of general studies.

Applicative Use of Schooling

The most serious limitation on the replicative use of any learning is its lack of flexibility. It works best when the new situation is almost a replica of those in which the learning was acquired. We are told that whenever new materials or new designs are introduced in house-building, even master craftsmen are disturbed. This is so because well-established habits and skills can no longer function replicatively.

Our technological civilization depends on the application of knowledge to particular problems of practice rather than on its replicative use. Mathematics and physics *applied* to problems of mechanics give us the profession of engineering, that in turn solves problems of transportation, construction, mechanical toasters, and space probes. Hence the enormous importance of applying school learning, or the *applicative* use of learning. Here a learning—usually in the form of some principle, generalization, or statement of fact—is used to solve a problem or to analyze a situation. The cues for what knowledge is needed and how it is to be used are limited and often hidden. Sometimes the situation is so unstructured and open that the bulk of the cues must come from the problem-solver himself. Accordingly, we rightly prize the applicative use of knowledge, for it greatly enhances our powers of understanding and control. The applicative use of knowledge is, however, more complicated than might first appear; otherwise we would not be so often chagrined that we had not applied knowledge that was in our possession all the time. If application of knowledge were a simple matter, would we not ourselves make those discoveries and inventions which seem so obvious after they have been made by others?

Knowledge is applied, of course, whenever one recognizes an object or an event as a member of a class or an instance of a generalization or a law. This is application by subsumption, and there is some justice in believing that it is a basic way of applying knowledge. In the more complex case one does not, as a rule, deal with one object or event. Rather, one deals with problems or problem situations, and to solve them one seeks some resemblance to a familiar problem or situation. This type of application may be thought of as filling in the missing terms of a proportional equation.

We have

$$\frac{\text{Familiar problem}}{\text{New problem}} = \frac{\text{Familiar solution}}{?}$$

As an example, we might consider the familiar situation of boys in slum neighborhoods resisting delinquency when an extensive recreational program is introduced. If another neighborhood is afflicted by a high rate of juvenile delinquency, it occurs to us to apply a familiar solution, namely, instituting recreational facilities.

This is, of course, an argument by analogy. Whoever first applied his knowledge of the power of an electric current to magnetize a bar of iron within a coil of wire, and thus to operate a bell, completed the analogy $\frac{\text{hand}}{\text{clapper}} = \frac{?}{\text{clapper}}$ and hit on the notion of using the magnetized iron bar to activate the clapper as the hand ordinarily does. Someone had to note the resemblance between the power of steam in a kettle and in an engine; between the phenomenon of parallax and the possibility of measuring the distance to inaccessible yet visible objects by sightings from differing positions.

Another example of applying knowledge is furnished when we work backwards and ask, "What will tell us how cold or warm it is?" In measuring other properties of objects such as weight or size, we often rely on pointers that move over a numerical scale. What in the temperature situation would move a pointer? If we know (or can use replicatively) the fact that heat and cold affect the volume of metals or liquids, we are on the road to completing an analogy and devising some kind of thermometer. One could illustrate the same sort of thinking process by raising a question such as, "What will turn salt water into fresh?" Here, knowledge about evaporation might furnish the clues to the solution, or knowledge about the chemical reactions that produce precipitates might be the starting point.

Applying knowledge is, therefore, not simply to recall it or to recite it. It is to use it for problem-solving, and, if we are not to use "application" trivially, we mean dealing with problems whose solutions are neither easy nor easily available from an expert or a handbook.

It is noteworthy that after we have solved the same type of problem many times, another problem of the same sort elicits a response that *replicates* at least part of the previous response. When this happens, one no longer applies knowledge, but rather uses a *skill*, much as one uses the skills of reading, writing, and spelling. In other words, even when we observe someone solving a problem, perhaps a difficult problem, we cannot be sure that he is applying knowledge; he may be merely replicating a skill. The human race has inherited the earth not because it can have knowledge or apply it, but primarily because it makes a habit of doing so.

For the curriculum designer, the important point is that in ordinary life the applicative use of knowledge is relatively rare. We do not solve many of our problems by thinking our way through them. On the contrary, we consult someone who has the solution for sale, or we look up the answer in some manual. Our behavior follows the law of least cognitive strain; we think no more than we have to.

As the next chapter explains more fully, it is the specialist in the exercise of his specialty who is most likely to use knowledge applicatively, and even he does so only when confronted with problems that are not routine. The highest applicative use of knowledge is to expand knowledge itself, as in the work of the scholar and researcher. The generalist is satisfying the requirements of thinking and intelligence when he uses knowledge interpretively.

Why do we stress the relative rarity of the applicative use of knowledge? Because in educational thinking it has generally been taken for granted that it is the applicative use of knowledge that justifies schooling in general and the teaching of any subject in particular. At times the schools have operated on the assumption that a large repertory of facts, rules, and principles learned for replication on cue would automatically be used applicatively when the life situation became problematic. At other times, disappointed that automatic application of school learnings did not occur, the schools urged that the pupil be given practice in application, so that applying a piece of knowledge became a standard part of a lesson. These Herbartian applications, usually practiced on problems within a given subject, served as an admirable test of the pupil's understanding, but they did not guarantee that the learning would be used to solve nonschool problems.

This was due partly to the fact that life problems are "molar," that is, more complex and massive than problems in a single discipline like mathematics or physics or chemistry. It was also due to the technological complexity of our culture. In such a culture, one depends more and more on specialized problem-solvers who have the knowledge, tools, and skills required. In such a state of affairs, to justify a curriculum on applicative uses is neither practically nor theoretically defensible, unless it is the curriculum for the training of specialists.

Interpretive Use of Schooling

Much of what in ordinary language we call application of knowledge is better regarded as interpretation, a process related to application but far less specific and detailed.

Experience becomes intelligible only as we categorize it, conceptualize it, or classify it. In other words, experience becomes intelligible and intelligently manageable insofar as we impose form upon it. But which forms, and from whence do they come?

The ultimate answer to this question is still a profound philosophical mystery, but for our purpose it is safe to say that every intellectual discipline, every science, every poem, and every picture is a source of forms or molds into which experience must flow and be shaped if we are to understand it at all. Our language is the great prefigurer or premolder of ordinary everyday experience; the sciences use molds or categories that allow us to understand our world in terms of atoms and electrons, galaxies and solar systems, acids and bases, causes and effects; our works of art enable us to feel the world as pervaded by human values.

Whenever we use our school learnings in these areas to perceive, understand, or feel life situations, we say that we are using our learnings primarily for interpretation, and not replicatively, associatively, or applicatively, although, strictly speaking, these uses do not necessarily exclude each other. There is a sense, however, in which the interpretive use of knowledge is the most fundamental of all, for without a prior interpretation of the situation we are not sure what we shall replicate, associate, or apply.

The interpretive use of schooling, accordingly, is primarily for orientation and perspective rather than for action and problem-solving. Although interpretation is a necessary preliminary to all the other uses of knowledge, there are many situations in which orientation toward a problem is as far as we can go, that is, in virtually all of the situations in which we cannot function as specialists.

Critical Thinking

What about critical thinking? Is critical thinking interpretive or an applicative use of schooling? Is it confined to the specialist, or must we all make use of it? There is little doubt that all citizens are expected to think critically and to be good at it in all domains of life. By critical thinking, we mean the scrutiny of discourse for truth and validity. We think critically when we attend closely to such questions as, "Is this statement true?" "Does this statement follow from the evidence presented in its behalf?" "Is this statement more or less probable on the evidence than alternative statements?"

Good thinking has both form and content. The form is provided and regulated by logic, or the rules for correct definition, classification, and inference. Good thinking or critical thinking also involves knowledge *about* the field in which the thinking is being done. It is this content that enables us to judge the truth and relevance of the alternatives presented to us in life situations. But it is precisely with respect to content, that is, with respect to knowledge about situations, that the citizen is not a specialist.

It turns out, therefore, that although content is used applicatively only by the specialist, logical form is the same when used by specialist or nonspecialist;

it must be used applicatively if used at all. This means that all subjects, if logically organized, must be studied with respect to both their logical form or structure and their specific content. Except by the specialist, the content is used interpretively and associatively, but the logical form of the subject (mathematics, chemistry, physics, history) is used applicatively, and this means only that the logical form of a subject matter is used applicatively to regulate our interpretations. When this occurs, we are thinking critically.

The discussion of the various uses of school learnings has been admittedly schematic and abstract. It may be helpful, therefore, to examine in some detail a task that confronts us so commonly that we forget its importance as a test of schooling—the task of reading a newspaper or magazine.

Suppose that the task is to read the following excerpt from the *Saturday Review:*

> In a few weeks, Albert Schweitzer will have completed fifty years of service at the jungle hospital bearing his name in Lambaréné, now part of the newly independent state of Gabon, in West Africa.
>
> In establishing a medical center in the heart of Africa, Albert Schweitzer subordinated careers as organist and organ builder, musicologist, theologian, philosopher, and historian. His initial funds came from his book on Johann Sebastian Bach. Much of the carpentering he did himself. What he built was not a "hospital" in the Western sense; he built an African village in which medical care was available to people most in need of it. He knew that Africans would be apprehensive about coming to a frosty white modern clinic. He wanted to meet the Africans on their own terms. He had a concept of human purpose that didn't permit a life of comfortable theorizing—even about matters of the gravest importance for renowned philosophers or theologians. He also had ideas about the nature of Christianity that didn't completely coincide with what he had been taught as a student. These ideas were related to a concept of the indwelling God and the way the reality of human brotherhood asserted itself. Rather than teach other students what he himself could not accept, he decided to leave the seminary and make his life his argument. If what he believed had genuine validity, it would be proved in his work.[2]

In this quotation from a Norman Cousins editorial, there is a typical cognitive task for modern man. The article assumes that the reader has some knowledge about Albert Schweitzer. In response to the name Albert Schweitzer, one typically ten-year-old boy gave the following associated items: "missionary," "mustache," and "doctor."

Although a specialist could give a precise definition of "musicologist," "theologian," and "philosopher," this youngster could not. He made a stab at "musicologist," but a "theologian" was defined as a man "interested in theories," and a philosopher was "you know, a sort of brainy type."

[2] March 16, 1963, p. 30.

The following few sentences were adequately interpreted, but when he got to "These ideas were related to a concept of the indwelling God . . .," the task of interpretation was too severe, and a vague "it has something to do with religion" was the best he could manage. "To make his life his argument" also gave trouble, requiring, as it did, some understanding of an unusual metaphor.

How was the youngster using schooling in this reading situation? Replicatively, he was using skills of pronunciation and syntax as well as visual habits involved in reading. Associatively, his previous learnings were functioning well enough that the words had sufficient meaning to give sense to most of the sentences. He had enough knowledge to interpret a good portion of the passage. He could say what it was about. Roughly, he could set the scene of a doctor in an African jungle, a learned man who gave up life among learned men because of some difficulty with religious belief. In the terminology of this book, the young reader had cognitive maps on which these sentences could be plotted.

The plotting, however, was exceedingly rough. What would refine it? More knowledge about Schweitzer and Africa, to be sure, but also a clearer notion of the subject matter of philosophy, musicology, and theology, Note, however, that there is no problem to be solved by the reader. He does not need to "apply" his knowledge to solve any problem. He uses some of his schooling to interpret these paragraphs; this particular boy achieved a marginal interpretation.

What in this example would be an applicative use of knowledge? A theologian might scrutinize the article for accuracy of statement and cogency of argument, and so might a student of the emerging new countries. A specialist in these fields would apply his theoretical knowledge and practical experience to evaluate Mr. Cousins' analysis and perhaps to suggest an alternative analysis or solution. An expert editorial writer would examine the passage for details of literary construction and rhetorical effect.

It will be pointed out that in applying knowledge, the specialist uses knowledge replicatively, associatively, and interpretively as well. Of course this is true, inasmuch as the applicative use of knowledge is the most highly developed use. The difference between the interpretive and applicative uses is that application carries interpretation to the degree of detail and precision needed to deal with a problem; it does not simply identify the focus and nature of the problem. Interpretive use leads to meaningful discourse and understanding; application is aimed at problem-solving.

Clearly, interpretation is a necessary condition for application, but not a sufficient one. Schooling that is adequate for interpretation may not be adequate for application, while some applicative study may be too narrow for adequate interpretive use. General education has for its goal the interpretive rather than the applicative use of schooling, whereas special schooling has the applicative use as its ultimate goal.

In terms of logical operations, interpretation can be achieved when a given cognitive task is subsumed under a class of cognitive tasks. For example, "This material has to do with chemistry," or "This is a sample of English poetry." More concretely, the test of acceptable interpretation is translation of the material to be cognized into roughly equivalent terminology, or giving an example. Thus, "gravitational field" is acceptably interpreted when the respondent says, "the pulling of the earth on things" or "it's what keeps people from flying off the earth." Definitions need not be precise nor explanations adequate; minimal interpretation is satisfied when identification is correct.

It follows that interpretation can be made highly precise by appropriate study, but it does not follow that it will automatically shade into application. Thus, a philosopher of science can be highly precise about the nature of scientific method, but remain helpless before a bubble-chamber problem in physics. One can become highly precise in interpreting number theory and yet be awkward in solving quadratic equations or translating problems of mechanics into mathematical terms.

Application presupposes interpretation but logically goes beyond identification. The whole series of acts—formulating a problem, observation, hypothecation, experimental imagination and design, verification procedures and criteria, judgments of adequacy—is involved in applying knowledge. Clearly, it involves a degree of detailed knowledge of fact as well as of theory, experience as well as adequate conceptual frames.

Questions for Discussion

What reason does Aristotle give for master workers being wiser than manual workers? Why does he believe that artists can teach but men of "mere experience" cannot? Distinguish theoretical, practical, and productive knowledge from one another and indicate the reasons given by Aristotle for one being more closely related to "Wisdom." What is the difference between making and acting? What connection does this distinction have with art and moral decisions? Not all sciences, according to Aristotle, are of the same exactness. What determines exactness? What is the object of highest knowledge? What ideas about the organization of the curriculum did you gain from Aristotle's analysis? Reappraise Aristotle's approach in light of today's interpretation of the organized disciplines.

Comte divides the natural sciences into two categories and bases the second category on the first. What criteria does he use to do this, and does he adequately support what he has done? Comte then establishes a hierarchical order, based on his criteria, for the ordering of the disciplines. Has he provided an adequate rationale for this order? Would it be possible to develop a different order by using Comte's criteria? What arrangements for curriculum and the sequence of teaching follow from Comte's proposals?

Schwab reviews earlier classifications of the disciplines, then states three basic problems for the structure of the disciplines. State the problems, indicate why they are important, and list their interconnections. What, then, is the structure of the disciplines approach to the curriculum? In what respect does it differ from past curriculums based on separate subjects found in traditional schools? Does it constitute an improvement of both the organization of knowledge and the involvement of the student in the learning process? How does Schwab suggest that the disciplines be taught?

What are Bellack's objections to the structure of the disciplines approach? Why does he believe that the school's responsibility extends beyond organized fields of learning and inquiry? Bellack argues that the curriculum builder must envision relationships among the disciplines; he then presents three forms in which these interconnections may be conceived. Evaluate each of these. He also briefly mentions a plan of general education based on four modes of intellectual activity. What are the advantages and disadvantages of structuring general education in this manner? Is this proposal a rapprochement with Schwab's position? Compare and evaluate the positions of Schwab and Bellack.

State the four uses of knowledge, their interrelationships, and the chief characteristics given in the essay by Broudy, Smith, and Burnett. Which of these uses would have a relationship to the arts? To skills? To problem solving? Have the authors underestimated the values of associative learning for students? Do they underestimate the extent to which applicative use is made of knowledge? Have they explored the full range of operations used in applying knowledge? Evaluate their analysis of the uses of knowledge in critical thinking. Do they distinguish critical thinking from problem solving? What teaching recommendations can be drawn from their essay?

Suggested Reading

Several texts provide an overview and interpretation of problems and issues in this area. An analysis from the point of view of the classical realist is presented by Harry S. Broudy in *Building a Philosophy of Education*, 2d ed. (Englewood Cliffs, N.J.: Prentice-Hall, 1961), chaps. 5–7. A discussion of knowledge and education and a look at the contours and epistemic problems in the sciences and humanities is found in John Martin Rich's *Humanistic Foundations of Education* (Worthington, Ohio: Charles A. Jones, 1971). Philip G. Smith offers a clear introduction to problems of knowledge and its structures in *Philosophy of Education: Introductory Studies* (New York: Harper & Row, Publishers, 1965), chaps. 4 and 6. Two useful collections of essays on the structure of the disciplines are G. W. Ford and Lawrence Pugno, eds., *The Structure of Knowledge and the Curriculum* (Chicago: Rand McNally

& Co., 1964); and Stanley Elam, ed., *Education and the Structure of Knowledge* (Chicago: Rand McNally & Co., 1964).

Two particularly important books on general education take a philosophical approach. Philip H. Phenix formulates a philosophy for general education based on the premise that the purpose of education is the fulfillment of meaning. This is accomplished through the delineation of six types of meaning in *Realms of Meaning* (New York: McGraw-Hill Book Co., 1964). A work based on the conviction that the content of general education should be the same for all, while differences in ability can be accommodated through sophistication and detail of the content, is Harry S. Broudy, B. Othanel Smith, and Joe R. Burnett, *Democracy and Excellence in American Secondary Education* (Chicago: Rand McNally & Co., 1964).

Israel Scheffler approaches problems of knowledge, belief, truth, and teaching through analytic philosophy in *Conditions of Knowledge* (Atlanta: Scott, Foresman and Co., 1965). A pragmatic approach which examines warranted beliefs, inference and fallacy, meaning and language is found in the treatment of H. Gordon Hullfish and Philip G. Smith, *Reflective Thinking: The Method of Education* (New York: Dodd, Mead & Co., 1961).

Among the books of readings the sampling is wide, with essays on epistemological problems, the structure of different disciplines, behavioral objectives, determining priorities and selecting content for the curriculum, and the like: Donald Vandenburg, ed., *Theory of Knowledge and Problems of Education* (Urbana, Ill.: University of Illinois Press, 1969); Robert S. Guttchen and Bertram Bandam, eds., *Philosophical Essays on Curriculum* (Philadelphia: J. B. Lippincott Co., 1969); Jane R. Martin, ed., *Readings in the Philosophy of Education: A Study of Curriculum* (Boston: Allyn and Bacon, 1970); and Martin Levit, *Curriculum* (Urbana, Ill.: University of Illinois Press, 1971).

CHAPTER SIX /

EDUCATIONAL CONCEPTS

CONCEPTS are the building blocks of a discipline. Although some disciplines, especially in the social sciences, may draw on concepts from related disciplines, a set of concepts is usually developed in each discipline for advancing research and inquiry. For example, we associate the concepts *proton*, *neutron*, and *energy* with physics; *molecule*, *valence*, and *element* with chemistry; and *socialization*, *social stratification*, and *social role* with sociology.

Education as a discipline or field of study has its own concepts; however, it has also borrowed many concepts from other disciplines, especially psychology. This is evident in the use of such terms as *learning*, *interest*, *needs*, and *adjustment*. But if education is a study concerned primarily with organized schooling and the teaching-learning process, some concepts seem to fall distinctly within its province: teaching, telling, indoctrination, curriculum, and the like.

Concepts are the elemental building blocks for theory construction, and they thereby serve heuristic purposes. But because educational policy and practice aim to gain compliance with prescribed behavior, educational concepts have frequently been employed as slogans to persuade people to conform to established policies and procedures. The use of concepts in this manner tends to vitiate their power to serve the ends of research and inquiry.

One way by which concepts can be understood better is by examining educational discourse. In this way concepts can be studied in use and their functional relationships discerned. One leading approach in ordinary language analysis suggests that the study of language and concepts consists of a number of activities that can be grouped together because they share a family resemblance. Analysts point out that there are a number of ways of operating with language. Some philosophers have tended to think of all languages as words whose "meanings" consist of the objects or ideas or activities that the words "stand for" or "name." But this is only one function of language, a naming function. One learns to name things by pointing to the thing denoted and pronouncing its name. But merely learning the names of things does not teach us how to use them; instead, we learn the meaning of a word by learning its use. There are language functions other than naming: reporting an event, giving an order, testing an hypothesis, telling a joke, solving a problem, describing an object, and others. To understand how to use a language is to understand how to operate by the rules embodied in various language functions.

The richness and the ambiguity of language is both its strength and its shortcomings. For example, our basic educational concepts are framed in a variety of ways and may also be expressed in an ambiguous or conceptually confused fashion. The search for alleged essences is anathema for analysis. Instead, conceptual analysis seeks to identify the uses of terms in educational discourse and to observe their linguistic movement. It also examines educational assumptions and the criteria and adequacy of arguments. After this primary work of analysis is completed, a logical reconstruction of the conceptual structure is made to remove the original source of perplexity and to render educational discourse more adequate for carrying its conceptual load.

Even though some have criticized ordinary language as a game or an intellectual exercise or a resurgence of neoscholasticism, it need not be taken in this way if analysis can illuminate and untangle conceptual problems that bear on educational theory, policy, and practice. For example, the meaning ascribed to the concept of equality is of great importance, just as various interpretations of the term *disadvantaged* affects policy. Divergent interpretations may lead to different policies, provisions, and forms of treatment. Likewise, much discussion today centers about *freedom* and *rights*, and each party may assume different meanings. Even when meaning is clear, persons may fail to note whether such important concepts are consistent with or call into question some aspect of one's philosophy of education. The term *relevance* is also frequently heard; yet because there are a multitude of different interpretations, the implied scope and the target of the students' criticisms and the recommendations that would follow are not clear. Turning specifically to the teaching process, a host of concepts are not always distinguished from one another: teaching, telling, indoctrinating, socializing, training, conditioning, and others. One function of philosophy of education is to overcome our conceptual muddles so that progress can be made in the development of educational theory and in the improvement of policy and practice. Attempts to do so are found in the selections in this chapter.

Paul Komisar first raises a paradox in educators' claims about equality. He distinguishes two kinds of equality: equal opportunity and equal treatment. An understanding of the differences between these two kinds of equality clarifies the paradox and makes clear the functions that can legitimately be expected of organized schooling in this area.

One way in which teaching can better be understood is to contrast it to other activities with a family resemblance. Thomas Green undertakes this task by first making a distinction between "teaching that" and "teaching to." He then shows possible similarities and differences between teaching and training, conditioning, instructing, and indoctrination.

Komisar and James McClellan explore the relatively neglected area of the use of slogans in educational discourse. They make a distinction between ceremonial and nonceremonial use of slogans, and it is important to note that they concentrate exclusively on the latter type. The essay makes clear the similarities and differences between slogans and generalizations, explains the functions of slogan systems, and points out both legitimate and unrealistic expectations held by educators in using and interpreting slogans.

24 / B. PAUL KOMISAR

The Paradox of Equality in Schooling

Except for the thoroughgoing materialist, everyone attributes to principles some leverage in the affairs of institutions. And even the unmitigated materialist will have to grant that principles are not all filigree, that they have at least nuisance value in the arena of public policy. I assume that the principle of equal opportunity is one of the more salient principles of educational policy today.

Being so premised, I want now to suggest that those who give weight to equality *as a principle of schooling* are flummoxed in paradox. The paradox is this: educators can not deny a place to equality in decisions about schooling; but neither can they, without self-contradiction, invoke equal opportunity in the dispensing of that schooling. There are ways of avoiding this paradox, I will claim, but these ways require some hefty shifts in our thinking about

B. Paul Komisar, "The Paradox of Equality in Schooling," from *The Record,* Vol. 68, No. 3 (December 1966), pp. 251–254. Reprinted by permission of the publisher and the author.

B. Paul Komisar (1926–) is a member of the Foundations of Education Department at Temple University. He has written on the concept of equality and is coeditor of *Psychological Concepts in Education.*

equality in education. But before exposing the paradox further, let me essay a few remarks about the idea of equality in general. These remarks will be helpful later.

Two Faces of Equality

Two different kinds of equality are referred to in discussions about education. One is the idea of equal *opportunity*, which is the main concern of this study and the idea to which we will return shortly. The second is the claim of equal *treatment*. These two notions of equality differ in ways that have a bearing on the paradox of equality in education.

The first difference is rather obvious. In speaking of equal treatment of students, we are referring directly to what is being done to or for the student. This is no more than to say that equal treatment is a claim about treatment, not results. So it's no good to say: "See, we gave these students equal treatment; they are both graduating from school." This won't do. The fact that the students are sharing in some dividend is not what we imply by equal treatment, for one student may have arrived at this result despite shoddy treatment along the way, while another may have enjoyed the pampering of special privilege. Equal treatment refers to what we do, not what the doing results in. Equal opportunity differs from this. It does not focus solely on what is done to the student *now*, but rather balances this against the sequel in the student's career. Equal opportunity is opportunity *to* achieve something, *to* get somewhere. The very term "opportunity" makes this clear; it is a relational term: to have an opportunity is to be vouchsafed a certain way to reach a designated goal. Thus, giving two boys identical books may be equal treatment, but whether it is also equal opportunity depends on the use to be made of the books.

The second difference between equal treatment and equal opportunity grows from the first. Equal treatment and not equal opportunity invites specificity when it is claimed. By "invites specificity" I mean that we can not talk of treating students equally without being prepared to specify *what treatment* we are alleging to be equal. Specificity of reference is necessary because the ways of treating students are numerous; there can be equality (or inequality) in: dispensing rewards, distributing largesse, inflicting penalties, apportioning tasks, presenting content, assigning duties, etc. And nothing in the bare idea of equal treatment is a clue to what service is being rendered equally.

Regarding equal opportunity, we are not required to specify the *treatment* we are referring to. Of course it can be asked: "Opportunity for what?" and the answer can be vocational proficiency, character development, enlightened mind, or any of the other supposed goods of education. But once the goal is clear, then further specificity is unnecessary. For equal opportunity consists in *whatever is a prerequisite to that goal.*

Specificity and Generality

The implications of these differences tell us the whole story. Equality of treatment is specific, it is context-bound; whereas equality of opportunity is general and goes beyond any immediate, especially institutional, context. Thus to promise to give equal treatment is to promise something that is or is to be specified within a given context. But a promise of equal opportunity is a *general* commitment to provide whatever it is that makes a designated achievement possible.

Now, the anomaly in equality of educational opportunity can be made clear. Presently this equality is conceived to be a principle *of* formalized education. That is, it is thought to be a principle whereby certain provisions of schooling are planned, debated, judged, and, ultimately, equitably distributed among those who receive schooling. This appears innocent enough, perhaps even admirable; but it propels us directly into a self-contradiction. For consider any accomplishment the school is said to foster (vocational competence, citizenship, etc.). I take it as indisputable fact that, for some students almost completely and for all students in some measure, the given accomplishment is *not* best served by some recognized form of schooling, and it is particularly not succored by continuous common schooling. Youth are simply not constituted all alike, they do not all take to formal schooling equally well. The flaw in conceiving of equal opportunity as a principle of schooling is as simple as that.

The point can be put more strongly. It is by definition true that the formal school charters just some of the diverse forms of socialization. Or to use Havighurst's more arresting phrase, just some of the "paths to maturity" pass through the halls of P.S. 27. One has to go to Plato for a conception of organized education which makes it coterminous with *all* forms of growth and development in a society.

Schooling vs. Equality

Now we all recognize these truisms yet fail to see their upshot: as we restrict developmental opportunities to schooling only, *we thereby* deny to students their right to equal educational opportunity. For not all students development is enhanced or enhanced to a similar degree by forms of schooling (again, especially common schooling). The point can be made stronger: as we restrict educational opportunity to schooling, it becomes *per se* unequal.

The conclusion virtually springs from the argument. The principle of equal educational opportunity (in virtue of its general reference) is not a principle of schooling; and those who believe it is are making a fundamental (because a moral) mistake.

Am I reading "education" too narrowly in restricting it to its institutional forms? I would say, first, that this is how many educators do in fact read the term in order to cite equal opportunity as a consideration in determining and adjudicating school policy and practice. But more than this, if we interpret the term more generously as, say, "any developmental activity found in a culture," then we are forced to the same conclusion: Equal educational opportunity is not particularly a principle of schooling but a general principle, one which serves to regulate the distribution of *all* paths to maturity.

The upshot, as I said in the beginning, is a paradox. For surely we want to say that schools must conform to considerations of equality in the conduct of their internal affairs; we do not want the school to champion inequality! But the principle of equal opportunity leads to self contradiction. Ergo, the school seems to defeat equality even as it salutes it.

Necessary Distinctions

As with paradoxes generally, this one is susceptible to dissolution by a distinction. In this case the necessary distinction is the one made earlier between equal treatment and equal opportunity. Despite all those who make schools the locus of equal educational opportunity, we had better locate this principle in society taken largely, and make the principle applicable to *all* social institutions. This puts us in a position to say that by providing for the schooling of Student A and the travel (or apprenticeship or work or specialized tuition or service corps or "private" schooling, etc.) of Student B, a society advances their equal opportunity for development in some area. The very linguistic change I slipped into would encourage this proper view of equal opportunity. That is, if we would henceforth speak of equal opportunity *for growth* or equal *developmental* opportunity in place of the customary wording, we would be less apt to conceive of this sort of equality narrowly, in terms of schools alone.

The equality which *is* internal to the policies and operations of schools is equal treatment. The principle of equal treatment is admirably restricted in scope to match the limited forms of beneficence schools are privileged to offer (and have difficulty enough in achieving). For a principle of equal treatment does not imply that *all* educational advantages for youth are found in schools; nor does it imply that schooling is one of the more important educational advantages. The principle of equal treatment announces only that whatever a school does have to offer, these offerings should be distributed equitably.

This is more modest promise, as befits an institution with limited resources. For in the end, the principle of equal educational opportunity is too grand a thing for something as narrow and pedestrian as mere schooling.

Contributions to Insurgency

The lunge in this discussion has been toward the new insurgency in educational thought. I refer to the radical view that the compulsory, common public school should be abolished in favor of a variety of independent publicly subsidized educational institutions. However, though this argument contributes to the insurgent position, the contribution has to be hedged on several points.

First, I do not want to deny the *historical legitimacy* of the identification of equal opportunity with (public) schooling. Conditions of the past justified taking the common school as the strategic focus in the campaign for equal educational opportunity. After all, the denial of schooling is as much a violation of equality as is the continual insistence on it. But historical legitimacy is not logical necessity, and there is no need now to confuse the felicitous with the formal. At present, we have both schools and affluence. The first achievement cancels the strategic focus. The second—affluence—makes new foci both possible and practical, since affluence should free us from cant (and can't) as well as want.

Second, the conclusion that schools alone cannot guarantee equal opportunity to grow can be avoided by denying the assumption that youth vary muchly in styles of development. For this is the axial premise on which turns the claim that protracted required schooling is incompatible with equal opportunity. But if I am wrong in taking seriously the idea of individual differences, then a belief even more cherished than equality (as judged by frequency of allusion) is tottering. For it is awesomely unbelievable that students are marvelously various in school but their nature is such that all experiences out-of-school are of precisely the same degree of irrelevance to their development. But once variation is granted, then one must conclude that equal opportunity and compulsory schooling are not fit companions.

A Right to Schooling?

We sometimes disguise this incompatibility by positing that the experience of formal education is itself a basic right of all youth. Then one speaks of equal educational opportunity as demanding schooling for all. The rationale for this bit of legerdemain is that each student is being given a chance to realize his right to schooling! But this argument works only if the "opportunity" is conceived not as a means to something beyond itself, but as an intrinsically valued experience in its own right. This seems to me to distort the idea of equal opportunity, but it is a plausible distortion. One can claim (as Dewey did in *Democracy and Education*) that one thing made possible by a contrived culture is a new kind of experience, namely the experience of contrived schooling. And as with any experience with a zing to it, it ought to be commonly shared. Let the point be granted, although it seems to be a backhanded way of putting a bold face on a bald necessity. But it does not follow that (a) schooling ought not to serve further ends; or (b) that schooling should be the sole subsidized provision for these ends; or (c) that even this premise necessitates all this much schooling for all. And certainly we should not delude ourselves that this unique experience of schooling enhances everyone equally well.

In fact this is an argument from right, not from necessity. So the only equality this argument supports is that of equal treatment in admission to schools. Or, if it is preferred, each person should have an equal opportunity to go to school, without being required to do so.

To read continuously compulsory attendance into this argument requires still other values. One such value is society's alleged need for a common culture. Once this notion is invoked we begin to see a plausible brief for protracted compulsory common schooling. But by arguing in this way, we have argued equal growth opportunity right out of the picture. The only equality that remains is equality of treatment.

25 / THOMAS F. GREEN

The Modes of Teaching

"Teaching That . . ." and "Teaching to . . ."

At the outset, let us acknowledge the existence of a major difference of emphasis. There are some teaching contexts within which we are concerned primarily to shape behavior, to mold habits. There are other contexts,

Thomas F. Green (1927–) is a member of the faculty at Syracuse University, where he teaches courses in the philosophy of education. He is the author of *The Activities of Teaching* and *Work, Leisure, and the American Schools*.

however, in which our primary interest is to shape beliefs or to communicate knowledge. This distinction is embedded in the linguistic contrast between "*teaching someone to do* so-and-so" and "*teaching someone that* so-and-so is the case." By the first of these expressions we clearly mean to focus on the formation of behavior and by the second to focus on the transmission of knowledge.

The exact relationship between these two emphases in teaching is immensely important to the philosophy of education; for there may be a temptation to say that one of these emphases is more fundamental than the other, and whole different philosophical views of education may result, depending on which of the two is regarded as the more basic. If "teaching that" is understood to be the more fundamental, then we are likely to view education as more centrally concerned with the transmission of knowledge and the formation of belief. If "teaching to" is taken as the more fundamental perspective then we are likely to think of education as more centrally concerned with the formation of ways of acting. In short, implicit in this contrast between "teaching that" and "teaching to" is the difficult problem of the relation between thinking and knowing, on the one hand, and doing or acting on the other; and quite different philosophies of education can be made to turn on the way that this relation is understood. At the moment, we must be content simply to observe that there is an important problem here. It shall be discussed more fully in another context.[1] It seems undeniable, nonetheless, that there is a difference to be observed between those teaching contexts in which we are concerned primarily to shape behavior and those in which we are concerned primarily to transmit knowledge, and that this contrast is embodied in the difference between the phrases "teaching someone to do so-and-so" and "teaching someone that so-and-so is the case." We may represent this fact diagrammatically as follows:

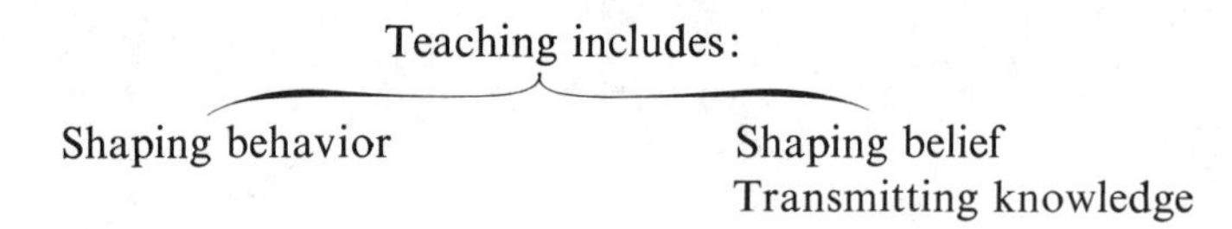

"Teaching" and "Training"

The concepts "teaching" and "training" are closely related. How do we know? Simply because there are many contexts within which either of these terms may be substituted for the other without changing the meaning of our statement. We may speak of teaching a dog, or of training a dog, to heel or to retrieve, and it apparently makes no difference to our meaning whether we

[1] See Chaps. 4 and 5 on "knowing" and Chap. 6 on "learning."

use the word "training" or the word "teaching." Or again, we may speak of an airline pilot who needs additional training in order to qualify to fly a new airplane, and it apparently does not alter our meaning whether we speak of teaching him or training him. There are many contexts, therefore, within which it is a matter of indifference whether the term "training" is used or the term "teaching," and this is a good reason for concluding that the meaning of the two terms overlap. They are closely related.

Nevertheless, however closely "teaching" and "training" may be related, it would be a mistake to conclude that they are the same thing. They are not. For there are many contexts in which it would be a rank distortion of meaning or just plain nonsense to substitute the one idea for the other. Not all teaching is a kind of training. For example, it is possible for a pilot to be trained to fly a certain airplane, and a part of his training may involve learning the stall properties of the airplane. But although we may speak of training him to fly the plane, we do not speak of training him that the stall properties are such and such. We may teach him or tell him that the plane will stall at 100 knots, but we do not speak of training him that it will stall at 100 knots. We could multiply examples, but the point is clear. In general, the term "training" may be substituted for "teaching" in any context where we are concerned with "teaching someone to . . .," but that substitution cannot be made with equal ease when we are concerned with "teaching someone that . . .." This observation suggests that the primary focus of the concept of training is on shaping behavior, whereas the concept of teaching is somewhat broader and includes both the shaping of behavior and the transmission of information.

We have observed that there are contexts in which we may speak of teaching but not of training. Similarly, there are contexts in which we may speak of training but not teaching. For example, we train a vine; we do not teach it. Also, we may speak of training certain muscles, particularly, though not exclusively, in cases of physical rehabilitation. But we do not speak of teaching muscles. We may teach a person to perform certain operations or exercises which have the consequence of strengthening his muscles, but we do not speak of teaching his muscles. Similarly, we speak of training the eye to see certain forms and colors, but we do not speak of teaching the eyes to see.

What is the importance of these rather simpleminded observations? It is simply that the contrasting usage of these two concepts, "teaching" and "training," indicates that there is a certain distinction concealed in our thinking. The analytic problem is not to invent a distinction here but to make explicit the principle which seems to underlie a distinction we in fact already make. I would like to propose a hypothesis that may help to formulate the principle and which may be confirmed, rejected, or modified by subsequent investigation. The hypothesis is that the distinction between teaching and training turns upon the degree to which the behavior aimed at in teaching or training is a manifestation of intelligence. The growth of the vine which we seek to direct by training does not express intelligence; hence, we do not speak of teaching the plant. Intelligence is a property which belongs to the behavior of a person and not to his muscles or to some organ such as his eyes. We do not say of a man that he has intelligent eyes or fingers or feet.[2] Hence, we speak of "teaching a person" but of "training his muscles." We may express the point in a principle, namely, that *in the proportion that the behavior aimed at in training manifests intelligence, it is easier to use the words "teaching" and "training" interchangeably; in the proportion that the behavior aimed at does not manifest intelligence, the term "training" continues to have application when the concept of "teaching" does not.* This principle says nothing about the intelligence of the creatures being trained or taught. The dependent variable between teaching and training has to do rather with the degree of intelligence displayed in the behavior we are seeking to shape.

"Training" and "Conditioning"

Our principle is designed to tell us why and at what points the concepts of teaching and training overlap in meaning. What it says is that they are related not because both are concerned with shaping behavior, but because both can be directed toward shaping behavior that manifests intelligence. The central feature of teaching seems to be that it focuses upon the display of intelligence. Let us ask, then, what happens in proportion as training is aimed less and less at the display of intelligence. In that case, the concept of training fades off gradually into what we would more and more clearly recognize as a case of simple conditioning, and it becomes increasingly difficult to apply the idea of teaching. Perhaps one reason why we can speak indifferently of training a dog or of teaching him is that we regard the actions of a trained dog as expressive of intelligence. We give an order and he *obeys.* He does not merely *respond* to a command in the sense in which a car may respond to a heavy foot on the accelerator. He obeys. Indeed, a well-trained dog is one that has passed obedience trials. Hence, it is perfectly natural to speak of training a dog to fetch, to heel, to sit, and to stay. It is equally appropriate and proper to speak of teaching him. But it is a distortion to speak of teaching a dog to salivate at the sound of a bell. Salivating at the sound of a bell is not an act of obedience. It is not an expression of intelli-

[2] It is interesting, I think, that we may speak of a potter's having educated fingers or of a field goal kicker as having an educated toe. These may be metaphorical expressions, but they suggest, nonetheless, that in some respects the concept of education is more closely related to training than to teaching, and this may be one reason why it is easy to think of education as training.

gence; it is an automatic and invariable response to a stimulus. We teach or train a dog to fetch or heel; we *condition* him to salivate at the sound of a bell.

These are distinctions of emphasis and are not indications of clear-cut boundaries between concepts; but these differences of emphasis seem to reveal a pattern, and it is this pattern that we want to discern. No one would point to the training of a pilot as the paradigmatic case of conditioning, although his training might include a clear case of conditioning. Therefore, what may be a good example of teaching or training may be a poor example of conditioning. The concepts are related but not identical. Similarly, one might point to the training of a person's eye muscles as a clear case of conditioning, but it would be a poor example of teaching. In short, *as the manifestation of intelligence aimed at in training declines, the concept of teaching seems to be less and less clearly exemplified and the concept of conditioning more and more clearly exemplified.* This, then, is the pattern we have been trying to discern. We can make it explicit in the form of some definite conclusions.

1. The concept of teaching is ambiguous in the respect that it may have to do either with "teaching someone to . . ." or "teaching someone that . . .." It includes both the shaping of behavior and the shaping of knowledge and belief. The concepts of "training" and "teaching" are closely related because training is a method of shaping behavior, "teaching someone to . . .."

2. There is another reason, however, why teaching and training are so closely related. Teaching seems to be essentially an activity aimed at shaping behavior that manifests intelligence; hence, training is an activity more and more closely identified with teaching in proportion as it aims at shaping behavior which more and more clearly expresses intelligence.

3. Finally, the concept of conditioning seems to be related to the concept of training in the respect that both have to do with shaping behavior. In that respect, conditioning is also related to teaching. But conditioning is an activity *unlike* training in the respect that the behavior it aims at shaping is not expressive of intelligence. Therefore, conditioning seems to be an activity less closely related to teaching than training is. Conditioning seems to be related to teaching primarily through its resemblance to training.

4. It would be a mistake to conclude that simple conditioning is not a method of teaching. On the contrary, simple conditioning enters into the teaching concept insofar as it can be shown to have a place in a teaching sequence or pattern of training which in itself is not mere conditioning but is aimed at shaping behavior expressive of intelligence. The concept of conditioning is, as it were, peripheral to the concept of teaching but enters into our thinking because of its resemblance to training, which is not peripheral.

5. If we may imagine the concept of teaching as represented by a circle, then we can describe this conceptual pattern as a continuum in which the

different modes of teaching are distributed so that some appear to display the central properties of the concept and others appear to be only peripheral. The continuum will then be represented as having a direction extending from the center of the concept to its borders.

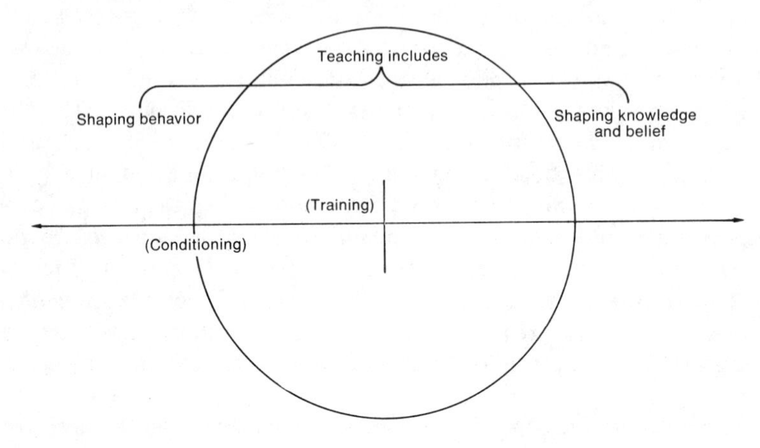

"Teaching" and "Instructing"

Employing the same method of study, let us examine the remaining two modes of teaching—instructing and indoctrinating. "Instructing," like "training," is a concept very closely connected with "teaching." The evidence for this is simply that the phrase "giving instruction" seems only another way of saying "teaching." The two terms, in many contexts, are synonymous. Nonetheless, teaching and instructing are not the same thing. There are almost endless instances of teaching which do not involve giving instruction, and the examples which most readily come to mind are those in which the focus of teaching falls most heavily on the side of shaping behavior to the exclusion of shaping belief. For example, we may speak of teaching or training a dog to heel, to fetch, to sit, or to stay. It would be less accurate, however, and perhaps even incorrect to speak of giving a dog instruction in sitting or fetching. In other words, when the teaching activity centers almost exclusively upon "teaching someone to . . .," as opposed to "teaching someone that . . .," then the concept of instructing has less application.

Why? Why is it more awkward in such contexts to speak of instructing than to speak of teaching or training? We need not go far to discover the answer. When we train a dog, say, to sit, we give an order and then push or pull and give reward or punishment. We do so precisely because we cannot explain the order. We cannot elaborate its meaning. The dog does not ask "Why?" or "What do you mean?" It is this limitation of intelligence or communication which disposes us to speak of training a dog rather than giving him instruction. What we seek to express by the phrase "giving instruction" is precisely what we seek to omit by the word *training*. Instructing seems, at least, to involve a kind of conversation, the object of which is to give reasons, weigh evidence, justify, explain, conclude, and so forth. It is true that whenever we are engaged in giving instruction, we are engaged in teaching; but it is not true that whenever we are engaged in teaching, we are giving instruction.[3]

This important difference between training and instructing may be viewed in another way. To the extent that instructing necessarily involves a kind of conversation, a giving of reasons, evidence, objections, and so on, it is an activity of teaching allied more closely with the acquisition of knowledge and belief than with the promotion of habits. Training, on the contrary, has to do more with forming habits and less with acquiring knowledge and belief. Instructing, in short, is more closely allied with the quest for understanding. We can train people to do certain things without making any effort to bring them to an understanding of what they do. It is, however, logically impossible to give someone instruction without at the same time attempting to bring him to some understanding. What this means, stated in its simplest and most ancient terms, is that instructing always involves matters of truth and falsity, whereas training does not—another reason for observing that instructing has more to do with matters of believing.

It is not, therefore, a bit of archaic nonsense to say that teaching is essentially the pursuit of truth. It is, on the contrary, an enormously important insight. The pursuit of truth is central to the activity of teaching because instructing is central to it. That, indeed, is the purpose of the kind of conversation basic to the concept of giving instruction. If instructing involves giving reasons, evidence, argument, and justifications, then instructing is essentially related to the search for truth.

[3] The reader should note that this point may be prejudiced by a curious limitation on the discussion which has been assumed, but so far has not been made explicit. The discussion of instruction here is confined to "instructing someone *in* such and such." Imagine a stockboy who, in taking inventory in a store, has been instructed to enter the total number of items on the shelf in his ledger in a certain way. Being "instructed to," in a context like this, is more akin to being "told to" or "ordered to" and may involve nothing in the way of explaining, justifying, questioning, or concluding. However, when we speak of giving someone instruction *in* taking inventory, presumably we have reference to a more complex activity which does involve explaining and so forth. The contrast is the difference between giving someone instruction, on the one hand, and giving someone *instructions*, on the other hand. We are concerned here only with the relation between teaching and giving someone instruction. Giving someone instructions may not be involved in teaching at all. For some important distinctions between teaching and telling, see Israel Scheffler, *The Language of Education*, chap. 5 (Springfield, Illinois, Charles C Thomas, 1960).

The point is not that instructing necessarily requires communication, although that would be true. The point is rather that it involves communication *of a certain kind*, and that kind is the kind which includes giving reasons, evidence, argument, and so forth, *for the purpose* of helping another understand or arrive at the truth. Scheffler makes the point with respect to the concept of teaching which I wish to make with respect to the concept of instructing. He says:

> To teach, in the standard sense, is at some points, at least, to submit oneself to the understanding and independent judgment of the pupil, to his demand for reasons, to his sense of what constitutes an adequate explanation. To teach someone that such-and-such is the case is not merely to try to get him to believe it. . . . Teaching involves further that . . . we try also to get him to believe it for reasons that within the limits of his capacity to grasp, are *our* reasons. Teaching, in this way, requires us to reveal our reasons to the student, and, by so doing, to submit them to his evaluation and criticism. . . .
>
> Even to teach someone *to* do something (rather than how to do it) is not simply to try to get him to do it; it is also to make accessible to him, at some stage, our reasons and purposes in getting him to do it. To teach is thus, in the standard use of the term, to acknowledge the "reason" of the pupil; i.e., his demand for and judgment of reasons, even though such demands are not uniformly appropriate at every phase of the teaching interval.[4]

It is this demand for reasons which I insist is essential to the conversation of instruction. But the important point is that although the purpose of instructing, in one sense, may be to get someone to do something or get someone to believe something, nonetheless, the purpose of the *conversation* of instruction is to get him to do it because he thinks he ought to, i.e., because he sees a good reason for doing or believing. In other words, the purpose is to shape someone's belief or behavior by helping him see that the belief is reasonable or the behavior justified. This is the sense in which the conversation of instruction has as its purpose the pursuit of truth or the acknowledgement of reasons.

"Teaching" and "Indoctrinating"

It is important to observe that the concept of instructing includes "teaching someone to do so-and-so" in the sense of *giving instruction* in doing so-and-so. In other words, instructing is like training in the respect that it can be

[4] *The Language of Education, op. cit.*, pp. 57–58.

directed at shaping behavior. But instructing also includes "teaching someone that . . .," and in this respect instructing differs from training in its relatively stronger emphasis on shaping belief or knowledge. In instructing, the concern is not simply that a person be taught to do or to believe, but that he be taught to do or to believe *for some good reason*, and moreover for a reason which *he* regards as good and sufficient.

Consider, however, what happens when this emphasis on shaping belief is rendered the sole concern of teaching. That is to say, what happens to the concept of instruction when our concern is simply to shape certain beliefs without a corresponding concern that the beliefs adopted are adopted for some good reason. No unusual powers of insight are needed to see that in that case, the concept of instructing fades off into what we would ordinarily call "indoctrinating" in the pejorative sense of that term. Instructing is transformed into indoctrinating when the concern to transmit certain beliefs because they are reasonable is changed simply into a concern to transmit beliefs. The difference between instructing and indoctrinating is a difference in the weight given to the pursuit of truth as opposed to the simple transmission of beliefs previously arrived at.

This difference of emphasis is reflected in the term "indoctrination" itself. Indoctrination is concerned with doctrine in a way which training and instructing are not. We indoctrinate people to believe certain things, but we train them or condition them to do certain things. Of the four modes of teaching we are studying, indoctrination seems to be the only one exclusively related to the formation of belief or transmission of doctrine. Moreover, and this is the telling point, the paradigmatic case of indoctrinating seems to be discoverable in an example of teaching some belief in which the primary purpose is simply to transmit a belief and get it adopted. Whether the belief is adopted for some good reason, whether it is grounded in evidence, or even whether it is a true belief is not of primary importance in indoctrinating as it is in instructing.

This point is of extraordinary importance. The different purposes involved in instructing and indoctrinating can be clearly seen in the different way each is judged to be a success. Consider the following rather simplified illustration. Suppose we find a person who does not know the identity of the discoverer of the American continent. We undertake to instruct him in American history with the idea of teaching him, among other things, that Columbus discovered America. Let us suppose that we present certain evidence, give explanations, enter into arguments with him, examine the statements of authorities, and that finally he concludes there are good grounds for the claim that the discoverer of the American continent was Columbus.

Let us suppose, however, that after extensive instruction he refuses to acknowledge that Columbus was the discoverer of the American continent.

Would it follow that our instruction had failed? Not necessarily. We would need to know for what reasons he refuses to assent to such a commonly held opinion. It may be, in fact, that the reasons for his judgment are better than those that can be offered for the more widely received opinion. He might say something like this: "There seems to be good evidence for the view that Columbus was not the first European to set foot on the American continent. Indeed, it seems a well-established fact that many years before Columbus's voyage, there were visitors of some Scandinavian descent to this continent. But the visits of these people seem not to have had the far-reaching historical consequences of Columbus's discovery. If you consider the historical consequences of great importance, then you might say that Columbus discovered America; but if you mean that his was the first discovery of America, then you would be mistaken."

You might think this an astonishing reply to get from an elementary student in American history. But perhaps it is not so extraordinary. In any case, the point is that such a reply would not signal a failure of instruction. On the contrary, it would be a sign of spectacular success. Oddly enough, however, if our purpose were to *indoctrinate* our student into the particular belief that Columbus discovered America, then his reply would constitute decisive evidence of failure. Indoctrination is an activity which aims at establishing certain beliefs or "matters of doctrine." It aims at inculcating the "right answer," but not necessarily for the "right reasons" or even for good reasons. Instructing, on the other hand, is an activity which has to do not so much with arriving at the "right answer" as with arriving at *an* answer on the right kind of grounds.

It is no valid objection to point out the many areas of knowledge in which it is important to lead students to the right answer. For all that is usually pointed out is that there are many areas of knowledge in which the grounds of decision are decisive and in which, therefore, there *is* a correct answer which it is important to know. Even in mathematics, however, where a "right answer" is often thought to be discoverable, a concern simply to lead students to that answer or to equip them to find it is a fundamentally defective kind of instruction. To focus simply on securing a right solution without understanding the nature of mathematical operations is the mathematical equivalent of indoctrination. Indeed, when indoctrination is seen to involve a certain style of knowing or believing, we can discover the possibility of indoctrination in nearly every area of human knowledge and not simply in those having to do with what we would commonly call "matters of doctrine." In other words, in teaching when we are concerned only to lead another person to a correct answer or correct belief without a corresponding concern that they arrive at that answer or belief on the basis of good reasons, then we are indoctrinating as contrasted with instructing.

These distinctions between indoctrinating and instructing are also partly differences of emphasis. But, here again, the differences of emphasis reveal a pattern, and it is a pattern we wish to make explicit. The following points may suffice:

1. Instructing and indoctrinating, like training and conditioning, are concepts that overlap. The distinction between them is not clear-cut at every point. They are alike in the respect that both have to do with the formation of knowledge and belief, but they are different in the respect that although indoctrinating has to do entirely with "teaching someone *that* . . .," instructing is a concept also used in connection with "teaching someone *to* . . .." This means that instructing is more closely related to training than is indoctrinating.

2. The most striking difference, however, turns on the fact that instructing and indoctrinating have different criteria for success. A successful attempt at instructing may at the same time be an unsuccessful attempt at indoctrinating. This clearly shows that instructing and indoctrinating are different activities at least in the sense that they have different purposes.

3. The reason why instructing and indoctrinating have different criteria for success is that they place a relatively different weight on the *grounds* of belief as opposed to the *content* of belief. Instructing is an activity of teaching in which relatively greater weight is given to the grounds of belief, and hence instruction may still be successful when *for some good reason* the student rejects the belief the teacher meant him to accept. Indoctrinating, by contrast, is an activity in which relatively little weight is given to the grounds of belief and relatively more to the content; hence indoctrination is successful if and only if the student accepts the belief the teacher seeks to transmit, even when the student may have no good reason for accepting it.

4. Instructing seems to aim at a way of believing which manifests intelligence, whereas indoctrinating does not. In this respect, indoctrinating is like conditioning. Conditioning is an activity which can be used to establish certain modes of behavior quite apart from their desirability. It aims simply to establish them. If a response to a certain stimulus is conditioned, the same stimulus will produce the same response even when the person admits it would be better if he responded otherwise. This is an unintelligent way of behaving. In an analogous way, indoctrinating is an activity which aims simply at establishing certain beliefs so that they will be held quite apart from their truth, their explanation, or their foundation in grounds or evidence.

5. If the hypothesis is true that teaching is an activity primarily concerned with enlarging the manifestation of intelligence, then it will follow that instructing is an activity which more perfectly displays the properties of teaching than does indoctrinating. If we represent this relationship

diagrammatically, then we can complete the continuum of the modes of teaching as follows:

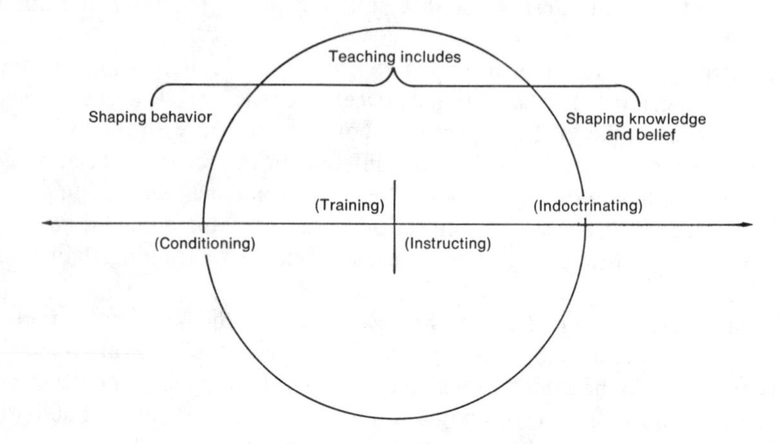

The analysis shows that although the different modes of teaching are distinguishable, still they bear a striking family resemblance. They all seem to be distributable along a continuum which represents a greater or lesser degree of attention to the manifestation of intelligence—either intelligence in behaving or intelligence in believing. There is no intention in this kind of analysis to argue that conditioning or indoctrination are not ways of teaching. The point is rather to see that sometimes they are and sometimes they are not. Nor is it any part of this sort of analysis to develop clear-cut and always applicable distinctions between the different modes of teaching. The intent is instead to understand clearly why it is that these concepts overlap, why it is that sometimes they seem synonymous and sometimes not. The purpose, in short, is not to propose a particular definition of teaching, but to see how the modes of teaching enter into our ordinary thinking, how they are related to one another and to the concept of teaching itself. The result is a kind of conceptual map, a representation of one kind of relationship that exists in the family of concepts that we ordinarily include in the idea of teaching itself.

26 / B. PAUL KOMISAR and JAMES E. MC CLELLAN

The Logic of Slogans

It is simple enough to notice that educational literature contains a surprisingly large number of such expressions as "Education for Life Adjustment," "Return to the Fundamentals," "The Ideal of Disciplined Intelligence," and "Pursuit of Excellence." These expressions *apparently* do not give any specific information, and we disparage them with the title of "slogans." When we find slogans in educational language we frequently become indignant. Moreover, our umbrage is magnified if the convicted slogan-user, be he administrator or philosopher of education, is not properly shameful when his error is pointed out to him.

Why is this so? Why should we hold pedagogical slogans in such disdain? Is it because of our failure to understand how slogans actually function in educational discourse? Do we not tend to judge pedagogical slogans according to models taken from other linguistic domains and applied uncritically to the language of education? If we would escape being the victims of both the sloganizers and the anti-sloganizers, we should ask ourselves these questions: What role do slogans play in educational language? How can we judge whether a particular slogan is playing its appropriate role? If so, is it acquitting itself well in this role?

1. The Ceremonial and Non-ceremonial Uses of Slogans

It requires no exceptional perspicacity to recognize that slogans are chosen to appeal to the feelings of the listener or reader. Sometimes slogans are used to do *only* this. Let us call this the ceremonial use of slogans, from the

B. Paul Komisar and James E. McClellan, "The Logic of Slogans," in B. Othanel Smith and Robert H. Ennis (Eds.), *Language and Concepts in Education*, pp. 195–214.

James E. McClellan (1922–) is a member of the Foundations of Education Department at Temple University. He is the author of *Toward an Effective Critique of American Education* and coauthor of *Education and the New America*.

context in which this use is most typically encountered[1]—a dedication, a convocation, an inauguration, or the like. On such a propitious occasion, a slogan may be a very useful device for emotive purposes, arousing interest, inciting enthusiasm, engendering loyalty, or achieving a unity of feeling and spirit. "Educational Leadership for a Free World" is a recent and notable example of a slogan used in this way.[2]

When used ceremonially, slogans do not usually refer or point to anything in particular. But this lack of concrete reference, while it infuriates many, probably confuses very few people. From the point of view of the sloganizer, the only criterion to apply to the ceremonial use of slogans is an empirical one: Does the slogan arouse the intended feelings? As the level of sophistication of the average educationist rises, slogan-makers will probably find it increasingly difficult to satisfy this criterion.

We call attention to this use of slogans only to avoid it. The study of how the ceremonial use of slogans may be handled more effectively (or avoided more skillfully) is not a matter for logical inquiry; it is a matter of skill in public relations or personal sanity. All slogans are chosen to appeal to feelings to some extent, but not all have this as their sole or primary function. Slogans sometimes occur in textbooks, lectures, seminars, and in meetings of educational policy-makers. Here slogans are used to give information and direction to educational activity, to create and establish rather definite language customs for the profession. These we call non-ceremonial uses of slogans, and our analysis is intended to apply to them.

Rarely, it would appear, does one have genuine difficulty in distinguishing between the ceremonial and non-ceremonial uses of a slogan. If a person asks for the meaning of *Lux et veritas*, we should ordinarily respond by translating the Latin into English. But suppose he then says, "Oh, I know how to translate the words. But I want to know what the motto means; that is to say, in what way an educational institution is different because it adopts this slogan as its motto rather than, say, *In lumine tuo videbimus lumen*."

Now this represents a case of mistaking a ceremonial use of slogans (putting them on the covers of college catalogues) for a non-ceremonial use of slogans (to convey, in a distinctive sort of way, information and directions). But usually we know when slogans are being used purely ceremonially, and we know that one does not ask from slogans so used, "What does it mean?" or "What should I do?"

[1] It's very doubtful that these ceremonial occasions are the most *usual* instances of a ceremonial use of slogans. But the ceremonial occasion provides the "point" of the slogan when used on other kinds of occasions.

[2] The expression was the "theme" of the Inauguration Year at Teachers College, Columbia University, 1955–56.

2. The Logic of Slogans

Slogans Considered as Summarizing Assertions. The educationally important uses of slogans are not the purely ceremonial ones. The important uses are those for which it does make sense to ask of a slogan, "What does it mean?" To understand these uses we propose the general rule: *When trying to find out what a slogan means, see what other assertions it summarizes.*[3] Some insight can be gained into the functioning of slogans by comparing them with generalizations, the assertion-form which they most closely resemble. Up to this point we have mostly used expressions as examples of slogans. If we are to compare them with generalizations, we must extend the word "slogan" to include utterances which have the grammatical form of assertions. Please note that we are using "assertion" in its most general sense, to include optative and prescriptive as well as descriptive utterances.

Slogans and Generalizations: Similarity. The first point is one of *resemblance* between generalizations ("all teachers are college graduates") and slogans ("we learn what we live"). Both are typically used to summarize other assertions not explicitly stated in the general assertion itself. How is this done? Imagine a hypothetical foreign lecturer who tells his audience that the disciplinary methods of teachers, standards of pupil achievement, and course of study found in his country differ from those he has observed here. He might stop there or go on (later in the lecture, perhaps) to state that public education in this country differs from public education in his homeland. In this case the general statement "public education differs in the two countries" is simply a restatement in *general* form of the many *particular* differences discussed in the lecture. The general statement summatively asserts the particular assertions; these *are* its meaning. Slogans in educational language often function in this way. On specific occasions when they are so used, they literally *mean* some list of other assertions.

The matter we want to call attention to is the relation between assertions of great generality on the one hand and particular assertions to which they are related on the other. The former act as (or are used as) summaries of the latter. For our purpose a particular assertion can be viewed as one in which

[3] The word "slogan" is applied even more widely than we will here consider it. The expression "Boost Soap Sales," bandied about by the salesmen of a soap company, would commonly be called a slogan. The expression is relatively specific; it does not resemble a generalization. In the remainder of this chapter we will concentrate on *general* slogans since an elucidation of the features of general slogans is important for understanding educational language.

a unique reference is made, and some simple, non-ambiguous assertion is then made about this reference; for example, "Miss Jones, teacher of Grade 5B in Smith School, should stress phonetics."

It is not uncommon for a generalization or slogan to summarize other generalizations or slogans. But these sub-slogans or generalizations may be reducible to more specific assertions. For example, we may be told that the task of a liberal education is to liberate the student to freedom through discipline (a very general slogan). Asking what this means, we may be told that, in part, this includes "Emphasizing the Rational Faculties of Students" (sub-slogan). More specifically (or prosaically), we might find that a proposal is being made to give instruction in logic and semantics. The last, when given a unique reference, would constitute a particular assertion subsumed under the slogans stated.

Slogans and Generalizations: Differences. When slogans are used as summaries, they differ from generalizations in several respects. When we speak of a generalization we ordinarily mean a general statement that is itself a descriptive assertion and summarizes more particular descriptive assertions. Of course, we can speak of prescriptive generalizations, but we must add the qualification "prescriptive" explicitly, else the descriptive will be understood. But in either case there is agreement in logical form between the generalization and its particulars: if the generalization is descriptive, all of its particulars will be descriptive; if prescriptive, all prescriptive.

Educational slogans, however, *always* contain a prescriptive element. There is a very good reason for this. Since education is a practical enterprise, aimed at the achievement of certain results through action, the language of education will inevitably be studded with assertions that are prescriptive. These particular assertions will be proposals and recommendations for action. The slogan itself may even be in the imperative form (e.g., "Make Learning Meaningful for Students"). But even if the slogan itself is in the indicative form, many of the assertions summarized by the slogan will not be. For example, the slogan "Good Teaching is Meaningful Teaching" may be summarizing, among others, such *proposals* to teachers as "discuss the practical application of the ideas presented," "give students reasons for the rules they are expected to obey," and "use visual devices."

Slogans, then, that seem to be nothing but *descriptions* of practice, to the extent that they are summarizing at all, end up summarizing assertions that do not merely describe educational practice but recommend, advise, exhort, hint, or suggest that certain educational practices should be followed and others avoided.

Let us look at the logic of this a bit more closely. When our foreign lecturer mentioned above says "education differs in the two countries," we realize in the context of his speech that he is summarizing what has gone before. Since his statement is not being used as a slogan and since it is in the indicative mood, we know that *all* the particular statements summarized by it will be indicative statements also (e.g., education differs in the two countries with respect to the average length of the school year). But contrast the slogan "Good Teaching is Meaningful Teaching." Although this assertion also has the form of an indicative statement, at the level of particulars it will be found to summarize not only descriptive statements but also, and more importantly, proposals for action. In fact, the descriptive statements and definitions it summarizes receive their relevance from their relation to the proposals. For example, in the context in which the slogan is used, perhaps an article in an educational journal, we might find the descriptive statement, "Miss Jones of Smith School reports a 50% greater enjoyment in the study of history by students who were shown films regularly in their history course." The point of this descriptive statement is to be found in its support of the proposal to the reader, "Use more visual devices in *your* teaching."

Slogans, then, may have one or more of these features usually not found in generalizations. (1) A slogan invariably summarizes, among other things, proposals for action. (2) There may be a disparity between the form or mood of the slogan and the assertions summarized by the slogan. (3) Slogans usually summarize assertions of differing logical types (descriptions, definitions, prescriptions), while a generalization does not.

Slogans and Generalizations: A Theoretical Explanation. Both slogans and generalizations may summarize particular assertions, but slogans summarize with much broader latitude than do generalizations. In explaining the differences, we wish to make two points: (1) Generalizations imply their particulars in a way that slogans do not; (2) Slogans are systematically ambiguous, in a demonstrable sense, until the systematic ambiguity is eliminated through a process of arbitrary delimitation of meaning.

(1) What we would call a generalization in common-sense or in scientific discourse can be said to *imply* a definite (or defined) set of particulars. Now this is no startling revelation, nor is it a statement likely to be contested on any philosophical grounds. Philosophers of different persuasions may wish to explain or interpret the concept of implication in different ways, but none would wish to deny that it holds between a generalization and its own defined set of particulars. In a perfectly straightforward, if not completely precise, fashion we may say that "all roses are red" means that if any object is a rose (thus defining a set of particular statements—"Object O_1 is a rose," "Object O_2 is a rose," and so on), then that object is red. The inverse square law of gravitation defines a set of particular statements—those describing the masses

and distances of all objects in the same physical universe—and implies the existence of a certain accelerative tendency between any two such objects. The latter example should make clear, if the first did not, that a set of particular statements need not be finite in length nor even knowable in principle.

Now this last feature of generalizations makes it possible to speak of the meaning of a generalization as something over and above any limited set of particulars that are offered as evidence or explanation of the generalization. Thus we may say that the meaning of "all roses are red" is not exhausted by any finite list of statements like "the rose in John's garden is red," "the rose in Mary's hand is red," and so on. From this it is a short step to the Whiteheadian idea that the complete explication of (i.e., making explicit what is necessarily implied in) any true generalization must reveal the necessary structure of the universe.

This may seem far removed from the logic of educational slogans; and so it is. But its relevance is not far to seek. When pedagogical slogans are translated into complete sentences, they typically take the form of statements of the purposes, aims, goals, ends, ideals, or ultimate values of education, and these statements closely resemble generalizations. Hence arises the quite common notion that the proper way to decide upon practices in a concrete situation is to formulate generalizations of aims or purposes of education and to draw the implications of these statements for the particular situation. If slogan-like statements of purposes or ends were logically identical with generalizations, and, further, if it were possible to formulate true statements of purposes or ends, then this commonly accepted procedure would have much to recommend it.

Sad to say, however, neither of these conditions can be met. We can assert at this point what remains to be demonstrated just below: slogans and generalizations differ in *how* they summarize their particulars; slogans do not *imply* their particulars in the way generalizations do. Slogans merely become connected or attached to a more or less clearly specified group of proposals, together with definitions and empirical evidence used as argument in favor of the proposals made. (Therein lies the genius or horror of slogans, however you would have it.) Assuming the satisfactory demonstration of that point, it follows that seeking to find the particulars summarized by a slogan is logically a quite different kind of procedure from that of finding the particular implications of a generalization. Between the generalized slogan and its application to a particular case stands a somewhat arbitrary act of interpretation.

(2) Initially, slogans are systematically ambiguous. Consider, for example, "More Democracy in the Classroom," a sometimes popular pedagogical slogan. There is no limit to the variety of conceivable practices this slogan could be summarizing. Does it propose ability grouping within the classroom

or not? Is a student government being recommended or a discussion of problems of democracy? The list could be extended indefinitely. Some proposals that might be made under this slogan will probably be inconsistent or, at least, incompatible with other possible proposals ("leadership by the teacher" or "more pupil planning"; "same instruction for all" or "vary instruction with ability"). This is what we mean when we speak of the *systematic* ambiguity of a slogan. A slogan that remains in this state is empty; it does not summarize. This is the sense in which we speak of a slogan as meaningless. Not that it has no reference, but that it is embarrassingly rich in this commodity. So to say that a slogan is meaningless is to say that no attempt is made (or that there is no other way) to restrict this great diversity of *possible* particulars.

Now let us pull together these two comments on slogans; that they do not imply particulars, and that they are systematically ambiguous. The two are obviously related, but we must note a qualification before stating this obvious relation.

Insofar as a slogan has the grammatical form of a statement, we may say that the slogan implies what the statement of it implies. For example, "Good Teaching is Meaningful Teaching" implies "for any *X*, if *X* is not meaningful teaching, then *X* is not good teaching." This is a valid implication from the statement. Or again, "All Teachers Ought to Transmit the Culture" implies "if Miss Jones is a teacher, then Miss Jones ought to transmit the culture." But notice we did not say that slogans do not imply *something*; we said that they did not imply their *particulars*. The implications drawn from the slogans just above are quite clearly not the particulars, that is, not the proposals to teach one set of materials rather than another, by one method rather than another, etc., that we have in mind when we talk about what the slogan *summarizes*.

Now it is clear that the implications drawn from a generalization (descriptive or normative) exclude otherwise possible states of affairs. Thus it can*not* be the case that at the same time (1) all crows are black and (2) object *F* is a non-black crow. Therefore, the *acceptance* of a generalization is logically tied to the *denial* of certain possibilities. But, since slogans do not imply their particulars, to accept a slogan does not logically require one to deny any proposals for teaching. Thus when one accepts "More Democracy in the Classroom" he has logically denied "Less Democracy in the Classroom," but he still has a bewildering plethora of possible particulars not excluded by his acceptance of the slogan. For non-ceremonial (informative, directive) purposes, a slogan left in this state is useless.

Slogans and Their Interpretation. But slogans need not remain in such a useless state. Slogans may come to summarize some definite set of particulars.

That is, in our term, it can come to acquire an *interpretation.*[4] For we can reduce the initial systematic ambiguity of a slogan by *deliberately* restricting or delimiting its application to some limited set of proposals within the larger amorphous class. So from all the possible particulars a slogan could conceivably be used to summarize, the slogan is made to apply to some sub-set of them. Notice, however, that, when performed, this is not only a *deliberate* act but largely an *arbitrary* one as well.[5] Some person or group actually *makes* this slogan mean this or that kind of educational program. They *give* the slogan this interpretation. In a sense, they are legislating or establishing a rule for the interpretation of their slogan (or of *the* slogan when *they* use it).

This is the essential difference between generalizations and slogans. Those who make "Democracy in the Classroom" *mean* "more teacher-pupil planning" cannot claim to be drawing an implication. They are arbitrarily

[4] It might seem more natural to speak of the "meaning" of a slogan rather than employing the unwieldly term "interpretation." We do in fact quite often ask "What do you mean?" when we want someone to interpret their slogan, i.e., give us the proposals they are summarizing with it. But the question "What does this slogan mean?" can be asked for different purposes. It could be a request for its historical or sociological significance ("What has the slogan 'Child-Centered School' meant to the Progressive Education movement?"). Or it might be taken as a request for a personal reaction ("What does it mean to you?"). To avoid these and other possible confusions, we use the word "interpretation" to refer to the proposals or program a slogan is used to summarize, and "interpreting a slogan" refers to the act of elucidating (indicating, specifying) the proposals. This retains one sense of the question "What does the slogan mean?" while avoiding contamination with the other senses.

[5] There is a sense of "arbitrary" in which it means "without justification." This is not the sense of the term we adopt. Actually, there may be good reasons for any particular restriction of meaning, not the least of which is the act of delimitation itself. For this act reduces the slogan to manageable form.

We call the giving of an interpretation an arbitrary act for two reasons: (a) Language permits the interpretation but does not demand it as it does with generalizations. (b) It is always possible to give an entirely new interpretation to an old slogan even when the slogan enjoys a standard interpretation.

To explain our use of "arbitrary" we must return to the difference between ambiguity and vagueness. The systematic ambiguity of a slogan is to be found in the range of linguistic expressions which it summarizes. The vagueness of a generalization is in the range of concrete objects to which it applies. In the latter case, for example, a court may have to exercise an arbitrary judgment in deciding whether "breaking and entering a building" applies to an act of forcing a latch on a chicken coop. But there is nothing arbitrary linguistically: If it is breaking and entering, then it is a felony. But whether the recommendation "Use more visual aids" is or is not included in the slogan, "Good Teaching is Meaningful Teaching," must be decided in a manner not determined by the rules of common sense language but by the preference of the user of the slogan. *In that sense*, it is arbitrary.

No one, of course, is required to provide an interpretation *de novo* each time he uses a slogan. Indeed, to the extent that a person wishes to take advantage of well known programs, he is not even permitted to. The logic is seen more clearly in simpler cases when it is possible to identify one man with one interpretation. See Section III, below, *Slogan Systems.*

legislating one into existence (for they might have ignored this point and made it *mean* something else, such as "teaching the Constitution"). Suppose generalizations got their meaning through the same kind of arbitrary act. Imagine, for example, a basketball coach who refers to a roomful of boys and says, "All those boys are on the second team." We can legitimately infer that for *each* boy it is true to say that "he is on the second team." This is what it means to draw implications from a generalization. But suppose the coach really did not want to include boys over six feet tall in his statement, though he neglected to tell us. This would be an arbitrary reservation (restriction), and we could not be expected to be aware of it. We could properly claim that he is misusing language or that on this occasion he is not using the assertion as a generalization at all. The fact that we can blame the coach for his use of language marks an important difference between slogans and generalizations. The arbitrary element is always present in slogans; it is not present (or should not be present) in generalizations.

This feature of slogans has the consequence that we cannot discover a slogan's interpretation by examining only the slogan itself. If some group asserts the slogan, "Teach the Structure of the Subject," they must explicitly inform us (or in some way let it be known) what educational program they have in mind. They must inform us what pedagogical practices are being prescribed and what proscribed with this slogan. There are two qualifications to this requirement. (1) It is not necessary for each and every detailed proposal to be made explicit. Vagueness, in the sense of incompleteness and lack of precision, may remain after systematic ambiguity is removed or reduced. (2) Logically, an arbitrary act of delimitation has to occur, but there are different ways of conducting it; that is, there are different procedures for reducing systematic ambiguity.

(1) As noted above, the difficulty we encounter when dealing in slogans is discovering the educational proposals some slogan is being made to summarize. From a larger array (or disarray) of possibilities a selection must be made. But this does not require that a complete detailed list of precise proposals be given. It is usually acceptable if some indication is given of the *kind* of educational program that is being proffered. Though this will probably be done by giving actual sample proposals embraced by the program, the proposals may lack precision, and the entire program may never be completely specified. Thus, under the same slogan, "Produce Students Who Think," one person may indicate an educational program wherein "the basic disciplines are rigorously taught." Another may author a program in which "significant social problems are exhaustively studied." Now, the programs have not been stated with any exactness; yet the systematic ambiguity has been considerably reduced. We now have a fairly good idea of the kind of thing that is meant by the slogan in each case. So the systematic ambiguity may be reduced, though a kind of vagueness remains.

(2) There are diverse modes of communication a spokesman may adopt to interpret his slogan. Of course, the usual procedure is to list some of the intended proposals. Or the sloganizer may indicate his interpretation by referring us to previous writings of his own or his colleagues. Or he may attach himself publicly to some well-known public-school program. But some writers on educational matters eschew such procedures. A Broudy or a Ulich will indicate his meaning by a wealth of allusion. The very language they choose to present their views may suggest (by form and cadence especially) the kind of education they are proposing. This latter mode of presentation serves the additional purpose of attracting favorable attention to the interpretation being offered. Yet even in these cases the act of delimiting the usage of a slogan is precisely the legislative, as opposed to the implicative, procedure that has been pointed out above as the necessary condition for eliminating the systematic ambiguity of slogans.

Slogans and Standard Interpretations. A mark of exceptional success in interpreting slogans is, without doubt, the occasion when others accede to or adopt it. Thus, custom comes to bless some slogans with a standard interpretation (though it is doubtful if this common awareness will ever extend down to the level of specific proposals). For example, educationists in general are aware of (if not always in agreement with) the proposals commonly summarized by the slogan "Education for Life Adjustment." This slogan has come to be a summary of the program expressed by the Ten Imperative Needs of Youth. (Note: The needs themselves are sub-slogans that probably receive various interpretations in practice.) The man who utters this slogan on some occasion, *to mean this program*, need not present an explicit interpretation of the slogan. He can assume, under normal circumstances, that his audience is familiar with the proposals being offered to school people.

Much of the accepted activity of educational debate and discussion is to establish and disestablish standard interpretations of certain slogans. Educators spend a good deal of time attempting to capture slogans for one set of proposals rather than for another. They try to get such adjectives as "vital," "democratic," and "creative" attached to one program rather than another. Perhaps the natural history of such a dispute might run somewhat as follows. A foreign country's scientific achievements lead many to want more highly trained scientific personnel than our schools currently produce. A rash of slogans appear as promissory notes for programs that will yield more such people than are currently available. Interpretation provides a few postulates; research (some of it of high quality, most not) is carried on in the interest of determining whether a given set of particulars in the program will produce people who have the skills required by employers. Then a contradiction appears: some of these new particulars are seen to be just those rejected in some rather well accepted slogan. So a reinterpretation of the older slogan (e.g., "Education for Democratic Citizenship") is called for, and usually provided. What occurs simultaneously is that certain administrators take the promissory slogans and provide their own interpretations for them in practice. At one time all these may be going on at once, and the uninitiated may find the controversy very disconcerting. This is one situation in which argument over words is not trivial. He who can successfully claim squatter's rights on, say, "developing the leadership potential of American youth" has gained a real advantage over the man who has to call his program "I.Q.-segregated training program for future military executives."

Of course, other educational strategy and tactics may be viewed as attempts to alter or even dissolve standard interpretations. Criticism is aimed at showing that some proposals should be added or deleted or revised. Continued debate on these matters may lead to the formation of different camps, each campaigning for a slightly different version of a slogan which once enjoyed a standard interpretation. "Traditional Education" and "Teaching the Fundamentals" seem to have suffered this fate, and it is probably no longer appropriate to speak of these slogans as possessing a common interpretation.[6] At least three claimants for the appealing "Basic Education" are currently disputing the title.

Résumé. The distinction we have drawn between interpreted and uninterpreted slogans tends to be irrelevant to an examination of the ceremonial use of slogans. For that use, however, we are not at all interested in the meaning of the slogan but solely in its emotive impact on the hearers.

This laissez faire attitude is inappropriate, however, when slogans are used non-ceremonially. On these occasions a failure to maintain this distinction can result in abuses. Rugg's use of "future-centered education" is an example of such an abuse. The context (a textbook) calls for a slogan with some more or less definite interpretation. This is made obvious when educators are charged with *failing* to have supplied a "future-centered education." Rugg does not interpret his slogan, but without an interpretation there is no criterion of success; and without a criterion of success it makes no sense to speak of failure. A similar case is the administrator who gets support for his policy at *only* the slogan level. He may take this as sufficient warrant to engage in all kinds of *particular* activities never explicitly connected with the slogan. This, too, is an abuse of slogans. It comes from a failure to realize that when a slogan is used non-ceremonially, an interpretation is required.

Note that we do not require that a slogan be *completely* interpreted. There

[6] The process of reinterpreting (or interpreting out of existence) certain summarizing assertions in education can be seen clearly in the contemporary public discussion of education. See C. Winfield Scott and Clyde M. Hill, eds., *Public Education Under Criticism* (New York: Prentice-Hall, Inc., 1954), esp. Chaps. II, III, and IV.

is a sense in which we do not know exactly what a slogan means until we know all the particulars (with specific time and space restrictions) summarized by it. But there is a difference between knowing what the slogan means and knowing *exactly* (in that sense) what it means. Let us therefore modify the rule announced above to read: *When trying to find the meaning of a slogan, seek its interpretation.* Corollary: *Never use a slogan in such a way that you encourage asking for its meaning without being prepared to offer an interpretation.* Corollary: *Do not change interpretations without giving clear, and preferably prior, notice.*

Perhaps someone might object that ours is an unwarranted application of the term "slogan." The objector might claim that this label is reserved for assertions that are uninterpreted and *only* used to arouse feelings. In the next section we apply the term to a body of educational writing that is renowned for its seriousness and austerity of purpose. It is essential, therefore, that we answer this objection.

Now, it is true that there may be a few people who persist in employing the term "slogan" to defame statements found in educational discourse. These people will no doubt be incensed at our failure to condemn sloganizing in general. But there are many general assertions encountered in educational writing and discussion that are neither descriptive nor prescriptive generalizations. The logic of slogans fits them. In educational psychology and methods textbooks they are often called principles or even general methods. Now when we apply the label and logic of slogans to them, we are not making an unwarranted extension of usage. We merely clarify an established practice. There are, for example, political expressions such as "Fifty-Four Forty or Fight," "Speak Softly but Carry a Big Stick," "Manifest Destiny" which are called slogans. Though these expressions quite obviously have a hortatory function, they do more than merely exhort. They summarize, but do not *imply*, a rather clearly specified program. This program includes *proposals* for what to do in the field of foreign relations as well as other assertions in the indicative form. Now these are the logical features of interpreted slogans as we have discussed them. These political slogans are the counterparts of similar assertions found in the educational literature ("Education is not Preparation for Life; It is Life"). Since they share the logical characteristics of slogans, why call them by any other name?

3. Slogan Systems

Analyzing Slogan Systems. Up to this point we have devoted exclusive attention to the isolated educational slogan and its interpretation. This approach seemed necessary in order to explain the distinctive logical characteristics of interpreted slogans. But in educational discourse, it is not the individual slogan that is of most significance; it is the slogan which, in context with other slogans, serves to unify a range of different proposals for education.

The activity commonly called "philosophy of education" (or its product, called sometimes by the same name and sometimes "theory of education") is in large part a matter of constructing and interpreting slogans. Customarily, one grand slogan—in which the fundamental "purpose" or "definition" of education is stated—is used to summarize many sub-slogans covering the accepted areas of educational activity. For example, consider Professor Ulich's statement, "Education, rightly conceived, is the process by which a growing person, according to his individual capacity, is prepared to understand himself, his relation to the universe, and to act upon this understanding."[7] This assertion, itself clearly a slogan in the sense of this essay, does not answer directly any educational questions. It does not propose that certain materials be taught to certain kinds of students under certain administrative conditions. Nor is there a standard interpretation for "rightly conceived education." But in Professor Ulich's own works and in those of his followers we see that this slogan summarizes more particular slogans which are interpreted by Ulich in such a way that systematic ambiguity is reduced to a minimum, and more importantly, those various sub-slogans have an interconnectedness that permits us to call the whole a slogan system.

In this sense a philosophy of education is literally a *system* of slogans. It is, indeed, the apex of educational sloganizing. In a well-constructed philosophy of education we find not only interpretations given for sub-slogans, we find also more general slogans which encompass the sub-slogans and give to the whole scheme an inner consistency and an outward charm.

The manifold advantages of a slogan system as compared with other forms of educational discourse can be seen clearly if we glance at two quite similar slogans, "The Objective of Self-Realization," as found in the 1938 statement of the Educational Policies Commission, and "The Principle of Self-Realization," as found in Broudy's *Building a Philosophy of Education.*[8] In the E.P.C. statement we have a congeries of slogans; in Professor Broudy's work, a system. In the former the interpretations of the slogan are crude, abrupt, disconnected. According to what we have already said, the E.P.C. has a perfect right to use this slogan to summarize such sub-slogans as "The Educated Person Knows How to Write the Mother Tongue" and "The Educated Person Knows How to Read the Mother Tongue." But the transition is neither smooth nor appealing.

[7] Robert Ulich, *Crisis and Hope in American Education* (Boston: Beacon Press, 1951), p. xi.

[8] Educational Policies Commission, *Policies for Education in American Democracy* (Washington: The Commission, 1946), pp. 193–213. Harry Broudy, *Building a Philosophy of Education* (New York: Prentice-Hall, Inc., 1954), Chap. 3.

In Professor Broudy's work, however, an entire language system has been skillfully developed just in order, or so it would appear, that the general slogan merges easily downward to the particulars he proposes and upward to still more general ethical and epistemological assertions. This slogan system enables him to relate the proposed changes in educational practice to the basic moral commitments and spiritual aspirations of his society. What appear at first blush to be mere metaphysical impedimenta actually function as quite useful baggage. A fully developed slogan system must necessarily cover a lot of ground; the metaphysical slogans, those of greatest generality, make it possible to take this journey in comfort.

But these advantages of a slogan system may be bought at too high a price. If we confuse the slogans with generalizations, if we try to argue the metaphysical assertions of a slogan system as if they had a meaning over and above their summarizing function, the price may be exorbitant. The most promising solution would seem to be the issuing of a general caveat to the users of slogan systems. If slogans are unavoidable in educational discourse, then we would do well to attend to the slogan systems; for in these we find slogans in their most useful form. But we must not permit the generalization form, in which we express well-developed slogans, to conceal from us their true nature. The slogans in a slogan system mean what the system's author interprets them to mean; or rather, the particulars summarized by the slogan system are those the system's author has decided it shall summarize. Any given statement within a slogan system may have a non-slogan meaning over and above its slogan function, but that meaning is ordinarily carefully distinguished (it must, in any event, be distinguished) from its meaning as a statement in a slogan system. This last injunction is nothing but common sense. If we have before us a statement such as "the school should promote self-realization," and we are asked what it means, we know, if we are at all wise, to ask where it comes from, what is its context, before trying to explain its meaning. The meaning of a statement within a slogan system is determined by the interpretation of that system.

At this point an objection might be raised against the analysis of philosophies of education as slogan systems. Imagine Mr. B raising the point in this way:

> *Mr. B:* "You say, then, that educational theories or philosophies of education are helpfully analyzed by the logic of slogans. The very general assertions encountered in these theories do not resemble generalizations, but slogans. And the specific assertions made in the same contexts are not descriptions *implied* by generalizations but proposals *arbitrarily attached* to slogans."
>
> "Yes, that is essentially correct."
>
> *Mr. B:* "But you know as well as I that we often charge people with misinterpreting or misapplying the theories of someone else.

> What could this charge mean but that improper implications have been drawn from general statements given in the theory? But on your account this is impossible. Since you do not admit the existence of an implicative track, how can you account for these implicative derailments? On your view, how can anyone ever misinterpret the intent or meaning of another's theory?"

This is a serious objection. We do in fact frequently speak of someone violating or misinterpreting in practice a theory invoked to justify the practice. Any analysis that is unable to account for misinterpretation is automatically suspect.

But Mr. B is mistaken in his contention that misinterpretation is an implicative fallacy. This notion that from a number of general statements in an educational theory, we deduce some specific statements is just another philosophical myth. Rather, misinterpretation is sometimes just what the name suggests—a "missed" interpretation. The practitioner might completely overlook the relevant specific proposals actually given somewhere in the context of the theory. But this is not so much misinterpretation as simply an error.

The occasion for misinterpretation arises when proposals are offered that go beyond those found in the theory itself. The interpreter develops additional practical proposals not given by the original author of the theory. In this sense the practitioner is extending the interpretation of the author's slogans. Since there is no strict rule dictating these extensions, how can we say that they are rightly or wrongly made? Though it is not uncommon to find the charge of misinterpretation leveled, there always is some difficulty in substantiating it. We *do* have trouble in deciding whether extensions of some theory are justified. The matter is not as simple as the "implicative model" would have us believe. We are rather generous in our appraisal of different interpretive extensions of the same root theory when these interpretations do not differ radically. Is it proper to interpret Dewey, a leading educational philosopher, as a supporter of the "planned curriculum"? Did he *really* have a strong social dimension in his theory? These are difficult questions, and we are quite willing to entertain differences of opinion over answers to them.

But if pressed to give a positive or negative appraisal of someone's interpretation of Dewey, how might we answer? Ultimately, the only test we have is whether the author of the theory himself would have welcomed this additional interpretation of his slogan. But, of course, when we charge someone with misinterpretation, we do not resort to this ultimate test. In deciding whether a person has properly interpreted some slogan in a slogan system, we take into account two aspects of the system. First, if the original theorist gave any interpretation to this slogan at all, we judge whether the later interpreter is giving the same *kind* of interpretation. Secondly, we judge the interpretation of one slogan against the backdrop of the other slogans (the "metaphysical baggage") in the system. Every teacher of philosophy of education has learned to fear the day when a student takes an isolated assertion from Dewey and offers the practical implications of it. Yet if Dewey's famous general assertions were generalizations rather than slogans, this procedure would be quite acceptable.

In principle, the process of judging whether a theorist has been misinterpreted is relatively simple. If Mr. *X* gives an interpretation of Dewey's slogan system, we ask whether Mr. *X*'s interpretation is the sort of proposal Dewey would have included, given Dewey's slogans and the kind of interpretation Dewey himself gave them. *In practice*, of course, it is excruciatingly difficult to make such a judgment. But if it were simply a matter of checking a new proposal by whether or not it can be deduced from the theory, this difficulty would not make sense.

Mr. B, in raising this objection, has actually pointed to a major difficulty in the "generalization-deduction" model of educational philosophy. As it turns out, when we use the model of a slogan system, we can account for both the existence of misinterpretation and also the difficulty we encounter in judging whether a charge of misinterpretation is justified.

Appraising Slogan Systems. (1) Any student recently emerged from instruction in philosophy can recite the standard tests of good "theory." Among other things, to be acceptable, a theory must be consistent, comprehensive, and parsimonious. That is, the constituent elements in the theory must be internally consistent, all the relevant "facts" must be accounted for by the theory, and this must be accomplished with the fewest possible number of basic terms.

These tests, of course, apply also to slogan systems; they do so, however, quite differently from the way they might be applied to a scientific theory. In dealing with slogan systems, these tests become simply convenient names for an indefinite number of challenges a slogan system might be exposed to. So when we say that a slogan system has passed these tests, we are not calling direct attention to any *particular* feature present in the slogan system. Instead we are attending to a whole assortment of features and indirectly reporting that the theory has either forestalled certain questions or has been able to answer them satisfactorily by adroit manipulation within the system.[9]

Thus, for example, under the label of comprehensiveness a slogan system might be challenged because it failed to make proposals concerning the

[9] These concepts (consistency, comprehensiveness, and parsimony) are *defeasible* in much the same way as certain legal concepts ("voluntary") and ordinary concepts ("responsibility"). See H. L. A. Hart, "On the Ascription of Rights and Responsibilities," in *Logic and Language*, A. G. N. Flew, ed., First Series (Oxford: Basil Blackwell, 1952), pp. 145–66.

emotional development of children or because it contained no provisions to help students prepare for careers in science. Such demands, however, vary with time and social context, and a mark of deficiency at one time may be a positive boon at another. These factors account for the difficulties one encounters in trying to specify, exactly, how much "ground" an educational theory has to cover to be comprehensive. These positive features are not easily identifiable, but we do know specifically that a theory is not comprehensive if we detect a certain particular and currently relevant deficiency.

Similarly with the tests of parsimony and consistency. Suppose a theory contained proposals aimed at refining the emotional responses of young children constituting an interpretation of the slogan "Teach the Whole Child." We might question whether these proposals might not be better summarized under another slogan already included in the same system. In the name of parsimony, then, we would request that the theorist expunge all reference to "the whole child" in his slogan system.

A special difficulty arises when applying the test of consistency. The questions we ask of a slogan system under this label are not concerned, by and large, with issues of formal contradiction as the name might suggest. This may be part of the story, of course, but we mainly ask whether certain proposed practices are compatible with others on sheer empirical grounds even though no formal contradiction is involved. We might take account of this by construing the test as one of compatibility. For example, there is no formal contradiction between these two proposals: (1) Schools should focus attention on the great literary heritage of our civilization; and (2) Schools should provide essentially the same education for all youth. But for quite obvious reasons, the person who tried to act on both these proposals would find them incompatible.

Finally, it is important to note that none of these tests (i.e., the challenges they summarize) can be applied to slogans *per se*. This follows from the very nature of a slogan. Except in a very trivial sense, one slogan cannot contradict another, although their interpretations may conflict. It is amazing that such a number of critics overlook this very obvious point. It is not at all uncommon to find people who criticize slogans without paying the slightest attention to the interpretation or interpretations given to them in educational discourse. The critic feels perfectly free to give his own interpretation (which is legitimate) and then to criticize it as if his constituted the standard interpretation. A further analysis in these terms of certain writings on public education by people only superficially acquainted with education discourse would be instructive.

(2) Some charges that might be leveled against a slogan system cannot be satisfactorily categorized by the three standard tests discussed above. For example, granting that some educational theory has a slogan covering the emotional development of children, we can ask whether this slogan has been

sufficiently interpreted. But once again this positive sounding criterion, "a philosophy of education must be interpreted," does not demand a certain predetermined level of interpretation. We only require that present demands for specification be met. So this criterion, also, is simply a convenient general label for an assortment of specific questions that might be put to a sloganizer, specifically, in this case, questions concerning the systematic ambiguity of his slogans (e.g., "What do you mean by 'logical order of knowledge'?" or "What do you mean by 'adjustment to the universe'?"). We may say that a slogan system must be capable of interpretation, not already interpreted, to any level of specificity desired. The amount of interpretation required depends on how much is asked for. As long as the questioner will detail the actual conditions under which the theory is supposed to operate, the author or supporter of the slogan system must be prepared to offer practical proposals. But, as indicated below, he is unwise if he interprets in too detailed fashion within his general statement.

Finally we may test a slogan system against the criterion of attractiveness.[10] The theory must have the power to charm. For if it fails to attract serious defenders and critics, if it does not enlist disciples and opponents, it has failed as a slogan system. It may still serve some ends; it may be an interesting intellectual exercise or contribute proposals to other slogan systems. But as a slogan system its days are numbered outside of academic circles. Here, more obviously than anywhere else, it is apparent that a successful slogan system does not possess some one feature not found in other, less fortunate, theories. This single criterion is a label for a concatenation of features and the way they are organized. We might be asking about any one of these features by questioning its attractiveness.

[10] In connection with this discussion, see Joseph Justman's plea for a new slogan system in *School and Society*, May 12, 1956. Jerome Bruner's *The Process of Education* (Cambridge: Harvard University Press, 1960) seems the most promising slogan system to appear in many years. Indeed this book represents an almost classic case of the natural history of a slogan system as discussed earlier, especially in passages like the following (p. 9): "We may take as perhaps the most general objective of education that it cultivate excellence [a most persuasive slogan-word currently]. . . . It here refers . . . to helping each student achieve his optimum intellectual development. [This is hoary but still effective.] Good teaching that emphasizes the structure of a subject is probably more valuable for the less able student than for the gifted one. . . ." Here not only are currently conflicting slogans reconciled, but the key word in the synthesis, "structure," has such a solid sound that one is not put off when regard is shown for the currently unfashionable less able student. If Mr. Bruner and his associates can provide the necessary interpretations of the slogan system when called on, they may perform a most valuable function, perhaps providing at least a linguistic basis for overcoming the "tragic" fragmentation between academics and educationists. *Cf.* Gordon B. Turner: "A Report on the Conference of the National Commission on Teacher Education and Professional Standards," *Newsletter* of the American Council of Learned Societies, Oct. 1960. This group also had a slogan, "New Frontiers in Teacher Education and Professional Standards," but they lacked a common slogan system.

Let us give attention to one component of charm. Confronted with a slogan system, we can always ask if it has the potential for growth and development. As indicated above, some theories may be over-interpreted to the level of stultifying detail. There is a strong presumption tha tover-interpretation reduces a slogan system's attractiveness. Such a system may not enlist creative minds to its camp, since it leaves so little working room for imagination. A little too much interpretation may be a dangerous thing.

At the practical level the situation is reversed. For whether or not teachers and administrators are actually influenced by the theory is apt to depend upon the presence of specific proposals. The slogan system must tell the practitioner what, where, when, and how to do something. In this requirement we have one goad to system building in education. The educational theorist finds himself facing a task that only the most imaginative and disciplined mind could complete successfully. The sloganizer must produce a system that is, at one and the same time, *vague* enough to attract theorists and sufficiently *specific* to direct the practitioner. No mean assignment!

The only appropriate response is a slogan system. The logic of slogans admits the richness, flexibility, and subtlety in using language that are essential to doing the jobs that an educational theory must do. The history of Western educational thought is a rich storehouse for those who wish to understand the logic of slogans.

As a criterion against which to appraise slogan systems, attractiveness may well be a general test embracing all the others that have been mentioned. For slogan systems do not die from explicit rejection, but through lack of attention. With theories, as with lovers, it is the little attentions that count. When the general slogans in the system fail to capture imagination, no longer command loyalty, and creative disciples fade away, the system dies. But the less general sub-slogans survive, become modified and temporarily involved with other systems. Some of the proposals attached to these sub-slogans become accepted tools in the teacher's repertoire regardless of theoretical commitments. After a time we even cease to speak of these as parts of slogan systems; they become simply good advice to teachers. Prospective teachers may be advised to organize their subject matter into units of study that have some degree of wholeness in themselves and also some point of initial interest and appeal to students, without the prospective teachers ever being aware of the existence of the systems of Kilpatrick or Morrison. Research is done at this level, testing the consequences when this advice is followed. But the stimulus to significant, imaginative research comes from the slogan system in which the proposal is temporarily housed, although the positive results of this research outlive, usually, the slogan system that inspired it. This is the level at which we can speak of progress in pedagogical knowledge. This advice accumulates and one can always criticize a slogan system for failure to include it or otherwise take account of it.

Questions for Discussion

Komisar begins his essay with a paradox. State and explain the paradox. What are the important differences between equal opportunity and equal treatment? Has the author made a defensible case for these distinctions? Keeping the two types of equality clearly in mind, would you agree that "The principle of equal opportunity (in virtue of its general reference) is not a principle of schooling . . ."? Does Komisar's conception of equal opportunity differ significantly from some of the more prominent ones in the educational literature? If so, in what respects? What is the importance of Komisar's distinction between the "historical legitimacy" of equal opportunity in schooling and that of "logical necessity"? Komisar draws some important conclusions about compulsory schooling. Give reasons for your agreement or disagreement with these conclusions.

Green makes a number of important distinctions in his essay on teaching. The first distinction is between "teaching that" and "teaching to." What use does he make of this distinction, and how do the differences between the two operate later in his analysis of teaching? Distinguish teaching from training, conditioning, instructing, and indoctrination. In what sense are there "family resemblances" among these processes? Does Green primarily derive the meaning of his concepts from an analysis of ordinary language? If so, then is ordinary language, in view of its impreciseness and ambiguity, a suitable source for the development of concepts? Does ordinary language need to be refined or reconstructed? Although the author's purpose is not to pose a particular definition of teaching, he seems to offer one. On what does he base it?

Komisar and McClellan concentrate their attention on the nonceremonial, rather than ceremonial, use of slogans. Note the difference between the two. What are the similarities and differences between slogans and generalizations? What are slogan systems and how are they used in educational discourse? How can it be determined whether a person has properly interpreted a slogan in a slogan system? What do the authors mean when they say that the "advantages of a slogan system may be bought at too high a price"? They also claim that in a sense "a philosophy of education is literally a *system* of slogans. It is, indeed, the apex of educational sloganizing." Explain why you concur or disagree with this conclusion.

Suggested Reading

Concepts pertaining to teaching, knowing, intelligence, morality, and others are analyzed by James Gribble, *Introduction to Philosophy of Education*

(Boston: Allyn and Bacon, 1969). A brief introduction to concepts of education, subject matter, knowledge, learning, and the like are developed by Jonas F. Soltis in *An Introduction to the Analysis of Educational Concepts* (Reading, Mass.: Addison-Wesley Publishing Co., 1968). C. D. Hardie was one of the first to deal systematically with educational concepts and arguments in *Truth and Fallacy in Educational Theory* (Cambridge: Cambridge University Press, 1942). Another early approach, one which places restrictions on the role of philosophy of education, is D. J. O'Connor's *An Introduction to Philosophy of Education* (New York: Philosophical Library, 1957). Israel Scheffler deals with definitions in education, educational slogans and metaphors, and teaching and telling in *The Language of Education* (Springfield, Ill.: Charles C Thomas, Publisher, 1960).

Two works provide the opportunity to examine educational arguments in considerable detail. Bertram Bandman's *The Place of Reason in Education* (Columbus, Ohio: Ohio State University Press, 1967) is principally concerned with the use of metaphysical and moral arguments in education, whereas Robert Ennis' *Logic in Teaching* (Englewood Cliffs, N.J.: Prentice-Hall, 1969) is a full-scale study with exercises of deductive logic, definition, explanation, and justification as they relate to education.

There are several valuable collections of essays on educational concepts. A number of American educators address themselves to concepts and cognate concerns in B. Othanel Smith and Robert H. Ennis, eds., *Language and Concepts in Education* (Chicago: Rand McNally & Co., 1961). Two collections of essays, primarily by British authors, deal with a number of important concepts and problems: R. D. Archambault, ed., *Philosophical Analysis and Education* (New York: Humanities, 1965); and Richard S. Peters, ed., *The Concept of Education* (New York: Humanities, 1967).

Finally, one should not overlook George F. Kneller's clear and accurate survey of the entire field of formal and informal logic in education in *Logic and Language of Education* (New York: John Wiley and Sons, 1966).

PART THREE /

THE STUDY OF EDUCATION

CHAPTER SEVEN /

EDUCATION AS A DISCIPLINE

SOME educators in recent years have been interested in whether education is a discipline. To speak of the study of education as a discipline is in a sense honorific: it bestows higher status on such a study. Moreover, few would want to devote a professional career to an activity that has no scholarly substance or any promise of achieving it. Yet other issues are also involved. A number of persons are interested in advancing the study of education to the point where it would be considered a science. Still others have the somewhat more modest aim of making education a recognized scholarly study based on a substantive body of knowledge and reasonably distinctive methods of inquiry. If education became a science it would be able to explain and to predict educational phenomena and outcomes, resulting in the improvement of educational practice. Making education a scholarly study would lead not only to greater recognition in the academic community but ultimately to some improvements in educational practice. These predicted improvements in practice would most likely accrue as the scholarly study of education learned how best to bridge the gap between theory and practice and uncovered more effective ways of developing, disseminating, and implementing educational findings.

Part of the difficulty may lie in different meanings ascribed to the terms *education* and *discipline* and the lack of agreement on the definitions. The normative definitions of *education* are far too numerous to list. The situation is somewhat less complicated with the concept of *discipline*; however, the different definitions and interpretations may create an initial point of confusion. Obviously the more common meaning of the term *discipline*—prescribed conduct or training that perfects or molds the individual's intellectual abilities or moral character to some desired end—is not under consideration here. One notion is that a discipline is a field of study governed by a set of guiding rules. Under this definition physical education and industrial arts, both of which have rules that guide practice, would be disciplines. A second interpretation is that it is either a substantive body of knowledge or an area of inquiry that in some respects is distinct from other disciplines, which may also have some distinctive methods of inquiry. For instance, both physics and biology would qualify because they have substantive bodies of knowledge and areas of inquiry that in certain respects are distinct from other fields. Physical education and industrial arts would fulfill this interpretation only in a much more limited sense. A third way of speaking of a discipline is to say that an area of inquiry has its own laws and theories. Physics would be an example par excellence. Although the social sciences and education have their own theories, their explanatory and predictive power is far more limited than the physical sciences; in contrast to the physical sciences, it is also questionable whether they have laws or are limited to law-like statements and principles. Finally, there is the social sense of discipline, in which individuals identify themselves with a learned society, its meetings, activities, and publications. Through communication and social interaction on problems and issues of joint concern, and through the sharing of common modes of inquiry that enable their findings to be meaningful to their fellows, the bonds among them are strengthened, and their activities become more systematically organized in light of these shared interests. Of the four interpretations of a discipline, the second is probably most commonly employed.

There are a number of arguments why education is not a discipline and a number of responses to those arguments. It is commonly said that "education is an art, not a science." According to proponents of this position, teaching is essentially an art that can never be fully captured by scientific study. Great teachers display genuine artistry in their activities, an artistry that cannot be reduced to scientific formulas and empirical data. However, in another sense this may be beside the point, for the *practice* of every science is an art. Further, if teaching is an art, most teacher education programs have been seriously misdirected; for systematic preparations for art are limited undertakings. However, many educators believe that scientific approaches to teaching may yield more reliable knowledge and eventuate in improved practices, and they present studies to corroborate their findings.

For some, education is an applied field, as engineering is an application of the physical sciences, as politics applies political science, and as social work applies sociology. These applied fields are not primarily devoted to research and knowledge for its own sake; instead, they are designed to effect changes and improvements in policy and practice and to prepare practitioners for service. Education is the application of findings and methodologies from psychology, sociology, philosophy, and other disciplines for the purpose of improving educational policy and practice. The upshot of this position is that in order to be fully competent to improve policy and practice, an educator would need a degree of expertise in many disciplines. Should the educator have competence in only one discipline, his understanding and abilities would be limited to areas in which the discipline could be applied, and he would be unable to envision the problems of education in full perspective. Thus this position demands that the educator, should he wish to be truly effective, become an encyclopedist in an age in which such a goal is virtually impossible. Moreover, this position overlooks the fact that those who study education have a domain of investigation not usurped by other disciplines—namely, organized schooling. This does not mean that educative experiences in the family, neighborhood, in voluntary groups, and other areas of the larger society are ignored; findings in these areas by sociologists and other investigators must be considered in terms of their impact on formal schooling. Perhaps what is borrowed from other disciplines is not the area of study but many of the methods of inquiry and, to a considerably lesser extent, the technical terminology.

Because education still borrows from other disciplines rather heavily, perhaps it should not be considered a discipline. However, the physical sciences borrow from mathematics and are therefore not completely independent disciplines, and mathematics, in turn, is derived from logic. The social and behavioral sciences have borrowed from the biological and physical sciences and from mathematics and statistics. Consequently, if this was the sole criterion for considering an area of inquiry a discipline, only logic would qualify.

Whether a body of subject matter is a discipline is not an either–or question but a matter of degree—the degree to which a body of subject matter fulfills a set of stipulated criteria. What is at issue are the criteria. Nonetheless, whether education is a discipline or is capable of becoming a discipline is not simply an academic question but one with considerable bearing on the direction and progress of educational research and theory and the possibilities that their advancement will improve policy-making and practice.

These and other points are examined in the following selections. Marc Belth shows the dangers of viewing education as an applied discipline and indicates what he believes to be the characteristics of a discipline. He distinguishes schooling from education and shows that the public and educators assume different roles with respect to each. Belth argues that no discipline is a substitute for the study of education and then presents his unique interpretation of the discipline of education.

Foster McMurray first evaluates two positions: that theories of education can be derived from philosophy, or that by starting with education the theorist can reduce the material to problems of philosophy. He notes the difficulties posed for education when it borrows theories from other disciplines and develops a conception of education or an educative event. McMurray points out the significance that this definition has for education's autonomy and shows areas from which educational theory can legitimately borrow.

Israel Scheffler investigates whether there is an autonomous body of knowledge underlying educational practice and whether educational activities derive their guiding principles from a distinctive realm of theory. He considers several arguments why education should be considered a discipline. He offers a definition of the term *discipline* and shows the limitations of construing a discipline in terms of a peculiar realm of objects and in terms of pure phenomena. Scheffler concludes with the effects it would have if education was found not to be a discipline.

27 / MARC BELTH

Education as an Applied Discipline

A familiar defense of education as a distinctive subject for study is that it is an "applied" discipline, akin in character to engineering, medicine, or law. For education is always engaged in the application of the theories of learning which it is the realm of psychology to develop. It also applies the theories of society, social organization, and social behavior with which the science of sociology is concerned. Moreover, education is applied philosophy, since it is the means by which we communicate the moral values of a people, a society, a civilization, to the oncoming generation.[1] In this vein, education is also strengthened by the contributions of other prevailing disciplines, including literature, economics, and the Classics. It is, in short, the study which is undertaken if one is to become a teacher, an applier of the source disciplines

Marc Belth, "Education As An Applied Discipline," from *Education As A Discipline* (Boston: Allyn and Bacon, Inc., 1965), pp. 2–20. Reprinted by permission of Allyn and Bacon, Inc.

Marc Belth is a member of the faculty of Queens College, where he teaches courses in the philosophy of education. His publications include *Education as a Discipline* and *The New World of Education*.

[1] *Cf.* V. C. Morris, *Philosophy and the American School* (Boston: Houghton Mifflin Company, 1961), in which several forms of this view are given.

of psychology, sociology and philosophy, and, above the level of the elementary school, of one specific additional field of knowledge.

This conception of education as an applied discipline is an inadequate defense of its distinctness from other disciplines. In fact, it sustains, in a way, the charge that there is no such subject as education. For if education has identity only as an applied discipline, what one studies when he studies teaching is psychology, in so far as he is concerned with concepts of learning; sociology, in so far as he is concerned with the forms and effects of society on developing individuals; anthropology, in so far as he is concerned with the force of civilizational patterns in the shaping of the institutions which nurture men; philosophy, in so far as he is concerned with examining and understanding the justification for the values to which one commits himself.

Furthermore, those who have accepted this explanation in order to enhance the importance of a special program for educators have placed themselves in a logically precarious situation. They have taken it upon themselves to become versed in the very best, deepest, and widest ranges of the conclusions of at least four, perhaps even more, very complicated disciplines. They have assumed the responsibility of becoming encyclopedists in an age when this has become all but impossible. In this position they can hardly avoid being identified by the more knowing as dabblers in a host of little intellectual endeavors, each of which becomes more of a private, gratifying, aesthetic activity than a developing intellectual pursuit. What follows is a genuine absurdity: the educator finds himself engaged in an intellectual career, but is not himself considered an intellectual.

An immediate consequence of this has been the development of an unfortunate kind of anti-intellectualism which says that only one who is a teacher and has actually worked in the classroom with children, helping them to learn, truly understands theories of learning, or of motivation, or of interest, or of social struggling, or of the force of value commitments in the behavior of human beings.[2]

There is one further, perhaps surprising, corollary to this view of education. Where education is seen as an applied science, clearly any activity of application becomes primary and crucial in a program. It appears that teachers, members of the discipline of education, should be produced by introducing students of education directly to the experience of teaching. It is often held that almost everything now being offered in education programs could be eliminated except practice teaching, where the principles of the parent disciplines can be

[2] See, for example, S. E. Sarason, K. S. Davidson, and B. Blatt, *The Preparation of Teachers* (New York: John Wiley & Sons, Inc., 1962). For an interesting essay on anti-intellectualism, *cf.* M. G. White, "Reflections on Anti-intellectualism," in *Daedalus*, Summer 1962.

applied. Such a conclusion is indeed consistent with the concept of applied science.[3]

No one would attempt to deny that practice teaching produces the results which are intrinsic to experience. But just what is intrinsic calls for analysis. Moreover, it does not do so automatically. For no one will derive from an experience what he has not been intellectually disciplined to comprehend and undergo. The fact that all too many teacher-training programs do depend on trial-and-error and are able to produce what appear to be effective teachers only adds to the difficulties of the discipline itself. For if we dispense with the need for understanding, anything untoward which occurs is likely to leave us quite helpless.

In their concern to establish uniqueness of education as an area of study, those who defend education as an applied science have confused the application of principles *as* a discipline with the application of principles *to* a discipline. Thus it is interesting to note that especially in education the notion of an applied discipline is a contradiction in terms. It is as if we were to decide suddenly that physics is applied mathematics, rather than a discipline in which mathematics can be applied fruitfully.

Establishing a Discipline of Education

If a discipline is to take on a direction of its own, its character and goals must be clearly defined. Identification merely as an "applied" science does not afford such clarification. One of the major problems which education faces derives from the obscurity about meanings of the concept of education itself, the sources of its objectives, the objectives themselves, and the limits of the concern. Without some basic understanding of what is and what is not meant by the terms of an activity, of what is included within it, of what is and what is not the relationship between the activity identified and other activities apparently like it, how can we evaluate what we are doing? How can we come nearer to an understanding that what we are doing is correct and defensible?

One of the intentions of this book is to develop a distinctive and defensible definition of education. In doing so, it will be helpful to go back over some of the ideas which have led education to where it is today.

The Source of Current Problems. At about the same time that Teachers College was being told that it had no subject matter, the kind of analysis of the character of education with which we are most familiar today was already under way. It began by pursuing the meaning of individual political in-

[3] *Cf.* esp. A. Bestor, *The Restoration of Learning* (New York: Alfred A. Knopf, Inc., 1955).

dependence, as a method by which a free man confronted day-to-day problems. In this pursuit, the political-social meaning of the role and the method of intelligence was produced which is so much a part of modern pragmatism. The conclusions which began to develop concerning how social theories of freedom directed the shape of education were more complicated and resistant to simple distillation than any previous views had been. When distillations were offered, a series of statements emerged which became clichés almost upon pronouncement. The effort to bring education's consequences into the arena of experience resulted in a series of slogans asserting that experience is the ultimate teacher, living through an event is the only way of learning, and human potentialities are released only in the context of congenial human relationships.[4]

In reaction against the establishing of educational activity on the basis of slogans, however worthy, serious minds turned away from further exploration of the subject. Even when there was sympathy for the profession, there was only an acceptance of the "applied" terminology, and then an urging of those in the profession to take seriously what was implied by that term. Thus psychologists, sociologists, and philosophers gave occasional attention to those aspects of their own pursuits whose implications might contribute to the improvement of educational practices. The practical concern of education, however, was accepted.

The interesting thing to note, however, is that John Dewey did much analysis on the problem of the social conditions for human freedom and bound the goals of education to this aspect of his social concern. But at other times he insisted on considering education in its own terms, subject to no goals other than those derived from the intrinsic demands of its own continuity. That he was not always sharp about this distinction is evident in the fact that almost without exception those who followed him developed the social-political-economic implications of the pragmatic sense of the goals of education. They followed his institutional concerns more than his strictly conceptual ones.[5]

But it is possible to read Dewey in places and see that his was a fundamental concern with the tenability of certain beliefs about education and with the educational consequences of various beliefs about man, nature, knowledge, and value. This did not free him altogether from error, but it does free him from the error of using social efficacy as a criterion for a discipline or study of education.

[4] *Cf.* esp. W. H. Kilpatrick, *Foundations of Method* (New York: The Macmillan Co., 1936), and *Remaking the Curriculum* (New York: Newsom & Company, 1936). *Cf.* also L. Cremin, *Transformation of the Schools* (New York: Alfred A. Knopf, Inc., 1961), and I. Scheffler, *The Language of Education* (Springfield, Ill.: Charles C Thomas, Publisher, 1962).

[5] J. Dewey, *Democracy and Education* (New York: The Macmillan Co., 1916), Chs. 13, 14.

From a more direct examination of his analysis, and from others which have been made in the intervening years, we can recognize that the real error lay in the method of trying to establish a unique discipline of education by comparing it to other, familiar disciplines. In other words, he used physics, psychology, history or philosophy as analogues in order to set forth the discipline of education. This, of course, is dangerous. For in these terms, there is nothing which education studies that is not already being studied in one of the prevailing disciplines. Seen as the activity of absorbing knowledge or that of nurturing the ability to know or to create knowledge, to become a member of a society or a culture, and to perpetuate the accrued, tested truths and faiths of the past, education merely does deliberately what other disciplines and other institutions do in non-deliberate ways, as additional results of more primary intentions. The only possible distinction that could then be made between education and other disciplines would be one of theory and application, with education always identified as the latter.

There is, in fact, a difference between instructing in a specific area and the process of education *per se*. But whether this process constitutes a separate discipline cannot be determined by direct comparison with other disciplines. This must be discovered by the use of basic criteria which are applicable to all disciplines. We shall consider four such criteria throughout this book.

Criteria for a Discipline. Disciplines are distinct from one another in one or more of the following:

1. In the level of abstraction of the concepts with which they are concerned.
2. In the modes of thinking by which they are characterized.
3. In the objectives they seek.
4. In the types and manifestations of the moral rules by which they are limited and evaluated.

The quality of education varies as the characters of these criteria operate more or less fully. Examination of these will occupy large sections of the books, but it will be worthwhile first to offer a brief explanation of each in order to make possible a proper expectation of what is to come.

Level of abstraction. In examining the familiar disciplines, we discover that however they differ from one another in modes of thinking, one could conceivably recommend an explanation of the processes of inquiry which would be equally applicable to all. Of course, a statement so inclusive would be on a highly abstract level. But if it is possible to make this case, then it is also possible to make a logical distinction between all of the disciplines within this frame and the activity, or discipline, of framing them. This would have great significance for a study of education.

For example, it is a function of psychology to develop theories and laws of human conduct which can be used to form explanations of the ways in which men undergo experiences. Such theories and laws become instruments of prediction and control of human behavior.

In recent times, philosophy has also become more emphatically a study of the meanings of concepts, their inclusions and exclusions, their logical relationships to other concepts, and the force they have in the lives of men. But though philosophy and psychology are both concerned with human beings, the types of concern differ.[6]

Education does not operate on either of these levels of abstraction, but on an entirely different level. It is not concerned with the use of concepts in experience, as psychology is, or with the meanings of concepts both logically and in relation to other concepts in experience, as philosophy is. Education deals with the relationship between concepts and powers nurtured in learners, and with the methods of creating concepts as the inventions of intelligence, in whatever fields these methods come to be employed. It concentrates not so much on the merits of particular ideas and their inclusions in the context of experience, as on the methodology of thinking, of which ideas themselves are the consequences. Once this is recognized, we can set aside a primary error which has plagued us. Education cannot be compared with psychology, or sociology, or philosophy, because it is not on the same plane with these. It is concerned, rather, with procedures for developing or creating the ideas used by each of these disciplines in performing its own activities.

In the simplest of terms, it is not possible to compare *Rover*, *Rex*, or *Champion Waffledale of Hillsboro* with *Canine*. Nor can you compare any of these with Boxer, Terrier, or Pekingese. The individual dogs can be compared with each other for all sorts of qualifications; the types of dogs can be compared for traits of size, color, docility, and the like. But the species *Canine* can be compared only with other species of animals, such as *Feline* or *Bovine*. And when such a comparison is made, traits of life functions, modes of generation and regeneration, patterns of behavior, and range of inclusion of who are and who are not members of the species itself are examined. In other words, the level of abstraction is identified by what traits are acceptable as being pertinent to that particular level.[7]

The discipline of education, then, is determined by a level of abstraction on which the models for explaining, exploring, describing, and inventing are established and studied in relationship to the methods by which these capacities operate.

[6] For example, R. M. Hare writes: "It is no use hoping by philosophy to convince . . . people to make them change their behavior. Here a deep understanding of psychology is required before any progress can be hoped for." (*Freedom and Reason* [New York: Oxford University Press, Inc., 1963], p. 203.)

[7] For an analysis under slightly different terms, but having the same general intent, *cf.* C. M. Turbayne, *The Myth of Metaphor* (New Haven: Yale University Press, 1962).

From this admittedly odd analogy, we can suggest that the levels of abstraction of the familiar disciplines of physics, psychology, mathematics, and sociology are identified by their concern with the specifics of human experiences. But the level of abstraction of education is identified by the methods by which ideas are produced, tested, and recreated—that is, by what is connoted in the phrase "method of intelligence." The role played by experience within the discipline of education will be a very different one, on this basis, than has usually been envisioned. This is a matter which will occupy us deeply. But what we will say of education as method will have defensible explanatory power if what is now known about each of the methods of the particular disciplines can be shown to be exemplifications of this general thesis.

Modes of reasoning. There seems to be a general acceptance of the view that there are three distinctive modes of reasoning, or thinking. There is mathematical thinking,[8] which is a matter of deducing conclusions from axioms which are themselves not subjects for investigation. There is scientific thinking, which uses deduction, but which differs from mathematical thinking because it is concerned with more than just logical adequacy. Scientific or experimental thinking is characterized by the processes which are used to make judgments and predictions about the material world.[9] There is philosophical thinking, which uses deduction, but whose concern is to understand, or expose to the understanding, meanings and commitments which are implicit in statements or judgments made. Man thinks philosophically when he addresses himself to the implicit grounds of value and meaning which have heretofore been accepted or rejected, but which have not been consciously examined.[10] There are other modes of reasoning which seem to defy easy categorization, and which will be considered in a later chapter, but for the moment these three make the point.

There is much that is different in each of the three modes of reasoning described above. They differ in the data confronted and in the kinds of conclusions they attempt to develop. Some can be tested experimentally; others, only logically. Still others are not tested at all, in either of these senses. Philosophical conclusions are not so much tested as they are examined for their significance, their acceptability, their justification, and the range of meaning of experience made available by them. In philosophical thinking, it is the clarity and the pertinence of the claims we make about the experiences we have and the laws and theories and other systems developed to sort out and explain those experiences which are tested.

[8] *Cf.* esp. C. J. Kayser, *Pastures of Wonder* (New York: Columbia University Press, 1929), Part I.

[9] E. Nagel, *The Structure of Science* (New York: Harcourt, Brace & World, Inc., 1961), Chs. 1 and 2.

[10] J. Dewey, esp. *Experience and Nature* (New York: W. W. Norton & Company, Inc., 1929), and *Reconstruction in Philosophy* (Boston: Beacon Press, 1948).

Educational thinking, however, has a quality of its own, though it probably runs closer to the philosophical at this point than to the other two. For thinking in education is directed not so much toward the logic of concept relationships, or of the judgments about the experienced world, but, rather, toward the models of thinking which enter into the process of reasoning, the judgments which result, and the form, range, and quality of experiences made possible by the models.

By examining the procedures which are common to all disciplines—exploring, describing, explaining, reasoning, and inventing—we can reach an understanding of how education differs from the other disciplines in the modes of thinking employed. The specific activities of each discipline in exploring, describing, explaining, reasoning, and inventing and the forms into which it organizes its recorded results give the clearest insight into the differences among the distinctive modes of reasoning which occur. Further, the different family views within each discipline can be identified by noting what function is assigned to each.[11] Suffice it to say at this point that the study of education, quite unlike any other study, is concerned with making possible newer modes of description, exploration, explanation, reasoning, and invention. It also seeks to explore the ways in which these processes result in human powers producing in each man his unique capacities. Thus, the thinking which is distinctively educational is not carried on merely by the use of prevailing models. Nor is it an inquiry into models for the purpose of exposing such meanings as might have escaped attention. It reflects, rather, on how models are produced, altered, tested, and extended, and otherwise affected. For this, it will be shown, is what is basic to the matter of learning to think.

Objectives. The problem of objectives is, without doubt, the most difficult problem to cope with, because most people, if they have any convictions at all about education, have them specifically regarding the proper goals of education. But invariably the premises from which these convictions are derived remain hidden, no matter how vigorously they are fought over. In fact, passion has made objectives the least examined, indeed, the least examinable, but the most verbalized of all issues.

Consider again the familiar disciplines. We can state briefly that the objective of science is the development of laws and theories, in terms of which we can make true statements about the world as we experience it or as we can expect to experience it.[12] The objective of mathematics (and that

[11] So, for example, within psychology and philosophy, some distinguish between description and exploration, and others do not, holding that certain types of description are explorations. Representing the latter in psychology, see B. F. Skinner, "Are Theories of Learning Necessary?" 57 *The Psychological Review*, pp. 193–216 (1950); in philosophy, see Scheffler, *op. cit.*

[12] N. O. Campbell, *Foundations of Science* (New York: Dover Publications, Inc., 1957), Part I.

of logic, for they are especially close in this) is to penetrate into the relationship between thought and thought in order to formulate rules setting forth the basis on which statements validly follow certain statements and not others.[13] The objective of philosophy is to draw out and set forth clearly and understandably, in order to discover the range of their meanings, the presuppositions on which we undertake all of our pursuits—physical, logical, and valuational.[14] In each case, acceptance of the objective depends on agreement upon an operation intrinsic to the discipline.

The objective of the study of education, then, would be to improve the methods of inquiry and creativity by which science, mathematics, and philosophy perform their functions and pursue their objectives.

However, the problems of educational objectives are drowned in the confusion between education and schooling. The error of fastening upon objectives for education which are, strictly speaking, objectives of schooling in a particular country is the most serious consequence. For example, the schools in a democracy are ever concerned with developing intelligence in a context of freedom to think and act. Thus, one of their aims is to produce self-directive individuals who can undertake their own inquiries and come to independent decisions. Others are to nurture a sense of fair play among the citizenry; a quality of adventure in experience; a sense of community among the members of present and future societies. Surely these are most worthy school objectives. But, in fact, they are quite different from educational objectives.

Public disputes over the aims of education are not likely to be resolved, because they are disputes of total outlooks in opposition to one another. They are the cultural disputes that prevail among well organized social units when each is trying to extend the scope of its influence by urging assent to its own vision of the world. They are disputes among philosophical systems, which are never resolvable. The best to be hoped for is the compromise of eclecticism, which is certainly not an educational resolution.

Only with schools, because they are societal institutions and must therefore be responsive to the plural stresses, does society itself force compromise. But school compromises serve no positive educational functions. The prevalence of such conflicts are deterrents to the process itself, and the resolution offers no contribution. For the real paradox lies in the fact that schools have social, political, and moral responsibilities of perpetuating what others have invented and given to ensuing generations, whereas education seeks to develop inventive intelligence. To be effective in the former is not

[13] B. Russell, *An Introduction to Mathematical Philosophy* (London: Allen and Unwin, 1948), Ch. 18.

[14] See J. Dewey, *Philosophy and Civilization* (New York: G. P. Putnam's Sons, 1931), Ch. 1.

necessarily to be fruitful in the latter. That is, efficiently transmitting concepts created by our fathers does not necessarily produce intelligent individuals. The goal of education is not only to develop a knowledge of these concepts, but, much more important, to nurture the ability to examine how they were arrived at and how they are tested, as well as to develop the understanding and skill needed to invent new meanings and new relationships. Strictly speaking, as Dewey has said on occasion, education has no objectives other than the improvement of its own quality and scope,[15] for its intrinsic growth.

If we remember that schools are societal institutions which are brought into existence to perform functions imposed upon them by society, then we will recognize that its educational goals are indeed only part of a wider list. But we cannot derive educational goals from schools, contrary to most views. They are *assigned* to schools, as are social, economic, psychological, and other goals. Insofar as the school is a societal institution, the society itself is properly concerned with retaining its controls over the schools. Insofar as education is a distinct discipline, educational responsibilities are *not* a matter for public decision, any more than mathematical analysis is a matter for public vote, or explanation of the laws of thought is a matter for public agreement.

Intrinsic educational objectives have really nothing to do with a particular society of a particular moral commitment. They are, rather, the developing principles by which the school guides itself to pay its respect to its educational obligations, as it pays its respects to the principles set forth by sociologists and to what the psychologists have helped to determine are individual patterns of interest, motivation, and development.

In short, the familiar disciplines of physics and psychology employ methods, the philosopher inquires into the meanings of method and its varieties, if any, and the educator has as his objective the study of the impact of method on acts of intelligence, and the invention of method as the irreducible condition for the operation of intelligence. Education becomes a way of raising and answering a question not otherwise asked, a question centering on the problems of improving the ability to think.

The objectives of the study of education are an understanding of the role played by the elements of inquiry in the operation of thinking, as well as the conditions which are called for in order to incorporate their functions into human capacities.

[15] Compare the views of goals of education of representative men in the field in J. S. Brubacher, ed., *Modern Philosophers and Education*, 54th Yearbook of the National Society for the Study of Education (Chicago: The Society, 1955). Examine also, for explicit and implicit concepts of goals, J. B. Conant, *The American High School Today* (New York: McGraw-Hill Book Co., Inc., 1959), and *Slums and Suburbs* (New York: McGraw-Hill Book Co., Inc., 1961); W. Griswold, *Essays on Education* (New Haven: Yale University Press, 1954); R. N. Mason, *Educational Ideals in American Society* (Boston: Allyn and Bacon, Inc., 1960).

Moral manifestations. Every discipline is guided by a basic set of rules which enable it to perform its proper functions, in the direction toward which it is turned, and in the character by which it is to accomplish its goals. These rules not only direct action and choices, but they serve as evaluative-corrective criteria. The more they serve as necessary for action the more evidently they come to serve as a kind of moral limitation within which action is permitted. So a violation of rules appears to be a defiling of the discipline itself. For example, where science is concerned with writing laws and theories by which explanations of material nature can be made and tested, it is an act of immorality to expect laws to be held as true even though all evidence denies the accuracy of those laws.[16]

In education, however, the moral dimension which has been pronounced has invariably been derived not from the educative rules, but from some social-psychological rule system. In such a context, certain textbooks have been called immoral and pressures are exerted to eliminate them. Those who have exerted the pressures have been called immoral, also, for not permitting students to have access to works which are personally disturbing. On the one side, the making of "wrong" choices is called immoral in education; on the other, the suppression of choice-making by limiting the choices is called immoral.

All of these and others are, to be sure, moral problems of great significance. But it is not always understood under what auspices the educational dimension of this moral issue can be held up to public scrutiny in order to determine what is and what is not justifiably moral in educational terms.

If we accept the principle implied in this brief discussion, namely, that moral principles, as rules for maintaining intrinsic functions, cannot be divorced from the character of the function involved, nor from the primary objectives for which the operations are pursued, then it is also correct to say that education alone has the duty to establish its own rules of procedure. The moral involvement would be the obligation to pursue its internal objectives by rejecting the intrusions of all external demands. Strictly speaking, the school is in society. It is, however, not so simple a matter to say that education as a field of study is also in society. The study of education, like any other study, or discipline, has a highly complicated relationship with society. At once, there must be concern with how its consequences are manifest in the lives of men in society, and yet a complete freedom in the study itself, regardless of the aims, needs, and obligations which the society has imposed upon itself. If education does have objectives outside itself, then it cannot be

[16] *Cf.* two works which ought to be read completely: M. Otto, *Science and the Moral Life* (New York: Mentor Books, 1949); J. L. Childs, *Education and Morals* (New York: Appleton-Century-Crofts, 1950).

restrained from pursuing what it seeks to discover, understand, and communicate. If the aim is to foster the powers of creation in and of communication, it does not mean communicating just *this* set of ideas and not *that.* If its aim is to develop the power of making value judgments, which it is then the realm of philosophy and science to explore and employ, it does not mean a development of the power to make just *these* value judgments, and not others.

In fact, where the study of education involves not the absorbing of others' tactics of exploration, description, explanations, and invention, but rather the critical analysis of the making of each of these, then it is clear that the moral dimension is limited by this type of inquiry. It would be immoral if, in place of studying how we have thought and judged, we indicated that not only is it not possible to study these, but that it is wrong to do anything but accept both the methods and the conclusions which wise men before us have set down.

The moral obligation which defines the study of education is best identified as including the obligation to explore and explain every system of exploration and explanation which is employed by anyone, anywhere.

Operational Distinctions

The purpose of this section is to recommend a relationship between the various accepted disciplines and the study of education. In terms of the distinctions offered thus far, we can deduce that no discipline which we know or engage in is a substitute for the study of education. Neither separately nor together do they exhaust all of the traits of method, or of the methodological inquiry which is the very *process* of education. This can be understood better, perhaps, if we observe what is genuinely alternative to deliberate education. Such alternatives at least enable us to see the limits of what we are to study.

The alternatives to education as a disciplined concern with an aspect of human experience are not such studies as physics or philosophy, but those approaches to the problems of experience which are not consciously methodological or intellectual. These would be commitment to such concepts as intuition, revelation, or inspiration. An interesting and important conclusion should be noted here. The moment that one begins to examine the alternatives to education and uses an intelligently planned procedure in the examination, education is already at work. It is present in the means of inquiry employed to confront the noneducational procedures which men often substitute for reason itself. This is entirely consistent with the view that the study of education calls for inquiry into methods, or claimed methods, of inquiry.

In terms of this methodic process, let us make one more distinction. Consider the fact that every study which we look into is in some way a human invention. If this is so, then education is actually the study of the nurturing of conceptual invention. Now this can be very vague, however persuasive it may sound, but it need not be. Consider, for example, the question: Who makes history? The most naive answer is that men and women, undergoing experiences in living their lives, make history as they relate to one another in pursuing goals and cross-goals. But when this is asked as an educational question, we get a very different answer. History is made by historians who connect together the evidences of experience within a context of theories and laws, presuppositions, and systems of explanation. In doing so, the historian generates meanings for events which would otherwise not have those meanings. The next phase of such a question, of course, is a study of historical thinking, inventing, and explaining.

Who makes the discipline of physics? The physicist, of course, when he "does" his physical inquiries. So it is with sociology and psychology, and every other study which becomes part of the curriculum of every school.

It is possible to approach the specific parts of a curriculum in several ways. Each subject can be studied as an area of invented, funded meanings, inquiry into which produces knowledge of the world and its inhabitants as consistent within the context of rules and concepts identified. That is, each subject can be studied as a well organized and tested body of conclusions which have been made by competent students of a field and tested by others.

A second level of abstraction shades into a philosophical approach, though it need not. For example, one can study history as historiography (which is a kind of historical tool and method making), or one can study the philosophy of history. Even more interesting is the difficulty of distinguishing the physicist's study of the basis of his operations as a physicist from the philosophy of science. Compare, for example, the writing of Norman Campbell,[17] who was a physicist, with that of Ernest Nagel,[18] who is not. Campbell's book, *Foundations of Science*, and Nagel's *The Structure of Science* are concerned with the same focus of inquiry.

But there remains that focus of interest in which we are concerned with the relationship between the world as we inherit it, with its cultural patterns, and its conceptual instruments, man's powers as we understand them at a given period. Now, if it is the responsibility of education to develop the ability to think, then the characteristics of the thinking process are primary to the concerns of the educator. From this there develops the need to study the relationship between the modes of thought available to us, and the range

[17] Campbell, *op. cit.*
[18] Nagel, *op. cit.*

of knowledge which is possible within prevailing modes of thinking, as well as developing awareness of the limits those modes fix upon what can be known.

Perhaps this distinction among the three types of concern will become clear in the two illustrations which follow.

Consider the writings of Plato. The historian examines them in the context of Greek history for the insight they provide on the lives, expectations, and behavior of the Greeks. The philosopher looks into the writings for the meanings of the concepts set forth and their relationship to other concepts in terms of consistency, implication, and significance of the meanings of the major (and minor) concepts in the work as a whole. If historical concerns enter, they enter only as corroborative materials, not as substantive facts which prove the philosophy's warrant. But when the educator turns to the *Dialogues*, he is looking for the models of the educative procedure which were unique to Plato. In this, he is not concerned with the significance of the concept of Justice, or of Courage, or of Knowledge, as these are argued in the various dialogues. He is, instead, looking for a much broader element—the role played, for example, by Myth, or Analogue, or Allegory, in the act of developing in others ways of fostering and using powers of reason. He seeks out the relationship between the basis for certain models used and the concepts of the world which are embedded in those models. And then he is concerned with analyzing the limits which the use of Plato's models, in mythic or allegoric, analogic or religious forms, places upon the student's power to reason, as well as the ways of employing those models.

Exactly the same threefold division can be made in a consideration of the works of Aristotle. But some interesting additional observations can be offered. The historian is more likely to keep the two, Plato and Aristotle, together in his explorations and the accounts he offers, for historically they were contemporaries, the one a student of the other, and both were affected by the common conditions of Athenian Greece. When the philosopher approaches Aristotle, at the point of attempting to understand and analyze his concept of science, he will certainly recognize the Euclidian model which is basic to the Stagirite's science. And he will note especially how Aristotle employs this model on medical and physical problems rather than leaving it exclusively in the realm of mathematics. Primarily, however, the philosopher's concern is to identify the concept of science for Aristotle, and to interpret how science is performed and what it is capable of accomplishing. But again, for the educator, the problem is not only what science, in this case, means for Aristotle, but the way in which the use of certain models gives the meaning to science that it comes to have, how such models can be used more broadly in unfamiliar experiences, and what alternatives are conceivable to such models. In short, it is not the validity of the model which is of concern to the educator, but the force of the model on the ability to think about the world and about experience.

Much more needs yet to be said about the distinctiveness of the educational approach, but for now, the above discussion will suffice. It is what education as a study strives to reveal, or expose, that more truly sets it apart from other disciplines. The first two levels of abstraction prove to be important supports to the study of the third and most abstract level, but of themselves they do not constitute that level. To be sure, we can detect the historical and the psychological, the philosophical and the sociological procedures which appear in an educational inquiry. But that inquiry is obviously not simply the collection of the findings of these other disciplines. The larger concern of education is to operate on some of those findings, to explore the consequences of their use, and to study the foundations of the disciplines themselves.

Perhaps the best demonstration of this function of education is to be found in the informal observation that the deeper the interest of any member of a discipline in the fundamental character of his discipline, and the greater his concern for the future of it, and of those who will one day enter into it, the closer he comes to discovering the necessity of confronting education directly, in itself, for understanding, and in hopes of recommending improvement. The increasing attention given to education today by diplomats, chemists, mathematicians, military men, historians and physicists is evidence of the fact that men grow toward the need to explore education in educational terms.

It has been suggested earlier in this chapter that one of the errors produced by a naive approach to education is the belief that one learns to teach by teaching, and that, therefore, the experience induced in the activity of student teaching is the most basic, most important event in the education program. If what has been argued above is conceded, then in the act of teaching, whether before the attainment of a license or after, we have opportunity for the manifestation of the outcome of the study of education. As such, the practice of teaching is the experience in and by which we learn more of what we have already begun to learn, within which we test out the fuller meanings of what we have learned. And it provides the opportunity for continuing the study of education with newer evidences to be considered. Just how important this is we shall discover in analysis of the evaluating and corrective aspects of the study of education, later in the book.

It is when we are able to see this relationship between the act of teaching and the study of education that we are able to recognize that the discipline of education demands of each member a continuous study, of which there is cumulative development from his own analyses and experiments and those of others. (But they will be experiments in an educational sense, which are quite different from social or psychological experiments.) For then we can also observe that the relationship of the study of education, in its greater level of abstraction, to the practice of teaching is analogous to the more familiar one between the writing of scientific laws and theories and the experiments conducted in the laboratory. As a continuous study, education stands alternative to every possible tactic of indoctrination, for its primary purpose is more knowledge of truth-making, meaning-making, and clarifying the conditions which give to human experience its variety of qualities and ranges.

Still further, if the concepts of method and the models which enclose them as subjects of inquiry are as we explained earlier, then education most assuredly is a subject to be studied. It is, in fact, the "subject of subjects"—perhaps the most creative, certainly the most demanding, of all areas of study. For there could not be a single consciously developed discipline were there not, to begin with, the deliberate intention to set forth and explore the implicit rules by which the raw data of human experience has been organized and given meaning. In this, we have fashioned the specific disciplines which have become so familiar to us. The study of education is the study of the role of models and methods, of how knowledge comes to be, how it comes to take the various forms it does, its consequences in the experiences of men, and how it alters and develops newer forms. It is the study of the creation and uses of models on which the operation of reason depends. It is the study of the methodological basis on which one makes the wide range of judgments necessary in common and uncommon pursuits.

Because the notion of a separate discipline of education implies that no other inquiry has antecedently existing subject matter of its own, education must be seen as the most complicated, the most subtle, the most perplexing of all studies. For it is the study of how subjects are developed and improved, and how they acquire the meanings and the intellectual force they come to have. Education explores how these subjects are related to the world of experience while collecting and arranging data into meaningful classes of information, and how they are also free from experience as methods of making new experience possible. It is concerned with the function of cognition which produces the subjects men study in order to come to know more about themselves, their societies, the world as a physical event, the expressions about that world, and the enjoyment of the world. In this sense, education as a study appears to borrow from other disciplines. But in reality it only "borrows" the consequences which it has enabled those disciplines to produce. For without education, is it likely that there would ever be a psychologist, a biologist, or a sociologist in the world?

28 / FOSTER MCMURRAY

Preface to An Autonomous Discipline of Education

My purpose is to offer a concept of educational theory as a unique discipline. By a unique discipline I mean one which has its own problems, its own line of inquiry clearly staked out, such that anyone who pursues it may find his theoretical materials and his procedures of validation contained within the discipline itself rather than in some other.

A self-contained discipline, if it should appear, would contrast in obvious ways with "philosophy of education" in its present form. In spite of differences among specialists in beliefs about philosophy of education, there is a fair measure of agreement that it is most intimately related to philosophy proper. According to the opinion of one group, the relationship is one in which theories of education are derived by implication from systematic philosophy. It is this view which dominates competitive textbook production and hence, no doubt, academic course work in philosophy of education throughout the country. A related view is different by reversing the order of inquiry. Starting with the problems of education, an educational theorist reduces his initial materials to problems in traditional philosophy. By either view, the outcome is the same: doctrines of education are grounded in philosophic doctrine. Our situation, therefore, is one in which a professional educator who seeks a comprehensive and consistent viewpoint toward the educative enterprise cannot do so on an informed and deliberate basis unless he is first able to choose one of the major systems of philosophy as his own. He must decide for or against idealism, realism, pragmatism, etc., for it is in these systems that one must find ultimate justification for an educational doctrine. A theory of education developed as a unique discipline, by contrast, would offer doctrines justified within the discipline itself.

Foster McMurray, "Preface to An Autonomous Discipline of Education," from *Educational Theory*, Vol. V, No. 3 (July 1955), pp. 129–140. Reprinted by permission of the publisher and the author.

Foster McMurray teaches courses in the philosophy of education at the University of Illinois. He has contributed articles to a number of journals.

I

When theory of education is constructed as a kind of elaborate deduction from philosophy, the most serious consequence is that theory of education tends to become a matter for individual choosing according to the peculiarities of individual taste. Each person, that is, either chooses or constructs his own philosophy of education from the alternatives supported by his culture. For some a realist philosophy is most compatible with personal values, for others an idealist philosophy seems most to accord with basic attitudes toward the world, etc. This is a situation to which we are so accustomed that it seems a virtue rather than a defect. Indeed, it must be admitted that a primary function of systematic philosophy is to give coherent expression to ways of organizing one's intellectual and evaluative overview of the universe. Furthermore, the continuous vitality of all major systems indicates that each is very nearly as valid as the other. The method of philosophic inquiry is such that a philosopher can neither establish the superior truth of his system as against others nor refute with universally acceptable finality any of the contending doctrines. To express the situation crudely, we might say that anyone has a perfect right to choose any of the available philosophic stances, and no one can challenge his reasonableness nor his intellectual responsibility. For philosophers and consumers of philosophy this situation is probably good. It is good to the extent that philosophy is less a science and more a rationalized poetry, expressing and integrating schemes of value. In this role, philosophy vindicates our assurance that freedom of choice is a necessary condition for being human. But if this role is extended to include theory of education, then theory of education is a luxury of no use to the enterprise of schooling.

Somehow the uselessness of educational theory, when tied to philosophy, has escaped notice. Nevertheless, the fact should be obvious. When theory of education is, like philosophy itself, a matter for personal choosing, then the program of a school, its curriculum, its aims, and its methods, must be determined independently from theory. Because a school is an institution and its activities are practical, a school program must be both unified and continuous. The work of one teacher must be integrated with the work of others. And the nature of the school program in its entirety must be sufficiently crystallized that it becomes a public object, available, that is, for objective examination. Granted even a large amount of freedom for teachers to vary their procedures and contents, the learnings and activities of pupils must reveal a progressive pattern that can be made intelligible to educators in general, and to the public, and hence free from determination by the individual tastes of particular teachers. To recognize this is not to urge an imposition of some particular value system upon all teachers. Quite on the contrary, it means that a democratic school program is that kind of thing which people of many value systems, holding different philosophies of life, must be able to agree upon, and agree upon without feeling that their own highest values are either jeopardized or given an undemocratic ascendency over the equally legitimate highest values or philosophies of other people in their society. If it were really true, as sometimes claimed by uninformed critics, that our public schools are dominated by pragmatism, and are inculcating pragmatism in the younger generation, then everyone, pragmatists included, would have a legitimate complaint. To base a public school program upon any particular system of philosophy would be no different in its anti-democratic character from basing a program upon the tenets of some particular religious group. The fact that we do not do so typifies our present situation: while educational "philosophers" engage at second hand in the controversies of systematic philosophy and in finding implications for education, practical educators with no training in theory proceed with their own tasks of constructing and changing school programs.

The effects upon philosophy of education, in addition to removing it from significant contact with schooling, are ones which teachers of graduate courses in the discipline can best appreciate. A specialist in educational theory must choose to become either a follower or a leader, either a disciple or an independently creative theorizer. If he chooses the latter, and thereby aims for the highest rewards, then he is obligated to show that earlier theories are inadequate, to be replaced by his own. The history of educational theory is a story of one giant replacing another. So long as this situation continues, theory of education cannot share the advantages most usually accruing to a discipline. There is no co-operative endeavor by many experts to build upon one another's findings and to pass them on for further refinements and additions. For teachers in advanced educational philosophy this means that supposedly advanced courses must be taught in a field where no advanced literature has come into existence. Consequently, instructors are forced to draw instructional materials from philosophy itself, and the more sophisticated the instruction the more closely it resembles training in a department of philosophy.

The resemblance is close, but a significant difference remains. The difference is one of professional competence and professional responsibility. An educational theorist who divides his time between work in philosophy and work in education is at best a master of neither. At worst, he is a man who lectures and who writes about philosophy to an audience of non-philosophers, thereby unable to profit from critical exchanges which usually accompany communication to an audience of professional peers.

Anyone who finds our present situation undesirable must have discovered difficulties standing in the way of change. Implicit in our semantic understandings is a distinction which seems to make good sense, and which seems also to favor a continuation of the present state of affairs. It is a distinction between "philosophy" and "theory". According to this usage, any large scale enterprise such as education should be conducted under the general direction of a philosophy. The function of a philosophy is to clarify the aims of professional action and to give a sense of relative importance among the values of which action might realize. The function of a theory, on the other hand, is to guide scientific investigation. A theory guides the enterprise of finding facts, rather than of reaching desired goals, and is neutral concerning alternatives among values. By enlargement of a technical vocabulary, theory is supposed to generate hypotheses for empirical testing. This way of seeing a division of labor between philosophy and theory suggests to educators that both are needed, and that their peaceful co-existence is a desirable state. On the one hand we must have a philosophy of education as a normative discipline, guiding educative action toward desirable outcomes, and on the other hand we need a science of education to provide the sort of knowledge that might help us become more effective in realizing the philosopher's norms. Taking one step further in this direction, the traditionalist then proposes that philosophy is *the* normative discipline, the one discipline into which any inquiry into ultimate values must find its way. Therefore, it is said, an educational program must be based, in final analysis, upon presuppositions of a philosophic nature.

This traditional separation of philosophic from scientific investigations sounds persuasive. What seem to be grounds for persuasion disappear completely, however, when appropriate distinctions are made.

To simplify a kind of distinction that could be explored profitably through many pages, we might speak of philosophy as being two different kinds of activity. There is, on the one hand, that kind of philosophy which presumes to offer actual substantive norms of the good, the true, or the beautiful. On the other hand, there is that kind of philosophy which seeks only to clarify the language or meanings necessary for normative discourse. The former is by far the more common, and it is what most people think of when they think of philosophy. It is a reasoned argument in support of certain values as preferred over other possible values. It is within this kind of philosophy that we distinguish one system from others, each system being in effect a partisan plea for the superiority of its norms over the norms supported in others. The other kind of philosophy, relatively unknown to the general public, argues not that this value or norm is superior to that, but only that this way of using terms will be more useful or more self-consistent than that in anyone's efforts to discover what he sought to value. It does not presume to show grounds for preferring any particular set of ultimate values, but instead, to refine the meanings used in any normative inquiry, without predisposition toward any favored outcome.

When it is said that philosophy of education must reflect the issues of philosophy which kind of philosophy is meant? Suppose, for the sake of argument, that it is the first kind. In that case, we should find ourselves in the untenable position discussed in foregoing paragraphs. That is, we should have to choose some one or some combination of partisan points of view, taking sides with some philosophers as against others. If, as I am supposing, the differences which divide philosophers from one another are socially important, reflecting valid alternatives having their roots deep in our culture, then it is impossible to establish a good school program upon a partisan doctrine. In essence, the reason for this is that the institution of formal schooling exists primarily to transmit selected materials from our culture. Among those materials are the attitudes and beliefs which reach their most critical formulation in philosophy. The content of philosophy is inseparable from dialectic dispute and partisanship. This fact imposes upon the school a requirement that disputes be transmitted as disputes, and that alternatives be transmitted as alternatives. In other words, the only way to transmit philosophy with truth to its nature is to transmit it as a continuing dialectic, something like a never ending war or charges and counter-charges, with never any great advantage, and never any preponderance of justice, on one side as against any other. To impose any particular philosophy as though it were the settled and assured outcome of investigation is to misrepresent the kind of enterprise that philosophy is.

With respect to substantive philosophy and its relations to educational doctrine, the only conclusion which can be maintained, it seems to me, is that the nature of the educative enterprise forbids our establishment of school programs upon particular beliefs concerning what is good or true or beautiful. Contrary to the more typical view, we do not base educative action upon the kinds of norms which the various branches of philosophy seek to formulate. It is true that an educational doctrine expresses norms, and that to accept a doctrine is to accept the validity of those norms. But the norms which an educational doctrine embodies are those proper to educative action, as a particular kind of action rather than as action in general.

Perhaps it should be mentioned, by way of example, that a typical educator's norm has been invoked in the course of argument. Stated negatively, it holds that educators should not use the curriculum to advance any preferred set of values among the alternatives that have been accorded roughly equal legitimacy by society. Stated positively, it holds that a good educative program is one which increases the probability that our present intellectualized conflicts will be pushed with vigor into the future. This, it may be noted, is a norm by express reference to educative action and its consequences.

It might seem possible to protest that a realist or an idealist or a pragmatist philosophy of education need not require of its adherents that realism or idealism or pragmatism be especially favored in the schools. But such a protest would be self-defeating. If it means anything at all to say that a philosophy of education is, for example, a realist philosophy, then it means that the methods and the curriculum proposed are those which the philosopher believes best suited to reveal the world and its values in that particular perspective which the term "realism" connotes.

Next in order of argument is consideration of philosophy as clarification of terms rather than as substantive doctrine. What relation could obtain between this kind of philosophy and a theory of education? It must be acknowledged that an educational theorist cannot get along without certain terms which philosophers are accustomed to exploring. Such words as "knowledge," "truth," and "art" are the most obvious examples. Could an educator profit from the definitions of technical philosophy?

To some extent the influence of philosophic analysis upon the vocabulary of educated people is unavoidable. Like anyone else, an educational theorist must show the influence of cultural accumulations. But he is also like anyone else who is not a professional philosopher, in this respect: in using the terms which philosophers analyze, he is under no special obligation to provide a technical analysis. Just as scientific discourse is not epistemological analysis, and art criticism is not esthetics, so also educational theory. The obligation of an educational theorist is to refine the vocabulary of his own discipline, and beyond this, to use terms consistently, and with clarity sufficient for the purposes at hand. To achieve sufficient clarity, a common technique even in technical literature is to use the language of common sense wherever a specialized meaning is not under construction. This avoids raising difficulties to which philosophers are especially sensitive. At some points, however, an educational theorist will find it important to remove some of the vagueness and ambiguity which characterize the language of common sense. Where that occurs, he may find it helpful to borrow from philosophers such clarification of terminology as they have offered.

There is a serious difficulty here. Few, if any, of the terms about which philosophic argument revolves have been clarified except within a particular one of the systems. Hence to accept a philosopher's language is to risk accepting his substantive doctrine as well. The simplest way for an educational theorist to avoid this trap is to do his own defining of professional terminology rather than to incorporate the language of a neighboring discipline. If his own usage should happen to coincide at some points with that of systematic philosophy, this would be no disadvantage if the theory as a whole were established upon a foundation other than systematic philosophy. It seems, therefore, that educational theory cannot establish itself as a derivative from philosophy.

If theory of education is to become a self-contained discipline, then what would such a discipline be like? The answer, in most general terms, is that theory of education must have its own province, its own area for investigation, one which is not now the province for inquiry within any of the older disciplines. To express the same idea in a different form, we might say that educational theorists must find their own way of asking questions. If they could agree upon a common set of problems, then a concerted attack and the pooling of findings by any and all investigators is more likely to occur.

A tendency frequently discernible in contemporary research is an attempt to mark out a kind of inquiry especially appropriate for investigators employed by colleges of education. An educational psychologist will propose to investigate learning as it occurs in school rooms, feeling that this geographic localization is sufficient distinction of his own province. Or an educational sociologist will direct research upon the school as an institution interacting with other institutions, believing that this focus upon schools sets him apart from sociologists in general and justifies describing his professional role with the adjective "educational." However useful and scientifically proper this may be, it is not what I mean by a unique discipline of education. The educational psychologist is a psychologist with special interest in education. The educational sociologist is a contributor to the discipline of sociology rather than to education. This is no mere semantic distinction. What is important to recognize is that the empirical findings of research conducted in or concerning the schools, when problems and procedures are those of the recognized social sciences, do not tell us how to teach nor what to teach. In the same way that application of pure science to industrial process is not found by simple deduction from basic knowledge, but is rather the product of creative invention, so also the "meaning" of the social sciences for education must be discovered by activities of a higher intellectual order than following suggestions, analogies, or supposed "implications" from foundational sciences. That, however, is not the point. The point is that we cannot expect a true discipline of education to arise simply by localizing the questions of some other discipline within a school setting.

From the preceding paragraph it might seem that an educator's discipline is comparable to technological application of generalizations or laws appropriated from the pure sciences. That, however, could not possibly be our situation, for two reasons. In the first place, the scientific materials which, if available, would be most directly useful to educators are not yet available. In the second place, we are lacking a unitary point of view around which to gather the resources of several "parent" disciplines.

If educators were in a position to construct educational doctrine by applying the established conclusions of science, then surely one of the most fundamental items of knowledge upon which to build would be the psychology of learning. From psychology we should like to know precisely what sort of thing learning is and how best to control it. But this is a kind of knowledge for which psychologists are still seeking. Rather than proven generalizations we find alternative theories, each theory claimed by its sponsors to be more valid than the others. Although many facts about learning have been made known, they are as yet relatively isolated facts, the broader significance of which is a subject of systematic dispute. Whether learning is a matter of conditioned responses, or of SR bonds, or of insights, is a question still to be answered. The same kind of situation exists in other social sciences. One of the most important questions an educator might ask of a sociologist is how to make social change more amenable to deliberate control. The only answers available are purely speculative theories, of which there are many. Further examples of ignorance about the processes which educators try to control could be listed indefinitely, all supporting the same conclusion: if education is to achieve the status of a rigorous discipline, it cannot do so by way of technological application of scientific knowledge.

This does not mean that educators are totally without resources. Nor does it mean that the few facts available, plus the greater bulk of theory, are to be spurned by educators merely because of their limited validity. Whatever we have should be used. But the separateness of the foundation disciplines makes it exceedingly difficult to find their potential significance for an internally consistent solution to the problems of education. What is most required is a discipline standing between the basic sciences on the one hand and practical pedagogy on the other. Such a discipline must be theoretical, and it must reflect the sophisticated theoretical domains concerning personality formation, learning, social change, institutional process, cognition, esthetic apprehension, and so on. It would be impossible to blend such a diversity of raw materials unless the educational theorist at the same time constructed his own basic concepts by which to judge relevance and coherence. Furthermore, no matter how freely he might borrow theoretic instruments from social sciences, his educational discipline must be an independent theory, such that it can be examined in its own right rather than by a multitude of backward references. If this were not the case, then an eclectic heaping together of theoretical and largely speculative materials would reduce the probable validity of the outcome to a point well below the degree of credence we demand as a basis for deliberate action upon human beings.

II

A necessary first step in the founding of an independent discipline is the construction of a unique point of view, guiding perception to those features of the world that are to be subject matters for inquiry. Given the multitude of things and processes in the world around us, or even in the limited environment of the school, an educator needs to know what aspects or what objects he should focus upon as his own special concern. To have found such a way of deciding upon the relevant and of eliminating the irrelevant is to have initiated a discipline.

The right place to begin is easily discerned. Education is a process, the significant outcome of which is some kind of change produced by educative action upon its object, the pupil. Hence, what is required is a concept of the educative change. In any school room changes of many kinds take place constantly, most of them interesting to the teacher. There are, for example changes of the kind called learning, and of the kind called personality development, and of the kind called growth. But each of these changes is subject matter of a particular discipline. If a teacher tries to use these disciplines to increase his command of what happens, he must limit his attention now to one kind of change and now to another, for he has no instrument by which to think about the over-all kind of change which synthesizes his wide concern. Unless a unitary concept of educative change is found, he must remain divided and atomistic in his attempts to improve performance.

Possibly, because of the language used, a false impression might have been made. It might be supposed that what I am proposing to find is a particular kind of existent thing, an object having the sort of obvious reality that we attribute when we point to an object and say that it represents what we mean by the classification "cat" or "salt shaker." Such a suggestion would be false. The events to be observed in a school are like events to be observed elsewhere; no special kind of happening is to be found. What we are seeking is an object unique only by an act of intellectual construction. A complex human event may be classified in innumerable ways. The same event that a psychologist might call an act of learning, a personality theorist might call a change in self understanding, and a sociologist might call an instance of socialization, and so on. Each specialist makes different inclusions and exclusions of all that is potentially there to be observed. The event to which he gives a name characteristic of his discipline is not there to be seen by everyone but is there only to someone who approaches the situation with a specialist's eye.

A simple way to begin looking for the educative change is to suggest that it is nothing other than the sort of change we commonly call learning. It is possible to define learning so broadly (as, for example, to define it as any change or modification of behavior) that the educative change would have to be classified as a special category under the broader heading of learning. But several objections to this procedure may be placed, further consideration of which leads to the kind of answer needed.

In the first place, an educative change is produced deliberately. This distinguishes it from those learnings which occur both outside of school and also within the school but only incidentally and in a manner beyond the teacher's intent. To exclude the so-called "incidental learnings" from the category of educative change might offend those who define the curriculum as including "all learnings which take place within or through the activities of the school." It should be obvious, however, that we cannot take responsibility for what we cannot control. And what we cannot control includes an infinite range of learnings even within the school, resulting from the interaction of children with each other, with adults, and with the mixtures of culture and personality they bear. As for the non-school learning of children, it is possible that culture picked up in out-of-school life is more fundamental, and perhaps also more important in determining character, than what is learned through deliberate instruction.

There is a second limitation. It results from the fact that we cannot intend to teach any content save that of which we are aware, and save that for the teaching of which we can offer a rationale. This means in effect that we cannot plan to teach any content other than cultural; other, that is, than the skills, ideas, information, and attitudes that have been found in our culture or in our cultural sanctions. The learning for which we assume responsibility is therefore a culturation process. Although all learning beyond the first few years of infancy is somehow tinged with culture, it is nevertheless true that some parts of human learning are not properly classified as cultural, and these kinds are excluded from the class of educative change. Hence, if we were to describe the educative change as a kind of learning, this might seem to classify it, in the categories of existent disciplines, as a psychological event, whereas in fact it is quite as much sociological as psychological, and, in further analysis, neither.

The culture of a complex civilization is never internally integrated and consistent. Information and evaluations communicated in school are often at odds with beliefs and values formed outside of school in normal or unplanned culturation. In his out-of-school life, for example, a pupil is likely to learn that the members of his own national or racial group are inherently superior to other national or racial groups. Later, in upper years of schooling, he learns facts and associated values that conflict with his already acquired pride and prejudice. The completeness of his education on such matters is measured by the extent to which older beliefs and emotions are reconstructed rather than allowed to remain in their original form. These sub-cultural oppositions and consequent demands for reconstruction are not, as the example might seem to suggest, encountered only now and then and here and there. They are universal and omnipresent, an inevitable feature of civilization. To have a civilization means to have built upon common sense a further refinement that is no longer in agreement with its starting point. Furthermore, it is from the refined portion of culture that a school draws its curriculum, and from common sense that out-of-school culturation draws its content. Even though it seems a little far-fetched, we may say truthfully that all increments of learning, if fully integrated, are effected by a change in prior learning rather than by simple addition. Ordinarily such reconstruction of belief and value is undramatic and painless, but often enough it hurts just a little, sufficient to remind us that learning is that sort of thing.

To introduce new ideas deliberately, and with awareness of how new culture modifies already established beliefs and attitudes, is to acknowledge at least implicitly a sense of direction. Ordinarily the direction is viewed at close range: toward increased reading skill, or new alertness to current events, or more courtesy in human relations. It is scarcely possible that a multitude of such proximate aims could ever be arranged in a hierarchy from most general to most specific. Still, it is impossible to describe educative change in general unless the direction of change is made part of the description. This requires a generalization so broad that all potential aims may be included within it; so empty of specific content that no-one could find his own cherished goals excluded or minimized; and so self-evident, when stated, that anyone might find himself inclined to acknowledge its inclusiveness.

For what reason do we think it a good thing that pupils shall appropriate to themselves selected parts of their culture? The answer, it seems to me, is that we expect pupils to become more capable than before of responding in the "right" way to selected realities. Just which realities are deemed most important, and the manner of defining the "right" way to respond, is a variable of widest latitude. In any period or culture, the relative importance attached to different aspects of the world is determined by values and world views dominant in society at large, or at least in the class which supports the school. At one time the language and literature of an ancient civilization may be valued highest, at another time "real life" problems may seem the most important reality. For any complex society, the common function of schooling is to assure a personality capable of responding to a world or a reality more complex than the uneducated person could manage.

For the sake of simplicity and convenience in discourse, it would be helpful to have a single and broadly meaningful term by which to designate the direction of educative change. What is needed is a word to serve as an adjective qualifying "behavior", which could then indicate the direction of improvement in behavior which education is expected to bring about. It seems to me that we have such an adjective in the non-psychological meaning of "intelligent." Although educators are now more accustomed to the noun "intelligence," and to thinking of intelligence as a native resource not much influenced by education, the adjectival form is broader and prior in meaning. To say that a person behaves intelligently is to pay tribute to actions and attitudes which contribute to success in achieving goals proper for an educated person. Not, however, any and all factors which contribute to success. If a person reaches his goals largely through what is called good luck, or if his goals are poorly chosen, then we would not say that his behavior, although successful, was especially intelligent. Successful behavior is to be called intelligent behavior only when the person might have done otherwise, and only when his actions were premised upon his understanding of what he was doing and why. This doubly relativistic feature of the term makes it particularly suited to describe the direction of improvement in behavior which education is expected to make. An educative change is one which increases a person's capacity for behaving intelligently.

An initial characterization of the uniquely educative event is very nearly complete. One further consideration remains: what is the medium or object within which the educative change takes place? Is it a change in the mind or intellect, for example, or a change in character?

Suppose that it should be called an intellectual or mental change. Given a liberal definition of either term, this could be made acceptable. But in customary usage it is consistent to say that there is sometimes little or no connection between intellectual events and capacity for intelligent behavior. We say that a man may have unusual intellectual capacities and a depth of intellectual learning and yet be unable to adjust successfully to many situations of the kind that are unavoidable, and in which failure has serious effects upon later living. By our inherited concepts pertaining to intellect, a person's over-all effectiveness in achieving his goals is determined not only by his mind but also, and perhaps even more, by his emotional organization. The question of whether it is right or wise to continue a traditional distinction between mind and emotions is not to be examined here. Even if the dualism were removed, the facts would still remain to be explained. The educative change is a change in capacity for effective behavior, and this is necessarily an integrative change, an integration of mind and emotions. For this reason the term "mind" is not well suited to designate the medium within which the educative event occurs.

The term "character" may be rejected because of a different kind of limitation. It is most commonly used in conjunction with moral judgment of a person's goodness or lack of it. There can be no doubt that ethical judgments are a component of intelligent behavior. But we cannot judge the quality of behavior by reference to any given and widely acknowledged set of moral standards. Whether or not a particular act is to be judged as contributing to the good life must be decided by consideration of the context in which the behavior occurs, and by reviewing many more facets than our moral training could circumscribe.

What, then, is it which must change in order that an increased capacity for intelligent behavior might result? The only term now available which seems roughly appropriate is "personality," not as the term is used in popular discourse, but as used by those psychologists who specialize in what is called personality theory. In this sense, personality is a term which includes mind, body, emotions, and the self, viewed as reciprocal and in greater or less integration. In other words, the infinite complex of structures and processes which together determine the course and the success or failure of behavior in all kinds of situations is what might best be called "personality." Even if, for some specialist's purpose, this definition might seem wrong, it is the kind of thing thus clumsily defined that an educator hopes to modify, and which might be called the object within which educative change occurs.

Given the meanings established, we are now in a position to characterize the educative event. An educative event is the deliberately initiated impact of cultural materials upon previously established learnings which modifies personality in the direction of increased capacity for intelligent behavior. Admittedly this definition is lacking in precision. Any of its terms might very well have been different. Still, I think it will serve to mark out a distinctive province for educational theory.

From the foregoing it is apparent that a problem in theory of education is a search for reasoned ideas about what kind of deliberate culturation will react with existent beliefs and predispositions to modify a learner's personality and thereby increase his effectiveness in dealings with himself and his world. A foundation for reasoned beliefs about such matters requires a self-consistent integration of information already available for our use from existent disciplines. The social sciences offer appropriate materials and so does philosophy. But the important observations to be made here are three in number. First, it should be noted that from any given discipline, including philosophy, only selected parts are directly relevant to educational theory. Second, by contrast with traditional views on the matter, a theory or "philosophy" of education is quite as dependent upon social sciences as upon philosophy for its raw materials. Third, an educational theorist cannot ask the same kinds of questions, or pursue his inquiry from the same perspective, as have other theorists in philosophy and in the social sciences from whose constructions he might borrow.

Concerning the first two considerations, allow me to suggest what seem to be the most necessary parts, as found in other disciplines, from which an independent discipline of education must draw. What might be called the foundations for an educational theory include most prominently a theory of intelligence, of what it is, how it works to guide conduct, and how it changes; a theory of the self or of personality as that which bears the educative change; a theory of the culturation process, of how culture propagates itself under controlled conditions, and of how the various levels of culture mingle and conflict with one another; and finally, a theory concerning the nature of reality as object of knowledge and how it is known, and of what powers a greater knowledge of reality confers upon those who have it as against those who have less. These are the most essential of the elements from which an educational theorist constructs an educational doctrine.

If the preceding paragraph should suggest a merely eclectic borrowing of theory from other disciplines, then a further word is needed to correct so false an impression. A necessary distinction may be clarified by consideration of an example. Perhaps the most fundamental of all materials for the foundation of an educational theory is a theory of knowing, drawing, of course, upon philosophic theory of knowledge. But a theory of knowing, as foundation for an educational doctrine, is not the same thing as a philosopher's theory of knowledge. One difference is that an educational theorist does not, as does the philosopher, inquire into the abstract possibility of knowledge. He presupposes the possibility of knowing, and develops his theory about the process by which a person comes to know, and about the function or the economy of knowing in human life. This brings him to discuss the nature of belief and doubt, meaning by these terms actual psychological processes found empirically. For a majority of philosophers such concern for psychological events is not a legitimate part of philosophy. Theory of knowledge is not about psychological events at all. It offers, as some philosophers would say it, a "rational reconstruction" of knowing rather than a description of how people do in fact come to know. It seems to me that rational reconstructions are an invaluable resource for educational theory. Nevertheless, the reconstruction is valuable to education only as a theorist uses it creatively to enlighten his understanding of knowing as a real process. This is in fact a difficult kind of appropriation to make. Nothing could be more naively mistaken and disastrous for the intellectual responsibility of educational theory than to treat a philosopher's rational reconstruction as if it were a description of knowing, and then, compounding the error, to convert the supposed description into an educational method.

If an educator's theory of knowing is a theory about actual processes characteristic of human existence, then a further obligation is to distinguish it from the psychology of learning. A study of believing and doubting is, one might suppose, within the specialized province of psychology. If the literature of psychotherapy be excluded from psychology, then it is relatively easy to distinguish the educational theorist's concern from the psychologist's. An educational theorist is interested in distinguishing true belief from false belief, or in distinguishing learning which accords with reality from learning which does not, and this is a kind of interest which a psychologist cannot share. For many psychologists at the present time, the process of learning what is in fact true is no different from the process of learning what is in fact false. And the construction of standards by which truth is distinguished from its opposite is not the psychologist's business. But it is the business of an educational theorist and very close to the heart of his concern.

29 / ISRAEL SCHEFFLER

Is Education a Discipline?

I. Introduction

Does the *enterprise* of education rest upon a *discipline* of education? Is there some autonomous branch of knowledge underlying educational practice? Does the art of education derive its guiding principles from a distinctive realm of theory?

These questions are most serious when they refer, not to the current state of the sciences, but to the principle of the matter. Granted that we do not now have a discipline of education, is there not necessarily such a discipline to be developed or discovered by investigation? Does not the hope of real educational progress depend, moreover, upon the success with which such investigation is carried forward? This rhetorical way of putting the matter is disarmingly simple and has undeniable persuasiveness. Yet we will do well to examine the grounds on which an affirmative answer might be defended.

II. Educational Practice

The practice of education is surely a discipline, it might be said. Some ways of educating are preferable to others; there must be rules distinguishing the better from the worse practices and enjoining us to choose the better. Educational skill is, furthermore, not instinctive but rather the product of training and experience, leading to a mastery of these rules. Such training and experience, as well as the finished art of the master teacher, serve, finally, to discipline the educator as all art disciplines the artist, through the continual challenge to exercise discretion and judgment, patience and foresight, to

Israel Scheffler, "Is Education a Discipline?" from Walton and Kuethe (Eds.), *The Discipline of Education*, pp. 47–61.

Israel Scheffler (1923–) is Victor S. Thomas Professor of Education and Philosophy at Harvard University. He is the author of *The Language of Education, Conditions of Knowledge, Anatomy of Inquiry, Science and Subjectivity*, and editor of *Philosophy and Education*.

sacrifice himself in the quest for excellence, to perfect his understanding and love of his material.[1]

This account of the practice of education is certainly plausible. Yet it does not have the slightest tendency to establish the fact that the practice rests upon some autonomous branch of knowledge distinctive to it. That rules govern educational practice may be sufficient ground for declaring such practice to be a discipline, in one sense of this word. It is no ground for supposing these rules to be drawn from a unique theoretical discipline, in another sense of this word. Engineering is governed by rules, but these rules are not drawn from a special science of engineering.

That educational skill is a result of training and experience may provide another reason for holding the practice of education to be a discipline. It gives no support, however, to the supposition that there must be a distinctive branch of science underlying the practice. Medical skill is a product of training and experience, though it draws upon a host of intellectual disciplines. That medicine is a practical discipline does not imply the existence of a unique science of medicine.

There is, finally, an important analogy between serious teaching and serious art. Each disciplines the agent through challenge. It is, however, fallacious to infer from the fact that an activity possesses disciplinary value, that it must therefore rest upon a distinctive discipline of inquiry. There is no science of poetry, though poetry disciplines and civilizes. Nor does painting, for all its creative challenge, presuppose an autonomous science of painting. We must, in short, be careful to distinguish the ways in which we apply the word discipline to activities in general, from the ways in which we apply it to branches of knowledge in particular, and we must avoid fallacious inferences from the one sort of case to the other.

III. The Educational Realm

Let us then resolve to speak here of theoretical disciplines exclusively—of branches of knowledge or bodies of science. Each such discipline, it may be said, strives to offer a complete, systematic account of some realm of things in the world. It seeks a comprehensive body of true principles describing and explaining the realm it takes as its proper object. The realm of physical things is the object of the discipline of physics, whose province thus embraces all significant truths concerning physical objects.

Consider now the realm of things involved in educational processes: schools, subjects, ideas, social practices and traditions, students, teachers,

[1] See, in this connection, M. Black, "Education as Art and Discipline," *Ethics,* LIV (1944), 290–94; reprinted in I. Scheffler, ed., *Philosophy and Education* (Boston: Allyn & Bacon, 1958).

methods, and curricula. Surely this important realm must form the proper object of some single theoretical discipline, comprehending all significant truths about the processes of education. Unless we are to abandon the assumption that the world is ordered, we must suppose that there is, for each realm, and, in particular, for the educational realm, some special and exclusive discipline, comprising within its scope all those principles capable of describing and explaining the peculiar orders which it exemplifies.

This argument takes the view that there is a one-to-one correlation between realms and disciplines, that not only does each discipline apply to a unique realm, but that each realm supports at least one, and at most one, discipline. If it were not so wrong, this view would be most appealing in its symmetry, embodying, as it does, the time-honored notion that reality and discourse are mirror images of one another.[2]

Unfortunately, however, a variety of disciplines may be supported by elements of the same realm, while some realms seem patently to support no discipline at all. It is not the case that if we were to collect all the significant general truths concerning elements of any given realm, they would fill one and only one box, representing *the* discipline of that realm. Indeed, this notion would appear to harbor a contradiction. For if there were a box for realm A and another for realm B, there would need to be still a third for the realm consisting of $A + B$, containing truths belonging, on the theory before us, exclusively to the first two boxes.

Much of the appeal of the theory derives from the example of physics, whose domain allegedly comprises *all* truths descriptive and explanatory of the realm of physical objects. But the appeal of this example evaporates once we take a good look at the contents of the physical realm. Some physical objects are, after all, linguistic tokens, some are fossils, some are plants or animals, some are people. Even the hardiest physicalist will find it embarrassing to maintain that the truths comprising linguistics, paleontology, biology, anthropology, and psychology belong, even in principle, to the single discipline of physics. And while chemistry is perhaps in principal easier to think of as reducible to physics, it is not (as construed now and in prior years) *actually* thus reducible though it applies to the same realm. It becomes obvious upon reflection that disciplines quite distinct in content and manner of expression may be supported by the same realm of things.[3] At its best, physicalism is thus a doctrine concerning the elements to which disciplines

[2] For a general discussion, see N. Goodman, "The Way the World Is," *Review of Metaphysics,* XIV (1960), 48–56.

[3] The independence of ontology from the conceptual apparatus of a theory is discussed in W. V. Quine, *From a Logical Point of View* (Cambridge, Mass.: Harvard University Press, 1953), particularly Chapter VII. A criticism of the notion that we explain *objects* is contained in the last section of my "Explanation, Prediction, and Abstraction," *British Journal for the Philosophy of Science*, VII (1957), 293–309.

apply, rather than a doctrine claiming exhaustiveness for the discipline of physics.

If the realm of physical objects is taken as our model for the educational realm, we have no reason to suppose that there is at most one theoretical discipline of education, comprising all those general descriptive and explanatory truths concerning the elements of education. Nor, considering certain other realms as examples, do we have any reason to suppose that every realm must support at least one discipline, on pain of violating some general assumption of an ordered universe. There is no discipline associated with the realm of chairs, but this does not mean that the mechanical behavior of chairs presents a baffling mystery to our sense of order. Chairs, as well as all other classes of physical objects, fall under the general principles of physics. It is clearly fallacious to infer, from the fact that every discipline takes some realm of things as its object, that therefore every realm of things must be the object of some discipline. If there is, in fact, no special discipline of education, it does not in the least follow that the realm of education must remain opaque to our understanding.

IV. Educational Phenomena

We have criticized the notion of a one-to-one correlation between theoretical disciplines and realms of things. Disciplines may differ, we have said, despite the fact that they are associated with the same range of objects. Perhaps the reason is that they give accounts of different classes of phenomena manifested by these selfsame objects or, alternatively, of different classes of aspects or properties possessed by them.

The idea is a natural one. Consider John Smith. His weight is a physical datum, his pulse a biological datum, and his conversation a psychological datum. He is simultaneously subject to physical, biological, and psychological analysis. What is more plausible than to suppose that, in addition to the concrete John Smith before us, there are a variety of related Platonic entities to be reckoned with, namely, the physical, the biological, and the psychological phenomena manifested by him? Each such set of phenomena, it might be said, forms the basis of some discipline applicable to Smith, providing an ethereal bridge between Smith and the object and the truths by which he is described within this particular discipline.

The variety of disciplines, on this view, thus arises out of the variety of types of phenomena. To each such type corresponds a single discipline, and every discipline corresponds to some single type. The existence of educational phenomena thus guarantees, at least in principle, a unique discipline of education, though, admittedly, any range of objects manifesting educational phenomena will certainly be manifesting other sorts of phenomena as well, and so be analyzable by several disciplines at once.

There is a certain attractiveness to this view, and it accords well with much of our ordinary thinking and talking; but it will not withstand serious analysis. Objections analogous to those previously discussed present themselves immediately. Not every set of aspects, properties, or phenomena supports a separate discipline. If there is no science of the class of chairs, neither is there a science of the phenomenon of chairhood. Nor is it the case that at most one discipline formulates the truth concerning any given set of phenomena. It is, to be sure, undeniable that linguistic studies, for example, do not address themselves to the physical properties of their subject matter, but such properties surely enter into disciplines other than physics, for example, chemistry and biology.

Formally, too, the contradiction noted above lurks here as well. If the class of phenomena K and the class of phenomena L have unique disciplines associated with them, and there is also a unique discipline for the class $K + L$, either some truths fall into two boxes or some box is not completely filled. At this point, however, the possibility of a new philosophical move presents itself. We may declare that we have an independent criterion for determining "pure" classes of phenomena and that this criterion prevents the formation of $K + L$, upon which the troublesome contradiction depends. Putting the matter another way, the one-to-one correlation of disciplines and phenomenal classes is now proposed to hold only for pure phenomenal classes, as determined by our supposed independent criterion. This criterion rules out, for example, the class of physical-biological phenomena, recognizing only the two classes of purely physical and purely biological phenomena. This move was inappropriate before, with respect to objects, for the notion of a purely biological or purely physical object is inconceivable. The notion of a purely biological or physical aspect, property, or phenomenon, however, is not at all inconceivable.

The Platonizing of our problem thus does accomplish something new by comparison with the previous formulation. In particular, it avoids the inconsistency noted, and it allows several disciplines to apply to the same realm of objects, claiming only a one-to-one correlation with pure classes of phenomena associated with this realm. But it fails to remove the other objections noted. For it will still be difficult to maintain that every pure class of phenomena supports a discipline. And it will still be true that more than one discipline is related to a given pure class of phenomena as, for example, anthropology and sociology are both concerned with social phenomena. Further, it is no longer clear that we still have an argument for the existence of an educational discipline, since it is not clear that educational phenomena are pure.

It might be said that at least one of the above criticisms is unfair: social phenomena are not pure; they must be split into anthropological and sociological phenomena, each group supporting at most one discipline. But how do we know this? What, after all, *is* our criterion for determining pure classes of phenomena? What, indeed, is a phenomenon, aspect, or property, as distinct from the thing which manifests it and the word which attributes it?[4] Presumably, the mass of a particular painting by Monet is one of its physical phenomena or aspects, while its being an instance of French impressionism is not. Presumably, Khrushchev's power is a sociological property, unlike his height, volume, and chemical composition, which are not. Are not these decisions, however, perfectly parallel to the judgments by which we decide that the term "mass" is a physical term while the term "instance of French Impressionism" is not, that the term "power" belongs to the vocabulary of sociology, whereas the terms employed in formulating height, volume, and chemical descriptions do not? This question gives rise to the nagging suspicion that the language of phenomena is a parasite on the language of language, that phenomena have no independent life but are projected on the world by the terms we use, that they are mere shadows cast on objects by our descriptions of them. Why not clarify the situation by eliminating this shadow world completely, and focussing our attention directly on the language in which our accepted descriptions and explanations of things are expressed?

V. Educational Terms

We began by trying to construe theoretical disciplines in terms of peculiar realms of objects and found this course unsatisfactory. The alternative attempt to attach such disciplines to distinctive classes of pure phemonena turned out to be equally frustrating, for new as well as old reasons. Shall we fare better by turning from objects and phenomena to words?

Some clear pitfalls in this new course are immediately evident. We must not, for example, proceed to explain the disciplines as characterized by special vocabularies, and then blithely go on to delimit these vocabularies in terms of what is required to account for distinct realms of phenomena or objects. For this would raise the old difficulties again. Nor must we characterize the discipline of physics, for instance, as one formulated in physical terms—understanding by physical term a term which is used in formulating physics. For such a procedure would be clearly circular. What then *can* be done?

The attractiveness of the present idea lies in the fact that the several theoretical disciplines may be construed as several bodies of systematized information, each such body presumably expressed by a distinctive linguistic

[4] See, in this connection, N. Goodman, "On Likeness of Meaning," *Analysis*, X (1949), 1–7, reprinted in *Semantics and the Philosophy of Language*, ed. L. Linsky (Urbana: University of Illinois Press, 1952), and M. White, *Toward Reunion in Philosophy* (Cambridge, Mass.: Harvard University Press, 1956).

apparatus. Assume, for simplicity's sake, a common core of logical terms and a common syntax for all disciplines. The extralogical vocabulary of each will then differ from that of each other in at least some degree. Thus, for example, biology, but not physics, will contain the extralogical term "cell," though both share a common logical structure. Some degree of overlap in vocabularies is thus compatible with the distinctiveness of each, taken as a whole. Can we not then specify the domain of each discipline as what is expressible by means of the extralogical vocabulary associated with it, with the help of logic and in accord with the assumed standard syntax? And is not a discipline of education thus guaranteed by the fact that the vocabulary of education is, at least in part, distinctive?

There are complex refinements to be made before the present idea can be put with even minimal clarity. Consider, for example, the extralogical vocabulary of biology; let us designate this vocabulary as *B*. Now let us designate the extralogical vocabulary of chemistry as *C*. We may reasonably assume that *B* overlaps *C*, that is, that certain extralogical terms belong to both the biological and the chemical vocabularies. How shall we now classify a statement *S*, whose extralogical constituents are all drawn from the area of overlap? Shall we, in particular, assign *S* to the discipline of biology or to the discipline of chemistry?

We may attempt to settle this question by introducing some notion of presuppositional order among the disciplines. We assume, for example, that physics presupposes logic, that chemistry presupposes physics and is in turn presupposed by biology. Now if *S* is composed of extralogical terms wholly drawn from the overlap of the biological and chemical vocabularies, but not at all from the overlap of both of these with physics, then we assign *S* to chemistry, since biology presupposes chemistry. In Morton White's phrase, *S* contains no *specifically* biological terms, but only specifically chemical terms, except for logic.[5]

What shall we now do with a statement of another sort, *T*, which *does* contain some specifically biological terms, as well as some specifically chemical terms, but no other extralogical terms? Here we may follow the rule recently suggested by White, that a statement is to be classified under a given discipline if, besides containing terms specific to that discipline, all other contained terms are specific to disciplines presupposed by it.[6] Thus *T* is to be assigned to biology.

Let us here waive the difficult question as to how the order of presupposi-

[5] See M. White, "Historical Explanation," *Mind*, LII (1943), reprinted with Postscript, in P. Gardiner, *Theories of History* (Chicago: Free Press, 1959), where the attempt is made to determine the status of history as an independent discipline.

[6] See his reply to a query by the present writer, in P. Gardiner, *Theories of History*, p. 372.

tion is to be interpreted, as well as all other problems arising out of the foregoing refinements. The basic idea is now that the province of a discipline is to be construed in terms of its specific extralogical vocabulary as well as its standing in the order of presupposition. Does it not now follow, from the existence of a specific educational vocabulary, that there must be a discipline of education?

Before we say yes to the last question, we must look critically at the basic idea underlying it. As a matter of fact, the general proposal has untenable consequences. Suppose, for example, that the terms "table" and "round" are each definable in physical terminology. Then the true statement, "Some tables are not round," is expressible in the specific language of physics. Yet this statement surely does not belong to the discipline of physics. Indeed, if this statement were considered to belong to physics because translatable into physical terms, its negation, "All tables are round," would also belong to physics by the same token, and the discipline of physics would turn out self-contradictory. Neither statement, in fact, belongs to the body of physical theories and laws, nor does either one follow from these. The term "table," though definable in physical terms, is, moreover, not a term that can properly be said to belong to the discipline of physics. It does not now figure in the formulation of physical laws or theories, nor is it ever likely to do so. The range of a discipline, if these reflections are correct, is considerably narrower than what is theoretically expressible by means of the discipline's distinctive linguistic apparatus. Much of what is thus expressible falls outside the discipline, and two disciplines may conceivably share the same apparatus. The range of a discipline thus seems to be a function, not of the expressive power of a given linguistic apparatus, but rather of the availability of a body of laws and theories which have been formulated and established within its scope. The point may be put in terms of the reduction of one discipline to another. If one discipline is to be reduced to a second, it will not in general be enough to show its terminology to be wholly definable by means of the second discipline's terminology. It will, in addition, be necessary to show its principles to be derivable from those of the second discipline.[7] This is another way of saying that the range of a discipline is set by a body of laws and theories, rather than by a particular vocabulary of terms.

While the derivation of a given statement from the principles of a particular discipline shows that the statement has indeed been reduced to, and hence belongs to, that discipline, it does *not* follow that every unreduced statement belongs to *some other* discipline. Recall our recent statement, "Some tables

[7] See E. Nagel, "The Meaning of Reduction in the Natural Sciences," in *Science and Civilization*, ed. R. C. Stauffer (Madison: University of Wisconsin Press, 1949), and *The Structure of Science* (New York: Harcourt, Brace, and World, 1961).

are not round." Though we may here assume each of its extralogical terms to be definable by means of the vocabulary of physics. it does not, I have argued, belong to the discipline of physics. Nor is there any necessity of supposing that, because it falls outside physics, it must therefore fall within the scope of some other discipline.

Note that, in the statement we have just considered, every extralogical term is definable in physical terminology and yet the statement as a whole is not "significant" in any theoretical sense; it is not likely to figure as a principle of any scientific discipline, though it is true. In general, the fact that a term is definable within the language of a discipline in no way guarantees that there must be significant principles formulable with its help. Carl Hempel some years ago illustrated an argument of his by inventing the term "hage."[8] A person's "hage" is his height, in inches, multiplied by his age, in years. Now my hage happens to be 2,698. Assume that I can be identified by my present spatio-temporal position, within the language of physics. It is obvious that, though the object with this position can then be said, within physical terminology, to have a hage of 2,698, this statement is not part of the discipline of physics. There is, furthermore, surely no necessity that the term "hage" will be fruitful in the formulation of any theoretical or lawlike principle within any discipline, despite the fact that it is definable in physical terms by means of which significant principles are expressed.[9]

Is it not even more obvious that disciplines cannot be created simply by producing new terms not definable within the vocabularies of established disciplines? Assume that educational terminology is distinctive, and thus allows us to express more than could be expressed without it. The crucial question remains whether this surplus is scientifically significant: Are there laws and theories forming a systematic and comprehensive body of assertions that are both expressible by means of this terminology and true, or at least, interesting in the scientific sense, and well supported? This condition is not necessarily met by every term. The fact that a term belongs to none of the hitherto established disciplines does not therefore guarantee that there must be some as-yet-undiscovered discipline to which it will belong. Whether the condition will in fact be met in a given case is determinable, if at all, by investigation rather than by a priori arguments. The mere distinctiveness of educational terminology, were it established, would not in itself guarantee the existence of a discipline of education.

[8] C. G. Hempel, *Fundamentals of Concept Formation in Empirical Science* (Chicago: University of Chicago Press, 1952), p. 46. I have here taken the liberty of specifying inches rather than Hempel's millimeters.

[9] By "principles" I here intend lawlike principles rather than bare generalizations. See N. Goodman, *Fact, Fiction, and Forecast* (Cambridge, Mass.: Harvard University Press, 1955).

VI. Educational Principles

I have suggested that disciplines are dependent on the availability of established scientific principles, that is, theories and laws, and that the terms of a discipline are those by means of which such principles are formulated. Does this imply that there is no connection between a given discipline and terms or statements that fall outside it? I think the answer is No. For to suppose that there is no connection is to construe the disciplines as completely isolated and self-contained. It is to deny the applicability of the disciplines to the concrete affairs of everyday life.

To illustrate: I have above suggested that the term "table" does not belong to the discipline of physics in the sense that it does not represent a fruitful category in the formulation of physical principles. But imagine that someone drops a lighted cigar on my new coffee table and burns it. The question, Why did my new coffee table show a burn when I came back into the parlor with the cheese? is a question to which physics supplies a relevant answer. Suitably supplemented with the particulars of the case, physical principles explain the disaster, despite the fact that physics includes no laws of the burning of new coffee tables nor references to cheese or parlors. The term "abstract painting" is not, I suppose, even definable (at least in any obvious way) in physical terms, but physics will explain why a particular abstract painting fell from the wall yesterday. The terms peculiar to common affairs may belong to no discipline at all, but they normally figure in applying the disciplines to life. This they do in helping to formulate both the initial problems arising in practice, and those particulars which serve to bring problematic cases within the scope of disciplinary principles.

Suppose, now, that the terms peculiar to educational institutions and practices never yield a discipline of education in the sense outlined. Does this imply that education is cut off from all established disciplines, and must forever lack theoretical illumination? If the previous considerations are correct, the answer must clearly be in the negative. The problems of education, the questions arising in educational practice, will be framed in familiar educational terms. Whatever explanatory principles are at all relevant will receive their educational applications through being linked with these terms. The latter may not figure explicitly within the principles themselves, but to suppose these principles therefore irrelevant is to suppose an absurdity. It is to suppose, in effect, that these principles are generally useless because generally inapplicable.

A crucial issue, it thus seems to me, is whether we can establish reliable principles to explain how and why children learn, schools develop, curricula change, ideals conflict, perceptions alter, societies differ, standards of taste and culture are formed. That *any* discipline is likely to be developed capable of answering these questions systematically and reliably is still a matter of some controversy. Ernest Nagel, a distinguished student of logical and methodological issues in the social sciences, has recently written that

> In no area of social inquiry has a body of general laws been established, comparable with outstanding theories in the natural sciences in scope of explanatory power or in capacity to yield precise and reliable predictions. . . . Many social scientists are of the opinion, moreover, that the time is not yet ripe even for theories designed to explain systematically only quite limited ranges of social phenomena. . . . To a considerable extent, the problems investigated in many current centers of empirical social research are admittedly problems of moderate and often unimpressive dimensions. . . . In short, the social sciences today possess no wide ranging systems of explanations judged as adequate by a majority of professionally competent students, and they are characterized by serious disagreements on methodological as well as substantive questions.[10]

The problem, it seems to me, is thus to advance the state of social inquiry —in particular, of all those studies which seem likely to yield explanatory principles relevant to the concerns of education.[11] Whether, however, it turns out that one or several theoretical disciplines develop, and whether any of these is a discipline of education specifically, seem to me quite unimportant issues.

As educators, we will continue to ask all sorts of questions arising in the course of our work. If the arguments presented above are at all convincing, we ought not to isolate ourselves from attempts to formulate principles relevant to our work, no matter what their disciplinary labels. Nor ought we build our professional identity upon the faith that a unique discipline of education will one day be found. Rather, we should encourage relevant investigations by psychologists, anthropologists, sociologists, economists, educationists, and still others, and we should strive to link them with the concerns of schooling. There is surely enough substance in such an enterprise to support a genuine and important professional identity, indeed, several such identities. If it turns out that, in the place of a unique discipline of education, we get a variety of systematized laws and principles *applicable* to the practice of education, I cannot see that we will have serious cause for complaint.

Questions for Discussion

According to Belth, what are the undesirable outcomes when education is considered an applied discipline? Does he convincingly show that it is not an applied discipline? Why is it an error to try to establish a discipline of

[10] E. Nagel, *The Structure of Science*, pp. 447–49.

[11] See the related comments in my *The Language of Education* (Springfield, Ill.: Charles C Thomas Co., 1960), Chapter IV, pp. 71–75.

education by comparing it with other disciplines? If education is a discipline, what are its identifiable characteristics? The public, he states, should have a voice in organized schooling but not in the discipline of education. Why? Explain why he believes no discipline is a substitute for the study of education. Show how he arrives at the conclusion that education is the "subject of subjects." Has he adequately supported this conclusion?

What position does McMurray take on the advisability of deriving educational theory from philosophy? Of starting with educational theory but reducing it to problems of philosophy? What are the bases for his arguments? McMurray takes considerable care to develop a conception of education. Why does he consider this activity so important, and what use does he make of his conception? If it is possible to borrow "theoretic instruments" from other disciplines, can education still have autonomy? Compare McMurray's approach to that of Belth.

Are Scheffler's reasons why the three arguments for a discipline of education cannot be sustained adequate? Are these the most important arguments? Why is the attempt to construe theoretical disciplines in terms of a peculiar realm of objects or as pure phenomena an unsatisfactory approach? What does Scheffler mean by *discipline*? In what way does his conception affect his analysis? Would distinct terminology guarantee a discipline of education? If by its very nature education is not a discipline and cannot become one, what consequences are likely to follow? Compare Scheffler's essay to the two preceding ones, and then develop your own position and be prepared to defend it.

Suggested Reading

Marc Belth has attempted, in considerable detail, to demonstrate that education is "the discipline of disciplines" in *Education as a Discipline* (Boston: Allyn and Bacon, 1965). A recent attempt to establish the basis for education as a discipline is John Walton's *Introduction to Education: A Substantive Discipline* (Waltham, Mass.: Xerox, 1971). John Walton and James L. Kuethe have edited a series of addresses and rejoinders, *The Discipline of Education* (Madison, Wis.: University of Wisconsin Press, 1963). The debate focuses on whether education is a discipline, a field of study, or the handmaiden of the social and behavioral sciences. A number of British educators approach the issue by examining the fields of educational inquiry, particularly the foundational fields, to determine their contours and interrelationships. This approach is found in J. W. Tibble, ed., *The Study of Education* (London: Routledge and Kegan Paul, 1966). Finally, an attempt to develop educational theory through the use of models is found in Elizabeth Steiner Maccia and George S. Maccia, *Development of Educational Theory Derived from Three Educational Theory Models* (Columbus, Ohio: Ohio State University Press, 1966).

CHAPTER EIGHT /

PHILOSOPHY OF EDUCATION

PHILOSOPHY began in ancient Greece before the time of Socrates and relied on the best reasoning the human mind could devise to explain the world and the nature of man. It posed an alternative to other approaches, such as myths, superstition, tradition, mysticism, and dogma, which have persisted as modes of dealing with life during man's short stay on this planet. Since philosophy antedates the discoveries of modern science, some philosophers sought knowledge and understanding of physical phenomena in the world around them as well as knowledge about the nature of man and the good life; these investigations have resulted in important contributions to mathematics and sciences.

The philosophic quest, generated by a sense of profound wonder about human life, attempts to sort, sift, and analyze phenomena and then to reorganize them into a logically consistent, embracing framework. This process enables the philosopher to see life in broader perspective and with greater depth and meaning; it makes possible the organization and systematization of human experience. The philosopher traditionally has raised questions about man and the cosmos, such as What is mind and what is matter? Is the universe purposive, or does it seem to have purpose only because of our imaginations? Can man ever have definite knowledge? How do we determine what is good and bad? What is beauty and how can it be recognized?

With the advent of modern science and the division of knowledge into numerous disciplines, some have come to see the role of philosophy as limited to those remaining areas where science does not investigate or have special competences in gaining knowledge. Philosophers who accept this point of view contend that some philosophical problems have been formulated in such a manner that no evidence could be adduced for either their support or refutation, and thus statements are philosophically meaningless unless they can be reformulated. With advancements in philosophy and with the need to conduct precise and penetrating analyses of the type previously mentioned, philosophy (as is the case with other disciplines) has become more specialized. Some philosophers still attempt to formulate major systems of thought, but there also has been a growth in the number of specialists who operate with great precision on more limited problems. There also are modern movements, such as existentialism, which believe that in traditional philosophy man and his individuality were too often absorbed into large-scale metaphysical systems. To rectify this condition they have sought as their starting point individual man and human existence as fundamental categories in which to undertake their inquiries.

Philosophy of education began with the writings of Plato, but as in philosophy itself, philosophy of education is undergoing reexamination to clarify its role in the study of education. There are presently numerous interpretations of the nature and function of philosophy of education, several of which will be briefly discussed.

A long-standing interpretation views philosophy as the parent discipline and philosophy of education as connected to it in some way. There are several versions of this interpretation. Philosophy of education may be thought to derive its theories, problems, and methodology from philosophy. In some cases education is considered a field in which the findings from general philosophy or the abilities of a general philosopher could be applied. Others have thought that by starting with education the material could be reduced to problems of philosophy. The most common variant, however, is the belief that from general philosophical systems a philosophy of education can be derived, including recommendations for policy and practice.

Several serious objections have been lodged against the position that philosophy of education is subordinate to or derivative of general philosophy. It has been argued that the problems of philosophy are not those of education and that the philosopher with little or no knowledge, experience, and interest in education has scarcely any contribution to make to the study of education. Neither are there plausible grounds for believing that the material of education can be reduced to problems of philosophy so long as it can be argued that there are distinctive characteristics in the study of education. Finally, there are not necessarily any logical relations between a particular metaphysical and ontological system and education.

A second proposal is that the function of philosophy is to follow a more inductive approach than the previous interpretation. Philosophical positions can be discerned from case studies of the teaching process or from examining the assumptions underlying educational problems. The advantage of this approach is that it focuses on the phenomena of education rather than philosophy. But it also misleadingly assumes that a close, direct relationship exists between certain teacher activities and a systematic philosophy of education.

A third interpretation holds that the purpose of philosophy of education is to develop a directive doctrine for organizing and prescribing the course for educational policy and practice. The point that a philosophy of education should have some bearing on the process of education is well taken, but it would stifle inquiry if every investigation must relate directly to practice or lead to policy changes. Theoretical and metatheoretical studies may not have an immediate impact on practice; to insist that they do would impede the development of the field and would also likely lead to an ineffectual doctrine for guiding practice because the philosophical and theoretical side would remain underdeveloped.

More recently some educators have been impressed with the importance of developing and refining a discipline of education, and they consider the philosopher of education to be the principal contributor to this enterprise. This undertaking is conceived as the primary purpose of philosophy of education. It would first have to be shown, however, that education approaches a discipline or can become a discipline, and further, the unique role of the philosopher of education in this undertaking must be established. Even then it could be plausibly argued that this should not be the exclusive function of philosophy of education.

A fourth interpretation, which arose from the application of analytic philosophy to education, envisions philosophy of education as a study of the language and logic of education. Studies of the use and misuse of basic educational concepts and the logic of education arguments constitute the areas of inquiry. Such studies are ultimately designed to improve educational research and to lead to a refinement in the conceptualization of education. One need not deny the importance of such investigations to believe that philosophy of education is not limited solely to this function. To deny other functions it would be necessary to show that on logical grounds they are impossible, or on pragmatic grounds they will fail to achieve the desired results, or for prudential reasons it would be unwise to undertake them (for example, policy-makers will ignore such studies).

Strongly opposed to this position is the conviction that the function of philosophy of education should enlarge the educator's range of vision and perspective. Few educators are too abundantly endowed with these attributes, and because the educator needs to lift this gaze occasionally from classes, meetings, and paperwork in order to chart his direction and find a center of meaning, philosophy of education can perform no greater service. However, analytic philosophers would question whether the philosopher has a special pipeline to truth or is blessed with greater vision and understanding than other specialists. Thus the philosopher of education should limit himself to functions he is best and uniquely able to fulfill: studies of the logic and language of education. Nonetheless, even though the philosopher of education cannot claim a special ability to comprehend truth, there is nothing inherent in a logical, systematic philosophy of education that prevents it from offering educators greater vision and perspective. But these outcomes are usually a by-product of a job well done rather than a consciously sought end.

Finally, there is the belief that philosophy of education is not a directive doctrine but a subject that promotes a liberal education. In other words, its purpose is to serve as a liberal and humane study that needs no justification on utilitarian grounds. It should assume a respected place in the pantheon of letters, arts, and sciences, revered for its powers to liberate man from the idols of the mind. In addition to those who doubt that philosophy of education possesses such powers, others would charge that it is abdicating its function to influence the course and direction of education and that it fails to help develop a discipline of education.

Several interpretations of philosophy of education are presented in the following selections. William Frankena provides a schematic system to enable us to better understand a philosophy of education. He first indicates what a normative philosophy of education includes, and then shows sequentially how these content items are likely to be arranged and connected. Finally, he notes exceptions to the full sequence that might be found in an actual normative philosophy of education.

John Dewey envisages the nature and function of philosophy of education in a special sense. His essay can be understood better if we recognize that he stipulates his own definitions for philosophy, science, and education and conceives a special purpose for philosophy (a purpose, by the way, with which many philosophers may not concur). In many of Dewey's writings he argues forcefully that the tendency to conceptualize in dualistic terms is the cause of some of the problems in philosophy and social life. These dualisms are quite common: labor and leisure, interest and discipline, mind and body, experience and thinking, liberal and vocational education, subject matter and method, and the individual and society. Dewey attempts to avoid dualisms in this essay and his other writings; in some instances he seeks to dissolve existing dualisms.

Elizabeth Maccia examines Dewey's conception of philosophy of education and finds it inadequate on several grounds. She also criticizes aspects of Frankena's ideas on the subject and then develops the distinctive features of her interpretation. One should be able to see clearly why she believes that philosophy is not the general theory of education.

30 / WILLIAM K. FRANKENA

A Model for Analyzing a Philosophy of Education

There are two sorts of things that go by the name of philosophy of education today, one traditional and one newish. The newish sort of thing is what is called "analytical philosophy of education." It consists in the analysis of educational concepts, arguments, slogans, and statements. For example, if one tries to define what is meant by teaching, to distinguish teaching from indoctrination, and to relate teaching to learning, or if one tries to determine what is meant by the slogan "Learn by doing!", then one is doing analytical philosophy of education. The analytical philosophy of education consists entirely of such inquiries. Since I am here seeking to show how to analyze a philosophy of education, this essay is itself an example of analytical philosophy of education. I say that this sort of thing is newish because, although educational philosophers have always included some of it in their works, it is only recently that some of them have come to think that their work should include nothing else.

The other kind of philosophy of education is what educational philosophers have done historically and what some of them still do. I shall call it "normative philosophy of education." It may be eclectic or non-eclectic; idealistic, realistic, or pragmatic; naturalistic or supernaturalistic; traditional or progressive. In all its forms, however, what distinguishes it from analytical philosophy of education is that it makes normative statements about what education, educators, and the schools do or not do, about what the aims, content, methods, etc., of education should be or not be.

I

Now consider any such normative philosophy of education, for example, that of Aristotle, Rousseau, Dewey, Whitehead, Russell, Maritain, Brameld,

William K. Frankena, "A Model for Analyzing a Philosophy of Education," from *The High School Journal*, Vol. 2 (October 1966), pp. 8–13. Reprinted by permission of the publisher and the author.

William K. Frankena (1908–) is professor of philosophy at the University of Michigan. He has published *Three Historical Philosophies of Education* and *Ethics* and has edited *Philosophy of Education*.

or Phenix. Our problem is to find a scheme for analyzing it, that is, for understanding it and seeing how it is put together, for taking it apart and putting it together again. One cannot evaluate it in any systematic way until one has analyzed it to see just what it says and what its arguments are.

In general, a normative philosophy of education will include statements of three kinds. (a) It must include normative statements about the aims, principles, methods, etc., of education, as Dewey does when he says that the schools should teach reflective thinking. (b) It will probably include—and it should include—some bits of analysis, for example, definitions of education, teaching, and learning. (c) Almost certainly it will contain some statements of empirical fact, hypotheses about their explanation, psychological theories, experimental findings, predictions, and the like, for example, Russell's statement that a child can be made to feel the importance of learning the dull parts of a subject without the use of compulsion. (d) It may also contain statements of a fourth kind—epistemological, metaphysical, or theological ones such as Phenix's assertion that the meaning of a proposition is defined by the method of validating it or Maritain's doctrine that man is a sinful and wounded creature called to divine life. It is not always easy to tell which kind of a statement is being made in a given sentence, and many sentences in works on the philosophy of education are ambiguous and hard to classify.

To analyze a philosophy of education one must find out what statements of these different kinds it contains and how they are related to one another in the author's reasoning. This is relatively easy to do in the case of some authors, for example, Maritain, harder to do in the case of others, for example, Dewey or Whitehead. What follows is an attempt to provide a guide for doing so.[1]

II

Education is primarily a process in which educators and educated interact and such a process is called education if and only if it issues or is intended to issue in the formation, in the one being educated, of certain desired or desirable abilities, habits, disposition, skills, character traits, beliefs, or bodies of knowledge (if it is intended to but does not, it is called *bad* education), for example, the habit of reflective thinking, conscientiousness, the ability to dance, or a knowledge of astronomy. For convenience, I shall refer to all such states as dispositions. Then education is the process of forming or trying to form such dispositions. Note that what I have just done is a rough analysis of the concept of education.

If this is so, then (1) the *main* task of a normative philosophy of education is to list and define a set of dispositions to be fostered by parents, teachers,

[1] For similar attempts on my part, see "Toward a Philosophy of the Philosophy of Education," *Harvard Educational Review*, 26, 1956; *Philosophy of Education*, Macmillan, 1965, pp. 1–10; *Three Historical Philosophies of Education,* Scott, Foresman, 1965, pp. 6–12.

and schools (and by the pupil himself). That is, it must say what dispositions are desirable and ought to be cultivated. In saying this it will, of course, be making normative statements, but the definitions of the dispositions listed will be bits of analysis. A complete normative theory of education will, however, do two more things. (2) It will give a line of thought to show that the dispositions listed by it are desirable or should be cultivated. Such a line of reasoning may take various forms, but they must all have the same general pattern. They must bring in some basic premises about the aims or values of life or about the principles to be followed in life—about what is desirable or obligatory. These, again, will be normative judgments, the most fundamental ones. Even Dewey brings in such premises, though he often writes as if he does not. In addition, they must show or at least give reasons for thinking that, if we are to live in the way that is desirable or in the way in which we ought to—if we are to live a good or a moral life—then we must acquire the dispositions listed. It is in this part of a philosophy of education that epistemological, ontological, or theological premises most often appear, but they are not logically required. What *is* logically required is, first, some normative premises stating basic goals or principles, for example, Aristotle's premise that the good life is a happy one consisting of intrinsically excellent activities like contemplation, and second, factual claims stating that certain dispositions are conducive to the achievement of those goals or to the following of those principles, for example, Aristotle's further claim that, if we are to achieve the good life as he sees it, we must cultivate such dispositions as moderation, practical wisdom, and a knowledge of mathematics, physics, and philosophy. If we think of basic normative premises as belonging to Box A, the other premises used here, whether they are religious, philosophical, or empirical, as belonging to Box B, and the conclusions as to the dispositions to be fostered as belonging to Box C, then we can represent this part of a philosophical education as follows:

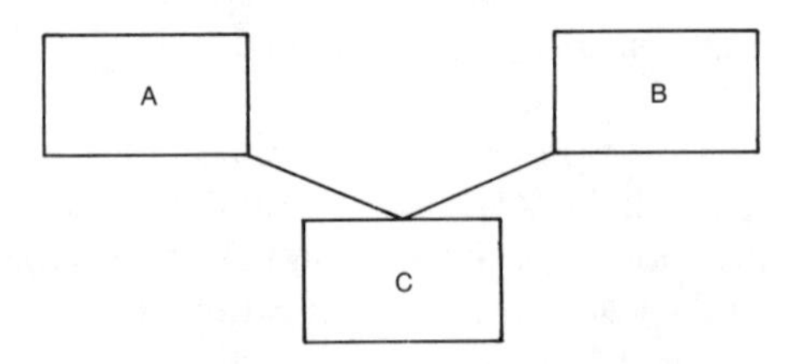

(3) Finally, a complete normative theory of education will tell us what we should do in order to acquire or foster the dispositions recommended by it in Box C, that is, it will make further recommendations about means, methods, curriculum, administration, etc., hopefully accompanying them with its reasons for making them. This means that it will make normative state-

ments of yet a third kind, and that it will support them by giving empirical evidence (discovered by observation and experiment or borrowed from psychology and other disciplines) to show that the methods and measures it advocates are necessary, helpful, or effective in the formation of the dispositions in its Box C (and that other methods are not). The example cited from Russell earlier will do here; in it he argues that compulsion should not be used, since children can be gotten through even the dull parts of a subject without it. This example also shows that premises from Box A may come in even in this part of a philosophy of education, for Russell is assuming the normative principle that compulsion ought not to be used unless it is necessary. Actually, epistemological premises or other premises from Box B may also appear at this stage; for instance, Cardinal Newman uses his epistemological premise that theology is a body of genuine knowledge in an argument to show that theology should belong to the curriculum of a university. Neglecting such important points, however, we may represent this part of a philosophy of education as follows, taking Box C as giving the dispositions to be fostered, Box D as containing factual statements of the form "Method X is necessary, effective, or at least helpful in the formation of one or more of these dispositions (or the opposite)," and Box E as including recommendations of the form "Method X should (or should not) be used":

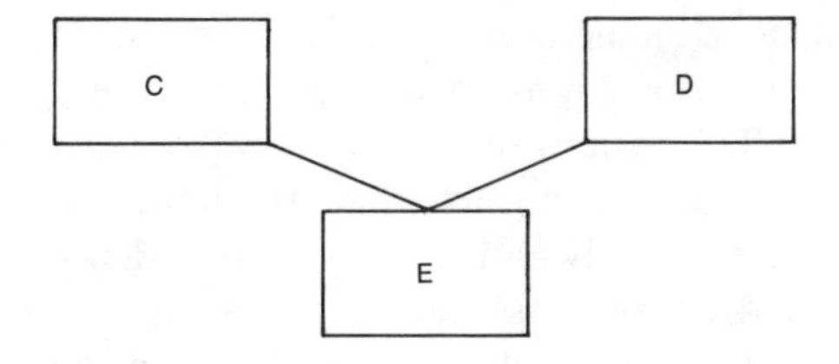

It should be added that bits of analysis may also show up in this part of a theory, for example, in a distinction between indoctrination and teaching or in a definition of compulsion.

III

It will now be clear that a full-fledged normative philosophy of education will have two parts, each probably including some bits of analysis; one part falling into the ABC pattern given above and the other into the CDE pattern. In its actual presentation, however, the two parts are often mingled and the patterns are often left unclear, for instance, in Whitehead's essays on education. Of the two parts, the first is the more properly philosophical, and the second is the more practical. Combining the two parts, we may represent a complete normative philosophy of education as follows:

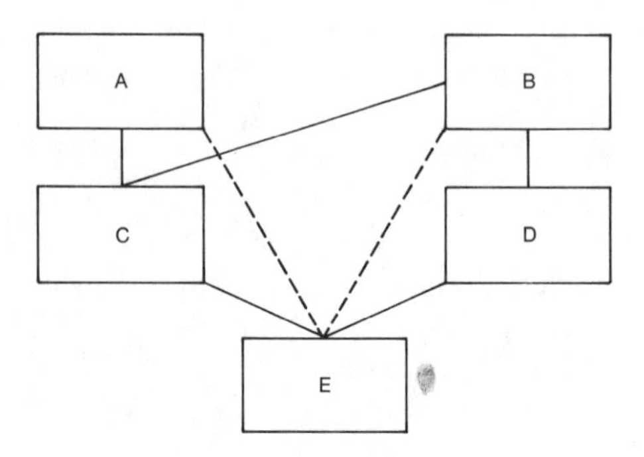

Here the dotted lines are intended to take care of the fact, noted earlier, that premises from Boxes A and B may be used in arriving at the recommendations made in Box E.

It will also be clear that there may be three kinds of normative philosophy of education: (a) one that is complete in the way just indicated; (b) one that does only what was described as the first part of the complete task, giving us what falls into the ABC pattern, that is, one that provides us only with a list of dispositions to be fostered together with a rationale showing us that they should be fostered and why, leaving the task of implementation to educational scientists, administrators, and teachers; and (c) one that simply begins with a list of dispositions to be cultivated and goes on to give us what falls into the CDE pattern or into what was referred to as the second part of the complete task, telling us what we should do to foster the dispositions listed most effectively and giving us the evidence and arguments to show why we should adopt those methods and procedures. A writer who does the third kind of thing might take his list of dispositions from some more philosophical work, or he might be eclectic, picking up the dispositions on his list from various sources, or he might simply take them to be the dispositions regarded as desirable by society, parents, the state, the church, school boards, or even the pupils themselves—remember how Bianca complains to her would-be educators in *The Taming of a Shrew:*

> Why, gentlemen, you do me double wrong,
> To strive for that which resteth in my choice:
> I am no breeching scholar in the schools;
> I'll not be tied to hours nor 'pointed times,
> But learn my lessons as I please myself.

We can also now see just what one must do in order to understand any complete normative philosophy of education that is placed before one (an analytical philosophy of education is another matter). If one knows this, one will also be able to analyze any less complete normative philosophy of education.

(1) One must first look to see what dispositions it says education should foster (Box C).
(2) Next, one must try to determine the rationale given to show that education should foster those dispositions. To do this one must:
    (a) See what its basic normative premises are—its basic values, principles, or ends (Box A).
    (b) See what factual premises are brought in (implicitly or explicitly), empirical, theological, or philosophical (Box B).
    (c) See how these go together to make a line of argument of the ABC pattern to show that the dispositions listed should be cultivated.
(3) Then one should look for recommendations about ways and means of teaching, administering, etc. (Box E).
(4) Fourthly, one must seek to discover the rationales for these recommendations. To do this one must:
    (a) See what factual statements based on observation and experience are brought in (possibly borrowed from psychology, etc.) (Box D).
    (b) See if any premises from Boxes A or B are used here.
    (c) See how these go together to make a line of argument (or a battery of separate arguments) to show that the ways and means recommended should be used in the cultivation of the dispositions listed (Pattern CDE).
(5) All along, of course, one should notice any definitions or bits of analysis that occur and see how they fit into the discussion.

Finally, it can also be seen from the above analysis of a normative philosophy of education what is involved in "building" one of one's own. However, this should now be so obvious that it need not be spelled out.

31 / JOHN DEWEY

Philosophy of Education

. . . Our further task is to extract and make explicit the idea of philosophy implicit in these considerations. We have already virtually described, though not defined, philosophy in terms of the problems with which it deals; and we have pointed out that these problems originate in the conflicts and difficulties of social life. The problems are such things as the relations of mind and matter; body and soul; humanity and physical nature; the individual and the social; theory—or knowing, and practice—or doing. The philosophical systems which formulate these problems record the main lineaments and difficulties of contemporary social practice. They bring to explicit consciousness what men have come to think, in virtue of the quality of their current experience, about nature, themselves, and the reality they conceive to include or to govern both.

As we might expect, then, philosophy has generally been defined in ways which imply a certain totality, generality, and ultimateness of both subject matter and method. With respect to subject matter, philosophy is an attempt to *comprehend*—that is, to gather together the varied details of the world and of life into a single inclusive whole, which shall either be a unity, or, as in the dualistic systems, shall reduce the plural details to a small number of ultimate principles. On the side of the attitude of the philosopher and of those who accept his conclusions, there is the endeavor to attain as unified, consistent, and complete an outlook upon experience as is possible. This aspect is expressed in the word "philosophy"—love of wisdom. Whenever philosophy has been taken seriously, it has always been assumed that it signified achieving a wisdom which would influence the conduct of life. Witness the fact that almost all ancient schools of philosophy were also organized ways of living, those who accepted their tenets being committed to certain distinctive modes of conduct; witness the intimate connection of philosophy with the theology of the Roman church in the Middle Ages, its frequent association with religious interests, and, at national crises, its association with political struggles.

This direct and intimate connection of philosophy with an outlook upon life obviously differentiates philosophy from science. Particular facts and laws of science evidently influence conduct. They suggest things to do and not do, and provide means of execution. When science denotes not simply a report of the particular facts discovered about the world but a *general attitude* toward it—as distinct from special things to do—it merges into philosophy. For an underlying disposition represents an attitude not to this and that thing nor even to the aggregate of known things, but to the considerations which govern conduct.

Hence philosophy cannot be defined simply from the side of subject matter. For this reason, the definition of such conceptions as generality, totality, and ultimateness is most readily reached from the side of the disposition toward the world which they connote. In any literal and quantitative sense, these terms do not apply to the subject matter of knowledge, for completeness and finality are out of the question. The very nature of experience as an ongoing, changing process forbids. In a less rigid sense, they apply to *science* rather than to philosophy. For obviously it is to mathematics, physics, chemistry, biology, anthropology, history, etc. that we must go, not to philosophy, to find out the facts of the world. It is for the sciences to say what generalizations are tenable about the world and what they specifically are. But when we ask what *sort* of permanent disposition of action toward the world the scientific disclosures exact of us we are raising a philosophic question.

From this point of view, "totality" does not mean the hopeless task of a quantitative summation. It means rather *consistency* of mode of response in reference to the plurality of events which occur. Consistency does not mean literal identity; for since the same thing does not happen twice, an exact repetition of a reaction involves some maladjustment. Totality means continuity—the carrying on of a former habit of action with the readaptation necessary to keep it alive and growing. Instead of signifying a ready-made complete scheme of action, it means keeping the balance in a multitude of diverse actions, so that each borrows and gives significance to every other. Any person who is open-minded and sensitive to new perceptions, and who has concentration and responsibility in connecting them has, in so far, a philosophic disposition. One of the popular senses of philosophy is calm and endurance in the face of difficulty and loss; it is even supposed to be a power to bear pain without complaint. This meaning is a tribute to the influence of the Stoic philosophy rather than an attribute of philosophy in general. But in so far as it suggests that the wholeness characteristic of philosophy is a power to learn, or to extract meaning, from even the unpleasant vicissitudes of experience and to embody what is learned in an ability to go on learning, it is justified in any scheme. An analogous interpretation applies to the generality and ultimateness of philosophy. Taken literally, they are absurd pretensions; they indicate insanity. Finality does not mean, however, that experience is ended and exhausted, but means the disposition to penetrate to deeper levels of meaning—to go below the surface and find out the connections of any event or object, and to keep at it. In like manner the philosophic attitude is general in the sense that it is averse to taking anything as isolated; it tries to place an act in its context—which constitutes its significance.

It is of assistance to connect philosophy with thinking in its distinction from knowledge. Knowledge, grounded knowledge, is science; it represents objects which have been settled, ordered, disposed of rationally. Thinking, on the other hand, is prospective in reference. It is occasioned by an *un*settlement and it aims at overcoming a disturbance. Philosophy is thinking what the known demands of us—what responsive attitude it exacts. It is an idea of what is possible, not a record of accomplished fact. Hence it is hypothetical like all thinking. It presents an assignment of something to be done—something to be tried. Its value lies not in furnishing solutions (which can be achieved only in action) but in defining difficulties and suggesting methods for dealing with them. Philosophy might almost be described as thinking which has become conscious of itself—which has generalized its place, function, and value in experience.

More specifically, the demand for a "total" attitude arises because there is the need of integration in action of the conflicting various interests in life. Where interests are so superficial that they glide readily into one another or where they are not sufficiently organized to come into conflict with one another, the need for philosophy is not perceptible. But when the scientific interest conflicts with, say, the religious, or the economic with the scientific or aesthetic, or when the conservative concern for order is at odds with the progressive interest in freedom, or when institutionalism clashes with individuality, there is a stimulus to discover some more comprehensive point of view from which the divergencies may be brought together, and consistency or continuity of experience recovered. Often these clashes may be settled by an individual for himself; the area of the struggle of aims is limited and a person works out his own rough accommodations. Such homespun philosophies are genuine and often adequate. But they do not result in systems of philosophy. These arise when the discrepant claims of different ideals of conduct affect the community as a whole, and the need for readjustment is general.

These traits explain some things which are often brought as objections against philosophies, such as the part played in them by individual speculation, and their controversial diversity, as well as the fact that philosophy seems to be repeatedly occupied with much the same questions differently stated. Without doubt, all these things characterize historic philosophies more or less. But they are not objections to philosophy so much as they are to human nature, and even to the world in which human nature is set. If there are genuine uncertainties in life, philosophies must reflect that uncertainty. If there are different diagnoses of the cause of a difficulty, and different proposals for dealing with it; if, that is, the conflict of interests is more or less embodied in different sets of persons, there must be divergent competing philosophies. With respect to what has happened, sufficient evidence is all that is needed to bring agreement and certainty. The thing itself is sure. But with reference to what it is wise to do in a complicated situation, discussion is inevitable precisely because the thing itself is still indeterminate. One would not expect a ruling class living at ease to have the same philosophy of life as those who were having a hard struggle for existence. If the possessing and the dispossessed had the same fundamental disposition toward the world, it would argue either insincerity or lack of seriousness. A community devoted to industrial pursuits, active in business and commerce, is not likely to see the needs and possibilities of life in the same way as a country with high aesthetic culture and little enterprise in turning the energies of nature to mechanical account. A social group with a fairly continuous history will respond mentally to a crisis in a very different way from one which has felt the shock of abrupt breaks. Even if the same data were present, they would be evaluated differently. But the different sorts of experience attending different types of life prevent just the same data from presenting themselves, as well as lead to a different scheme of values. As for the similarity of problems, this is often more a matter of appearance than of fact, due to old discussions being translated into the terms of contemporary perplexities. But in certain fundamental respects the same predicaments of life recur from time to time with only such changes as are due to change of social context, including the growth of the sciences.

The fact that philosophic problems arise because of widespread and widely felt difficulties in social practice is disguised because philosophers become a specialized class which uses a technical language, unlike the vocabulary in which the direct difficulties are stated. But where a system becomes influential, its connection with a conflict of interests calling for some program of social adjustment may always be discovered. At this point, the intimate connection between philosophy and education appears. In fact, education offers a vantage ground from which to penetrate to the human, as distinct from the technical, significance of philosophic discussions. The student of philosophy "in itself" is always in danger of taking it as so much nimble or severe intellectual exercise—as something said by philosophers and concerning them alone. But when philosophic issues are approached from the side of the kind of mental disposition to which they correspond, or the differences in educational practice they make when acted upon, the life-situations which they formulate can never be far from view. If a theory makes no difference in educational endeavor, it must be artificial. The educational point of view enables one to envisage the philosophic problems where they arise and thrive, where they are at home, and where acceptance or rejection makes a difference in practice.

If we are willing to conceive education as the process of forming fundamental dispositions, intellectual and emotional, toward nature and fellow men, philosophy may even be defined *as the general theory of education*. Unless a philosophy is to remain symbolic—or verbal—or a sentimental indulgence for a few, or else mere arbitrary dogma, its auditing of past experience and its program of values must take effect in conduct. Public agitation, propaganda, legislative and administrative action are effective in producing the change of disposition which a philosophy indicates as desirable, but only in the degree in which they are educative—that is to say, in the degree in which they modify mental and moral attitudes. And at the best, such methods are compromised by the fact they are used with those whose habits are already largely set, while education of youth has a fairer and freer field of operation. On the other side, the business of schooling tends to become a routine empirical affair unless its aims and methods are animated by such a broad and sympathetic survey of its place in contemporary life as it is the business of philosophy to provide.

Positive science always implies *practically* the ends which the community is concerned to achieve. Isolated from such ends, it is a matter of indifference whether its disclosures are used to cure disease or to spread it; to increase the means of sustenance of life or to manufacture war material to wipe life out. If society is interested in one of these things rather than another, science shows the way of attainment. Philosophy thus has a double task; that of criticizing existing aims with respect to the existing state of science, pointing out values which have become obsolete with the command of new resources showing what values are merely sentimental because there are no means for their realization; and also that of interpreting the results of specialized science in their bearing on future social endeavor. It is impossible that it should have any success in these tasks without educational equivalents as to what to do and what not to do. For philosophic theory has no Aladdin's lamp to summon into immediate existence the values which it intellectually constructs. In the mechanical arts, the sciences become methods of managing things so as to utilize their energies for recognized aims. By the educative arts philosophy may generate methods of utilizing the energies of human beings in accord with serious and thoughtful conceptions of life. Education is the laboratory in which philosophic distinctions become concrete and are tested.

It is suggestive that European philosophy originated (among the Athenians) under the direct pressure of educational questions. The earlier history of philosophy, developed by the Greeks in Asia Minor and Italy, so far as its range of topics is concerned, is mainly a chapter in the history of science rather than of philosophy as that word is understood today. It had nature for its subject, and speculated as to how things are made and changed. Later the traveling teachers, known as the Sophists, began to apply the results and the methods of the natural philosophers to human conduct.

When the Sophists, the first body of professional educators in Europe, instructed the youth in virtue, the political arts, and the management of city and household, philosophy began to deal with the relation of the individual to the universal, to some comprehensive class, or to some group; the relation of man and nature, of tradition and reflection, of knowledge and action. Can virtue, approved excellence in any line, be learned, they asked? What is learning? It has to do with knowledge. What, then, is knowledge? How is it achieved? Through the senses, or by apprenticeship in some form of doing, or by reason that has undergone a preliminary logical discipline? Since learning is *coming* to know, it involves a passage from ignorance to wisdom, from privation to fullness, from defect to perfection, from non-being to being, in the Greek way of putting it. How is such a transition possible? Is change, becoming, development really possible and if so, how? And supposing such questions answered, what is the relation of instruction, of knowledge, to virtue?

This last question led to opening the problem of the relation of reason to action, of theory to practice, since virtue clearly dwelt in action. Was not knowing, the activity of reason, the noblest attribute of man? And consequently was not purely intellectual activity itself the highest of all excellences, compared with which the virtues of neighborliness and the citizen's life were secondary? Or, on the other hand, was the vaunted intellectual knowledge more than empty and vain pretense, demoralizing to character and destructive of the social ties that bound men together in their community life? Was not the only true, because the only moral, life gained through obedient habituation to the customary practices of the community? And was not the new education an enemy to good citizenship, because it set up a rival standard to the established traditions of the community?

In the course of two or three generations such questions were cut loose from their original practical bearing upon education and were discussed on their own account; that is, as matters of philosophy as an independent branch of inquiry. But the fact that the stream of European philosophical thought arose as a theory of educational procedure remains an eloquent witness to the intimate connection of philosophy and education. "Philosophy of education" is not an external application of ready-made ideas to a system of practice having a radically different origin and purpose: it is only an explicit formulation of the problems of the formation of right mental and moral habitudes in respect to the difficulties of contemporary social life. The most penetrating definition of philosophy which can be given is, then, that it is the theory of education in its most general phases.

The reconstruction of philosophy, of education, and of social ideals and methods thus go hand in hand. If there is especial need of educational reconstruction at the present time, if this need makes urgent a reconsideration of the basic ideas of traditional philosophic systems, it is because of the thoroughgoing change in social life accompanying the advance of science, the industrial revolution, and the development of democracy. Such practical changes cannot take place without demanding an educational reformation to meet them, and without leading men to ask what ideas and ideals are implicit in these social changes, and what revisions they require of the ideas and ideals which are inherited from older and unlike cultures. . . .

32 / ELIZABETH STEINER MACCIA

The Nonidentity of Philosophy and Theory of Education

I. The Problem Stated

> If we are willing to conceive education as a process of forming fundamental dispositions, intellectual and emotional, toward nature and fellow men, philosophy may even be defined *as the general theory of education.*[1]

Is Dewey correct in defining *philosophy* as the general theory of education? This is the question I shall attempt to answer in this paper. Obviously in answering this question, the consequential relation of the definition of *philosophy* to the conception of education must be considered. Moreover, Dewey's conception of education as a process of forming fundamental intellectual and emotional dispositions toward nature and fellow men must be inquired into.

Elizabeth Steiner Maccia (1925–) is professor of philosophy of education at Indiana University. She has done extensive work in educational theory construction and is co-author of *Development of Educational Theory Derived from Three Educational Theory Models.*

[1] John Dewey, *Democracy and Education* (New York: Macmillan Co., 1916), Paperback Edition, 1961, p. 328.

II. The Consequential Relation

Dewey relates the consequent, "philosophy may even be defined *as the general theory of education*," to the antecedent, "we are willing to conceive education as the process of forming fundamental dispositions, intellectual and emotional, toward nature and fellow men." In this section I shall explicate the bases of this relation. The exceptions which should be taken are in sections to come.

Dewey maintains that *philosophy* must be defined from two sides: subject matter and method. The subject matter side he equates with general theory of education and the method side with education. From the subject matter side philosophy consists of conclusions which are general theory. ". . . philosophy is an attempt to *comprehend*—that is to gather together the varied details of the world and of life into a single inclusive whole. . . ."[2] From the method side philosophy is an "endeavor to attain as unified, consistent, and complete an outlook upon experience as possible."[3] "Philosophy might almost be described as thinking which has become conscious of itself—which has generalized its place, function, and value in experience."[4]

Thinking which is generalized in its place, function, and value in experience is a general attitude or fundamental disposition, "not to this or that thing nor even to the aggregate of known things, but to considerations which govern conduct."[5] Reflective thinking, therefore, is forming fundamental intellectual and emotional dispositions toward nature and fellow men. Philosophy from the method side is the process of education.

Reflective thinking also produces considerations which govern conduct or intellectual and emotional dispositions. Considerations which so govern are general theory about the formation of dispositions and hence about education. Consequently, philosophy from the subject matter side is general theory of education.

The following schemata summarize the explication of the bases of the consequential relation.

$$(P^S \equiv T)\ (P^M \equiv R)\ (R \equiv D)\ (D \equiv E^P) \supset (T \equiv E^T)$$
$$(P^S \equiv T)\ (T \equiv E^T) \supset (P^S \equiv E^T)$$

where

$\equiv$ stands for is
$\supset$ stands for only if

[2] *Ibid.*, p. 324.
[3] *Ibid.*
[4] *Ibid.*, p. 326.
[5] *Ibid.*, pp. 324–325.

P^S stands for philosophy from the subject matter side
T stands for general theory
P^M stands for philosophy from the method side
R stands for reflective thinking
D stands for fundamental intellectual and emotional dispositions toward nature and fellow men
E^P stands for education as process
E^T stands for education as general theory

III. Philosophy as Subject Matter and Method

Although Dewey views philosophy from two sides, it is patent from the explication in Section II that he conflates philosophy as subject matter and philosophy as method. But more, he dissolves philosophy as subject matter in philosophy as method which has been psychologized.

> It is of assistance to connect philosophy with thinking in its distinction from knowledge. Knowledge, grounded knowledge, is science; it represents objects which have been settled, ordered, disposed of rationally. Thinking, on the other hand, is prospective in reference. It is occasioned by an *un*settlement and it aims at overcoming a disturbance. Philosophy is thinking what the known demands of us—what responsive attitude it exacts.[6]

General theory thus is not propositional in nature. The totality expressed in general theory rather is "*consistency* of mode of response in reference to the plurality of events which occur."[7]

The conflation of the two sides of philosophy arises from a failure to discern orders of discourse. Through such discernment the conflation can be avoided. Philosophy from the subject matter side is a different order of discourse than philosophy from the method side. Philosophy from the subject matter side is discourse about certain events, whereas philosophy from the method side is discourse about philosophy from the subject matter side. So relative to the events, philosophy from the subject matter side is first order and philosophy from the method side is second order. Second-order discourse relative to first order is called *meta-discourse.* Therefore, philosophy from the method side more properly is a part of meta-philosophy, which leaves *philosophy* as the term for philosophy from the subject matter side. Schema 1 succinctly expresses these matters.

[6] *Ibid.*, p. 326.
[7] *Ibid.*, p. 325.

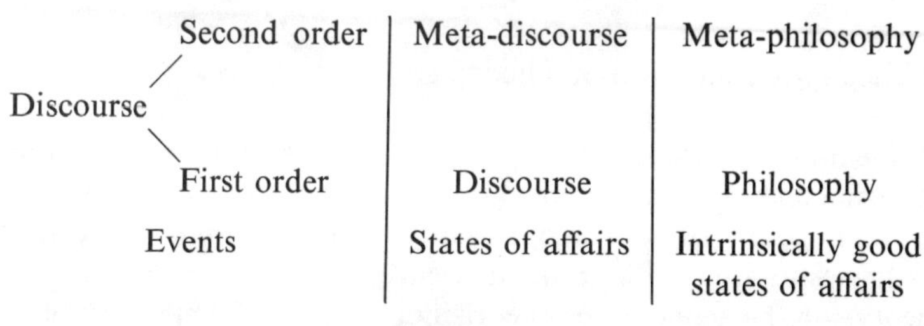

Schema 1

The dissolution of one side of philosophy in the other and the psychologizing of method follows from the identification of philosophy on the subject matter side with general theory. The totality demanded in general theory, where *theory* is taken in its usual propositional sense, rightly is seen by Dewey as hopeless. This leads to his taking general theory as psychologized method.

> . . . "Totality" does not mean the hopeless task of a quantitative summation. It means rather *consistency* of mode of response in reference to the plurality of events which occur.[8]

By not identifying philosophy on its subject matter side as general theory, its dissolution in psychologized method can be eliminated. As indicated in Schema 1 and as I shall argue in the next section, philosophy is not discourse about all events but about only those states of affairs which are intrinsically good.

As seen above, philosophy from the method side is meta-philosophy; it is discourse about philosophy. Nevertheless it is philosophical discourse about philosophy, and so ought not be psychologized even on the meta-level.

To be methodic is to be ordered in one's behavior. To be ordered requires one to meet certain standards in his behavior. Logic is the branch of philosophy that provides such standards through a description of structure: function, form, and content. Psychology cannot provide such knowledge, for it treats of behavior whether it is ordered or not and does not attempt to set forth order that can be used to judge behavior. The psychologist's concern instead centers on factors relating to behavior including that which is methodic.

With respect to philosophy then, philosophy from the method side is not the psychology of philosophy but the logic of philosophy. Philosophy from the subject matter side is, of course, philosophy.

[8] *Ibid.*

IV. Philosophy as a Kind of Theory

The identity of philosophy with general theory has its origin in an outcome of theorizing and in a philosophical tradition. Theorizing has as an outcome higher-order generalizations about reality, and philosophy has a tradition which defines its field as the general science of reality.

Theory, or the outcome of theorizing, consists of sentences which are knowledge claims—that is, which express propositions asserting universal connections within or between states of affairs. It is such expressions which could describe—that is, connect every state of affairs of a certain sort to one or more properties and connect properties within or between states of affairs. Theory, moreover, involves ordering between its generalizations of unrestricted range in space and time. This ordering arises due to degrees of complexity and generality. The greater the complexity and generality, the more states of affairs are claimed to be linked together. General theory obviously would be theory that has the highest degree of complexity and generality. It would attempt to gather together all of the states of affairs into a whole.

If *philosophy* is defined as the general science of reality, then a philosopher is supposed to discover the principles which underlie all the specialized sciences of reality. The philosopher is supposed to be a general theorist of reality. The tradition, therefore, carries with it a claim to matters that belong to the sciences. Also it claims a matter that belongs to the sciences but which the sciences would take as impossible of treatment (if not from the logical standpoint at least from the standpoint of the stage of the development of the sciences). It claims unification of the sciences.

Given the scientific enterprise as treating of reality to the extent it can be treated, many philosophers have come to define their field in a more restricted way, as one of analysis of meanings. Such restriction is at once too broad and too narrow. It is too broad because scientists also in their theorizing seek to set forth meanings. One cannot set forth descriptions without involving oneself in the definitional task. It is too narrow because philosophers are engaged in a certain kind of pursuit of truth, not the kind pursued by the scientist. Surely Schlick is wrong in holding that *science* should be defined as the pursuit of truth and *philosophy* as the pursuit of meaning.[9] Philosophy is the pursuit of truth about intrinsic goodness.

To be the pursuit of truth about intrinsic goodness is to be theorizing about what is worthwhile or good in and of itself. Philosophy consequently is a different kind of theory than is science. Philosophy is a description of ideal states of affairs, whereas science is a description of states of affairs which

[9] "The Future of Philosophy," *Basic Problems of Philosophy*, ed. D. J. Bronstein, Y. H. Krikorian, and P. P. Wiener (New York: Prentice-Hall, 1947), p. 739.

are or which will necessarily be. An excellent illustration is found in Plato's *Republic*, a treatise on the ideal man and the ideal society or state, and his words make this clear:

> "Well," said I, "in heaven, perhaps a pattern of it is indeed laid up, for him that has eyes to see, and seeing to settle himself therein. It matters nothing whether it exists anywhere or shall exist; for he would practice the principles of this city only, no other."[10]

Ethics, which treats of the good man, and social or political philosophy, which treats of the good society or state, are the branches of philosophy that are primarily illustrated. Epistemology, which treats of truth, and logic, which treats of order, are two other branches. The descriptions of the philosopher are said to be normative insofar as they provide standards for judging whether states of affairs are good, true, or ordered.

There are yet other normative descriptions that are not philosophical. One can describe states of affairs that are good for something else, that are instrumentally good. This third kind of theory, over and above science and philosophy, is praxiological in nature. Praxiological theory consists of descriptions of practices. A practice is a group of interrelated human actions which may or may not include material objects as instruments in such actions. Practices by their very nature are means-ends relationships, for they are devised by man to be effective with respect to what he has in mind. Praxiological descriptions thus are normative insofar as they provide standards for judging effectiveness.

To summarize this section, there are three kinds of theory: scientific, philosophical, and praxiological. Philosophy, therefore, is not general theory of reality. Philosophy is not science. Also philosophy is not general theory but one kind of theory. Three kinds of theory, scientific, philosophical, and praxiological, would constitute general theory, if such theory be possible.

V. The Concept of Education

Surely Frankena has stated rightly that "a distinction must be made between education as a process and education as an academic discipline."[11] Unfortunately our discourse has not been refined to reflect that distinction. *Education* has been made to do double duty. *Education* refers both to what is inquired into, a process as an object of inquiry, and to the results of that inquiry, an academic discipline constituted of knowledge about education.

[10] W. H. Rouse did the translation and these words of Plato are found in Book 9, 592.

[11] William K. Frankena, "Toward a Philosophy of the Philosophy of Education," *Harvard Educational Review* 26, no. 2 (Spring 1956), p. 95.

Knowledge about education obviously would be adequate theory about education. To refine our discourse I have introduced *educology*[12] for the academic discipline, and so permit *education* to do single duty. *Education* would refer only to the process. Dewey, of course, in his conception of education conflated education and educology. He failed to distinguish between the object, the process of education, and propositional discourse about the object, theory about education.

Turning to education as a process, it has been taken as equivalent to that of living, to all of life. Development of an individual, whether it is physical or emotional or intellectual, has been equated with education. This sense of education would make it broader than learning, since physical maturation (as growing taller) would be included and learning is a change in behavior (covert or overt) which persists and which does not arise solely through such maturation. Dewey's conception of education is clearly a conception of learning. Only intellectual and emotional dispositions are taken as involved in the process of education. His conception, therefore, cannot be criticized as including too much embracing nonlearning instances.

Dewey's conception, however, does refer to instances of learning which are not deliberately brought about. Learning without teaching is conceived as education. Consequently his conception can be faulted on the grounds that it includes too much. It includes learning without design.

Implicit in what has been argued thus far is a conception of education as a teaching-learning process—that is, a process in which someone teaches something to someone somewhere. This conception was arrived at, for it is neither too broad nor too narrow. It does not include instances of noneducation—development which is not learning or learning which is not designed. It does not exclude instances of education. Neither training, which is designed learning through direct experience, nor instruction, which is designed learning through symbolic experience, are excluded. Then too education in this sense is not limited to one way a group could arrange itself for the teaching-learning process—for example, schooling. Finally, education in this sense is not limited to good education. One can be educated badly, even though it might be conceivable that a teacher would not deliberately attempt to bring about bad learning. A teacher could be mistaken about what is good.

Dewey's conception is not too exclusive in the sense of limiting education to either training or instruction or schooling, but it does limit education to good education. It does not hold the formation of any dispositions, intel-

[12] In "Logic of Education and of Educatology: Dimensions of Philosophy of Education" (*Proceedings of the Philosophy of Education Society*, 1964) I introduced the term *educatology* for the study of education. Following W. Gruen's suggestion, I changed to *educology*. See "Analysis as Metatheorizing" (*Proceedings of the Philosophy of Education Society*, 1970).

lectual and emotional, toward nature and fellow men to be education but only the formation of fundamental ones. The formation of these fundamental ones are good, as these are the dispositions of a thinking man who has become conscious of himself. These are the dispositions of a reflective thinker or a philosopher.

To put the matter quite simply before moving to a discussion of theory of education, Dewey takes education as all learning which is good and so takes it in too inclusive and exclusive a sense and in only one ambiguous sense. Education should include only learning within the teaching-learning process and should not exclude bad learning therein. Furthermore, education should be taken also as distinct from educology.

VI. The Nature of Theory of Education

Given the negative results of the above analysis—that is, the rejection of the following:

> the conflation of philosophy as subject matter and as method
> the identity of philosophy and general theory
> the conflation of education as theory and as process
> the identity of education and the process of forming fundamental dispositions, intellectual and emotional, toward nature and fellow men

the question raised in this paper has been answered. Dewey is incorrect in identifying philosophy as general theory of education. The positive results, however, permit a statement as to the relationship of philosophy and theory of education. Here too nonidentity will be seen.

The analysis in Sections IV and V permits setting forth general theory of education as a system of sentences which could describe the teaching-learning process, and also permits delineating three kinds of theory within general theory of education. Scientific theory of education could describe what is or necessarily will be in the teaching-learning process. Philosophical and praxiological theories of education are normative. Philosophical theory of education could describe what is intrinsically good (worthwhile in and of itself) in the teaching-learning process, while praxiological theory of education could describe what is instrumentally good (effective relative to selected ends) in the teaching-learning process.

Since adequate theory of education not only could but does describe the teaching-learning process, adequate theory of education is knowledge of education or educology. Educology thus consists of three branches: science of education, philosophy of education, and praxiology of education.

Contrary to the parts of educology set forth here, Frankena marks off factual, normative, and analytical parts.[13] The factual part is the same as the scientific part, which is clear from the following statement:

> First, there is the factual "science" of education. This is especially concerned to gather facts, particular and general, about the process of educating.[14]

The normative part conflates the philosophical and praxiological parts, for:

> It proposes ends, goals, or norms for this process which teachers and administrators are to promote, and it advocates the means by which these ends are to be achieved.[15]

Moreover, Frankena's conception of the normative is not solely descriptive. To advocate is to prescribe. The analytical part

> . . . would be concerned partly with analyzing concepts of the factual science of education, for example "intelligence" or "growth," and with evaluating the assumptions and methods of this science. But it would also be interested in the normative part of education, analyzing its concepts, for example, "good," "justice," etc., and scrutinizing the methods by which it seeks to justify its recommendations.[16]

This part is not a distinct part of educology. Insofar as it is concerned with analyzing concepts of either the factual or normative parts, the analytical part is those parts. As argued in Section IV, setting forth meaning is one of the theory construction tasks and so is not a task over and above theorizing. Insofar as the analytical part is concerned with methods, it is not at all a part of educology but is a part of meta-educology. In Section III method clearly is seen to be a meta-concern. In the light of the above, Frankena's analytical part should be dropped as should the prescriptive part of the normative. The remaining descriptive part of the normative part should be separated into philosophical and praxiological ones. Thereby the three parts of educology (science of education, philosophy of education, and praxiology of education) would emerge.

VII. Philosophy of Education and Philosophy of Educology

The discussion of the nature of theory of education has made patent that philosophy of education is not identical with theory of education. The results

[13] Frankena, *op. cit.*
[14] *Ibid.*, p. 96.
[15] *Ibid.*
[16] *Ibid.*

of Sections III and V support a distinction between philosophy of education and philosophy of educology. Furthermore, the results of Sections III, IV, and V can be utilized to clarify what philosophy of education and philosophy of educology are.

Given that education is a teaching-learning process or a process in which someone teaches something to someone somewhere, education involves a teacher, curriculum, a learner, and a setting. The something taught or curriculum is taken from man's culture. Language is a vehicle for both the expression and transmission of culture, and so the teacher and learner behave linguistically. Adequate linguistic behavior, adherence to rules or ordered linguistic behavior, results in expression or transmission of the culture selected. Selection depends on what kind of learner behavior (learning) is taken to be good. For instance, if knowing is taken as good, truth is selected from the culture. The teacher then attempts to bring the learner to a state of true belief. In addition to questions about good learning, there are questions about goodness of the behavior of one individual relative to another in the educative process. Teacher and learner interact as could other persons, such as administrators, counselors, and custodians. The setting need not be one without persons. Therefore, since descriptions of education require those of good learning, truth in the curriculum and its transmission, order in the language behavior of teacher and learner, and goodness in the interaction of persons in the teaching-learning process, ethics of education, epistemology of education, logic of education, and social or political philosophy of education can be delineated. All of the branches of philosophy discussed in Section IV are represented in philosophy of education.

Not only can one philosophize about the process of education but one can do so about the academic discipline of education. One can philosophize about educology. Since educology is produced by persons and since such production involves interaction of persons, ethical and social or political philosophical questions about educology arise. Instances would be:

> Is it good to utilize students as subjects to advance educology?
> Is it good to engage in educological research of little significance because it is funded?
> Is it good to engage in educological research which does not result in immediate amelioration of educational ills?
> Is it good to copyright educological ideas?

That epistemological and logical questions about educology exist is probably more apparent. Educology after all is knowledge or truth about education and it is expressed in language. An example of the logic of educology is the analysis of methods that Frankena referred to. Again all of the branches are represented in philosophy of educology.

VIII. The Significance of the Nonidentity

If philosophy is taken as general theory of education, then educology and meta-educology are hindered in their development. In the case where general theory is taken simply as general theory of reality, philosophy becomes general scientific theory. Clearly philosophy of education and praxiology of education are neglected. In the case where general theory is taken simply as general theory, the distinctive efforts of neither the philosopher of education nor the scientist of education nor the praxiologist of education are furthered. In both cases levels of discourse are conflated, and so the distinctive efforts of neither the educologist nor the meta-educologist are furthered.

If philosophy of education is taken as theory of intrinsic good with respect to the teaching-learning process, science of education as well as praxiology of education can be honored. Educology in all its branches can develop. Meta-educology can too, because there is no longer a conflation of levels of discourse. Philosophy of education is distinct from philosophy of educology, which is theory of intrinsic good with respect to knowledge about education.

Questions for Discussion

According to Frankena, what does a normative philosophy contain? Is his a complete list? How does each of the content areas enter into his analysis of a normative philosophy of education? Probably the best way to determine the adequacy of Frankena's schema is to apply to one of the more clearly stated, less complex philosophies of education. Are you able to identify the different elements of the philosophy and place it into the appropriate blocks within the schema? Remember too that not all philosophies follow the complete pattern. To what extent did the exercise help you to better understand the philosophy? Should confusion still exist after completing the exercise, is it due to choosing a philosophy less amenable to analysis or to some inadequacy in Frankena's framework? Does the essay help you to understand how to build your own philosophy of education? Does it help in any way to assess the adequacy of a philosophy and the cogency of its arguments?

For Dewey, what is the function of philosophy? What dangers does he find in the traditional conception of its role? At what point does science merge into philosophy? Does Dewey's essay carefully avoid any dualisms? Why is Dewey unwilling to define philosophy from the side of subject matter alone? There is a discussion of the role of theory in education. Is Dewey's interpretation of theory's role sound? State and evaluate the arguments that lead Dewey to define philosophy "*as the general theory of education.*" What then becomes of education? How is it conceived and in what way does it function?

Maccia contends that Dewey conflates philosophy as subject matter and philosophy as method. If this argument is sound, what consequences follow for philosophy? Moreover, it is also claimed that philosophy as method has been psychologized and philosophy as subject matter is dissolved into it. How can this difficulty be overcome? What is meant by "meta-discourse" and what use is made of it? What is Maccia's interpretation of philosophy from the method side? She holds that philosophy should be defined neither as "the general theory of reality" nor as "analysis of meanings." Explain why she takes this position and then evaluate her own interpretation of philosophy. Distinguish *educology* from *education.* What was the consequence, according to Maccia, of Dewey's failure to distinguish the two? What are the shortcomings of Dewey's conception of education? Distinguish scientific theory of education, philosophical theory of education, and praxiological theory of education. Explain and evaluate the weaknesses found in Frankena's conception of the study or discipline of education. What difference is there between philosophy of education and philosophy of educology? Which do you believe has the most defensible interpretation of philosophy of education—Dewey or Maccia?

Suggested Reading

Christopher J. Lucas has edited a collection of essays devoted to the topic, *What Is Philosophy of Education?* (New York: Macmillan Co., 1969). Both philosophers and philosophers of education participated in discussing the nature, characteristics, and uses of philosophy of education in an entire issue devoted to the topic: *Harvard Educational Review* 26, no. 2 (1956). A number of essays in George Barnett, ed., *Philosophy and Educational Development* (Boston: Houghton Mifflin Co., 1966), are concerned with this topic. The largest collection of articles on the subject can be found in the journal *Educational Theory*, 1951 to the present.

A number of basic texts in the field present an overview chapter on the problems and issues of clarifying philosophy of education and its relation to education in general and to other disciplines: Philip H. Phenix, *Philosophy of Education* (New York: Holt, Rinehart and Winston, 1958), chap. 1; John S. Brubacher, *Modern Philosophies of Education*, 4th ed. (New York: McGraw-Hill Book Co., 1969), chap. 15; Philip G. Smith, *Philosophy of Education: Introductory Studies* (New York: Harper & Row, Publishers, 1965), chap. 3; and G. Max Wingo, *The Philosophy of American Education* (Boston: D. C. Heath and Co., 1965), chap. 1.

INDEX